Palgrave Shakespeare Studies

Palgrave Shakespeare Studies takes Shakespeare as its focus but strives to understand the significance of his oeuvre in relation to his contemporaries, to subsequent writers and to historical and political contexts. By extending the scope of Shakespeare and English Renaissance Studies, the series aims to open up the field to examinations of previously neglected aspects or sources in the period's art and thought. Titles in the *Palgrave Shakespeare Studies* series seek to understand anew both where the literary achievements of the English Renaissance came from and where they have brought us, and provide the reader with a combination of cutting-edge critical thought and archival scholarly rigour.

James W. Stone • Catherine Bates
Editors

Shakespeare and Psychoanalysis

Method in the Madness

palgrave
macmillan

Editors
James W. Stone
American University
Paris, France

Catherine Bates
University of Warwick
Coventry, UK

ISSN 2731-3204 ISSN 2731-3212 (electronic)
Palgrave Shakespeare Studies
ISBN 978-3-032-07896-4 ISBN 978-3-032-07897-1 (eBook)
https://doi.org/10.1007/978-3-032-07897-1

This Palgrave Macmillan imprint is published by the registered company Springer Nature Switzerland AG.
The registered company address is: Gewerbestrasse 11, 6330 Cham, Switzerland

The philosophers have only interpreted the world, in various ways; the point, however, is to change it.

Karl Marx, *Theses on Feuerbach*

In memory of Christian A. Smith
1963–2022
Shakespearean. Marxist. Activist. Colleague. Friend.

Preface

This book looks backward and forward. The photograph on the cover both recalls and resurrects a past. More than one past. The Freud Museum in London used this image to promote a lecture, in January 2013, entitled "The Formative Influence of Shakespeare on Freud and the Development of Psychoanalysis." The lecturer was Christian A. Smith. An American from Los Angeles, Christian had moved to England, with his wife Annie Barker, in order to work and to study. He finished his doctoral thesis at the University of Warwick shortly before his engagement at the Freud Museum. As an historical materialist, who would publish the magisterial *Shakespeare's Influence on Karl Marx: The Shakespearean Roots of Marxism* (Routledge, 2021) eight years after his lecture in London, Christian understood how the remains of the past haunted and determined the course of thought and ideology. His sudden death a year later meant the second part of his great project, Shakespeare's influence on Sigmund Freud, remained unconcluded, a work in progress tragically stopped in its tracks before its time. Our aim in this volume is to let Christian's project start its journey in the company of fellow travelers, many of whom knew him and his work.

In 1938 Freud translated from Vienna to London his old furnishings, his works accomplished and still in progress, his antiquities, his library. His beloved daughter Anna accompanied him. In his office and at his desk (at both Berggasse 19 in Vienna, and 20 Maresfield Gardens in London), Freud surrounded himself with ancient gods from Egypt, Mesopotamia, China, Greece, and Rome. Analogous to the method of the archeologist is the doctor's and the literary critic's exhuming long-buried strata.

Beneath a modern play like *Hamlet* lay an old play by Sophocles (and lay too a further history not well known to Freud: at least one *Ur-Hamlet* and a tradition of revenge tragedies). Literary and critical histories repeat themselves. The past and its translations of cultures are a palimpsest of fragments and ruins: Quartos bad and good, cruxes, sources, and allusions both manifest and recondite, the unknown, the irrepressible stirrings of the unconscious. In London as in Vienna, Freud practiced and wrote surrounded by the statuettes, the figures on his desk and on the shelves of his library. At hand, in his library, he took inspiration from the works of Shakespeare in English and in German.

We editors and our contributors stand upon these foundations in order to forge something new.

Paris, France
Coventry, UK
August 2025

James W. Stone
Catherine Bates

Acknowledgments

Our first thanks go to Annie Barker, widow of Christian A. Smith, whose loss we continue to mourn and to whose memory this volume is dedicated. We thank Annie for her openness to this commemorative project and for her involvement in editing the chapter by Christian which launches the present volume. Annie herself would like to thank Susan Wells (Temple University) for, in her words, "her editing and emotional support in getting through the arduous task of editing a work that feels so painfully present and yet is trapped in a snapshot of history."

This project would not exist without the good offices of Eileen Srebernik, Commissioning Editor at Palgrave Macmillan, to whom we owe a debt of gratitude. We are most thankful to her for the receptiveness and generosity she has shown toward the volume from the beginning. Thanks also go to the team at Palgrave, including our production manager Sivaranjani Siva. We are delighted that the volume forms part of the Palgrave Shakespeare Series and would like to thank its General Editors Dympna Callaghan and Michael Dobson for welcoming it into this prestigious grouping.

We are grateful to Jane Hanenberg, Editor of *American Imago*, for permission to reproduce a longer version of Catherine Bates's essay "The Imaginary and the Symbolic in Shakespeare's *Venus and Adonis*," which was first published in the journal in Volume 81, No. 4, 2024, pp. 335–66, as winner of the Julius Silberger Prize (2023).

On behalf of the contributors of this volume, we would also like to extend our thanks to the following: Bernard Burgoyne, Maud Ellman, John Gillies, Gregg Horowitz, Helena Kottman, Karl A. Kottman Jr.,

Toni McNaron, Jacques Mauger, Élyse Michon, James Newlin, Adam Phillips, Avgi Saketopoulou, Emily Schoenbeck, the late Mike Schoenfeldt, Ted Tregear, and Anthony Welch.

Contents

Notes on Contributors

Catherine Bates is Research Professor in the Centre for the Study of the Renaissance at the University of Warwick. She is author of *The Rhetoric of Courtship in Elizabethan Language and Literature* (Cambridge UP, 1992), *Play in a Godless World: The Theory and Practice of Play in Shakespeare, Nietzsche, and Freud* (Open Gate Press, 1999), *Masculinity, Gender and Identity in the English Renaissance Lyric* (Cambridge UP, 2007), *Masculinity and the Hunt: Wyatt to Spenser* (Oxford UP, 2013), winner of the 2015 British Academy Rose Mary Crawshay Prize, and *On Not Defending Poetry: Defence and Indefensibility in Sidney's 'Defence of Poesy'* (Oxford UP, 2017), winner of the 2019 *Studies in English Literature, 1500–1900* Elizabeth Dietz Award. She is also editor of *The Cambridge Companion to the Epic* (Cambridge UP, 2010), *A Companion to Renaissance Poetry* (Wiley Blackwell, 2018), *Sixteenth-Century British Poetry*, co-edited with Patrick Cheney (Oxford UP, 2022), *The Oxford Handbook of Philip Sidney* (Oxford UP, 2025), and *The Routledge Companion to Renaissance Literature* (Routledge, 2026).

Drew Daniel is Professor in the Department of English at Johns Hopkins University in Baltimore. His articles have appeared in journals such as *Shakespeare Quarterly, TELOS, Social Text, Film Quarterly, Opera Quarterly, Early Modern Culture, The Journal of Early Modern Cultural Studies, Art in America*, and *English Studies*; he has contributed chapters to edited collections on early modern political theology, affect studies, queer studies, Shakespeare studies, Milton studies, early modern poetry, early modern drama, premodern critical race studies, sound studies, and musical performance. He is the author of three books: *Twenty Jazz Funk Greats* (Bloomsbury, 2008), *The Melancholy Assemblage: Affect and Epistemology in the English Renaissance* (Fordham UP, 2013), and *Joy of the Worm: Suicide and Pleasure in Early Modern English Literature* (U of Chicago P, 2022). He lives in Baltimore and is one half of the electronic group Matmos.

John Fletcher is Emeritus Professor of the Department of English and Comparative Literary Studies at the University of Warwick, and honorary senior research associate of the Psychoanalysis Unit at University College London. His publications include *Freud and the Scene of Trauma* (Fordham UP, 2013), and he has written extensively on the work of Jean Laplanche: *Seductions and Enigmas: Laplanche, Theory, Culture*, co-edited and introduced with Nicholas Ray (Lawrence and Wishart, 2014); edited and co-translated a special issue of *New Formations*: *Jean Laplanche and the Theory of Seduction* (2003); translated, edited, and introduced Jean Laplanche's *Essays on Otherness* (Routledge, 1999); edited and (with Jonathan House and Nicholas Ray) translated Laplanche's *Freud and the Sexual: 2000–2006* (International Psychoanalytic Books, 2011). He has also published articles on Laplanche's work in the *British Journal of Psychotherapy*, *Psychoanalytic Quarterly*, *Sitegeist*, and *Textual Practice*; *La séduction à l'origine: l'oeuvre de Jean Laplanche*, ed. Christophe Dejours and Felipe Votadoro, (PUF, 2016); *Jean Laplanche: Seduction, Translation and the Drives*, ed. John Fletcher and Martin Stanton (ICA, 1992); and recently an entry with Nicholas Ray in *Vocabulaire de Laplanche*, ed. Hélène Tessier (PUF, 2024).

David Hillman is Associate Professor of English at the University of Cambridge and Fellow of King's College, Cambridge. He is the author of *Shakespeare's Entrails: Belief, Scepticism and the Interior of the Body* (Palgrave, 2007), and the *Shakespeare and Freud* volume of the Great Shakespeareans series (Bloomsbury, 2012). He has edited or co-edited *Companionable Thinking: Spenser with …* (a special issue of *Spenser Studies* vol. 37 (2023)), *The Cambridge Companion to the Body in Literature* (Cambridge UP, 2014), *The Book of Interruptions* (Peter Lang, 2007), *The Body in Parts: Fantasies of Corporeality in Early Modern Europe* (Routledge, 1997), *Authority and Representation in Early Modern Discourse* (Johns Hopkins U.P., 1996). He trained as a child and adolescent psychotherapist at the Tavistock before taking up his post in Cambridge.

Heather Hirschfeld is Distinguished Professor of the Humanities at the University of Tennessee, where she is a faculty member in the English Department. Her monographs include *Joint Enterprises: Collaborative Drama and the Institutionalization of the English Renaissance Theater* (U of Massachusetts P, 2004), and *The End of Satisfaction: Drama and Repentance in Shakespeare's Age* (Cornell UP, 2014), and she has edited *The New Cambridge Shakespeare Hamlet* (2019) and *The Oxford Handbook of Shakespearean Comedy* (2018). She is a long-time member of the Appalachian Psychoanalytic Society.

Daniel Katz is Professor of English and Comparative Literary Studies at the University of Warwick. A specialist of twentieth-century and contemporary literature, he is the author of *Saying I No More: Subjectivity and Consciousness in the Prose of Samuel Beckett* (Northwestern UP, 1999), *American Modernism's Expatriate Scene: The Labour of Translation* (Edinburgh UP, 2007), and *The Poetry of Jack Spicer* (Edinburgh UP, 2013), as well as of many chapters and articles. He is also the editor of *Be Brave to Things: The Uncollected Poetry and Plays of Jack Spicer* (Wesleyan UP, 2021) and is Founding Editor of the book series, Bloomsbury Studies in Critical Poetics.

Paul A. Kottman is Professor of Comparative Literature at the New School for Social Research, New York City. His books include *Love as Human Freedom* (Stanford UP, 2017), *The Insistence of Art: Aesthetic Philosophy after Early Modernity* (Fordham UP, 2017), *Tragic Conditions in Shakespeare* (Johns Hopkins UP, 2009), *A Politics of the Scene* (Stanford UP, 2008), *Philosophers on Shakespeare* (Stanford UP, 2008), *The Art of Hegel's Aesthetics: Hegelian Philosophy and the Perspectives of Art History*, co-edited with Michael Squire (Wilhelm Fink, 2017).

Adelais Mills teaches English at King's College, Cambridge. She was a visiting fellow at the Rothermere American Institute, University of Oxford, and a visiting scholar at Yale University. She has contributed essays on literature and psychoanalysis to a number of journals and collections. She is undertaking a psychoanalytic training at the Centre for Freudian Analysis and Research (CFAR).

Dominique Scarfone is honorary professor at the Université de Montréal, member emeritus of the Montreal Psychoanalytic Society (French branch of the Canadian Psychoanalytic Society) and honorary member of the Italian Psychoanalytic Society. He was for many years an Associate Editor of the *International Journal of Psychoanalysis.* He retired from psychoanalytic practice in 2021 but continues teaching, writing, and presenting. The author of numerous journal articles and book chapters, he also published a number of books, his most recent being *The Reality of the Message: Psychoanalysis in the wake of Jean Laplanche* (The Unconscious in Translation, 2023). In 2024 he received the Sigourney Award for Outstanding Psychoanalytic Work.

Christian A. Smith received his doctorate from the Department of English and Comparative Literary Studies at the University of Warwick. His thesis topic was "Shakespeare's Influence on Marx, Freud and the Frankfurt School Critical Theorists." He worked as a teaching fellow at Warwick English and was awarded an Honorary Shakespeare Research Fellowship at Kingston University, London. He published papers in *Shakespeare Studies*, *Marxist Studies*, and *Translation Studies,* and co-edited a Karl Marx Bicentennial special edition of the *Shakespeare* journal with Hugh Grady. He wrote the chapter on Marxist Shakespeare Studies for *The Arden Research Handbook of Contemporary Shakespeare Criticism* and is the author of *Shakespeare's Influence on Karl Marx: The Shakespearean Roots of Marxism* (Routledge, 2022).

Madelon Sprengnether is Regents Professor Emerita of English at the University of Minnesota, where she taught literature and creative writing for over forty years. Her scholarly books include *Mourning Freud* (Bloomsbury 2018), *Shakespearean Tragedy and Gender*, co-edited with Shirley Nelson Garner (Indiana UP, 1996), *Revising the Word and the World: Essays in Feminist Literary Criticism*, co-edited with Vèvè A. Clark and Ruth-Ellen Boetcher Joeres (U of Chicago P, 1993), *The Spectral Mother: Freud, Feminism, and Psychoanalysis* (Cornell UP 1990), and *The (M)other Tongue: Essays in Feminist Psychoanalytic Interpretation*, co-edited with Shirley Nelson Garner and Claire Kahane (Cornell UP, 1985). Her books of poetry include *Near Solstice: Prose Poems* (Holy Cow! Press, 2015), *The Angel of Duluth* (White Pine Press, 2006), and *The Normal Heart* (New Rivers Press, 1981). Her books of memoir include *Great River Road: Memoir and Memory* (New Rivers Press, 2015), *Crying at the*

Movies: A Film Memoir (Graywolf Press, 2002), and *Rivers, Stories, Houses, Dreams* (New Rivers Press, 1983). For more information consult her author website: www.madelonsprengnether.com.

James W. Stone is a lecturer on Shakespeare and early modern literature at American University and on Shakespeare at the Osher Institute at Johns Hopkins University. He taught at the American University in Cairo and at the National University of Singapore. He is the author of *Crossing Gender in Shakespeare: Feminist Psychoanalysis and the Difference Within* (Routledge, 2010) and articles on Shakespeare, Milton, the Renaissance Ovid, film theory, and contemporary Egyptian art. In 2024 James Newlin and he co-edited the essay collection *New Psychoanalytic Readings of Shakespeare: Cool Reason and Seething Brains* (Routledge, 2024).

CHAPTER 1

Introduction

James W. Stone and Catherine Bates

Let us return to the primal scene, at once destructive of foundations and re-foundational, the traumatizing and fecundating origin of Shakespeare and Psychoanalysis. A new allegory of reading and a compendium of *exempla*, *The Interpretation of Dreams* launched psychoanalytic Shakespeare criticism. This is a truism: neither worth stating, again, nor capable of resisting the compulsion to repeat it, to reiterate it and to re-examine its proposition, as will witness the chapters that follow our Introduction. The particulars of the Oedipus complex, its origins in the correspondence of Freud and Wilhem Fliess in the late 1890s, its motivation of the plot in Sophocles's play and its incorporation, with a difference, in *Hamlet*, and the contestation and modification of Freud's theory of seduction in the work of Jean Laplanche and his school—these perennials are explored in the chapters in our collection by Christian A. Smith, Dominique Scarfone, and John Fletcher. *The Interpretation of Dreams* theorizes and exemplifies

J. W. Stone (✉)
American University, Paris, France

C. Bates
University of Warwick, Coventry, UK
e-mail: c.t.bates@warwick.ac.uk

J. W. Stone, C. Bates (eds.), *Shakespeare and Psychoanalysis*, Palgrave Shakespeare Studies,
https://doi.org/10.1007/978-3-032-07897-1_1

in detail how the labyrinth of a patient's dream images gives rise through transference within the analytic session to a complex and consubstantial labyrinth of words uttered in free association (*freier Einfall*). In his narrative case studies, his dream works, and his unpacking of jokes and parapraxes, Freud sets as his goal to make the seemingly random and chaotic signifying chains yield a counterpoint that is comprehensible and therefore therapeutic. (In literary criticism, one tends to speak more in terms of pleasure (Roland Barthes) than of therapy, though the two realms are connected both metaphorically and organically.) Psychoanalysis is a method that permits one to translate and to find a reason in the abounding words that displace, condense, confound, and short-circuit themselves in metaphors (the vertical axis from René Descartes through Roman Jakobson) and metonymies (the horizontal axis of contiguity) as the two axes plot with/against each other. Psychoanalysis, like psychoanalytic literary criticism, allows one to find a method in the seeming madness (of dreams and of literary texts).

To state the case with neither nuance nor hyperbole, Freud invented close reading in its modern form. Psychoanalysis relishes explaining the work and function of mono- and multilingual puns. Small differences import in Freud's explanations, often the difference of a single letter. One dream interpretation hinges on the fertile conflation of, but also subtle differentiation between, "*Weise*" ("melody") and "*Waise*" ("orphan") (419n/374n); another rings changes on the declension of "*Non vixit*" ("he did not live") as a parapraxis for the intended "*Non vivit*" ("he is not alive") (421–23/429–30); in one of Freud's own dreams, he mocks the academic paper of a medical colleague for being "written in a positively norekdal style" (296/264), a neologism that is revealed under analysis to concatenate Nora in Ibsen's *A Doll's House* and Ekdal in *The Wild Duck*. In Freud's own dream of Irma's injection, the dream upon which psychoanalysis was founded, a key node or navel of interpretation is the condensation of "amyls" in the dream-thoughts and "propyls" in the dream-content. The latter, in turn, gives rise, via free association, to the "Propylaea," a ceremonial portico not only in Athens but also in Munich (294–95/262–63). Condensing and displacing signifiers in dreams elicit so many coinages and puns that the interpretation of their content "is over-determined" (292/260). The signifier that names Irma's person has multiple referents: Freud's patient Irma, his eldest daughter, a number of other patients with different first names whom Freud examined in the neurological department of the children's hospital in Vienna (where he was working in 1895), and Freud's wife. These associated figures "were concealed behind the dream figure of 'Irma,' which thus turned into a collective image with, it must be admitted, a number of contradictory characteristics. Irma became the representative of all these other figures which had been sacrificed to the work of condensation, since I passed over to *her*, point by point, everything that reminded me of *them*" (293/260–61). Proper and common names conceal multiple referents whose apparent randomness it is the work of analysis to unravel.

The challenge of transforming apparently random images and a seeming cacophony of sounds into a logical counterpoint is addressed as well in Freud's article "Über den Gegensinn der Urworte" ("The Antithetical Meaning of Primal Words"), published ten years after his epochal dream-work. In this short essay Freud locates linguistic ambiguity not in the paronomastic play across two or more words that are homonyms (or at least sound similar if not identical) but focuses instead on single words that signify both one meaning and the opposite of this meaning. Freud begins the essay by looking retrospectively in the mirror to perform a revisiting and a self-citation (if not a Borgesian *mise-en-abîme*):

> IN my *Interpretation of Dreams* I made a statement about one of the findings of my analytic work which I did not then understand. I will repeat it here by way of preface to this review:
>
> "The way in which dreams treat the category of contraries and contradictories is highly remarkable. It is simply disregarded. 'No' seems not to exist so far as dreams are concerned. They show a particular preference for combining contraries into a unity or for representing them as one and the same thing. Dreams feel themselves at liberty, moreover, to represent any element by its wishful contrary; so that there is no way of deciding at a first glance whether any element that admits of a contrary is present in the dream-thoughts as a positive or as a negative." (155/143)

As "a thing in a dream can mean its opposite" (155/143), so the "same" word may differ from itself; it defers univocal meaning. The following are some examples of such self-deconstructing (*différance*) words: the Latin *sacer* designates that which makes holy and that which desecrates the holy, the English contronym *cleave* is the dividing of a whole into parts and/or making parts adhere in order to form a whole, the word *ravel* means an entangling of strands and/or a disentangling of them. Let us take but one example, from the legions offered, by William Empson, of what he calls "a word which covers its own opposite": "a 'restive' horse, for example, is a horse which is restless because it has been resting for too long" (195).

Empson writes that his seventh type of ambiguity, "the most ambiguous that can be conceived, occurs when the two meanings of the word, the two values of the ambiguity, are the two opposite meanings defined by the context, so that the total effect is to show a fundamental division in the writer's mind" (192). He is not without precedent: "I invoke primitive languages on the authority of Freud (*Notebooks*, vol. iv, No. 10), and cannot myself pretend to understand their mode of action" (193). Although what he called (at various points in his career) "complex words" pose challenges, there is no cause for despair: "In so far, in short, as you know that two things are opposites, you know a relation which connects them" (195). Empson's Freud-inflected theory manifests itself in application in adducing and analyzing page after page of very short quotations from the English canon (from Shakespeare more than from any other poet). Ur-texts of modern theory like Empson's and Freud's read uncannily the condensations (the vertical axis of metaphor, to use the terminology of Roman Jakobson's structuralist rubric) and displacements (what Jakobson calls the horizontal axis of metonymy) of poets and dreamers. They rationalize the buried strata and striations of texts and dream-texts. In *A Midsummer Night's Dream*, Philostrate presents Theseus with a list of entertainments to celebrate his nuptials, including a "tedious brief" enactment of the *liebestod* of Pyramis and Thisbe, "very tragical mirth." The newlywed ruler wonders how he can resolve "the concord of this discord" (5.1.56–60).[1] (The comic oxymorons, by the way, are closer to the fifth than the seventh Empsonian type of ambiguity, hence not entirely identical to Freud's antitheticals or to Shakespeare's in his Sonnets or in the tragedies; but little matter.) The analyst-critic can help extricate analysand Theseus from the befuddling dream and make all these odds even. The analyst-critic and the analysand, like the lunatic, the lover, and the poet, are of imagination all compact. There is method in their madness (and, in antithetical counterpoint, there is madness in their method).

Not only is Freud someone who reads close to the bone and then penetrates to the marrow below. He is also, *avant la lettre*, a distant reader and a proto-structuralist, anticipating Jakobson, Claude Lévi-Strauss, and Jacques Lacan. The structural differences that a single word can make (or

[1] In the Introduction all quotations from Shakespeare's works are taken from the single-volume Arden, in its third series.

one or two letters within a single word)[2] can be writ large in the analysis of genre, theme, and groups of texts, as is evident already in *The Interpretation of Dreams.* In two foundational texts for literary criticism, and for Shakespeare studies, the astonishing "The Uncanny" and "The Theme of the Three Caskets," Freud amalgamates gleanings from many linguistic traditions and epochs to establish, respectively: 1. What seems disturbing, strange, and unfamiliar (*unheimlich*) is often what was once quite familiar or home-like (including one's primal-original home in the womb) and 2. the theme (*Motiv*) ("motif" or "motive")[3] of choosing among the three caskets is an analogue for the three women in every man's life (see the discussion of *Cymbeline* below). *King Lear* and *The Merchant of Venice* are analyzed in the essay on the casket choice, along with texts written in Greek, Latin, German, and French. In these two essays, Freud implicates himself in practices that would become familiar decades later under the rubric of "comparative literature." Limitations of space restrain one from going into detail, but our expectation is that those who plumb the following chapters will remark that several of our contributors read Shakespeare and psychoanalysis not primarily through attention to local linguistic slippage but rather through the framework of the structuring principles of thought and social relations—principles that reveal their action paradigmatically, at a distance from the local mesh of words (i.e., Empsonian close reading).

❦

From quite different perspectives (as is now well-rehearsed), the pincers of the New Historicism and of cognitive psychology strained to marginalize psychoanalytic approaches to Shakespeare. The former emerged in 1980, while the latter came on strong in the new millennium. The New Historicism dealt blows to any literary-critical methodology that analyzed a text (or a cluster of texts) closely, whether in its oldest version, in psychoanalysis, or in later versions like the New Criticism, structuralism, or deconstruction. In a controversial essay Stephen Greenblatt criticized

[2] For the difference that a single letter can make to psychoanalytic criticism, see the fifth chapter in our collection, by David Hillman and Adelais Mills. From the case study of the Wolfman they glean the "Roman V" which bars and castrates not only Freud's patient but also the name and person of Shakespeare's Coriolanus.

[3] Christian A. Smith offers a compelling analysis of errors in translation in the title of this essay as it appeared in the *Standard Edition*. See the first chapter in our collection.

as ahistorical the application of psychoanalysis to early modern literature: "Yet I think that in all the literary instances I have cited, identity is conceived in a way that renders psychoanalytic interpretations marginal or belated" (221).[4] Politicized historicists dismissed psychoanalysis and the various schools of formalist criticism that pretended to ahistorical, universal truths divorced from the embedded realities of culture and of material culture: of religion, of science and medicine, of law and politics, of Foucauldian sexuality, of race and colonialism. New historicists emphasized the grounding of literature within non-literary contexts and downplayed linguistic ambiguities. Often the emphasis was placed, usefully, on how the canon was informed by non-canonical texts like religious tracts and sermons, letters and journals, and travel writing. Both psychoanalytic and non-psychoanalytic formalists alike, by contrast, fetishized the warp and the woof of Shakespeare's text. For the formalists, whether they were not (think of Stephen Booth in his edition of Shakespeare's Sonnets) or were (think of Joel Fineman in his Lacanian analysis of the Sonnets) also partisans of psychoanalysis, literary texts whose every rift was loaded with ore were the end of literary analysis (Barthes's pleasures of the text and his

[4] In the Introduction to their recent collection of essays on Shakespeare and psychoanalysis, *New Psychoanalytic Readings of Shakespeare: Cool Reason and Seething Brains* (Routledge, 2024), James Newlin and James W. Stone refute Greenblatt's opposition to psychoanalysis (2–5), as do several essays within this earlier collection. Likewise, the editors of the present volume have mounted similar challenges to New Historicism elsewhere in their writing. Catherine Bates, for example, critiques Greenblatt's reading of Wyatt's lyrics and *Penitential Psalms* in *Renaissance Self-Fashioning*, in which the male critic aims to recuperate and to heroicize the poet's abject and masochistic personae. She suggests, rather, that one might "choose to take issue with this somewhat self-congratulatory portrait of what the ideal literary critic should look like" (*Masculinity, Gender and Identity* 12). Bates argues against the thesis that through his poetry Wyatt is able to subvert dialectically, and to triumph over, his fraught life at the Henrician court. She opposes Greenblatt's notion that there is an unproblematic, uncastrated agency that can ground or re-establish a lost masculinity by means of poetic sublimation. James W. Stone defends psychoanalytic formalism over against Greenblatt's historicizing reading of *Twelfth Night*. Whereas Greenblatt regards Feste's reference to the kid glove ("A sentence is but a cheverel glove to a good wit: how quickly the wrong side may be turned outward" (3.1.12–14)) that can be turned inside-out as a homology for male and female genitals, Stone sees the glove not as material object but rather as the signifier *glove*. Feste employs this signifier as a metaphor for the instability of words. Viola avers that "they that dally nicely with words may quickly make them wanton" (3.1.16–17). The reversibility of the glove describes the way that words may be turned inside out and so make of their speakers and bearers the confused and divided subjects of sexual desire and loss (24–42).

readerly *jouissance*). Overdetermined words and their unpacking were the be-all and end-all of Shakespeare's, and of the Shakespeare critic's, fecundity. For non-psychoanalytic and for psychoanalytic close readers alike, aporetic, ambiguous, and antinomian language yields consummate and uncanny verbal and thematic fruit. From the Sonnets alone one is presented with a vast array of examples whose complex wordplay, and structures of complex words (the figures of chiasmus, for example, and of *syneciosis*, which George Puttenham Englished as the "Crosse-Couple" in *The Arte of English Poesie*) recall the cento of exemplary fragments of mono- and multi-lingual wordplay cited from Freud above. Booth's mandarin comments on the words in the sonnets run to four hundred pages. (His commentary on a single sonnet can extend to several pages, reminiscent of the way that Freud employs a few sentences in italics in order to lay out the manifest content of a dream, then inundates his readers with a page or pages of detailed analysis that lays forth the latent meanings.) Freud, Empson, Booth: the dream of an antithetical or ambiguous language that yields meaning and is interpretable. Fineman too is a partisan of this dream, in his psychoanalysis of the Sonnets across the Lacanian registers of the Imaginary and the Symbolic, and in his readings of the thematics of misogyny and narratives of rape in other Shakespearean works. Fineman's redoubtable analysis, however, like Freud's, invited antithetical and antipathetic responses from feminist criticism.[5]

The shift from the phallocentric and the phallogocratic to the "hymeneal" spurred the creation of what may have seemed to some, initially, to be an oxymoron: feminist psychoanalysis. It would be neither unnuanced nor hyperbolical to advance the proposition that the many sexist assumptions in Freud's oeuvre proved to be fodder for (or, to follow a wont of feminist criticism, to *engender*) readings against his masculinist grain.

[5] Fineman's masculinist account of the difference between the sexes genders difference itself as feminine: "In a formula whose lusty misogyny is recognizably Shakespearean, we can say that in Shakespeare's sonnets the difference between man and woman is woman herself" (17). In a typical Neoplatonic schema, man is figured as the sun, woman as the moon (as in the debate between shrew-tamer Petruchio and shrew Kate), in service of an "orthodox erotics for which woman is the Other to man, the *hetero* to homo, precisely because her essence is *to be* this lunatic difference between sameness and difference" (120). Formulas that represent man as self-identical (always the same as himself) lend themselves to a feminist deconstruction. Shoshana Felman comments on how the uncanny feminine inhabits and subverts the notion of masculine sameness-unto-itself: "The feminine … is not *outside* the masculine, its reassuring canny *opposite*, it is *inside* the masculine, its uncanny *difference from itself*" (64).

Masculinist Freud proved fertile for his detractors; the bibliography of Freud's feminist critics grew large. It did cultural work on both sides of the Atlantic Ocean and in the Global South.

The hagiography of Freud evident in the opening paragraphs of our Introduction, redolent of Bardolatry, has its reverse side of the coin, its tain that backs (sub-verts) the shining mirror. To hold Freud in homage or to wish to destroy him, to consecrate or to desecrate (the two contrary meanings of *sacer*) the father or the oedipal father figure—both approaches may yield cogent literary criticism. Attempting to topple Freud's statue from its sacred pedestal (or to debase the coin of his reputation, or to tarnish or to "tain" the Freudian specular Imaginary), feminists in Europe and in the United States called into question the patriarchal orthodoxies of psychoanalysis: the hegemony of the phallus as the locus of signifying, of penis envy as a universal of feminine sexuality, of the father as the ultimate determinant of law, prohibition, and meaning, of the Oedipus complex as the dominant if not sole motive force of narratives of the family romance.

In France, the "apostasy" of the radical feminism of Luce Irigaray met with her banishment from the ranks of *l'École freudienne* in 1974. Irigaray's voice fell under the sign of erasure (~~Irigaray~~). This was a regrettable attempt to repress (*refouler*) and to purge an early progenitor of feminist psychoanalysis who revealed the internal contradictions within the tenets which this science held aloft for reflection.[6] Outside France, feminist Shakespeareans from the late 1970s through the end of the century often looked for inspiration more to the object relations psychoanalysis of Melanie Klein and D. W. Winnicott than to the penchant of foreign Theory (the noisome import from France) to avail itself of *écriture féminine* in its efforts to dethrone the phallus, to bar the bar of the regnant transcendental signifier. Emphasis on the preoedipal mother-child dyad

[6] Irigaray contrasts male masturbation by means of the hand to the way that a woman takes self-pleasure: "As for woman, she touches herself in and of herself without any need for mediation, and before there is any way to distinguish activity from passivity. Woman 'touches herself' all the time, and moreover no one can forbid her to do so, for her genitals are formed of two lips in continuous contact. Thus, within herself, she is already two—but not divisible into one(s)—that caress each other" (24) Woman escapes phallomorphism and the scoptophilic economy of the male gaze that would fix her as the object of its desire. The consequences of the fact that woman "*is neither one nor two*" and that "her sexual organ, which is not *one* organ, is counted as *none*" (26) extend far beyond the body into differences in the way that women think and practice philosophy, psychoanalysis, literary criticism.

supplemented a deficiency in Freud's hyper-masculine Oedipus complex. Janet Adelman, Coppélia Kahn, Carol Thomas Neely, and Madelon Sprengnether were leaders in this school of Shakespeare studies. Feminist critics rang the changes on male characters who blamed their madness (melancholy, hysteria, rage) on the women in their lives. Hamlet rants against his mother and girlfriend for the loquaciousness that he thinks causes his (oedipal) delay in avenging the murder of his father. The melancholy (steeped in the affront to narcissism) which makes Hamlet fall short of the male heroic ideal of revenge tragedy induces (and is induced by) a dilatory wordiness that effeminizes and bewhores him, he complains (at length). He "must like a whore unpack my heart with words / And fall a-cursing like a very drab, / A stallion!" (2.2.582–84). The hero's inaction stems from the fact that he is "as patient as the female dove" (5.1.276) and prone to what he characterizes as "such a kind of gaingiving as would perhaps trouble a woman" (5.2.195–96) (Adelman 11–37). King Lear berates the "mother" or "*hysterica passio*" for his being dispossessed of both kingdom and sanity:

> O, how this mother swells up toward my heart!
> *Hysterica passio*, down, thou climbing sorrow,
> Thy element's below. (2.2.252–54)

The etiology of the former king's self-diagnosed madness is the uterus that rises to (s)mother him.[7] Lear rages and rails against the depths of the female body, *his* female body, and that of the female body in general: "But to the girdle do the gods inherit, beneath is all the fiend's: there's hell, there's darkness, there is the sulfurous pit, burning, scalding, stench, consumption!" (4.6.122–26) (Kahn 33–49). Adelman and Kahn critique

[7] In his biography of Freud, Peter Gay details how Freud's visit to Paris (in 1885) to study with Jean Martin Charcot at La Salpêtrière reinforced his understanding that men as well as women suffered from hysteria and that the malady was more psychological than organic. When Freud returned to Vienna many months later, among the colleagues before whom he lectured about his French discoveries was a nationalistic "old surgeon" who asked whether the name "hysteria" itself, from the Greek word for "womb," did not "make it plain that women alone could suffer from hysteria?" (53). The old monoglot surgeon, untutored in and untouched by the literary, skeptical of the latest innovations from abroad, had little tolerance for ambiguous referents, contrarian senses, or the Shakespearean nihilisms of the sound of O that courses through Lear's body.

male misogyny by unveiling and unraveling the inconsistencies and contradictions in its putative logic.

In *Cymbeline*, Posthumus, wrongly confident that his wife Innogen has committed adultery with the rake Iachimo, inveighs against the physical parts that mark him as being of woman born: his navel, his mother's genitalia, and her womb. He locates in the woman's body the source of every moral debility and all the travails in men's lives: "Could I find out / The woman's part in me—for there's no motion / That tends to vice in man, but I affirm / It is the woman's part" (2.5.19–22). But neither exorcising nor surgically removing this anatomical part and its supposedly deleterious effects is any more possible than reversing the fact of having been born. Posthumus's soliloquy has proven fertile ground for feminist criticism because it encapsulates a major topos of misogyny: the problem of man's tendency to project difference onto the Woman whom he hypostasizes as Other. Many men cannot divorce themselves from blaming women, without whom, they aver in bad faith and non-factually, they would be self-identical (self-contented and self-contained), independent of the malaise entrained (so the hysterical male asserts) by sexual difference.

One wonders how to place this reified Female (this female object of a man's obsessive fantasy) within Freud's schema of the three women in a man's life in "The Theme of the Three Caskets": the mother who gives birth to the male child, the wife whose bed he shares, and Death, or mother earth, the woman to whom every man must return and with whom he must rest eternally. Innogen is Posthumus's wife, but she is not the unchaste wife he says she is. The possibility of a fourth woman in a man's life, the redemptive daughter, is absent from Posthumus's rant, as it is from Freud's schema, though such young women do exist in Shakespeare's late romances (including *Cymbeline*). In *Pericles*, Marina is lauded by her father as "Thou that beget'st him that did thee beget" (5.1.185). In the acts of begetting and bearing, Marina is both father and mother to her own father. In *The Tempest*, in marrying Ferdinand, Miranda allows her father Prospero to get back in retirement not simply his lost duchy but rather more than that: a dynasty that comprises Naples in the south and Milan in the north. Prospero gains through his daughter more than he ever lost through his naïvete and mismanagement in Milan; more than what was lost is found (to invoke and to vary a Christic and Pauline topos dear to Shakespeare). In Shakespeare's romances, daughters ultimately prove fecund for the interests of their prodigal and irresponsible fathers or husbands. Innogen contributes to the victory of her surrogate father (Belarius) and brothers over imperial Rome, to the redemption of her wayward Posthumus, and to turning her biological father Cymbeline into the parthenogenic mother-father figure he becomes and takes joy in at the end of the play ("O, what am I? / A mother to the birth of three? Ne'er mother / Rejoic'd deliverance more" (5.5.368–70)). The fourth woman in a man's life, the daughter whom Freud does not include in his schema, permits the reversal of many of the misogynistic charges that some men lay at the feet of the first three women.[8]

Madelon Sprengnether (the author of the third chapter in our collection) foregrounds not only the misogyny in the tragedies but also the celebration of female heroines who, in demolishing misogyny by deconstructing its "logic," create a "powerful matriarchal vision" (177): "The values that emerge from these plays are, if anything, 'feminine' values dissociated from the traditional masculine categories of force and politics, focused instead on the significance of personal relationships or the fact of human relatedness: the values of feeling, kinship, loyalty, friendship, and even romantic love" (179). Unlike Shakespeare's other tragic heroines, Cleopatra dies long after her husband. She is "the woman who betrays, a Circe, an Acrasia, an Eve, the Venus of *Venus and Adonis*," but she nurtures and "conceives" the Antony of our memory. She is "imaginative, fertile, identified with the procreative processes of the Nile" (179). From the inert mudflats of the receding Nile are spontaneously generated hermaphroditic serpents. Antony's "sword, made weak by my affection" (3.11.68) has the potential to be restored; he is not bound (even not bound after death) to remain forever "robbed ... of my sword" (4.14.23). Let us add: "I am dying, Egypt, dying" (4.15.19) is Antony's apostrophe to his lover in the throes of his death ecstasy. (One thinks of John Donne's lovers in "The Canonization" who "die and rise the same" by their sacred

[8] Not every man has a daughter, after all, so Freud cannot be faulted for omitting her as the fourth woman in a man's life. (Were Freud rigorous in his logic of inclusion and omission, he should have omitted the second woman in a man's life, for not all men have a wife.) Burton A. Melnick suggests that the fourth woman in a man's life, his daughter, symbolizes rebirth for her elderly father. He quotes a letter from Freud to James S. H. Bransom, in which Freud refers to "the secret meaning" of *King Lear* as being "the repressed incestuous claims on the daughter's love" (25). Ruth Nevo discusses Innogen in terms of one of Shakespeare's "beloved, thaumaturgic daughters" of the romances, who "supplement Freud's death-dominated triad" (93). Nevo recalls that Freud personally did not discover the value of daughters until his "Anna-Antigone" helped him in his illnesses (157n). She shepherded her father to a new life (albeit a short one) in London.

love.) Antony owes his resurrective prowess to his pharaonic Queen who both consumes him and conceives him anew. Posthumously, the joys and travails of Antony and Cleopatra, their deaths and resurrections, will be played time and again on the stage, in English and in global Shakespeares, in translation, in adaptation.

In 2024 James Newlin and James W. Stone published the first collection of essays devoted solely to psychoanalytic readings of Shakespeare since the influential anthology (which includes Sprengnether's chapter) edited by Murray M. Schwartz and Coppélia Kahn over forty years earlier, in 1980. In the Introduction to this recent book, the co-editors critique the New Historicism (see above) and cognitive psychology (5-7). Influential publications from 2001 onward gave cognitive psychology the upper hand over psychoanalysis as the primary psychological method of critique in Shakespeare studies. For many years Shakespeare journals and seminar offerings at annual meetings of the Shakespeare Association of America provided platforms for analytical prescriptions and quantifiable diagnoses (and remedies) for the fictional characters (e.g., Iago's "autism") in Shakespeare's works. These doses and overdoses of the dismal science left scant room for the unrepentant psychoanalysts' rehearsals of predilection: incest, parricide, revenge, violence and violation and their trauma, the compulsion to repeat (its morbidity, its fatality), the melancholy sickness unto death, masochism, the vagaries of repression, and the interpretation of dreams. Also regrettable was the fact that the cognitive approach had little or no interest in the Feminist Complaint against psychoanalysis, a complaint that was cognizant of its historical sources, whereas many a cognitive critic had little or no interest in the origins of psychiatry in Austro-Germanic culture, nor in its further developments elsewhere in Europe, the United States, and Latin America. The clinic of cognitive literary science repressed and desiccated the bloody themes, the perennials (by definition both ancient and modern), and the predilections of the founders of psychiatry.[9] But the repressed returns (one of the perennial themes of the old guard, formerly the vanguard), often with a

[9] In the American popular press, one reads that Freud's writings and those of his school are at times hard to find today in the libraries where students specializing in mental health do their studies, so much has the cognitive approach superseded psychoanalysis. At the same time, however, the press in Britain and the United States points to a revival of interest in psychoanalysis in popular culture.

vengeance.[10] In our collection Heather Hirschfeld, the author of the fourth chapter, makes brilliant use of Wilfred Bion in order to effect a reconciliation between cognitive science and psychoanalysis.

❦

Was Shakespeare Freudian or Freud Shakespearean? This is a question psychoanalytic and literary critics have routinely asked and routinely found unanswerable (see, e.g., Armstrong, Bates ("Recognitions"), Fineman, Hillman). Nonetheless, these two questions are indicative of distinct directions of travel: the profound influence which the works of Shakespeare undoubtedly had on Freud from the very inception of psychoanalysis, and the insights of psychoanalysis as they, in turn, are applied to the works of Shakespeare. This volume is interested in the traffic between the two, it being, of course, a two-way street. We aim to implement a "backward" look (typically psychoanalytic in the sense of what Freud called *Nachträglichkeit* or "Afterwardness," as Laplanche translates the term) which will encourage us to rethink both Shakespeare's role in the construction of psychoanalysis and the looping back which occurs when psychoanalytic theory, in all its later developments and reconfigurations, comes to be applied to his work. This will include looking at Shakespearean texts which Freud never mentions but which—this new way of looking suggests—may well have contributed to the subsequent shaping and development of psychoanalytic theory after all.

[10] Limitations of space permit only a glance at a few of the chapters in Newlin and Stone's recent collection that mine the strident return of the repressed literary-critical science that is psychoanalysis. One author is guided by Eric L. Santner's *On the Psychotheology of Everyday Life* in elaborating how Hamlet's ability to transcend religious injunctions and to take action in the secular world comes at a cost. In Santner's terms, Hamlet cannot truly inhabit the midst of life because he chooses to defend himself against the Other rather than tarrying with its unassumable excess. Another contributor engages with Nicholas Abraham and Maria Torok's "cryptonomy" of Freud's case study of the Wolfman in order to analyze physical and psychological entombment in *Romeo and Juliet*. Another contributor adduces Cynthia Marshall's work on the shattering of the self (her critique of Stephen Greenblatt's optimistic Renaissance self-fashioning) to show how the sadomasochism of the tragic hero is, paradoxically, the means for constructing his subjectivity. Drew Daniel (the author of our Afterword) reads closely Octavius Caesar's description of Antony drinking "the stale of horses and the gilded puddle" (1.4.63) to show how fantasies of transfer and contagion, abjection and waste, and anxiety about effeminization fuel the Caesarean project of empire and the racialized (Cleopatra as subversively "tawny" (1.1.6)), hypertrophied white masculinity that it presupposes.

To that end, we divide the volume into two equal parts. In the first, "Shakespeare and Psychoanalysis," five chapters look in different ways at the formative part Shakespeare's work played in the construction of psychoanalysis. In the second, "Psychoanalysis and Shakespeare," five chapters look at the many ways in which psychoanalysis so constructed might bear complexly on Shakespeare's poems and plays. Part I opens, then, with a chapter by Christian A. Smith which showcases Shakespeare's centrality to the formulation of psychoanalytic theory across Freud's career (from his studies in hysteria to *Beyond the Pleasure Principle*) by considering a range of texts from across Shakespeare's (*A Midsummer Night's Dream*, *Hamlet*, *1 Henry IV*, *The Merchant of Venice*, and *King Lear*). Although pride of place is given to *Hamlet*, a play Freud refers to more than any other by some margin—and especially to the part it played in his dramatic abandonment of the seduction theory to make way for the Oedipus complex in 1897—Shakespeare's influence is shown to be omnipresent in what might be called Freud's larger "literary turn": his realization that in analytic practice it often proved difficult if not impossible to differentiate memories from stories, fictions, and imagined scenes; and that these fantasies commanded absolute belief and turned out to play just as powerful a role in shaping the psyche and sexual life not only in hysterics and neurotics but all human beings.

It was this shift—momentous for the development of psychoanalysis as both a theory and practice—which made Freud the medically trained specialist of nervous disease into Freud the great analyst of culture. This literary turn shaped not only his thought but a new way of thinking: one that, in being open to the illogicalities of the imagination, of metaphor, of wordplay and wit, was more a poetic method than a scientific one. Like Smith, Dominique Scarfone also notes Freud's citation of Hamlet's famous line "The readiness is all" (5.2.172) to indicate that this switch to a newly open disposition or availability was itself drawn from literature. In his chapter, Scarfone takes this citation as the basis for an extended meditation on Freud's development of the analytic method: the "readiness" of analyst and analysand alike to be open to all that is unexpected, contradictory, even crazy-sounding, and to accept these without criticism or judgment. Like Smith, Scarfone finds it remarkable that Freud should look to Shakespeare—and specifically to *Hamlet*—at the critical moment of 1897. Yet, surprisingly, the collapse of what until that point had been Freud's etiological and explanatory matrix for the generation of neurosis and hysteria did not prompt despair in him but rather good cheer. As he confided to his friend and confidant, Wilhelm Fliess, "I vary Hamlet's saying, 'To be in readiness': to be cheerful is everything!" (Masson 265). Freud was cheerful because what remained "entirely secure" (266) was the method he had been evolving for interpreting dreams, free associations, symptoms, and unconscious material in all its baffling strangeness: namely, to accept—resorting to his second favorite quotation from the play—that there must be method in the madness and vice versa.

In the chapter that follows, Madelon Sprengnether takes the speech of Shakespearean characters to inform models of subjectivity subsequently developed by psychoanalytic theory. An intervention in the long-running debate between psychoanalytic and New Historicist literary practices touched on briefly above, Sprengnether's chapter argues that the Freudian and post-Freudian subject is the product of a distinct literary history: the transformative moment of the Renaissance in which pioneering early moderns such as Petrarch peered into the culture—and especially the *literary* culture—of classical antiquity and found it uncannily familiar (Latin) yet different (pagan) from their own. From this encounter emerged a subjectivity that was opaque to itself and as fragmented, layered, mysterious, and revelatory as the archeological ruins of Rome (Freud's go-to metaphor for the mental topography). Using *Romeo and Juliet* as a case study, Sprengnether shows how Shakespeare uses Juliet's speech to dramatize this move toward a complex subjectivity in rhetorical terms, as she transitions from a simple girl and object of Romeo's bland Petrarchism to a mature woman who can take the initiative, make decisions, express ambivalence, undertake deception, and experience desire, doubt, horror, aloneness, and a near descent into madness: in all these respects looking ahead to Shakespeare's later tragic heroes. For Sprengnether, this amounts to evidence that "without Shakespeare there could be no Freud" (60).

Heather Hirschfeld likewise considers the way Shakespeare uses speech to represent the thought processes of his characters (thinking being a process of symbolization), in this case, the distinctively *disordered* thought processes made evident in *Measure for Measure*. A contribution to cognition studies as a rich and fast-developing subfield in Shakespeare criticism, Hirschfeld's chapter shows how Shakespeare's problem play corroborates the work of Wilfred Bion, a British psychoanalyst in the Kleinian tradition, for whom the inability to process the dissatisfactions of everyday life gives rise to blanks or crises in thought. With its rigidly binary thinking ("measure for measure"), the play exemplifies such disordered thought in abundance—the failure to think laterally or outside the box, to see alternative points of view, to accommodate ambivalence, uncertainty, contradiction, and doubt, or to find a third way—and as a result takes increasingly desperate measures to solve problems of its own making. Characterized by inflexibility, legalism, and literalism, the speech and sometimes chaotic syntax of Angelo, Isabella, and the Duke (in both soliloquies and exchanges) shows thought, if you can call it that, going round in circles and getting nowhere—the play's logic of exchange being the opposite of equitable—right up to its unsatisfactory, problematic, and unresolved end.

In the chapter which closes Part I, David Hillman and Adelais Mills consider the logic of the supplement. As that which variously alters, adds to, and completes psychoanalysis, literature—and especially Shakespeare—has long laid claim to know something about what Hillman and Mills call "the unanalyzed of Freud," making psychoanalysis in large part a "precipitate of the literary" (105). Indeed, Shakespeare is not only present in Freud's many mentions of him throughout his work,[11] but even more so "when unmentioned than when he is cited," as Harold Bloom is quoted as saying (391). Of Shakespeare's thirty-eight plays, Freud refers to exactly half, some (notably *Hamlet*, *Macbeth*, and *Julius Caesar*) many times over. Perhaps one would not expect him to refer to every single play, but some absences are conspicuous, and Hillman and Mills make a compelling case that this is a category into which *Coriolanus* falls, all the more so, indeed, for its huge popularity in the German-speaking world of the 1910s to the 1930s. The play seems to speak to some of Freud's central concerns (not least his obsession with Rome) but, as a classic case of repression, also to his blind spots. Mining Freud's analysis of the Wolfman for clues as to Freud's silence regarding *Coriolanus*, they find castration anxiety, homosexual orientations, and an arrested and unresolved Oedipus complex. Most important of all for the purposes of the present volume, however, is their confirmation of the argument that "literature has a unique claim to bearing on Freud's psychoanalysis as the 'other scene' of the unconscious bears upon conscious thought" (108).

This observation leads directly to the chapters in Part II which return to the insights which psychoanalytic theory can bring to bear on Shakespearean texts which helped—in ways both obvious and unobvious—to shape it. In the opening two chapters, Catherine Bates and James

[11] See the chronological record of quotations from, allusions to, and mentions of Shakespeare and his works in Freud's writings set out in the Appendix at the end of the volume.

Stone consider Shakespeare's two narrative poems (often treated as a pair), neither of which Freud appears to have mentioned. Both chapters consider the role sexual violence plays in the formation of the speaking subject, and both take a broadly Lacanian approach. Discussing *Venus and Adonis*, Bates shows how its story of a mortal youth whose relation with a goddess is fatally severed when a boar gores him in the thigh neatly figures the fatal intrusion of the Phallus into the mother/child dyad, inaugurating the long process of separation, castration, and oedipalization by means of which the *infans* ("unspeaking") enters into both language and adult sexuality to become, in time, a speaking, desiring being. This shattering of an idyll can also be seen to figure the transition from the Imaginary (the register of fiction, fantasy, nostalgia, and the consolatory jubilations of the mirror stage) to the Symbolic (the register of absence, difference, insatiable desire, castration, perversity, taboo, law, guilt, shame, punishment, and repression). As if testing out the full potentialities of his medium here in 1593, relatively early in his writing career, Shakespeare would go on to associate the Imaginary with comedy, lyric, and romance, and the Symbolic with tragedy, satire, and complaint.

Discussing *The Rape of Lucrece* (written a year later in 1594), Stone considers the unspeakable crime of rape, contrasting what he calls the "contradiction-saturated logic of rape" (170)—in which No is taken for Yes and the antithetical meaning of primal words such as *let* (indicative of prohibition and permission alike) can be recruited into any rapist's charter—with forms of "speech" which are capable of countering such antithetical aporias. We put "speech" in inverted commas here, because the response to this unspeakable crime is classically one of speechlessness, as in the tapestry which Ovid's tongueless Philomela weaves in the book to which Shakespeare's tongueless Lavinia points in *Titus Andronicus*. In *The Rape of Lucrece*, Stone argues, the eponymous heroine likewise contemplates a tapestry—a wordless-because-visual tableau representing the fall of Troy (albeit one re-mediated through language in Shakespeare's ekphrasis)—and, by learning to read deceit in the pictured face of Sinon, finds herself able to reverse, remedy, and repair the duplicities of language to which she had earlier fallen victim. Unlike Philomel and Lavinia, Lucrece is able to speak after her rape—"My tongue shall utter all" (line 1076)—because the passage from Symbolic to Imaginary has been temporarily reversed. In her suicide (the archetypally Stoic act), she cuts off her own life in lieu of having her tongue cut out, thus making the ultimate sacrifice in order to "lend her tongue" as Stone puts it (179) to the story of her violation and that of her allegorical sisters: a fascinating take on the genre of female complaint.

In Part I, both Smith and Scarfone make reference to the work of Laplanche. Smith notes that what Freud had rejected in 1897 as hysteria's cause (seduction as historical experiences of childhood sexual abuse, subsequently repressed) Laplanche reformulates as "a universal feature of the encounter between the infant and the caring *other*" (39). For Scarfone, momentous as Freud's abandonment of the seduction theory was, Laplanche "spent lots of energy putting it back" (43). At stake here is what John Fletcher, in the chapter that follows, identifies as Freud's constant alternation between a radical decentering of the subject in relation to a primal other and a resurgent recentering on the individual as the origin of his or her own development (positions Laplanche characterizes as Copernican and Ptolemaic, respectively). If the Oedipus complex—which Freud had partly corroborated by moving from *Hamlet* to his theory—represented just such an "endogenous model of psychic causality" centered on "spontaneous, infantile impulses" (195), then Fletcher turns this round by moving from the theory back to *Hamlet*, and, in his own Laplanchean reading of the play, exploring the alternative "exogenous" model of psychic development which it manifests. Here, the traumatic intromission of enigmatic parental signifiers which confound the infant and destine the subject to the compulsive repetition of that primal trauma thereafter are figured in (among others) the Ghost's hair-raising "tale" of Purgatory (1.5.15), the repeated descriptions and representations of being poisoned in the ear, and the hideous sound of Troy crashing to the ground which (according to the Player's speech) "takes prisoner Pyrrhus's ear" (2.2.475). Just as Hillman and Mills found it significant that Freud should apparently avoid engaging with *Coriolanus*, a play in which the father figure is almost entirely absent, so Fletcher finds it "surprising for Freud of all thinkers to ignore the figure of the father and in this play of all plays" (215).

Concluding Part II, the chapters by Daniel Katz and Paul Kottman—which look at *Troilus and Cressida* and *The Winter's Tale*, respectively—both center on the theme of fidelity and the complex questions it raises concerning doubt and faith, identification and desire, envy and rivalry, love and violence. "Why," asks Kottman, "has the everydayness of skepticism been so hard to believe in?" (260). Or, to put it the other way round, why has infidelity so often been represented in literature—and in these two plays especially—as a cataclysmic breach of faith, a shattering of the status quo, a collapse in the belief that a good woman (like Descartes's good God) would not deceive us? One reason historically given, Kottman suggests, "has been something like the canonical 'Shakespearean' view of men as doubting, and of women as subject to either male doubt or male faith" (264), a position based on the assumed limits of male knowledge about the sexual life of women. Both Kottman and Katz use their chapters to revise this "canonical" view, and both do so by comparing the Shakespearean plays they discuss with modern remakes of them: Éric Rohmer's film *Conte d'hiver* (1992), and the American poet Jack Spicer's play *Troilus* (1955), respectively. In both cases, moreover, they find these modern texts enact that revision by turning specifically to the desire of women. As Kottman notes, in Shakespeare's late plays (romances like *The Winter's Tale*) men who learn the hard way eventually come to accept their exclusion from what women know and to awake their faith, as Leontes does through the ministrations of Paulina. But the revision of pathological jealousy and insecurity also requires that a general, pervasive, and ordinary skepticism toward the absolute knowability and reliability of another person be extended to women, too: to Félicie, the heroine of Rohmer's film who acts out her inability to believe, finally, in her "mad love" (272); and to Cressida in Spicer's play who finds peace, ultimately, in a universe which is not constantly required to mean something, relief from the constant need to test and know. This relaxing into skepticism not only takes the pressure off everyone but, more importantly, ensures that love can never be taken for granted, and—for that reason—might paradoxically come closer to being love after all.

It is notable that these two chapters on the theme of fidelity should belong to what might be called the field of "adaptation studies," for the fidelity in question extends from matters of sexual to matters of textual relation. What bearing do these secondary texts have on the Shakespearean plays they imitate, riff off, supplement, revise? Are they "unfaithful" to the original, as bad translations are supposed to be? Or do they add something, complete the original in some way, so that it needs them and vice versa? All of the above, Katz and Kottman conclude. In the case of Shakespeare's *Troilus and Cressida* these questions are especially pertinent because the play is itself obsessed with issues of emulation (the word and its cognates occur nine times within it, more often than in any other Shakespeare play),[12] such that Spicer's emulative project is, as Katz

[12] Aside from *As You Like It* where cognates of the word appear twice, they never appear more often than once through the rest of Shakespeare's oeuvre.

comments, "already found *within* the play it revisits" (235). The clashes of doubt and faith, identification and desire, envy and rivalry, love and violence which acts of fidelity arouse in and between the characters in both texts thus also play out at the metadramatic level between Shakespeare and Spicer, author and imitator—or author and author—and are similarly powered by mimetic desire: the desire to be like the other, to overcome the other, to be the other, to desire what they desire, to desire their desire. Although neither Katz nor Kottman makes the connection, it is tempting to put into this potent mix of imitation, identification, envy, rivalry, skepticism, and doubt, Freud's own denial in the last decade of his life that Shakespeare—"the man from Stratford" (266n/236n)—was the author of the plays (favoring the Earl of Oxford in his stead), a bizarre and frankly embarrassing episode which, probably for that reason, is little commented on.[13] Could this otherwise unaccountable betrayal on Freud's part have been a symptom of the deep debt he owed the bard and, in a skepticism which kept him from taking that connection for granted, a perverse expression of his love?

References

Adelman, Janet. *Suffocating Mothers: Fantasies of Maternal Origin in Shakespeare's Plays:* Hamlet *to* The Tempest. Routledge, 1992.

Armstrong, Philip. *Shakespeare in Psychoanalysis*. Routledge, 2001.

Bates, Catherine. *Masculinity, Gender and Identity in the English Renaissance Lyric*. Cambridge UP, 2007.

———. "Recognitions: Shakespeare, Freud, and the Story of Psychoanalysis." *The Cambridge Companion to Literature and Psychoanalysis*, edited by Vera J. Camden, Cambridge UP, 2022, pp. 41–53.

Bloom, Harold. *The Western Canon*. Penguin, 1994.

Booth, Stephen, editor. *Shakespeare's Sonnets*. Yale UP, 1977.

Empson, William, *Seven Types of Ambiguity*. New Directions, 1930, 3rd ed., 1953.

[13]As Freud himself wrote to Fliess in Draft N (1897), "Belief (doubt) is a phenomenon that belongs wholly to the system of the ego (the Cs.) and has no counterpart in the Ucs. In the neuroses belief is displaced; it is denied to that which is repressed if it forces [its way] to reproduction and—as a punishment, one might say—transposed onto that which is defending. Titania, who will not love her rightful husband, Oberon, is obliged instead to bestow her love on Bottom, the fantasy ass" (Masson 251). As Smith notes in his essay, fantasy is used in such cases to defend against an intrusive traumatic memory. As a result, the power of belief is displaced from the actual event (now unconscious) to the fantasy in which the subject now adamantly believes. Freud's Earl of Oxford might be his own fantasy ass.

Felman, Shoshana *What Does a Woman Want? Reading and Sexual Difference.* Johns Hopkins UP, 1993.

Fineman, Joel. *Shakespeare's Perjured Eye: The Invention of Poetic Subjectivity in the Sonnets.* U of California P, 1986.

Freud, Sigmund. *The Revised Standard Edition of the Complete Psychological Works of Sigmund Freud*, edited and translated by James Strachey, revised by Mark Solms. 24 vols. Rowman & Littlefield Publishers, 2024. (In-text references provide *RSE* page numbers immediately after *SE* page numbers).

———. "The Antithetical Meaning of Primal Words" (1910). *The Standard Edition of the Complete Psychological Works of Sigmund Freud*, edited and translated by James Strachey, vol. 11, Hogarth Press, 1957, pp. 153–61/*RSE* vol. 11, pp. 141–48.

———. *The Interpretation of Dreams* (1900). *SE* vols. 4 and 5, 1953/*RSE* vols. 4 and 5.

———. "The Theme of the Three Caskets" (1913). *SE* vol. 12, 1958, pp. 289–301/*RSE* vol.12, pp. 287–98.

———. "The Uncanny" (1919). *SE* vol. 16, 1955, pp. 217–52/*RSE* vol. 17, pp. 213–47.

Gay, Peter, *Freud: A Life for Our Time.* W. W. Norton, 1988.

Greenblatt, Stephen. "Psychoanalysis and Renaissance Culture." *Literary Theory/ Renaissance Texts*, edited by Patricia Parker and David Quint, Johns Hopkins UP, 1986, pp. 210–24.

Hillman, David. "Introduction: Freud and Shakespeare." *Marx and Freud: Great Shakespeareans Volume X*, edited by Crystal Bartolovich, Jean E. Howard, David Hillman, and Adrian Poole, Continuum, 2012, pp. 99–103.

Irigaray, Luce. *This Sex Which Is Not One.* Translated by Catherine Porter, Cornell UP, 1985.

Kahn, Coppélia. "The Absent Mother in *King Lear.*" *Rewriting the Renaissance: The Discourses of Sexual Difference in Early Modern Europe*, edited by Margaret W. Ferguson, Maureen Quilligan, and Nancy J. Vickers, U of Chicago P, 1986, pp. 33–49.

Masson, Jeffrey Moussaieff, editor and translator. *The Complete Letters of Sigmund Freud to Wilhelm Fliess, 1887–1904.* Belknap Press, 1985.

Melnick, Burton A. "Psychoanalysis as Poetry, Psychoanalysis as Rhetoric: Freud's 'On the Theme of the Three Caskets.'" *Studies in Psychoanalytic Theory* 4, no. 2, 1995, pp. 18–28.

Nevo, Ruth. *Shakespeare's Other Language.* Methuen, 1987.

Newlin, James and James W. Stone, editors. *New Psychoanalytic Readings of Shakespeare: Cool Reason and Seething Brains.* Routledge, 2024.

Schwartz, Murray M. and Coppélia Kahn, editors. *Representing Shakespeare: New Psychoanalytic Essays.* Johns Hopkins UP, 1980.

Shakespeare, William. *The Arden Shakespeare Third Series Complete Works*. Edited by Richard Proudfoot, Ann Thompson, David Scott Kastan, and H. R. Woudhuysen, Bloomsbury, 2021.

Sprengnether, Madelon [*published as* Madelon Gohlke]. "'I wooed thee with my sword:' Shakespeare's Tragic Paradigms." *Representing Shakespeare: New Psychoanalytic Essays*, edited by Murray M. Schwartz and Coppélia Kahn, Johns Hopkins UP, 1980, pp. 170–87.

Stone, James W. *Crossing Gender in Shakespeare: Feminist Psychoanalysis and the Difference Within*. Routledge, 2010.

PART I

Shakespeare and Psychoanalysis

CHAPTER 2

The Role of Shakespeare in the Development of Freud's Theory

Christian A. Smith

The year 1897 was a pivotal moment in the development of psychoanalysis, one in which Freud famously abandoned the seduction theory. Up until the autumn of that year, Freud had developed a theory of the causality of neurosis whereby sexual trauma was carried through life repressed in the unconscious, but always susceptible to being triggered back into consciousness. The individual's ego, which had carried out the repression in the first place, continued to defend the subject from this unwanted knowledge. Freud's developing theory had a temporality and a topology that could explain why the root causes were hidden and why psychoanalysis was needed to undo the structures of repression and uncover the hidden material to make it available for working-through. Before he could satisfactorily complete his theory, however, Freud encountered contradictions within it which caused him to abandon his original path and take up a new

This chapter is based on a paper delivered at the World Shakespeare Congress in 2021 and on Smith, "Fortune and Caskets."

C. A. Smith (deceased)
Berlin, Germany

J. W. Stone, C. Bates (eds.), *Shakespeare and Psychoanalysis*, Palgrave Shakespeare Studies,
https://doi.org/10.1007/978-3-032-07897-1_2

one which would become the foundation for Freudian psychoanalysis. The reversal occurred in September 1897, and a central concept—the Oedipus Complex—was in place by mid-October. By the end of the year, Freud's theory had undergone a radical alteration.

Freud did not abandon the seduction theory easily. His struggle was difficult, even traumatic, and he needed all the resources at his disposal to carry it through. Those resources included the reports of his patients and his own self-analysis; Freud also drew on literature and art to interpret the ideas he was developing and to bind the trauma associated with them. This chapter will trace Freud's engagement with literature at a critical juncture of his career, especially as it is recounted in the letters to his friend and confidant at the time, Wilhelm Fliess.

In the correspondence with Fliess during the fall of 1897, Freud worked out theories and recorded hunches as they arose. The letters include case studies, applications of theory, and theoretical modeling. Some of this content is written in the letters and some is written in attachments to the letters, known today as Draft L, Draft M, and Draft N.[1] In his 2 May 1897 letter to Fliess, Freud wrote:

> In the first place, I have gained a sure inkling of the structure of hysteria. Everything goes back to the reproduction of scenes. Some can be obtained directly, others always by way of fantasies set up in front of them. The fantasies stem from things that have been heard but understood subsequently, and all their material is of course genuine. They are protective structures, sublimations of the facts, embellishments of them, and at the same time serve for self-relief. (Masson 239)

Freud postulates a scenography in the structure of neuroses. Some scenes are remembered, and some covered up and replaced by fantasies as protective structures. It was in these letters that Freud began to use literature, especially Shakespeare and Goethe, to express, anchor, and conceptualize his developing theory. John Fletcher writes that "Freud turns to literary texts that exemplify a repeated pattern of traumatic scenes and that dramatize precisely a traumatic scenography" (xv). Fletcher argues that "Freud's engagement with literature at key moments of theoretical impasse and crisis, as well as his long study of Leonardo da Vinci, constitutes thought experiments in the imaginary space of literature and painting" (xv).

[1] For the letters in their German original see Masson, *Sigmund Freud Briefe an Wilhlem Fließ*.

In Draft N, included in the letter of 31 May 1897, Freud writes that "memories appear to bifurcate: one part of them is put aside and replaced by fantasies; another accessible part seems to lead directly to impulses. Is it possible that later on impulses can also derive from fantasies?" (Masson 250). He is working out the role of fantasy in repression and symptom generation. Then he uses three ideas from his reading of dramatic literature to develop these notions. In a section where he is investigating the role of fantasy and belief, Freud writes:

> Belief (doubt) is a phenomenon that belongs wholly to the system of the ego (the Cs.) and has no counterpart in the Ucs. In the neuroses belief is displaced; it is denied to that which is repressed if it forces [its way] to reproduction and—as a punishment, one might say—transposed onto that which is defending. Titania, who will not love her rightful husband, Oberon, is obliged instead to bestow her love on Bottom, the fantasy ass. (Masson 251)

The simile lines up as follows: When one represses the memory of an event—say, from Freud's case studies, an instance of sexual abuse—and uses a fantasy as a means to defend against the intrusive traumatic memory, the power of belief is displaced from the actual event—because it is now in the unconscious—to the fantasy. One now believes adamantly in the fantasy. This is a symptom and is construed, by Freud, as a punishment for repressing the truth. Similarly, in *A Midsummer Night's Dream*, Titania, the Fairy Queen, is angry with Oberon, the Fairy King, for stealing an Indian boy she vowed to raise for one of her votaries. She refuses to love Oberon and shuns his presence in the woods. Within the setting of the play, the consequences of this action are much more problematic than a marital fight, because Titania and Oberon are gods of nature; their fight causes a rupture in the harmony of the natural world. To punish Titania for withholding her love, Oberon obtains a flower juice that causes her to fall madly in love with the first thing she sees after he squirts it in her eyes. As a result, Titania falls in love with Bottom, who has been transformed into an ass/man hybrid by Robin Goodfellow, a mischievous puck. In Freud's simile, loving "Bottom the fantasy ass" is Titania's symptom and punishment for repressing her love for her rightful husband.

In the next section of Draft N, Freud writes that "the mechanism of fiction is the same as that of hysterical fantasies." He conjectures about the role that the novel *Die Leiden des jungen Werthers* (*The Sorrows of Young Werther*) played in Goethe's life:

> For his *Werther* Goethe combined something he had experienced, his love for Lotte Kästner, and something he had heard, the fate of young Jerusalem, who died by committing suicide. He was probably toying with the idea of killing himself and found a point of contact in that and identified himself with Jerusalem, to whom he lent a motive from his own love story. By means of this fantasy he protected himself from the consequences of his experience. (Masson 251)

In 1772, Goethe fell in love with a married woman, Charlotte Kestner, but curtailed his attentions to her at the insistence of her husband. In October of that year, Karl Wilhelm Jerusalem, an acquaintance of Goethe's, borrowed a pistol from Kestner and shot himself. These two events, set within the aesthetic influence and emotionality of the *Empfindsamkeit* movement in which Goethe and Kestner met, became material for Goethe's *Werther* (see Williams 14). According to Freud's developing theory, Goethe transformed his despair and shock about the impossible love and the suicide, respectively, into writing a novel. He thereby protected himself from falling victim to his own suicidal thoughts.

Freud then alludes to Theseus's speech at the opening of the final act of *A Midsummer Night's Dream*, where he explains to Hippolyta why the lovers' story about their night in the woods is so strange. Theseus says:

> The poet's eye, in a fine frenzy rolling,
> Doth glance from heaven to earth, from earth to heaven;
> And as imagination bodies forth
> The forms of things unknown, the poet's pen
> Turns them to shapes, and gives to airy nothing
> A local habitation and a name. (5.1.12–17)

Freud writes: "So Shakespeare was right in juxtaposing fiction and madness (fine frenzy)" (Masson 251). He interprets Theseus's lines as if they were a concept of literary criticism. Theseus lists three types of people who experience madness: lovers, madmen, and poets. Of these three, only poets have means to bind the madness. The poet "turns them to shapes" and gives them "a local habitation and a name" (5.1.16–17). For Freud, one role of fiction is to handle the distress of madness by binding it in poetic form and narrative; fiction is juxtaposed to madness. Goethe handles his suicidal ideation by writing a novel, and neurotics handle the traumatic material they repress by creating fictional fantasies as symptoms.

On 22 June, Freud writes that he went through "some kind of neurotic experience, curious states incomprehensible to Cs., twilight thoughts, veiled doubts, with barely a ray of light here or there" (Masson 254). He reports these feelings to Fliess as evidence for a theory of periodicity that Fliess is developing: the organic world, including human health and psychology, is under the sway of cycles of twenty-three and twenty-eight days. However, in a letter on 14 August, Freud reports:

> Things are fermenting in me; I have finished nothing; am very satisfied with the psychology, tormented by grave doubts about my theory of the neurosis, too lazy to think, and have not succeeded here in diminishing the agitation in my head and feeling; this can happen only in Italy. (Masson 261)

The semicolons (if one assumes the punctuation of the letter has been transcribed faithfully) display Freud's state of mind. His "ferment" is not simply due to periodicity. His thoughts are running along, pausing but not stopping, swerving from satisfaction to agitation. His admission that he has doubts about his theory of neuroses seems to foreshadow a bad ending. He longs to start his holiday in Italy, and it is there where the theory will meet its tragic end.

Like many Northern European people of letters and culture on their grand tour, Freud valued Italy as a primary destination. His exposure to the ruins and memory of the classical world offered an alternate framework for Freud's experience of an intellectual and emotional expansiveness that he could not find in Vienna. Freud was an ardent collector of antiquities. He brought them home and filled every nook of his office and consultancy room with them (see Burke). These statues and relics from the classical world carried in them scenes from classical mythology—which form a large part of the source material for literature and art. Freud's collection reproduced these scenes on his office desk, shelves, and tables.

After spending the month of August in the tourist Alpine town of Aussee, Freud traveled to Siena, Italy, and then on to Orvieto. On 6 September, Freud wrote to Fliess:

> In Italy I am seeking a punch made of Lethe; here and there I get a draft. One savors the strange kind of beauty and the enormous creative urge; at the same time my inclination toward the grotesque, perverse-psychological gets its due. (Masson 263)

In Book 11 of Ovid's *Metamorphoses* (lines 594–615), one drinks from the river Lethe to obtain a state of oblivion, and restful forgetfulness. In the heat and among the ruins of the ancient world, Freud found a space to re-evaluate and redirect his theory. The ferment and anxiety of August gave way to the resolution of September; supported by his encounters with the expressive culture of the ancient world, Freud was prepared to abandon the seduction theory.

Upon his return, Freud wrote Fliess a crucially important letter, known today as the "Letter of the Equinox":

> Here I am again, since yesterday morning, refreshed, cheerful, impoverished, at present without work, and having settled in again, I am writing to you first.
>
> And now I want to confide in you immediately the great secret that has been slowly dawning on me in the last few months. I no longer believe in my *neurotica*. (Masson 264)

He gives four reasons for this change. First, he states that he could not bring any analyses of his patients to a real conclusion. His patients would run away at the moment when they were getting close to revealing significant scenes from their life and working through them. Second, he found that for his theory to work in light of the widespread nature of neuroses, he had to declare all fathers, including his own, perverse. This seemed improbable. Third, he could not be assured of the truth of the remembered scenes, for there are no indications of reality in the unconscious. And finally, in some cases, with "deep-reaching psychosis" the therapist and patient cannot reach the memory and the cure remains elusive. It also needs to be mentioned that the preceding year, on 21 April 1896, Freud presented his findings on seduction to a meeting of the Society for Psychiatry and Neurology and was met with "an icy reception" (Gay 93). Richard von Kraft-Ebbing pronounced Freud's theory to be a "scientific fairy tale" (Gay 93).

Freud recognizes his decision to be the result of honest and vigorous intellectual work that could be merely "an episode in the advance toward further insights" (Masson 265). However, it is clear from what he writes next that Freud feels defeated and possibly devastated. He writes:

> I vary Hamlet's saying, "To be in readiness": to be cheerful is everything! I could indeed feel quite discontent. The expectation of eternal fame was so beautiful, as was that of certain wealth, complete independence, travels, and lifting the children above the severe worries that robbed me of my youth.

> Everything depended upon whether or not hysteria would come out right. Now I can once again remain quiet and modest, go on worrying and saving. A little story from my collection occurs to me: "Rebecca, take off your gown; you are no longer a bride." (Masson 265–66)

In the German original, Freud writes, *Heiter sein ist alles* ("To be cheerful is everything"). The adjective *heiter* also denotes serenity and carefreeness. In the following chapter in this volume which centers upon this line from the Letter of the Equinox, Dominque Scarfone, citing Yves Bonnefoy, holds that Hamlet's readiness is not so much a preparedness for the duel to come, but a disposition and availability, "*disponibilité*," to be open to what comes. Scarfone reminds his readers that this is the fundamental rule of psychoanalysis, to sit in a position of availability to all that arises from the mind without censoring. It appears that Freud did just that in Italy; he entered into a state of readiness and availability to whatever arose, and what arose was that his theory did not work. Even at the risk of his career, he knew that he had to abandon his formulation.

Freud must have had some degree of availability in his listening practice to hear the stories of trauma and perversion coming from his patients. However, similar to the way dream material requires secondary revision due to its fragmented, non-narrative quality, the content Freud was hearing required analytical construction and a theoretical model to work with it in a useful manner. His first model was not completely wrong, only not completely adequate. Freud would return to aspects of his theory of seduction (his "*neurotica*") many times in his later writings. However, at this point, the summer of 1897, the theory needed to be destroyed to make room for new information. Freud reached for literature to find a model for this deed.

During October, his patients had not yet returned to his practice and he had a lot of free time. He used this time to continue the state of availability he began in Italy, and he embarked on an intensive course of self-analysis. He used his letters to Fliess to report his findings. First, he discovered that it was not his father who had engaged him sexually as a child, but his nurse (see Masson 268). In these letters Freud remembers that the nurse taught him about sexual matters, possibly masturbated him, and combined this molestation with lectures about God and a mix of praise and ridicule. She bathed him in water that was stained with her menstrual blood. Freud reports all of this to Fliess in the October letters. In those same letters, he reports his memory of the first time he saw his mother nude, on a train when the family was moving from Moravia to Austria.

On 15 October, Freud reports a memory of a traumatic event when he frantically searched for his mother. The memory combines his mother and his nurse, a surrogate mother, into one figure. While his mother was confined, Freud's brother Philipp caught the nurse stealing from the family and had her arrested. Freud writes:

> Thereupon a scene occurred to me which in the course of twenty-five years has occasionally emerged in my conscious memory without my understanding it. My mother was nowhere to be found; I was crying in despair. My brother Philipp (twenty years older than I) unlocked a wardrobe [*Kasten*] for me, and when I did not find my mother inside it either, I cried even more until, slender and beautiful, she came in through the door. What can this mean? Why did my brother unlock the wardrobe for me, knowing that my mother was not in it and that thereby he could not calm me down? Now I suddenly understand it. I had asked him to do it. When I missed my mother, I was afraid she had vanished from me, just as the old woman had a short time before. So I must have heard that the old woman had been locked up and therefore must have believed that my mother had been locked up too—or rather, had been "boxed up" [eingekastelt]—for my brother Philipp, who is now sixty-three years old, to this very day is still fond of using such puns. (Masson 271–72)

In his 1900 text, *The Interpretation of Dreams*, when discussing children's experience of death in dreams, Freud writes:

> A child makes no distinction as to how this absence is brought about: whether it is due to a journey, to a dismissal, to an estrangement, or to a death. If during a child's prehistoric epoch, his nurse has been dismissed, and if soon afterwards his mother has died, the two events are superimposed on each other in a single series in his memory [...]. If their mother does actually make the journey to that "undiscover'd country, from whose bourn no traveller returns," children seem at first to have forgotten her, and it is only later on that they begin to call their dead mother to mind. (254–55/226)

Earlier, Freud had analyzed one of his dreams in which he saw three women in a kitchen. One of them is making *Knödel* ("dumplings"). He interprets the three women to be "der Parzen" (the Parcae, or the Fates) and the woman making the dumplings to be "the mother who gives life, and furthermore (as in [his] own case) gives the living creature its first nourishment" (204/181). However, there is no mother who gives life in the three Fates: Klotho/Nona spins the thread of one's life; Lachesis/ Decima measures life; and Atropos/Morta cuts life. They are associated with destiny, not with birth, feeding, fertility or any other quality associated with the mothering image in Freud's dream. The Moerae/Parcae are imagined as old women not young mothers. Instead, Freud has inserted his mother into the scene.

He explains:

> When I was six years old and was given my first lessons by my mother, I was expected to believe that we were all made of earth and must therefore return to earth. This did not suit me and I expressed doubts of the doctrine. My mother thereupon rubbed the palms of her hands together—just as she did when making dumplings, except that there was no dough between them—and showed me the blackish scales of *epidermis* produced by friction as a proof that we were made of earth. My astonishment at this ocular demonstration knew no bounds and I acquiesced in the belief which I was later to hear expressed in the words: "*Du bist der Natur einen Tod schuldig.*" (205/181–82)

This passage shows how dreams can be built from combinations of various traumatic scenes that had been repressed into the unconscious. The myth of the Fates is itself an explanation for the ultimate trauma, the fear of death. Freud's unconscious threw in a traumatic scene from his childhood where he learned, possibly for the first time, that he would die and return to nature as dirt. The second thing to notice is that Freud reached for Shakespeare to handle his mother's distressing lesson. He (mis)quotes a scene from *Henry IV, part 1.*

Freud began reading Shakespeare at eight years old, two years after the dust-to-dust lesson. In the Schlegel-Tieck translation of Shakespeare that he had been gifted, he would have found this line spoken by Hal in response to Falstaff's request for Hal's protection if he fell on the battlefield. Hal tells Falstaff that he "[owes] God a death" (5.1.126). Schlegel translates this line as, "du bist Gott einen Tod schuldig." Freud misremembered the line as, "you owe nature a death," and used it to make sense of his mother's frightening lesson. For Freud, literature protects the self against the shock of trauma. Scenes in literature and art bind and replace traumatic scenes, yet they also necessarily carry the trauma. They can make sense of the enigmatic, but they also always threaten to return to it.[2]

Freud himself would return to the motif of three women—and to Shakespeare—some twelve years later. In a discussion that anticipates what he would later call "the death drive," Freud once again turned to Shakespeare for support in framing difficult concepts. In the Spring of 1912, he wrote a paper that would be published in 1913 under the title of "Das Motiv der Kästchenwahl" ("The Theme of the Casket Choice"), a reference to the key scene in *The Merchant of Venice* (3.2) in which Bassanio, in search of a wife, is confronted with a choice between three caskets. Freud applies psychoanalytic dream analysis to the imagery in the casket scene, much as he did in his childhood memory of the traumatic event in which he "lost" his mother/nurse. He writes: "if what we were concerned with were a dream, it would occur to us at once that caskets are also women, symbols of what is essential in woman, and therefore a woman herself—like coffers, boxes, cases, baskets, and so on" (292/290). Understanding these as "symbolic substitutions," we see that the theme is "*a man's choice between three women*" (292/290). On this basis, Freud draws a parallel with the scene in *King Lear* in which Lear makes a choice between his three daughters.

In both plays—as in other versions of the motif in myth and fairytale—the quality that the women in the third position share is muteness.[3] When Lear asks his daughters to tell him which one of them loves him most, the third daughter, Cordelia, says, in an aside, "What shall Cordelia speak? Love and be silent" (1.1.62). When he turns to Cordelia and asks for her to speak, she responds by saying, "Nothing, my Lord" (1.1.87). Likewise, when Bassanio addresses the lead casket, he says, "Thy paleness moves me more than eloquence" (3.2.106). Editors often emend "paleness" to "plainness," since its competing quality in the sentence is eloquence, or speech. In the choice of caskets, gold and silver are "loud," while lead is dumb like Cordelia, who loves and is silent. Eloquence can be read as another version of flattery: the flattery that Morocco and Aragon read for themselves into the gold and silver caskets and the flattery that Regan and Goneril heap on Lear.

[2] The next six paragraphs are written by Catherine Bates, drawing closely on Smith, "Fortune and Caskets" and extensive input on the latter by John Fletcher and James W. Stone.

[3] Freud references the Judgment of Paris and Cinderella.

Freud solves the riddle. When the men choose the third woman, they choose death. The third woman's muteness identifies her as one of the three Fates, the Parcae or Moerae. The third Fate is Atropos, the inexorable. She is the representation of Death who cuts the thread of one's life. Atropos cannot be persuaded or entreated in any way to change her enactment of one's death (she is literally "the unturning one.") The Moerae represent the "ineluctable severity of the Law and its relation to death and dissolution [...] as though men had only perceived the full seriousness of natural law when they had to submit their own selves to it" (298/295). Yet every one of the third women chosen in the plays and stories is young and beautiful, the very opposite of death. In choosing the lead casket, for example, Bassanio gets the "fair and wise Portia" (291/289).[4]

Lear likewise chooses Cordelia when, early in the play, he says that "I loved her most, and thought to set my rest / On her kind nursery" (1.1.123–24). This is not the same "nursery" as his mother's when he was a boy, however. Rather, it will turn out to be that of Atropos, the third woman in a man's life. At the end of the play Lear is an old man who wants to "unburdened crawl toward death" (1.1.40). He knows that he is dying, but, Freud writes, "the doomed man is not willing to renounce the love of women; he insists on hearing how much he is loved" (301/298). He will die in the limp arms of the deceased Cordelia—Atropos the Goddess of Death, the Valkyrie who will carry the warrior from the battlefield.[5] Freud interprets the three women of the myths as the three relationships that men will have with women—"the woman who bears him, the woman who is his mate, and the woman who destroys him"—and as the three forms of the mother—"the mother herself, the beloved one who is chosen after her pattern, and lastly the Mother Earth who receives him once more" (301/298). Freud's last line of the essay is: "But it is in vain that an old man yearns for the love of woman as he had it first from his mother; the

[4] Portia is not described as fair and wise in *The Merchant of Venice*. Bassanio describes her as fair and wealthy ("a lady richly left" (1.1.161)) and A. W. Schlegel translates this as "*reich an Erbe*" and "*schön*" (1.1.164, 165). When she is acting as Balthazar in the court scene, Shylock calls Balthazar "a wise young judge" (4.1.224) when the judgment sways in his favor and Gratiano calls Balthazar "learned judge" (4.1.313) when the judgment swings to Antonio's side. Her status as fair and wise seems to exist uniquely in Freud's mind.

[5] Freud writes, "Lear carries Cordelia's dead body on to the stage. Cordelia is Death. If we reverse the situation it becomes intelligible and familiar to us. She is the Death-goddess who, like the Valkyrie in German mythology, carries away the dead hero from the battlefield" (301/298).

third of the fates alone, the silent Goddess of Death, will take him into her arms" (301/298).[6]

Freud accounts for the apparent contradiction that this figure so often appears as young and beautiful by noting that "there are motive forces in mental life which bring about replacement by the opposite in the form of what is known as reaction-formation" (299/296).[7] In what follows, he goes on to explain the historical development of this specific reaction-formation: "Man [...] makes use of his imaginative activity in order to satisfy the wishes that reality does not satisfy" (299/296). In this case, he rebels against the inexorability of death by replacing the Goddess of Death with the Goddess of Love: "The third of the sisters was no longer Death; she was the fairest, best, most desirable and most lovable of women" (299/296). The same consideration accounts for the motif of choice: "Choice stands in the place of necessity, of destiny" (299/297).[8] Nonetheless, this apparently free choice "is, properly speaking, no free choice, for it must necessarily fall on the third" (300/297). Death, that is

[6]There is the potential for some confusion here, since Freud interprets the replacement of the death image with an image of life, love, and beauty as a *reaction-formation*, but describes the reversal by which choice (life) replaces destiny (death) as a *wish fulfilment.* However, these are not the same processes in psychoanalysis. A wish-fulfilment may make use of such a wish to reverse and suppress another wish, but it is not a reaction-formation. Rather, Freud sees reaction-formations as the site of a conflict between opposed wishes (see Laplanche and Pontalis, *Language of Psychoanalysis* 376–78). A reaction-formation is a defence mechanism which serves in the repression of an unconscious drive or desire. It is used for blocking or withdrawing libido, by intensifying its opposite (see Freud, "Repression" 157/139).

[7]The first English translation of Freud's essay by C. J. M. Hubback in the 1925 *Collected Papers* is titled "The Theme of the Three Caskets," a title James Strachey keeps in his 1958 *Standard Edition* translation (290), but it is misleading. The German word *Motiv* translates both as theme/motif and as motive. Freud's essay supports both meanings. Freud quibbles on the word *Motiv*, slipping between its meaning as *theme* and its meaning as motive. About the theme of the caskets he writes, "*es behandelt ein menschlisches Motiv, die Wahl eines Mannes zwischen drei Frauen*" (*Gesammelte Werke. Zehnter Band* 26) ("It treats of a [has to do with a] human theme, a man's choice between three women") (translation by author). Here he means *theme*. About Bassanio's choice he writes, "*Stünden wir in der psychoanalytischen Praxis vor solcher Rede, so würden wir hinter der unbefriedigenden Begründung geheimgehaltene Motive wittern*" (*Gesammelte Werke. Zehnter Band* 24) ("If we stood in psychoanalytic practice before such a speech, we would suspect that behind the unsatisfactory reasons are kept secret motives") (translation by author). Here he means *motive.* In the title of the essay, the word *Kästchenwahl* suggests a reading of the word *Motiv* as *motive* as well as *theme.*

[8]Again, the English title "The Theme of the Three Caskets" is misleading since it drops the specific reference to choice (*wahl*) that Freud makes in his. The *Kästchenwahl* (literally, "casket choice") refers to the act of choosing performed by the character (a verb), while the emphasis of Hubback's and Strachey's English title is on the caskets themselves (a noun).

to say, remains inexorable. Freud moves toward a resolution of this contradiction by pointing out that the beautiful love goddess "has kept certain characteristics that border on the uncanny" (300/297).

When Bassanio finds Portia's portrait inside the leaden casket, he describes the effect it has on its viewer: "The painter plays the spider, and hath woven / A golden mesh t'entrap the hearts of men / Faster than gnats in cobwebs" (3.2.121–23). The gnat, of course, dies, eaten by the spider. Such hints of death contribute uncanniness to the scene (one might also ask why Freud does not finish interpreting Bassanio's reasons for choosing the third casket and switches instead to *King Lear*). Perhaps the *Kästchenwahl* essay provides a theoretical spark from which one could write a general psychoanalytic theory of comedy. Comedy (Eros) could be seen as a reaction-formation that represses tragedy (Thanatos). The life drive that powers the comedic plot could be interpreted as a defensive inversion of the death force that shadows the unconscious. Shakespeare presaged this notion by weaving many tragic fibers into the fabric of his comedies. Freud could have found a great deal of material for a theory of the relationship between Eros and Thanatos in *Romeo and Juliet*, a tragedy that includes a comedy (the joining of the two families in peace) which is possible only through the tragedy (the death of the two lovers). He could have also found much to work with in the Sonnets, where Eros defies death: "So long lives this and this gives life to thee" (sonnet 18, line 14). At this point, of course, Freud had not yet developed his theory of the death drive (*Todestrieb*) which would first appear by name in *Beyond the Pleasure Principle* (1920). Indeed, this may explain why he did not appear to notice the connection between the dream of his mother being "eingekastelt" and the caskets in *The Merchant of Venice*. But it is possible to see him working toward that concept in the *Kästchenwahl* essay, and it is significant that he draws on Shakespeare to do so, specifically, a comedy (albeit a problem one),[9] and a tragedy, *King Lear*.[10]

[9] Many critics have contested the generic attribution of comedy to the play: e.g., Drakakis 48–5; Halio 10–11, 18; Mahood 9–12; Bate and Rasmussen 414.

[10] Even though Freud did not coin the term until 1920, the development of the theory of the death drive spanned the length of his writing life. He began writing about the drive for quiescence and death in his unpublished 1895 *Project for a Scientific Psychology*. In his metapsychological works in 1915, especially "On Narcissism," Freud constructs the theoretical basis for his notion of the death drive. Freud's interpretation of *The Merchant of Venice*'s casket scene in the 1913 *Kästchenwahl* essay offers a glimpse of how Shakespeare's plays influenced the development of psychoanalytic theory. This influence was mediated through Freud's personal use of Shakespeare's plays to handle his own psychological trauma. This matter is discussed in Smith, *Shakespeare's Influence on Marx, Freud, and the Frankfurt School*.

In the years before his formal theorization of the death drive, Freud instead wrote a theory of a sexual drive (*Sexualtrieb*). In the key year of 1897, he discovered that he had been in love with his mother, and that this love and its consequent complications of jealousy against his father and guilt about his desire is represented in Sophocles's *Oedipus Rex*:

> A single idea of general value dawned on me. I have found, in my own case too, being in love with my mother and jealous of my father, and now I consider it a universal event in early childhood, even if not so early as in children who have been made hysterical. (Similar to the invention of parentage [family romance] in paranoia—heroes, founders of religion). If this is so, we can understand the gripping power of *Oedipus Rex*, in spite of all the objections that reason raises against the presupposition of fate; and we can understand why the later "drama of fate" was bound to fail so miserably. Our feelings rise against any arbitrary individual compulsion, such as presupposed in *Die Ahnfrau* and the like; but the Greek legend seizes upon a compulsion which everyone recognises because he senses its existence within himself. Everyone in the audience was once a budding Oedipus in fantasy and each recoils in horror from the dream fulfillment here transplanted into reality, with the full quantity of repression which separates his infantile state from his present one. (Masson 272)

The same issue is the solution to the long-standing question of Hamlet's problem:

> Fleetingly the thought passed through my head that the same thing might be at the bottom of Hamlet as well. I am not thinking of Shakespeare's conscious intention, but believe, rather, that a real event stimulated the poet to this representation, in that his unconscious understood the unconscious of his hero. How does Hamlet the hysteric justify his words, "Thus conscience does make cowards of us all"? How does he explain his irresolution in avenging his father by the murder of his uncle—the same man who sends his courtiers to their death without a scruple and who is positively precipitate in murdering Laertes? How better than through the torment he suffers from the obscure memory that he himself had contemplated the same deed against his father out of passion for his mother, and - "use every man after his desert, and who should 'scape whipping?" His conscience is his unconscious sense of guilt. And is not his sexual alienation in his conversation with Ophelia typically hysterical? And his rejection of the instinct that seeks to beget children? And, finally, his transferral of the deed from his own father to Ophelia's? And does he not in the end, in the same marvellous way as my

> hysterical patients, bring down punishment on himself by suffering the same fate as his father of being poisoned by the same rival? (Masson 272–73)

Freud's traumatic memory of his panic about his mother's and nurse's disappearance is swiftly replaced by a memory of being in love with his mother—Thanatos is replaced by Eros—and represented by two pieces of dramatic literature. Did Freud's belief in his new notion, which he will call the Oedipus Complex, replace his disbelief in and repression of a developing understanding of a death drive? Interestingly, his example in his 31 May letter about Titania and Bottom is applicable here. If Titania and Oberon are gods, and Titania switches her desire to Bottom, a mortal who stands in a filial role to the gods, then this scene from *A Midsummer Night's Dream* is also an Oedipal situation.

Jean Laplanche's General Theory of Seduction demonstrates that Freud's seduction theory was close to discovering the basis for the death drive. In Laplanche's theory, humans are born without a self and without sexuality. Instead, they are biopsychical beings in a state of helplessness, dependent on a mothering *other* for their survival. During the operations of infant care, enigmatic messages of adult sexuality can be delivered by the mothering *other* to the skin threshold of the child. The child carries out an active process of metabolization: a primal attempt of interpretation of the messages. This interpretive act creates the self, with the ego as its central mechanism. The failure to translate messages that are enigmatic, e.g. adult sexuality, results in the construction of the unconscious, the location where the self can hide and store that which it represses. Instead of conceiving of this encounter as a particular act of seduction that causes neurosis, as Freud did, Laplanche insists that this is a universal feature of the encounter between the infant and the caring *other*, and on this basis formulates a General Theory of Seduction.[11]

This primal seduction results in an implantation of sexuality on the child. From the child's active work with this implantation his subjectivity begins to be constructed. There is also a violent variant of implantation which Laplanche calls intromission. In this case, adult sexuality is shoved in past the child's threshold. This form of sexual abuse and intrusion is walled off by the body as a "body that cannot be metabolized [...] and short-circuits the differentiation of the agencies" (*Essays on Otherness* 136). This intromitted material sets up a compulsive repetition of the

[11] See Scarfone for a summary of this theory.

traumatic sexual scene, which unbinds and fragments the self. This is the sexual source of the death drive. This is what Freud was close to discovering in 1897, but he had not then formulated certain theoretical notions, for example, a theory of narcissism. In 1912, when he revisited the question in his "Casket Choice" essay, the necessary theoretical notions were still lacking.

Instead, in October 1897, Freud shifted his focus to the child's sexual desire for his mother and consequent guilt. It's not that he was wrong about it; after all he sourced it from his own analysis and discovered this desire in his patients. However, through this shift he recentered the focus on the subject and repressed the role of the *other* in the primal scene. Laplanche called this Freud's "Ptolemaic going astray" (*Essays on Otherness* 60). Freud used stories from literature to help move his concept from what is being repressed to that which defends, the Oedipus Complex.

The plays he chose to anchor his new theory—*Oedipus Rex* and *Hamlet*—both also reach deep into the historical narrative surrounding death. Freud could use them to carry his displacement of what he was discovering in the 1890s, because the plays both allowed him to protect himself—and his theory—from the trauma of what he was discovering, and to carry that trauma for a re-reading later. Indeed, both have been re-read by John Fletcher, using Laplanche's notions, to discover the role of the *other* and to uncover the circulation of trauma depicted.

On 27 October 1897, Freud writes to Fliess:

> I live only for the "inner work." I am gripped and pulled through ancient times in quick association of thoughts; my moods change like the landscapes seen by a traveler from a train; and as the great poet, using his privilege to ennoble (sublimate), puts it:
>
> Und manche liebe Schatten steigen auf;
> Gleich einer alten, halbverklungenen Sage,
> Kommt erste Lieb' und Freundschaft mit herauf. (Masson 274)

The quoted lines are from the Dedication of Goethe's *Faust*. Goethe writes:

> And many dear shades rise up
> Like an old half-faded legend
> Comes up first with love and friendship (lines 10–12)

The setting of literature, like that of the analytic hour, allows the subject to rest in readiness, to be open. Poetic and literary form carries all the information that arises, and all the scenes that clamor to be remembered. The role of aesthetics is not simply to capture trauma and replace with a story, but to put the subject in readiness for all.

Works Cited

Bate, Jonathan and Eric Rasmussen, editors. *William Shakespeare: Complete Works.* Modern Library, 2007.

Burke, Janine. *The Gods of Freud: Sigmund Freud's Art Collection.* Knopf, 2006.

Drakakis, John, editor. *The Merchant of Venice.* By William Shakespeare. Arden, 2010.

Fletcher, John. *Freud and the Scene of Trauma.* Fordham UP, 2013.

Freud, Sigmund. *Gesammelte Werke.* 17 vols. Imago Publishing. 1940.

———. *The Revised Standard Edition of the Complete Psychological Works of Sigmund Freud*, edited and translated by James Strachey, revised by Mark Solms. 24 vols. Rowman & Littlefield Publishers, 2024. (In-text references provide *RSE* page numbers immediately after *SE* page numbers).

———. *The Interpretation of Dreams* (1900). *The Standard Edition of the Complete Psychological Works of Sigmund Freud*, edited and translated by James Strachey, vols. 4–5, Hogarth Press, 1953/*RSE* vols. 4–5.

———. "Repression" (1915), *SE* vol. 14, 1957, pp. 141–58/*RSE* vol. 14, pp. 127–39.

———. "The Theme of the Three Caskets" (1913). *SE* vol. 12, 1958, pp. 289–301/*RSE* vol.12, pp. 287–98.

Gay, Peter. *Freud, A Life for our Time.* Doubleday, 1988.

Goethe, J. W. *Faust.* Deutscher Taschenbuch, 1997.

Halio, Jay L., editor. *The Merchant of Venice.* By William Shakespeare. Oxford UP, 1993.

Laplanche, Jean. *Essays on Otherness.* Edited by John Fletcher, Routledge, 1999.

Laplanche, Jean, and J.-B. Pontalis. *The Language of Psychoanalysis.* Translated by Donald Nicholson-Smith, Hogarth Press, 1973.

Mahood, M. M., editor. *The Merchant of Venice.* By William Shakespeare. Cambridge UP, 2003.

Masson, Jeffrey Moussaieff, translator and editor. *The Complete Letters of Sigmund Freud to Wilhelm Fliess, 1887–1904.* Belknap Press, 1985.

Masson, Jeffrey Moussaieff, editor. *Sigmund Freud Briefe an Wilhlem Fliess, 1887–1904, Ungekürzte Ausgabe.* S. Fischer, 1986.

Scarfone, Dominique. *Laplanche, an Introduction.* Translated by Dorothée Bonnigal-Katz, The Unconscious in Translation, 2015.

Smith, Christian A. “Fortune and Caskets: Necrophilia in *The Merchant of Venice*,” *Shakespeare Seminar* (published under the auspices of the *Deutsche Shakespeare-Gesellschaft*), vol. 12, 2014, pp. 37–47.

———. *Shakespeare’s Influence on Marx, Freud, and the Frankfurt School Critical Theorists*. PhD Thesis. University of Warwick, 2013.

Shakespeare, William. *A Midsummer Night’s Dream*. Edited by Sukanta Chaudhuri, Arden, 2017.

———. *Hamlet*. Edited by Ann Thompson and Neil Taylor, Arden, 2006.

———. *Hamlet*. In *Sämtliche Werke*, Translated by August W. Schlegel, Aufbau, 2003.

———. *King Henry IV, part 1*. Edited by David Scott Kastan, Arden, 2002.

———. *The Merchant of Venice*. Edited by John Drakakis, Arden, 2010.

Williams, John R. *The Life of Goethe: A Critical Biography*. Blackwell, 1998.

CHAPTER 3

The Readiness for Transference: Hamlet's Lesson

Dominique Scarfone

I

> I vary Hamlet's saying, 'To be in readiness': to be cheerful is everything! (Masson 265)

The sentence is by Freud.[1] It appears in the second part of the fateful letter of 21 September 1897 in which he reveals to Fliess he no longer believes in the theory of seduction he had elaborated and harshly defended in previous years. The loss is enormous for him, who adds, perhaps ironically: "I could indeed feel quite discontent. The expectation of eternal fame was so beautiful, as was that of certain wealth […]" (Masson 265–66).

Jean Laplanche considered that the abandonment of the theory of seduction is a real cataclysm, and he spent lots of energy putting it back,

[1] This is a modified English version of the paper "De la disponibilité au transfert. La leçon d'Hamlet" that appeared in *Revue française de psychosomatique*, vol. 53, no. 1, 2018, pp. 5–20.

D. Scarfone (✉)
Université de Montréal and Canadian Psychoanalytic Institute,
Montreal, QC, Canada

J. W. Stone, C. Bates (eds.), *Shakespeare and Psychoanalysis*,
Palgrave Shakespeare Studies,
https://doi.org/10.1007/978-3-032-07897-1_3

in a generalized form, at the gravitational center of psychoanalytic theory (see his *New Foundations*). But whereas he denounces Freud's "strayings," Laplanche is no less faithful to the Viennese founder, admiring his persistence in tracking down his object (see Laplanche, *Temptation of Biology*). Freud remains Freud: even when he temporarily loses the North, his thinking is all the same magnetized and rammed by his unceasing quest for the unconscious *Thing*.

In this chapter, I propose to work on one aspect of what might be called, in a buzzword, Freud's "resilience" at the time of the "cataclysmic" abandonment of the theory of seduction. In view of which I will let myself be guided by the very words of the letter in which he announces to Fliess the "great secret." At the end of that letter, after trying to talk about something else, Freud returns to the main event and concludes:

> In this collapse of everything valuable, the psychological alone has remained untouched. The dream [book] stands entirely secure and my beginnings of the metapsychological work have only grown in my estimation. It is a pity that one cannot make a living, for instance, on dream interpretation! (Masson 266)

As we know, Freud ended up not only making a living on dream interpretation and the method of treatment derived from it, but also obtaining the much-desired fame. Still, the "cheerfulness" he substitutes for Hamlet's "readiness" is surprising. After all, Freud has just lost sight of the "sources of the Nile" he thought he had found with infantile seduction.[2] At the moment of considering the sentence itself, I find it remarkable that in this dramatic hour Freud's thoughts turn to Hamlet. In fact, the tragedy *Hamlet* will be evoked again three weeks later, in another important letter dated 15 October 1897 where Freud exposes to Fliess his understanding of Sophocles's *Oedipus Rex* and wonders if one could not find the same plot in the famous Shakespearean play (see Masson 270–73); a parallel that he shall draw again and in more detail in *The Interpretation of Dreams* (see 261–66/232–36). What, then, of this appearance of the Prince of Denmark in the letter of 21 September, the "letter of the equinox," as Laplanche calls it?

[2] See Freud's letter to Fliess dated 26 April 1896 (Masson 184); the same analogy appears in "On the Aetiology of Hysteria" (1896), pp. 203/210.

Let us start by noting that the phrase from *Hamlet* that Freud quotes (and distorts) is not just any sentence. In the preface added in 1978 to his 1957 translation of *Hamlet* and *King Lear*, the French poet Yves Bonnefoy concentrates on this one and only sentence: "The readiness is all." In it he sees the major key to the interpretation of the play. Yet, in place of the readiness, whose meaning, as we shall see, is not as obvious as it seems, Freud puts "cheerfulness." In the German original it reads: "*Heiter sein ist alles*," whereas, according to the German publishers of his correspondence, the correct rendition of "*The readiness is all*" would have been "*Bereitschaft ist alles*" or "*Bereit sein ist alles*" (Freud, *Briefe* 285). The adjective *heiter* can also mean "serene," "clear," or "unclouded." And his serenity, his clear mind, seems to astonish Freud himself: he mentions that he would rather have reasons to be "quite discontent." Interestingly, the same word "*heiter*" was already present in the very first sentence of the same letter: "Here I am again, since yesterday morning, refreshed, cheerful (*heiter*), impoverished [...]" (Masson 264). This double occurrence of the word *heiter*, in addition to its replacing *Bereitschaft*, makes it stand out from the dramatic background. One could see here a reaction formation. But we will not go into the analysis of Freud-the-man. We shall see that the twice mentioned *heiter* will prove not so distant, after all, from Hamlet's *readiness*, and will even highlight an important aspect thereof.

II

Readiness has many meanings: among them the word can signify the state of being ready or prepared, or of being willingly disposed. This ambiguity is put to advantage by Shakespeare in the context of the play. On the one hand, the sentence is spoken when Hamlet prepares to meet Laertes in a sword duel (see 5.2.222). It is part of the answer the young prince gives to Horatio when the latter suggests postponing the duel because, in his view, Hamlet may not be fit enough. Readiness could therefore seem to mean "being sufficiently prepared (ready) for combat." But as the rest of the scene suggests, and as Bonnefoy points out, Hamlet has something else in mind. His readiness is rather a matter of accepting the inevitable, whatever it may be, since, he adds: "There is special providence in the fall of a sparrow" (5.2.219–20). Hamlet's readiness, therefore, is not truly, or not only, about being ready for the fight, for which he could have used another term: *preparedness* (we shall get back to this).

It is striking that, on the one hand, in 1957, Bonnefoy translated "The readiness is all" by "L'essentiel, c'est d'être prêt" ("The essential thing is to be prepared"), whereas in the preface he added some twenty years later, he contrasts Hamlet's *readiness* with King Lear's *ripeness* in these terms: "I will try to understand the 'availability' in *Hamlet*, the 'ripening' in *King Lear*" (Je vais essayer de comprendre la "disponibilité" dans *Hamlet*, le "mûrissement" dans *Le Roi Lear*, Bonnefoy 7.) Being ready is replaced with being available. Then, with regard to the willingness to accept fate, Bonnefoy specifies that Hamlet does not accept it in a "passive, discouraged" way, adding:

> The readiness [Hamlet] proposes is not to rely on the divine will as a guarantor of our effort, guardian of our meaning; it is, on the contrary, to stop doing what the God of old had expected of us: the bold and sustained exercise of our judgment in the world he has created, the appreciation of good and evil. To a thinking that foresees and organizes, and which can do so because it knows the values, [Hamlet] substitutes the reception of things as they come, as disordered and contradictory as they may be [...]. (My trans.; 14)

Remarkably, this commentary could, *mutatis mutandis*, apply to what Freud was experiencing when he wrote the letter of 21 September 1897, to which we shall now return. What Freud really announces in this missive is that he has given up not the theory of seduction itself, but the etiological role of the perverse acts of seduction that he had thought was the specific cause of psychoneuroses. This etiological theory indeed placed seduction in the light of the appreciation of good and evil; it therefore entailed a judgment both of value (these acts are bad, pathogenic) and of existence (the acts really took place). As for the reflection about them, it served to "plan and organize" according to these values, that is, yield a positive knowledge of the psychopathological becoming and its treatment. After abandoning this etiological theory on the basis of several arguments expounded in the letter, Freud falls back on what "stands entirely secure," i.e., the interpretation of dreams, which as we know requires precisely what Bonnefoy sees in Hamlet's availability: "the reception of things as they come, as disordered and contradictory as they may be [...]."

I am not the least suggesting that in writing the quoted lines Bonnefoy had in mind the Freudian method. However, I dare put his reading of Hamlet next to the fact that Freud—the great admirer of Shakespeare, strongly impressed by this great play—thinks precisely of Hamlet during this dramatic episode of his research. That Freud should indirectly quote Hamlet's *readiness* by substituting it with "cheerfulness" at the very moment when he, too, has somehow accepted fate, seems to me usefully enlightened by Bonnefoy's remarks about Hamlet's *availability*, as it evokes, unintentionally I suppose, precisely what Freud shall develop in the months and years following the dramatic abandonment of his *Neurotica*. Do not the words of Bonnefoy indeed recall the Fundamental Rule that Freud was soon going to formulate on the basis of the study of dreams? Freud is therefore right, at the end of his letter, to console himself by noting that "[i]n this collapse of everything valuable, the psychological alone has remained untouched. The dream [book] stands entirely secure" (Masson 266). It can therefore be said that Freud does not distort Hamlet's famous sentence that much after all. Freud's "cheerfulness" or "serenity" is indeed one aspect of Hamlet's *readiness*, as an acceptance of the inevitable to which Freud, just like Hamlet, does not resign himself in a "passive, discouraged" way.

In view of the method that Freud developed following—and despite—the "cataclysm" of 1897 by sticking to the solidity of his discoveries about the dream, there are grounds for paraphrasing another famous excerpt from *Hamlet*. We would indeed be tempted to say: "There is method in such [...] readiness." Indeed, the analytical method that emerged from the work on the dream contains two versions of readiness: free association on the part of the patient and evenly hovering attention on the part of the analyst. In both cases, it is recommended to suspend judgments of value and existence and to attend to what comes, "as disorganized and contradictory as it may be [...]." The parallel holds good up to the conclusion that Bonnefoy arrives at concerning availability: "I understand the readiness that appears in Hamlet as, simply, negatively, a survival technique of the soul [...]" (my trans.; 16).

III

Visibly, for the development of my topic, I must navigate between languages, which is what the work of translation—that of Bonnefoy regarding Hamlet; that of Strachey and of Laplanche regarding Freud—not only invites, but also greatly enlightens.

Whereas in his letter of 1897 Freud opts for "cheerfulness" (*heiter sein*) rather than readiness (*Bereitschaft*), he will, however, one day turn his attention to this second term. *Bereitschaft* and all that relates to it, such as the substantive *Bereitung* (preparation) or the verb *bereiten* (to prepare), will take on a major conceptual value in *Beyond the Pleasure Principle.* In it, Freud explains that trauma involves a breach in the stimulus barrier and that the ensuing fright (*Schreck*) is the result of "lack of any preparedness for anxiety (*Angstbereitschaft)*, including lack of hypercathexis of the systems that would be the first to receive the stimulus" (31/31; words between parentheses added).

"Preparedness *for* anxiety" is Strachey's way of translating the German compound word *Angstebereitschaft*, whereas the French translators of the Complete Works rendered it with "preparedness *by* anxiety" (*Apprêtement* par *l'angoisse*) (303). Such variance is not merely a different choice of terms, it is a theoretical choice. In purely linguistic terms, the two choices are equally justified (see Bourguignon et al. 81). But in the context of *Beyond the Pleasure Principle*, the French version gives anxiety a decisive role in the prevention of trauma, in that it triggers the preparations for the coming shock. In this regard, Strachey's choice for the English translation is surprising since, as a note by his own hand attests, he well knew that Freud, a few pages earlier, had written the following:

> I do not believe that anxiety can produce traumatic neurosis. There is something about anxiety that protects its subject against fright (*Schreck*) and so against fright-neuroses" (*Beyond the Pleasure Principle*, 12–13/12–13)

adding in a footnote, "Freud is very far indeed from always carrying out the distinction he makes here. More often than not he uses the word '*Angst*' to denote a state of fear without any reference to the future" (13n1/13n1). Clearly then, anxiety (*Angst*) not only differs from fright or terror (*Schreck*) but serves to avoid it. Freud later explains that this is done by triggering the overinvestment (hyper-cathexis) of the receiving systems, preventing the shattering of the stimulus barrier. However, though the choice between "for" and "by" anxiety is certainly significant, it is not our main concern here. More important for our present purpose is the fact that Strachey translated *Bereitschaft* by *preparedness* and not by *readiness.* This time it is a rigorous choice, since, as we have seen, readiness could mean the acceptance of the inevitable whereas, in *Beyond the Pleasure Principle*, there is no question of acceptance, but of preparation to *counter* a traumatic breach. Be it as a preparation *for* anxiety (Strachey) or a preparation *by* anxiety (Laplanche), the *preparedness* is what matters here, in that

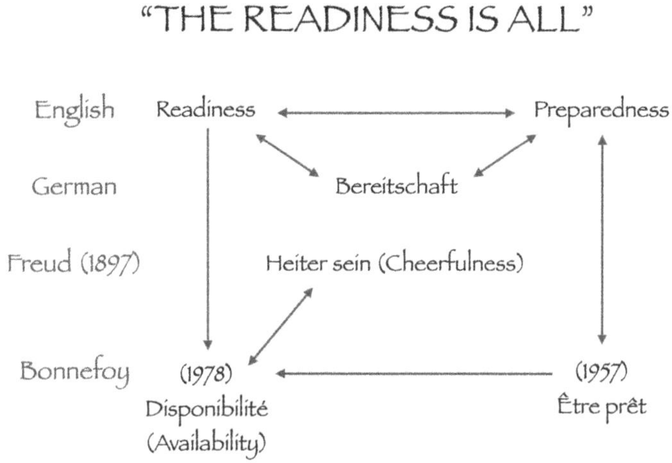

Fig. 3.1 Readiness, preparedness, cheerfulness

it emphasizes that in this case *Bereitschaft* does not involve any resignation.

So, in this back and forth between languages (see Fig. 3.1), we find that the German *Bereitschaft* can be either rendered by Hamlet's *readiness*—or his *availability* (Bonnefoy)—or by *preparedness* in Freud/Strachey or *apprêtement* in Freud/Laplanche. Let us keep at hand this readiness/preparedness polarity within the *Bereitschaft*, since it will help us to move further toward the question of transference.

IV

Let me quote Bonnefoy again:

> The readiness [Hamlet] proposes is not to rely on the divine will as a guarantor of our effort, guardian of our meaning; it is to stop, on the contrary, what the God of old had expected of us: the bold and sustained exercise of our judgment in the world he has created, the appreciation of good and evil. To a thinking that foresees and organizes, and which can do so because it knows the values, [Hamlet] substitutes the reception of things as they come, as disordered and contradictory as they may be [...]. (My trans.; 14)

I said above that this is redolent of the Freudian method and its fundamental rule. Now, it is interesting to note that in the very pages where Freud describes and justifies this rule, the *Bereitschaft* is indeed invoked—this time within the substantive *Vorbereitung*. Freud writes indeed about the analytic method that

> [It] involves some psychological preparation (*psychischen Vorbereitung*) of the patient. We must aim at bringing two changes in him: an increase in the attention he pays to his own psychical perceptions and the elimination of the criticism by which he normally sifts the thoughts that occur to him. [...]. It is necessary to insist explicitly on his renouncing all criticism of the thoughts that he perceives. We therefore tell him that the success of the psycho-analysis depends on his noticing and reporting whatever comes [*Einfall*] into his head and not being misled, for instance, into suppressing an idea because it strikes him as unimportant or irrelevant or because it seems to him meaningless. He must adopt a completely impartial attitude to what occurs to him [*Einfalle*], since it is precisely his critical attitude which is responsible for his being unable, in the ordinary course of things, to achieve the desired unraveling of his dream or obsessional idea or whatever it may be. (*Interpretation of Dreams* 101/90)

In this double requirement, the intensification of attention draws, on the one hand, on *preparedness*: the analysand must endeavor to scrutinize his psychic landscape more attentively; on the other hand, the setting aside of criticism requires *readiness*, the willingness to accept all that comes into the field of intensified attention. It is a two-tiered and apparently contradictory process that seems to try and sway the analysand's mind, bending it first in one direction (to pay more attention), then in the other (to avoid sifting what comes up). Freud will further develop the description of this method by distinguishing between reflexive attention and self-observing attention:

> In both cases attention must be concentrated, but the man who is reflecting is also exercising his *critical* faculty; this leads him to reject some of the ideas that occur to him after perceiving them, to cut short others, without following the trains of thought which they would open up to him, and to behave in such a way towards still others that they never become conscious at all and are accordingly suppressed before being perceived. The self-observer, on the other hand, need only take the trouble to suppress his critical faculty. If he

> succeeds in doing that, innumerable ideas [*Einfälle*] come into his consciousness of which he could otherwise never have got hold. (101–02/90–91)

V

Attention, then, is a central element of the method, as long as we distinguish between its two forms. I have indicated elsewhere from which source stems the importance that Freud has always given to attention (see Scarfone, "Free-association"). The British neuroscientist Karl Friston has brought back into the limelight the fundamental contribution of Hermann von Helmholtz, the leader of the physicalist school, of which Ernst Wilhelm von Brücke—Freud's director at the time of his laboratory research—was also part. What may be called the "Helmholtz Principle" states that the essential function of the central nervous system is to keep free energy as low as possible because a too-high free energy level interferes with brain function. The relation to the outside world therefore requires the binding of free energy. And if we ask how this translates into psychological terms, Friston specifies that it is ultimately a question of avoiding surprise (see "The Free-Energy Principle"; also Llinás). It is a question of putting some order in the world, giving the subject a capacity of foresight or prediction, of getting ready for any eventuality: a *preparedness,* then, intended to avoid big surprises.

This is clearly similar to what Freud wrote in *Beyond the Pleasure Principle* about the avoidance of trauma through preparation *by* anxiety. In this same text, Freud also posited, in terms very close to those of Helmholtz, that the binding of free energy (i.e., of the quantity of excitation) is a fundamental task of the psychic apparatus (see *Beyond the Pleasure Principle*, 26–31/27–31, 33–36/32–36, 62–63/59–60). The logic of the theory of trauma and of its possible avoidance is thus based on this primary function, on this principle of binding the energy. But if, in the light of this principle, we now examine what we have quoted above about the psychological preparation of the patient in analysis, we note that the Freudian method aims at somehow *diverting* the psychic apparatus from its tendency to preparedness. Remember that a greater attention paid to internal perceptions, coupled with a withdrawal of criticism, must favor the appearance of incidental ideas (*Einfälle*), that is to say, unexpected ideas quite literally "falling upon" the patient. The Freudian method of analysis therefore works *against* the fundamental principle of binding and seeks, on the contrary, to favor a certain surprise!

Thinking about it, what else could one expect from a method called psychoanalysis? Does not "*lysis*" mean precisely unbinding, decomposition? The analysand has done his best all his life to bind the "free energies" that assailed him, i.e., to master the consequences of events and situations for which the psyche was not prepared. The most primal of these situations is what, in *New Foundations for Psychoanalysis*, Laplanche calls the Fundamental Anthropological Situation containing an asymmetry, as for the sexual dimension, between the infant and the adult caretaker. In Laplanche's theoretical frame, we find an equivalent of Helmholtz's free energy in the non-metabolizable part of the excitation due to the enigmatic sexual lodged within the adult's messages of attachment. Following this model, a subject can be exposed to disturbing events of variable intensity that may lead to dead ends in symbolization. The subject will one day report his/her unproductive efforts and will start looking for more effective bindings. But these new links cannot be obtained without first unbinding, i.e., undoing the pre-existing links. Analysis, it must be remembered, proceeds *per via di levare.* The analysand would rather not have to go through such an ordeal, but as the work analysis is primarily devoted to unbinding, it cannot help temporarily raising the levels of free energy. This is not without causing moments of anxiety, a disturbance that the analysand would rather try to prevent.

Such affinity of the analytical method with the model of the traumatic breach certainly does not mean that analysts actually try to re-traumatize their patients! Yet, obviously, a well-understood Freudian method of analysis contrasts with a certain contemporary predilection for techniques that seek above all an empathic communication between patient and analyst (see Kahn, *Psychoanalysis, Apathy*), as if one tried at any cost to avoid raising the level of free energy in the analysand. Yet only such a raise can lead to the temporary unbinding needed for new symbolization to happen in the *après-coup.*[3] How indeed could the *après-coup* temporal dynamics operate if the analytic session did not offer opportunities for new *après-coup* events, which, in order to happen, include new "blows" ("nouveaux coups," see André)?[4]

[3] I use, as ever more Anglophone authors do, this French expression for *Nachträglichkeit*, given the unsatisfactory English translation as "deferred action."

[4] There is play here with the word "coup" (blow) that is part of "après-coup."

VI

As a counterpart to the unbinding that the method entails, the analytic frame with its containing function is there to ensure that the rise in free energy does not exceed a certain threshold. But within this framework, another phenomenon arises, custom-made, as it were, to ensure that the "surprise" is already partially countered by a new type of binding. This phenomenon is none other than the transference. As we have seen, the method that invites unbinding requires of the analysand a readiness to be surprised by the incidental ideas, thus to let the free energy rise. But that never goes without a movement in the other direction, as if something were already in place, ready to absorb some of the energy unleashed by the method. At one point, Freud speaks of "stereotype plates" (*Klischee*), something like printing plates ready at hand for issuing new editions of old relational and affective configurations ("The dynamics of transference" 100/94). This type of transference is dubbed by Laplanche "filled-in transference"; it is the analysand's response—almost predictable from what is known about the patient's history—destined at countering the unbinding provocation by the analyst (see Laplanche, "Transference"). Seen in this light, the binding effect of the transference works against the disposition to let the incidental ideas come in; it guards against any surprises by reproducing situations already experienced. As Freud noted in "Remembering, repeating and working-through," transference is resistance.

The parallel between the analytic and the traumatic unbinding still holds for what regards triggering the repetition compulsion. Indeed, if the "blows" due to the analytic method are like micro-traumatic events, the emergence of the transference is itself of the order of repetition. However, the containing structure offered by the analyst as guardian of the setting and of the method creates a situation very different from that in which full-blown traumas have occurred. The readiness of the patient to allow a certain unbinding combines not only with the analyst's capacity for containing and the reliability of the frame, but also with another *readiness*: the analyst's own readiness not only to hear, but also to let him/herself get caught, as it were, in the net of the transference (see Gantheret).

The analyst who, by the simple act of instituting the inevitably seductive analytic situation, provokes the transference, must therefore possess a double disposition: on the one hand, a *preparedness* manifest in setting up the framework and the refusals it imposes; on the other hand, a *readiness* to welcome the transference in its actuality, that is, not only as a repetition of a thing of the past, but as a new fact happening in the present (see Freud, "Remembering, repeating and working-through"), a fact which now truly concerns the analyst. The analyst's availability or, following a term borrowed from Lyotard (121, 127), his *passibility*, is thus engaged in a more radical way (see Scarfone, *The Unpast*). It is a matter of letting oneself be reached without colluding with the positive transference nor retaliating against negative transference—something which does not go without failures on the part of the analyst, but failures that Winnicott considered inevitable, even necessary (see Winnicott 91).

VII

The combination of preparedness and readiness, in the analysand as in the analyst, makes of transference a system that we could describe as metastable, in the sense that the philosopher Gilbert Simondon gives to this term. A metastable system or organization is one still capable of evolving because it has not exhausted its potential, i.e., it has not reached the zero level of available energy. Contrary, then, to what may ordinarily be wished for outside of analysis, the transferential link is not at all expected to stabilize itself, since its metastability is what allows the continuation of the working-through. The establishment and maintenance of the frame, on the one hand, and the provocation of the transference coupled with the availability or *passibility* of the analyst, on the other hand, allow for a somewhat contained unbinding and rebinding, yet still open to surprise.

Under the name of "psychological chimera," Michel de M'Uzan has formulated a powerful metaphor for describing this metastable, evolutive situation. The chimera is a "fabulous child" resulting from the meeting between the patient's and the analyst's unconscious (see M'Uzan, "La bouche de l'inconscient"). The life of this hybrid entity follows an original course, specific to each particular case. In this respect, the disposition of the analyst must, according to de M'Uzan, go so far as to tolerate a certain degree of depersonalization. Indeed, the chimera manifests itself as a "paradoxical system" (see M'Uzan, "Countertransference and paradoxical system") in which it is not easy to determine to whom the thoughts or incidental ideas obtained through the analytic method belong. This is certainly a radical conception, but a most important one in terms of *passibility*; it is the greatest possible *readiness*, offered jointly with—and yet opposite to—any *preparedness*. The chimera is a composite being, it metastabilizes the transferential process, but it also has a life of its own and is therefore not entirely subject to a will external to it. The two participants in the analytic situation are at the same time spectators of its autonomous course. The chimera therefore supposes in both of them a disposition to welcome the surprises brought about by its evolving nature; attenuated surprises, to be sure, and thus less likely to cause psychic paralysis, but surprises all the same, attesting the vitality of the analytic process.

A closer view suggests that the analyst who hosts the transference must lend him/herself to a sort of dissociation between the role of guardian of the frame and the disposition to welcome and contain paradoxical thoughts, i.e., a certain degree of depersonalization. To accept, therefore, a certain "madness" insofar as it is bound by a method. Polonius's phrase, "Though this be madness yet there is method in't" (2.2.205–06) could, again, be paraphrased thus: "Though this be method yet there is (some) madness in it."

VIII

On what, then, can the analyst rely when making him/herself available, so as not to skid uncontrollably? I propose that it is still on the "entirely secure" thing that comforted Freud in the Fall of 1897, after he lost sight of "the sources of the Nile": I am talking of the model of the dream and the metapsychology derived from it. Except that, nowadays, a misunderstanding reigns on this matter. While there still is a general agreement that *The Interpretation of Dreams* is Freud's major work, it is not at all obvious that its central tenets are currently taken into account. The impression one gets from many contemporary publications is that the dream is no longer an object of analysis and that analysts stay mainly at the level of the manifest content. The analyst's "reverie" is frequently invoked, but it often seems to be conceived as a direct provider of unconscious content rather than a precondition for a better listening. It is probably worth remembering that in good Freudian logic, the royal road to the unconscious is the *analysis* of the dream, not the dream itself, nor consequently the reverie. From the moment that the content of the reverie—be it that of the patient or that of the analyst—is taken as a direct access to the unconscious and not as something to be analyzed, the Freudian method is seriously distorted. I am not lamenting this deviation for the sake of orthodoxy; this is an eminently practical issue. The problem is that the celebration of reverie for itself, without calling upon the "witch" metapsychology, has the paradoxical effect of giving the analysts' associations a preponderant weight and, moreover, to shield them against the methodological doubt and suspicion required of any analyst confronted with what seems obvious.

Admittedly, it is indispensable during our listening to indulge in a "dreaming thought" (Pontalis's "pensée rêvante," 19) and to let oneself be caught up, as already mentioned, in the transference, but this does not dispense the analyst from maintaining an evenly distributed attention as a counterpoint to the associations of the patient. But "evenly distributed" does not imply that anything goes; it means above all a constant work of rebalancing, i.e., of opposing a healthy skepticism to what seems self-evident, being particularly wary of the possible misguiding role of affects due to their facile transferability from one representation to another (see Kahn, *L'écoute de l'analyste* 84 ff.). The reverie occurring in the session is not a point of arrival; it is still only one aspect of the readiness, of the analyst's disposition to hear better. The analyst's task is to take note of the crop of reveries and *analyze* them in order to get a better idea of where he/she stands with regard to the patient's transference. Nothing forbids the interpretation from taking a poetic turn, to be a dreaming utterance, even carrying something apparently "crazy." But if the "madness" of transference and countertransference must be tolerated, it does not exempt us from having to maintain a method within it.

The method that is called for in these circumstances is still made of readiness. But here caution is warranted. If the analyst is to indulge in his/her own reverie, he/she must avoid using it to saturate the paths of thinking that open up during the session. On the contrary, he/she must work to constantly offer a "hollow" to the transference of the analysand, a hollow likely to accommodate another "hollow" (see Laplanche, "Transference"). Indeed, another surprise of the analytic situation is that transference does not always present an identifiable content; it is not always a filled-in transference. On the contrary, transference can present itself as a void of representations, as a repetition of the subject's primordial confrontation with the enigmatic, as the actual experience of a failure of translation—a failure which Freud, in another famous letter to Fliess dated 6 December 1896, called repression (see Masson 207–15). The actualization of the primordial situation presenting itself as a hollowed-out transference requires that the analyst offer a matrix, so to speak, within which unconscious seeds for the processes of representation and fantasy-building can be patiently cultivated (see Scarfone, "Fantasme").

It goes without saying that, in practice, one cannot always neatly distinguish between "filled in" and "hollowed-out" forms of transference. As a clinical phenomenon, transference is structured in the manner of a dream or a symptom in which one can detect recurring patterns made of an "actual" nucleus (in this case, a hollow), coated with a properly psychic, representational layer (see Scarfone, *The Unpast*). What, on the other hand, is offered by the analyst as a hollow matrix is for Laplanche essentially made of the analyst's "refusals," first among these the things he refuses him/herself, such as the refusal to know—a refusal of preparedness with readiness taking its place. In a similar perspective, M'Uzan speaks of a necessary "fundamental silence" of the analyst, an atemporal silence which is "the mouth of the unconscious" (*La bouche de l'inconscient: essais sur l'interprétation* 42). By "fundamental silence," de M'Uzan does not trivially mean that the analyst should refrain from speaking; he rather means offering the analysand a listening like no other: "[a] fundamental silence, where the analyst collects and remembers all the messages coming from his own unconscious and especially that of his patient, this would be the active agent of healing" (my trans.; 43).

The analyst's refusals and fundamental silence indicate that the analytical procedure is a mixture of method and availability, of containment and openness to what comes forward. It is this—not the least passive—availability or passibility of the analyst that constitutes, as Bonnefoy said of Hamlet's *readiness*, a "survival technique of the soul."

Acknowledgment The author would like to thank Jacques Mauger, Élyse Michon, and Avgi Saketopoulou for their critical support.

Works Cited

André, Jacques. *Les désordres du temps*. PUF 2010.

Bonnefoy, Yves, translator. "Préface." *Shakespeare, Hamlet-Le Roi Lear*. Gallimard, 1978.

Bourguignon, André, et al., *Traduire Freud*. PUF, 1989.

Freud, Sigmund. *Au-delà du principe de plaisir* (1920a). *Oeuvres Complètes de Freud*, vol. 15. PUF, 1996, pp. 273–338.

———. *Briefe an Wilhelm Fließ*. Fischer Verlag, 1897.

———. *The Revised Standard Edition of the Complete Psychological Works of Sigmund Freud*, edited and translated by James Strachey, revised by Mark Solms. 24 vols. Rowman & Littlefield Publishers, 2024. (In-text references provide *RSE* page numbers immediately after *SE* page numbers).

———. *Beyond the Pleasure Principle* (1920b). *The Standard Edition of the Complete Psychological Works of Sigmund Freud*, edited and translated by James Strachey, vol. 18. Hogarth Press, 1955, pp. 1–64/*RSE* vol. 18, pp. 3–61.

———. "The dynamics of transference" (1912). *SE* vol. 12, 1958, pp. 97–108/*RSE* vol. 12, pp. 91–101.

———. *The Interpretation of Dreams* (1900). *SE* vols. 4 and 5, 1953/*RSE* vols. 4 and 5.

———. "On the Aetiology of Hysteria" (1896). *SE* vol. 3, 1962, pp. 189–224/*RSE* vol. 3, pp. 197–225.

———. "Remembering, repeating and working-through" (1914). *SE* vol. 12, pp. 145–56/*RSE* vol. 12, pp. 141–53.

Friston, Karl. "The Free-Energy Principle: A Unified Brain Theory?" *Nature Reviews Neuroscience*, vol. 11, 2010, pp. 127–38.

Gantheret, François. "Traces et chair." *Moi, monde, mots.* Gallimard, 1998.

Kahn, Laurence. *L'écoute de l'analyste. De l'acte à la forme.* PUF, 2012.

———. *L'écoute de l'analyste. De l'acte à la forme.* PUF. *Psychoanalysis, Apathy and the Post-Modern Patient.* Translated by Dorothée Bonnigal-Katz, Routledge, 2014/2018.

Laplanche, Jean. *New Foundations for Psychoanalysis.* Translated by Jonathan House, The Unconscious in Translation, 2016.

———. *The Temptation of Biology: Freud's Theories of Sexuality* (1993). Translated by Donald Nicholson-Smith, The Unconscious in Translation, 2015.

———. "Transference: its provocation by the analyst" (1991). *Essays on Otherness*, edited by John Fletcher, translated by Luke Thurston, Routledge, 1999, pp. 218–37.

Llinás, Rodolfo. *I of the Vortex.* MIT Press, 2001.

Lyotard, Jean-François. *L'inhumain. Causeries sur le temps.* Galilée, 1988.

M'Uzan, Michel de. "Countertransference and paradoxical system" (1976). *Death and Identity*, translated by Andrew Weller, Karnac Books, 2013, pp. 17–32.

———. "La bouche de l'inconscient." *Nouvelle revue de psychanalyse*, vol. 17, 1978, pp. 89–98.

———. La bouche *de l'inconscient: essais sur l'interprétation.* Gallimard, 1994.

Masson, Jeffrey Moussaieff, translator and editor. *The Complete Letters of Sigmund Freud to Wilhelm Fliess, 1887–1904.* Belknap Press, 1985.

Pontalis, J.-B. *Windows.* Translated by Anne Quinney, U of Nebraska P, 2003.

Scarfone, Dominique. "Fantasme et processus de fantasmatisation." *Revue française de psychosomatique,* vol. 50, no. 2, 2016, pp. 47–68.

Scarfone, Dominique. "Fantasme et processus de fantasmatisation." *Revue française de psychosomatique,* vol. 50, no. 2. "Free-association, surprise, trauma and transference." *Psychoanalytic Inquiry*, vol. 38, no, 6, 2018, pp. 468–77.

———. *The Unpast. The Actual Unconscious.* The Unconscious in Translation, 2015.

Shakespeare, William. *The Riverside Shakespeare.* Edited by G. Blakemore Evans et al., Houghton Mifflin, 1997.

Simondon, Gilbert. (1958) *L'individuation psychique et collective.* Aubier, 1989 and 2007.

Winnicott, D. W. "Fear of Break-Down" (1963). *Psychoanalytic Explorations*, Harvard UP, 1989, pp. 523–32.

CHAPTER 4

Representing Subjectivity in Shakespeare's *Romeo and Juliet*

Madelon Sprengnether

We live in a post-psychoanalytic era. By this I mean that our conception of individual subjectivity has been irrevocably altered by Freud and his successors. As a result, we imagine that we lead complex subjective and intersubjective lives, fraught with urges, inhibitions, fantasies, and conflicts, and dense with narrative meanings. At the same time, we neglect to historicize our condition, accepting it instead as a given. In the chapter that follows, I propose that Shakespeare played a major (if not defining) role in the representation of subjectivity that led to Freud and beyond.

I am neither the first nor the only scholar to suggest this. Nor am I unique in arguing that Shakespeare's dramatic representation of interiority anticipated Freud. Those who have argued some version of the former include, among others, Francis Barker, Catherine Belsey, Jonathan Dollimore, Joel Fineman, Christopher Pye, and Katharine Maus. The latter proposition has been put forward by Harold Bloom, Paula Cohen, David Hillman, Cynthia Marshall, and Sandra Young. These two groups represent major trends in Shakespeare studies over the past half-century.

M. Sprengnether (✉)
Minneapolis, MN, USA
e-mail: spren001@umn.edu

J. W. Stone, C. Bates (eds.), *Shakespeare and Psychoanalysis*, Palgrave Shakespeare Studies,
https://doi.org/10.1007/978-3-032-07897-1_4

Those who focus on the emergence of the "liberal humanist subject" propose that the Enlightenment construction of a coherent, unified self is the heir of Renaissance individualism. They seek to deconstruct such a subject through cultural/historical methods of analysis. Those who focus on Freud's indebtedness to Shakespeare emphasize the extent to which he relied on literature, and especially his oedipal reading of *Hamlet*, to underpin and validate his theories. These two groups do not speak directly to each other, as their aims are different. Philip Armstrong gives a concise summary of some of these developments:

> To credit the cultural materialist or new historicist version of English dramaturgical history, while remaining suspicious of the universalized and humanistic account of psychological evolution represented by the work of [Harold] Bloom, requires not only that the paradigm of the self as a deep, interior consciousness (and unconsciousness) be seen as an intervention which occurs at a particular time, in a particular corner of the world, but also that this invention should be examined in its political, cultural and imperial investments. This hypothesis provides a way to historicize the categories of psychoanalysis—albeit against its own will—and, in so doing, to gain a clearer sense of both their appropriateness and their limitations in the readings of texts. (41)

My analysis differs from the work of these fine scholars insofar as my focus is on literary history and its role in the development of modern psychoanalytic subjectivity. Further, I suggest that literary history offers a means to illuminate the path by which we have arrived at our present moment in time. In other words, without Shakespeare there could be no Freud.

In this chapter, I turn first to matters of literary history and its relationship to psychoanalysis as the premier rhetoric of interiority of our time. I then explore these questions by examining Shakespeare's portrait of Juliet, whose mentally anguished state leads directly to his creation of Hamlet. My emphasis is on the way Shakespeare represents the development of Juliet's character in increasingly complex rhetorical terms, ones that were available to him through the language of courtly love but which he advanced to new levels of sophistication. In this way, I suggest, Shakespeare anticipated future developments in Western literary culture which have flourished to the point that we no longer regard them as innovations, but rather as baseline assumptions about human nature. In the final section, I consider the extent to which literary history thus contributes to our understanding of both subjectivity and psychoanalysis.

The Renaissance acquired its name (in part) from Petrarch, who described his engagement with the literature of antiquity as a *rinascita*: a rebirth simultaneously of the previously hidden past and of the person who encountered it, whose very selfhood was altered as a result. From the perspective of the twenty-first century, it is hard to conceive of such a transformative moment. We can only compare it to more recent temporal and psychological shifts, such as the nineteenth-century discovery of deep geological time or Darwin's theory of the origin of species. But for Petrarch, whose love for antiquity was perhaps only matched by his literary ambition, the incorporation of the classical past into the warp and woof of his individual psyche was as destabilizing as it was enabling. The pagan world of antiquity was at once profoundly other while at the same time feeling deeply familiar, so much so that Petrarch was moved to write to one of his favorite authors, Cicero, as if he were his contemporary.[1] Jacob Burckhardt declared, rather more simply, that Petrarch was the "first truly modern man" (193), meaning that he focused on his individuality and his inner life in a way that separated him from the medieval understanding of self as defined by external criteria such as family, clan, and community. Despite the romanticization of Burckhardt's portrayal of Renaissance Italy, many (if not most) historians replicate this view.[2]

[1] Leonard Barkan describes the impact of the discovery of antiquity on writers and artists of the Renaissance through his lyrical exposition of the uses and transformations of Ovid's *Metamorphoses*. Like many others, Barkan regards Petrarch as a key figure in the creation of radically new rhetorical forms, which have served in turn to alter our conceptions of subjectivity. "It could be argued," he writes, "that all of Petrarch's works amount to an extended act of introspection and autobiography," concluding that his writings "probably represent the first sustained attempt at self-consciousness in Western writing" (206). For an analysis of the destabilizing effects of the Tudor adoption of humanist pedagogy (focused on the imitation of classical authors such as Cicero) on the evolution of the English language, see Catherine Nicholson.

[2] In an influential essay Stephen Greenblatt dismissed psychoanalysis (a late nineteenth- and twentieth-century conceptual framework) as a means of interpreting early modern texts. He based his argument on a sixteenth-century case of imposter identity, documented in the French court system of the time and revived by historian Natalie Zemon Davis in her book *The Return of Martin Guerre*. Greenblatt's position may be summarized as follows. The "fake" Martin Guerre, who was accused of appropriating the name, wife, and property of the "real" Martin Guerre, was exposed by external criteria, e.g. birth, baptism, marriage, and property records. In other words, individual identity in the early modern period was a matter of cultural and material construction and hence best understood in historical, rather than psychological, terms. His argument had a distinctly chilling effect on psychoanalytic interpretations of early modern texts, including the plays of Shakespeare. In my own view, Greenblatt's

Aldo Scaglione, for example, states that Petrarch "was responsible for introducing introspection at the very centre of cultural and literary activity" (137).[3] The authors of *A History of Private Life: Passions of the Renaissance* support Burckhardt's distinction between medieval and Renaissance conceptions of privacy and the inner life. Jean-Marie Goulemot maintains that "Medieval literature was oral and public" and "for the most part anonymous." As he explains:

> Writers belonged to the community: jongleurs, clerics, authors of sacred mysteries and profane plays existed only because a community—a convent, confraternity, or city "commissioned" their works. The community, in which specific cultural practices were embodied, was the writer's *raison d'être*, his work served its needs and brought it renown. (364)

For Goulemot, Montaigne and Ronsard mark turning point moments in the development of French (and European) literature, due to their portrayals of inwardness:

> Montaigne's *Essays* represent a mutation in the nature and status of knowledge. The work is in no way derivative of the medieval summa, or scholastic commentary. Where the summa is systematic, the *Essays* are fragmentary. Where the commentary refers to a unique work, of which it offers a gloss, the *Essays* are a compendium of many sources, a summary of wide reading.

essay conflates identity (how one may be viewed by one's place in the socio/political order) with subjectivity (how one may comprehend one's individual selfhood), failing as a result to consider Shakespeare's achievement in developing a radically new language of interiority.

[3] Scaglione's claim, however, does not necessarily imply the construction of a coherent, much less unified, subject. As Giuseppe Mazzotta maintains, Petrarch's vaunted focus on his inner life reveals a self that is elusive, fragmented, and finally impossible to represent in language. He describes his *Canzoniere* as "The quest for the signs of Laura, which ends by exposing the self-mystification as the presence of a nothingness, masks and hides another more painful and insoluble quest, the poet's quest for poetic language, for the signs that might be adequate to the poet's inner thoughts" (71). Cynthia Marshall regards the Petrarchan tradition in England (viewed through its lesser-known practitioners) as manifesting forms of sado-masochism whose aim is "jouissance," or the ultimate shattering of the self. Catherine Bates reads the Petrarchan tradition as dissolving the presumption of an autonomous, unitary subject at the heart of Enlightenment philosophy. Her book "takes as its point of departure the fact that the ego is not 'master' in its own house, that the subject is always 'in process,' that masculinity is never 'consolidated' nor gender identity 'achieved,' and that, in the final analysis we are the creatures not the masters of our words" (24).

> What makes them coherent is Montaigne himself, sole master of his references and queries and creator of his library. (365)

Of Ronsard, he claims that he "and with him the group of poets known as The Pléiade, can be credited with originating lyric poetry as the Romantics would later define it: poetry that expresses private feelings and experiences" (368). In other words, Montaigne and Ronsard move the needle further along the spectrum (presumably established by Petrarch) toward modern conceptions of selfhood and the inner life.

In an essay on *Romeo and Juliet*, Gail Kern Paster endorses this view:

> In England until the late sixteenth century, individual identity had been imagined not so much as the result of autonomous, personal growth in consciousness, but rather as a function of social station, an individual's place in a network of social and kinship structures. (258)

In accord with this line of thinking, she argues that "At the core of the play's evident accessibility is the importance and privilege modern Western culture grants to desire, regarding it as deeply expressive of individual identity and central to the fulfillment of women no less than men" (257–58). Although her commentary centers on Romeo as lover, her analysis applies equally (and more forcefully) to Juliet. "For Romeo, as for Petrarch," she states, "love is the formation of an individualistic identity at odds with other kinds of identity" (262). Individualism is the mark of the Renaissance transformation of Western conceptions of self in relation to society.[4] What role did Shakespeare play in this profound shift of consciousness?

[4]The concept of Renaissance individualism seems well established by now. At issue are its sequelae. For cultural materialist and Marxist critics, it led to the development of the liberal humanist subject, responsible, in turn, for various social ills, such as Western industrialization, European imperialism, and global capitalism. For others, it fostered a flowering of artistic, literary, and scientific achievements. I do not propose to adjudicate this matter. Rather, I wish to call attention to fissures in the concept of the individual subject. If Freud is the heir and beneficiary of this tradition, he can hardly be viewed as its celebrant. For Freud, the self is not only divided (and fractured) into conflicting parts but also undermined from within. For Lacan, the ego is further alienated by what he describes as the "mirror stage," in which the infant forms an image of itself as integral or whole as a necessary illusion. Preoedipal theory in general regards the process of infant development as variable, fragile, and contingent. In the past, psychoanalytic theory has been excoriated for its supposedly intrapsychic focus—as a sign of its failure to address the subject's cultural, racial, gendered, economic,

Shakespeare was most certainly familiar with the poetry of Petrarch. The opening scenes of *Romeo and Juliet* pay loving—as well as mocking—tribute to the tradition of love poetry established by him and carried forward by lyric poets such as Ronsard. It is unclear whether Shakespeare read Ronsard, but most scholars assume that he knew Montaigne through the translation of his contemporary John Florio. I am not arguing here for a direct line of influence, but rather for a change in sensibility signaled by the turn toward the individual, the nature of private experience, and inner life that Burckhardt (following the lead of Petrarch) attributes to Renaissance culture.

Yet, there is a difference between the form of lyric poetry and the essay (as Montaigne invented it), and dramatic literature in which characters may represent various aspects of the author's mental awareness but appear to have a life of their own independent of their creator. They are purely linguistic constructs, yet Shakespeare makes them seem "real"—to the extent that generations of readers and theatergoers (not to mention literary critics), have responded to his plays as if his dramatis personae were living human beings with passions and conflicts much like our own. Some have even tried to construct backstories for them or to analyze their words and actions as if they were patients on a couch.[5] What made Shakespeare so successful in convincing his audiences of the reality of his linguistic creations?

In what follows, I discuss several focal points in *Romeo and Juliet* which appear to mark Juliet's transition from a dutiful girl to a young woman who not only experiences inner conflict but who also weighs her options and chooses her own course. I attempt in my analysis to account for audiences' fascination with Shakespeare's creation of a character who seems to change before our very eyes. Romeo, in contrast, remains static—as

and socio-political components. The late twentieth-century revival of trauma theory has dramatically altered the terms of this critique by restoring the interpsychic (and intersubjective) dimensions of psychoanalytic theory and hence the complex interplay between internal and external factors in the formation of individual human subjects.

[5] Paul Menzer claims that "About the turn of the twentieth century, a vocabulary of the interior entered the professional theater review" (70). He attributes this phenomenon to the confluence of the work of Stanislavsky (theater), Freud (psychoanalysis), and A. C. Bradley (literary criticism), who were near contemporaries. The influence of Bradley and his character-based approach to literature can hardly be underestimated in the field of literary studies up to and including the New Criticism. Psychoanalysts who write about Shakespeare tend to follow Bradley's lead, interpreting characters in a play as if they were patients in the consulting room.

passionate and impulsive at the conclusion of the play as at its inception. It is Juliet who anticipates Shakespeare's development of his tragic heroes. I examine how, through the medium of language, he creates the illusion of a complex self-consciousness, as a prelude to his exploration of tragic subjectivity.[6]

At the beginning of the play, there is no suggestion that Juliet will defy her parents' will, much less reverse the conventional roles of lover and beloved by actively wooing Romeo. When not yet fourteen, she is asked by Lady Capulet: "Can you like of Paris' love?" she responds in the sing-song rhyming style of the opening of the play: "I'll look to like, if looking liking move / But no more deep will I endart mine eye / Than your consent gives strength to make it fly" (1.3.97–99).

Shakespeare's eloquent exchanges between the equally smitten lovers obscures to some extent how quickly Juliet takes charge of their fate. It is she, in the famous balcony scene, who thinks most practically, observing for instance that Romeo (as a Montague) is in mortal danger: "If they do see thee here, they will murder thee," and inquiring sensibly "By whose direction found thou out this place?" (2.2.70, 79). She also raises the question of Romeo's constancy by observing:

> Dost thou love me? I know thou wilt say "Ay,"
> And I will take thee at thy word. Yet if thou swear'st,
> Thou mayst prove false. At lovers' perjuries,
> They say, Jove laughs. O gentle Romeo,
> If thou dost love, pronounce it faithfully. (2.2.90–94)

Given what we (as the audience) know about Romeo's supposed passion for Rosaline, this is a very pertinent question. On further assurances, Juliet makes another prescient comment:

> Although I joy in thee,
> I have no joy of this contract tonight,
> It is too rash, too unadvised, too sudden,

[6] I explored the way that Shakespeare creates the illusion of interiority in "'All that is spoke is marred': Language and Consciousness in *Othello*": "Complex language in Shakespeare's plays is an index of complex consciousness. By examining the speech of Iago, Othello, and Desdemona, I hope to demonstrate the ways in which the use of language with more than one possibility of interpretation creates the illusion of a complex consciousness or a multi-layered sense of reality" (157). I remain committed to this view and extend it here.

> Too like the lightning, which doth cease to be
> Ere one can say "it lightens." (2.2.116–20)

Romeo, who asks for more "satisfaction," elicits an outright proposal from Juliet, accompanied by a plan of action:

> If that thy bent of love be honorable,
> Thy purpose marriage, send me word tomorrow,
> By one that I'll procure to come to thee,
> Where and what time thou wilt perform the rite
> And all my fortunes at thy foot I'll lay
> And follow thee my lord throughout the world. (2.2.143–48)

Nothing I have said so far will strike a reader (or interpreter) as remarkable. While Juliet appears to be capable of imagining uncertainty and even duplicity, she is single-minded, at this point, in the pursuit of her desire. What changes her course is Tybalt's death and her father's insistence that she marry Paris, both of which precipitate an alteration in her character which tests her ability to suffer and negotiate conflict.

Act 3, scene 2 begins with Juliet's anticipation of the consummation of her love for Romeo, commencing with the frank expression of her impatience:

> Gallop apace, you fiery-footed steeds,
> Towards Phoebus' lodging. Such a wagoner
> As Phaeton would whip you to the west
> And bring in cloudy night immediately,
> Spread thy close curtain, love-performing night,
> That runaways' eyes may wink, and Romeo
> Leap to these arms, untalked of and unseen. (3.2.1–7)

The arrival of Juliet's nurse turns this moment of unalloyed passion to one of pain and turmoil. Mistakenly believing Romeo to be dead, Juliet imagines her own demise:

> Hath Romeo slain himself? Say thou but "Ay,"
> And that bare vowel "I" shall poison more
> Than the death-darting eye of cockatrice.
> I am not I if there be such an "I,"
> Or those eyes shut that make thee answer "Ay." (3.2.45–49)

The relentless punning in this passage (on "Ay," "I," and "eye") obscures to some extent the splitting of Juliet's consciousness: into the realistic "Ay," the observing "eye," and the existential "I," now called into radical question. Fearing the worst, Juliet seems to lose her bearings. She does not know where she is, who she is, much less what has happened. Discovering the truth only intensifies her anguish.

Learning that Romeo has killed Tybalt, she at first condemns him:

> O serpent heart hid with a flowr'ing face!
> Did ever dragon keep so fair a cave?
> Beautiful tyrant, fiend angelical!
> Dove-feathered raven, wolfish-ravening lamb!
> Despised substance of divinest show!
> Just opposite to what thou justly seem'st,
> A damned saint, an honorable villain.
> O nature, what hadst thou to do in hell
> When thou didst bower the spirit of a fiend
> In mortal paradise of such sweet flesh? (3.2.73–82)

Juliet reverses the conventional pairing of opposite states of mind typical of courtly love poetry—where the idealized object remains constant, while eliciting contradictory emotions in her frustrated lover, who feels alternations of fever and cold, hope and despair, torment and delight. Here, in contrast, it is the beloved who is represented as two-faced and double-hearted. Who is Romeo, Juliet wonders, if he can woo her in one guise and kill her kinsman in another?

When her nurse concurs with this harsh assessment, dismissing all men as "perjured, / All foresworn, all naught, all dissemblers" (3.2.86–87), Juliet changes course again, professing her earlier love for Romeo, while also recalling her allegiance to Tybalt:

> Shall I speak ill of him that is my husband?
> Ah, poor my lord, what tongue shall smooth thy name
> When I, thy three hours wife, have mangled it?
> But, wherefore, villain, didst thou kill my cousin? (3.2.97–100)

She considers the possibility that Tybalt might have killed Romeo, a thought that leads her to the lesser, but equally distressing, prospect of her husband's banishment.

> To speak that word
> Is father, mother, Tybalt, Romeo, Juliet,
> All slain, all dead. "Romeo is banished."
> There is no end, no limit, measure, bound,
> In that word's death. (3.2.122–26)

Assuming that she will never see him again, Juliet tells her nurse to remove the ladder she has brought for Romeo to ascend to her chamber: "Come, cords—come, nurse," she says, "I'll to my wedding bed, / And death, not Romeo, take my maidenhead!" (3.2.136–37). Alarmed by Juliet's suicidal rhetoric, the nurse assures her that she will find Romeo and bring him to her bed. As a result, the consummation of the lovers' passion is marred by violence—of both action and emotion. But there are further challenges for Juliet to confront.

The temporary calm of the lovers' union is quickly disrupted by Capulet's insistence that his daughter marry the suitor of his choice. He sends his wife to deliver this message. The mother/daughter conversation that ensues prompts Juliet to develop a new mode of communication: a kind of double-speak in which she says one thing and means another. Concealing her distress over Romeo's banishment with her grief for Tybalt, Juliet tries to deflect her mother's questions about her state of mind. But when her mother condemns Romeo as a murderer, Juliet replies equivocally:

> Indeed, I never shall be satisfied
> With Romeo till I behold him—dead—
> Is my poor heart, so for a kinsman vexed.
> Madam, if you could find out but a man
> To bear a poison, I would temper it,
> That Romeo should upon receipt thereof,
> Soon sleep in quiet. O how my heart abhors
> To hear him named and cannot come to him
> To wreck the love I bore my cousin
> Upon his body that hath slaughtered him. (3.5.93–102)

Each of Juliet's statements, in this carefully crafted response, may be read in two ways: that she longs to see Romeo (dead), that she would temper any poison so that he should sleep (rather than die), and that she wishes to come to him in order to demonstrate (wreak) the love she bears her slaughtered cousin upon his body. These are some of the means by which

Shakespeare creates the illusion of a complex self-consciousness: a mind that is able not only to sustain conflicting thoughts and emotions but also deliberately to deceive. This newly acquired ability will be tested further when Capulet insists on enforcing his will. "Look to't, think on't, I do not use to jest," he ends their heated conversation, "Thursday is near. Lay hand on heart, advise. / An you be mine, I'll give you to my friend" (3.5.189–91). For the first time, Juliet finds herself completely alone, separated from her lover and abandoned not only by her parents but also by her nurse, who advises her to forget Romeo and marry Paris: "Then, since the case so stands as now it doth, / I think it best you married with the County" (3.5.216–17). There is no one, at this point, whom Juliet can trust—except, perhaps, Friar Lawrence. Inwardly, she turns away from her nurse (hitherto her closest confidante) with the words: "Thou and my bosom henceforth shall be twain. / I'll to the Friar to know my remedy," adding ominously "If all else fail, myself have power to die" (3.5.240–42).

Friar Lawrence's solution to Juliet's (and his) dilemma is to offer her a potion that simulates death as a means of preventing her marriage to Paris. Before she ingests the potion, however, she must make another difficult choice: she must deliberately lie to her father. On encountering Capulet on her return from Friar Lawrence's cell, she claims that she has "learnt me to repent the sin / Of disobedient opposition / To you and your behests ... Pardon, I beseech you. / Henceforward I am ever ruled by you" (4.2.17–22). She deceives her mother and her nurse as well, by reassuring them that "we have culled such necessaries / As are behooveful for our state tomorrow," assuring them both that she wishes now to "be left alone" (4.3.6–8). Once they have departed, however, she has second thoughts. In the lengthy soliloquy that follows, Juliet engages in the kind of self-questioning that reveals (or simulates) a mind in conflict with itself.

> I have a faint cold fear thrills through my veins
> That almost freezes up the heat of life.
> I'll call them back to comfort me—
> Nurse!—What should she do here?
> My dismal scene I needs must act alone. (4.3.15–19)

Having quelled her fear, she resolves to drink the potion. But even more distressing thoughts arise: "What if this mixture do not work at all?" she asks, "Shall I be married then tomorrow morning?" (4.3.21–22). Pushing this thought aside, she determines, once again, to follow the Friar's instruction, but almost immediately she imagines a more terrifying prospect:

> What if it be a poison which the Friar
> Subtly hath ministered to have me dead,
> Lest in this marriage he should be dishonored
> Because he married me before to Romeo?
> I fear it is. (4.3.24–28)

At this point, Juliet has not only appeared to experience profoundly dissonant emotions, learned to dissimulate her feelings in the presence of previously trusted others (her mother and her nurse) and lied outright to a figure of authority (her father), but she has also begun to imagine the deceptiveness of language and appearances in the world at large. In other words, she has demonstrated the range of emotion, capacity for introspection, and the depth of perception of a modern subject. The remainder of Juliet's soliloquy—one of the hallmarks of Shakespeare's tragic heroes—is unusual not only in its length but also in its rapid alternation of states of mind, culminating in a ghoulish fantasy that pushes her to the brink of madness. Not unlike Hamlet in his "To be or not to be" soliloquy, Juliet begins to fantasize what she might encounter on waking in her family's vault:

> How if, when I am laid in the tomb,
> I wake before the time that Romeo
> Come to redeem me? There's a fearful point.
> Shall I not then be stifled in the vault,
> To whose foul mouth no healthsome air breathes in,
> And there lie strangled ere my Romeo comes? (4.3.30–35)

Pursuing this nightmarish scenario, Juliet imagines what it might be like to wake up in the company of her ancestors' bones, not to mention the recently interred body of her cousin Tybalt:

> Or, if I live, is it not very like
> The horrible conceit of death and night,
> Together with the terror of the place—
> As in a vault, an ancient receptacle
> Where for this many hundred years the bones
> Of all my buried ancestors are packed;

> Where bloody Tybalt, yet but green in earth,
> Lies festr'ing in his shroud, where, as they say,
> At some hours in the night spirits resort—
> Alack, alack, is it not like that I,
> So early waking, what with loathsome smells
> And shrieks like mandrakes torn out of the earth,
> That living mortals, hearing them run mad— (4.3.36–48)

Juliet's imagination, gone wild, evokes the atmosphere of a contemporary horror movie. Nor does her fantasy end here. What if she should wake:

> ... shall I not be distraught,
> Environed with all these hideous fears,
> And madly play with my forefathers' joints,
> And pluck the mangled Tybalt from his shroud,
> And, in this rage, with some great kinsman's bone,
> As with a club, dash out my desp'rate brains? (4.3.49–54)

Having worked herself into a fever pitch of emotion, Juliet enters, briefly, into a state of delusion. She hallucinates the ghost of Tybalt:

> O look, methinks I see my cousin's ghost
> Seeking out Romeo that did spit his body
> Upon a rapier's point! Stay, Tybalt, stay! (4.3.55–57)

Here, Shakespeare seems to anticipate his portrayal of Macbeth, who speaks to the murdered Banquo at his feast. Unlike Macbeth, however, Juliet has no crime on her conscience, and quickly recovers herself, invoking Romeo's name as an antidote to her fears as she ingests Friar Lawrence's potion: "Romeo, Romeo, Romeo! Here's drink. I drink to thee" (4.3.58).

I quote so extensively in the above commentary to highlight Shakespeare's dramatic representation of a mind in urgent conversation with itself—a significant departure from the theatrical traditions (as in the medieval mystery and morality plays) that preceded him. Today, we tend to take this development for granted—so much so that contemporary productions of *Romeo and Juliet* cut many of Juliet's most powerful lines in the interest of speed and dramatic effect.[7] Because we, as twenty-first-century

[7] Baz Luhrman's film version (1996) of *Romeo and Juliet* tests the outer limits of how much of Shakespeare's language may be sacrificed for the sake of kinetic intensity. Even the

viewers, expect our fictional heroes (and heroines) to possess a sophisticated self-consciousness, we may gloss over the step-wise historical and literary processes by which we have arrived at these assumptions. Contemporary viewers, for instance, tend to regard Shakespeare's characters as fully rounded creations, such as we might find in a novel by a nineteenth-century author.[8] They appear to have minds of their own: capable of self-observation, reflection, awareness of inner conflict, alterations of mood, doubt, emotional instability, and even areas of self-blindness or obfuscation. Yet there were no novels as we would understand them in Shakespeare's day. British and European prose writers in the sixteenth and seventeenth centuries, with the notable exception of Montaigne, wrote political and religious tracts, fictional romances (in imitation of stylized ancient Greek models), and picaresque adventure narratives featuring unselfconscious protagonists. The rise of the novel (the premier literary genre of the nineteenth and twentieth centuries) was slow to gather momentum, gaining ground in Britain in the eighteenth century with the likes of Henry Fielding's *Joseph Andrews* and *The Adventures of Tom Jones* and the more introspective genre of the epistolary novel as established by Samuel Richardson's *Clarissa*.

We are the heirs of this tradition. To what extent do we take it for granted, assuming, with Freud, that our interior lives are as richly textured and layered as that of Juliet and as densely convoluted as that of Hamlet and Shakespeare's other tragic heroes?

In *Civilization and Its Discontents* (1930), Freud wrote:

> Now let us, by a flight of imagination, suppose that Rome is not a human habitation but a psychical entity with a similarly long and copious past—an entity, that is to say, in which nothing that has once come into existence, will

more leisurely paced interpretation (1968) by Franco Zeffirelli omits many of Juliet's lines and all but the conclusion of the soliloquy that precedes her ingestion of the Friar's death-like potion.

[8] Commenting on the evolution of the novel and its emphasis on the inner lives of its characters, Paula Cohen writes: "One of the salient marks of nineteenth-century literature is the way it shows us the internal life of characters, a focus that is developed in the twentieth century with the technique of stream of consciousness. The beginning of internalization occurred with Shakespearean soliloquy, but in the novel it is amplified and elaborated to a degree that makes the characters seem individualized and hence, more realistic" (345). For an extended treatment of the development of the novel and its relationship to the reading public in eighteenth-century England, see Ian Watt. See also Robert Scholes and Robert Kellogg.

have passed away and all the earlier phases of development continue to exist alongside the latest one. (70/64–65)

We are familiar with Freud's passion for antiquity, evidenced in part by his extensive collection of relics. We also know that his Viennese Gymnasium education introduced him to the classics of Greek and Roman literature and impressed him with the feats of heroes such as Hannibal (who warred on Rome), as well as the tragic fate of Sophocles's Oedipus.[9] He was witness in his lifetime, moreover, to the spectacular archeological discoveries of Heinrich Schliemann, who excavated the ruins of Mycenae and those (as he believed) of Homer's fabled Troy. One might argue that history, literature, and archeology fused in Freud's imagination in such a way as to alter our conception of the human mind.

For Freud, human consciousness is not only hidden and opaque but also stratified (as in the successive layers of an archeological dig), and finally unknowable—too deep, fragmented, lost in time, and mysterious to bring to light. Freud's shift from a topological model of mind (conscious/preconscious/unconscious) to a structural one (ego/superego/id) did not obviate or efface his initial emphasis on the division between conscious and unconscious ideation. The archeological metaphor he evoked in *Civilization and its Discontents* mediates between these two conceptions. That is to say, we retain all of our prehistory (in hidden and unconscious layers of the mind) even as we develop as individuals with specific, conscious thoughts, feelings, and memories. No one would seriously wish to argue that modern and postmodern art, literature, and culture have been unaffected by this view.

Returning to Shakespeare, what role does his portrayal of Juliet—and other tragic figures—play in our current understanding of self and mind? Juliet, as I have argued, presents the reader or viewer with several stages of mental development, including taking the initiative in love-making, expressing ambivalent feelings of love and hate toward the object of her passion, undertaking the deliberate deception of figures of authority, having concerns about the (possibly deceptive) motives of others,

[9] For an account of Freud's education in the classics and his engagement with Sophocles's *Oedipus Rex*, see Peter Rudnytsky. See also Freud's major biographers Ernest Jones and Peter Gay. My book *The Spectral Mother* focuses on Freud's phobic responses to the figure of the mother and hence his neglect of the preoedipal period. Freud's most recent biographer Joel Whitebook acknowledges this strain in his thought, although he does not explore its potential for subversion.

experiencing fantasies of horror, and a near-descent into madness. How might we comprehend this series of mental stages through the perspective of contemporary psychoanalytic theory?

Viewing Juliet through a Kleinian lens, one might say that she has arrived at the depressive position in her ability to hold radically conflicting emotions in tension, without succumbing to the paranoid projection of intolerable feelings of hatred and destruction onto an external object.[10] But what about her awareness of deception—not only in her own practice but also in her consideration of the motives of others? Here, we might turn to Attachment Theory for its insight into the development of mentalization or "theory of mind."

"Theory of mind" refers to our capacity as individuals to imagine that others possess inner lives (thoughts, feelings, beliefs, and desires) as various and complex as our own. Most of us take such an assumption for granted. Yet how we arrive at this understanding is not self-evident. Is it a matter of innate ability, brain development, or even social and environmental factors? For psychoanalyst Peter Fonagy and his associates, the relationship between an infant and his or her primary caregiver sets the stage for the emergence of this critical dimension of human interaction. As he and they maintain:

> A number of philosophers of mind assume that the experience of mental states is intrinsic; psychic reality is a "given," … The model that we propose places Freud's notion of psychic reality in a developmental perspective. We have already presented empirical evidence and developmental observations … to support the view that our understanding of the mental world is not a given, is radically different in the young child, and crucially depends for its healthy development on interaction with other people who are sufficiently benign and reflective. (256)

They conclude: "The social nature of thought is thus part of the very essence of subjectivity" (256). From this point of view, one might argue that Shakespeare's portrayal of Juliet has captured the process by which a

[10] Melanie Klein is the originator of this theory, which she considers an aspect of early childhood development. The depressive position, in her view, signals a major achievement, as it represents the infant's ability to hold or contain emotions of both love and hate towards its primary caregiver without splitting off and projecting feelings of anger or aggression onto her or an external object. Klein labels this less integrated phase the "paranoid-schizoid position." See her *Envy and Gratitude* for a fuller explanation of these two major concepts.

mind not only becomes aware of its own inner complexity but also the means by which it differentiates itself from the minds of others, similarly endowed. To put this another way: if Juliet can deceive her parents and her nurse, so too may Friar Lawrence seek to deceive her.

The art of deception, I suggest, lies at the heart of Shakespearean tragedy.[11] Those who cannot imagine it are victims: think of the hapless Duncan, naïve Othello, or even the supremely self-ignorant Lear as he entrusts his kingdom to his two-faced daughters.

Those practiced in deception, on the contrary, appear (initially) to thrive. Consider Iago (liar par excellence), and Shakespeare's other arch villains—not only Goneril, Regan, and Edmund, but also Macbeth and Lady Macbeth, King Claudius, and perhaps his wife Gertrude. One might even argue that the core of Hamlet's dilemma (hence his famed procrastination) is less a matter of suppressed oedipal desire than a question of who is deceiving whom.[12] On learning of the treachery of the Thane of Cawdor,

[11] Shakespeare's use of the word "lie," in all its possible meanings, goes back to sonnet 138, where the poet excoriates his mistress and himself for their mutual deceit. This sonnet, playing on the verbal and sexual referents of the word "lie" concludes: "Therefore I lie with her and she with me, / And in our faults by lies we flattered be." In "'All that is spoke is marred,'" I explore the complexity of the mind of the liar, as one who manifests a multilayered consciousness of reality (a possibly desirable trait) but whose use of this capacity is destructive.

[12] Hamlet has reason to be wary. He is the only (and conspicuous) mourner at a court engaged in festivity. The Ghost confirms his suspicion that his father was murdered by his uncle Claudius, who promptly married his mother, casting doubt on her involvement in her husband's death. Yet a ghost may also deceive. Even the well-meaning Polonius is caught up in this web of intrigue by spying on Hamlet's conversation with Ophelia, whose motives are thence also called into question. Rosencrantz and Guildenstern add to Hamlet's conviction that no one at court can be trusted by their admission that Claudius has sent for them to observe his seemingly erratic behavior. Once his suspicions are confirmed, however, Hamlet begins to act: first by killing the hapless Polonius (spying on him in his mother's bedroom), then Rosencrantz and Guildenstern (carrying instructions for his execution in England), next Laertes (in the treacherous duel to which he assents), and finally Claudius himself (once he detects his last poisonous deceit). Hamlet inhabits a world of lies, to which he responds with an understandable level of caution, adopting an "antic disposition" to disguise his investigations before escaping capture, via sea voyage, and returning to claim his fatal heritage. In the midst of this chaos, there is only one person whom Hamlet trusts: his university friend, Horatio, who acts as a neutral observer of the affairs at court and inherits the burden of relating his bloody history. To reduce this twisted plot to an oedipal reading of a son's unconscious wish to murder his father and have sex with his mother seems hopelessly reductive, however effective it may have been in supporting Freud's nascent theory. For a more compelling psychoanalytic reading of the play, see Janet Adelman's chapter on *Hamlet.*

Duncan mildly observes: "There's no art / To find the mind's construction in the face" (1.4.12–13), a comment that proves prescient, while also failing to alert him to the deeper threat posed by Cawdor's successor Macbeth. The Duncans of this world did not interest Shakespeare as much as those who not only discover the depths of their subjectivity but who are also fragmented, shattered, and ultimately destroyed by that process.[13]

Shakespeare's tragedies open a reservoir of violent and conflicting emotions, both within the hero and in the world at large. In his tragic universe, such an awareness leads inexorably to destruction. Juliet, in her rapid movement from simple girlhood to a sophisticated understanding of herself and the treacherous nature of the world she inhabits, prefigures this development. A careful reading of Shakespeare's tragedies raises the question of whether (and to what extent) he prepared the ground for Freud's and our understanding of subjectivity.

What do I mean by this?

If it is true—as Freud and his successors maintain—that in order to have a mind of one's own one must first separate from the matrix of one's primal caregiving environment, accept and integrate feelings of both love and hate toward cherished others, act independently of them, which involves the capacity to think (or feel) one thing and say (or do) another, then it also makes sense to ask how we arrive at such a complex state of awareness.[14]

Fonagy and his associates regard this process of development as time-sensitive, social, and contingent, rather than inevitable. Some people do

[13] I made this case in my essay on *Othello* where I argued that Othello's unitary sense of self is disastrously undone by his gradual comprehension of the duplicity of language and appearances. His tragedy is that he develops a complex consciousness of self and other at the expense of his warrior identity and integrity. Shakespeare's representation of this process is bivalent, as it is in his other major tragedies. To lose one's life and the lives of cherished (or hated) others for the sake of a nuanced understanding of one's own inner reality can hardly be considered a victory. It is a Fall, rather, into the chaos of self and world. For an entirely different reading of this process, see Cynthia Marshall, for whom the shattering of the self may be perceived as a welcome or (unconsciously) longed for release from the strictures of a unified or purely integral identity. I admire the sophistication of her argument, but do not concur with her conclusions, at least as they apply to Shakespeare's major tragedies.

[14] This is a highly condensed account of early childhood development, as represented in the works of Melanie Klein, D. W. Winnicott, and others in the Object Relations school, as well as members of the Attachment Theory group, whose adherents are too numerous to name. I am especially indebted to Billie Pivnick for the insight that a child's capacity "to hold a secret" may signal a step in the process towards developing a sense of inwardness.

not give evidence of an awareness of others as individual subjects like themselves, nor do they demonstrate more than a superficial comprehension of their own inwardness. Each of us can recall someone like this from our own personal history or circle of acquaintances. In the socio-political world, they appear most frequently in the guise of narcissists, bullies, autocrats, or dictators. These people strike us as flat and one-dimensional—like stock figures in literature, rather than fully realized characters.

The question I want to pose in this chapter is first, does our contemporary consciousness of inwardness derive as much from literature as from psychoanalytic theory? And second, to what extent does literary history contribute to our understanding of modern (and postmodern) subjectivity?

Harold Bloom, a highly individualistic (if not eccentric) critic of the late twentieth and early twenty-first centuries, makes the extravagant claim that Shakespeare altered our understanding of what it means to be human. He opens his audaciously titled book *Shakespeare: The Invention of the Human* with the words:

> Literary character before Shakespeare is relatively unchanging; women and men are represented as aging and dying, but not as changing because their relationship to themselves, rather than to the gods or no God, has changed. In Shakespeare, characters develop rather than unfold, and they develop because they reconceive themselves. (xix)

Concluding his opening chapter titled "Shakespeare's Universalism," Bloom states that his "originality in the representation of character will be demonstrated [in his book] throughout, as will the extent to which we all of us were, to a shocking degree, pragmatically invented by Shakespeare." He goes as far as to claim that "his principal characters have become our mythology, and he, rather than his involuntary follower Freud, is our psychologist" (17)

Bloom, I suggest, is as much of a Romantic as Burckhardt in his celebration of Shakespeare as the heir of Italian Renaissance individualism. Yet his claim that Shakespeare's representation of character was unique and prescient in its portrayal of complex subjectivity merits consideration in terms of literary history. What if he, Burckhardt, and his compatriots (including the *History of Private Life* collective and scholars such as Gail Kern Paster) are on to something? If the qualities of inwardness and self-reflectiveness we now take for granted are a matter of socio-historical and cultural development, how are we to understand the discipline of psychoanalysis, which Freud claimed to be founded on universal (hence fixed) principles?

Psychoanalytic theory, I maintain, is no more immutable than the matrix of history from which it arose.[15] In this respect, it also resembles literature, which takes different forms in different eras. What can be thought or said in one may seem stale or outmoded in another, requiring new modes of expression. The mobile and evolutionary quality of literature, as I suggest, offered fertile ground for Freud's invention of psychoanalysis, as he himself was quick to observe in his extensive references to literature, most especially to Shakespeare. Finally, if Shakespeare may be viewed as the precursor of Freud, then we may also begin to re-write both literary and psychoanalytic history.

Acknowledgement I am grateful to the University of Minnesota for a research grant that allowed me to hire Emily Schoenbeck, a doctoral candidate in the Department of English, who assisted me with essential research tasks. I also want to thank my friend and colleague Toni McNaron, Professor Emerita of English, for entertaining my rambling thoughts and first attempts to articulate the parameters of this project. Finally, I am grateful to the editors of this volume for their invitation to submit an essay to their collection, and especially to Catherine Bates for her thoughtful attention to my contribution and astute suggestions for revision.

Works Cited

Adelman, Janet. *Suffocating Mothers: Fantasies of Maternal Origin in Shakespeare's Plays,* Hamlet *to* The Tempest. Routledge, 1992.

Armstrong, Philip. *Shakespeare in Psychoanalysis.* Routledge, 2001.

Barkan, Leonard. *The Gods Made Flesh: Metamorphosis and The Pursuit of Paganism.* Yale UP, 1986.

[15] I regard this point as self-evident, although many may take issue with it. In my view, most innovators in this field take pains to affirm their fidelity to Freud—as if their interventions were only refinements or elaborations of his fundamental concepts. Jacques Lacan offers an outstanding example of this strategy. While retaining Freud's oedipal structure of society and culture, Lacan radically alters its meanings by recasting it in terms of Saussurean linguistics. Yet he represents his theoretical endeavor as a return to Freud. Melanie Klein, in a similar vein, assisted the preoedipal turn in psychoanalytic theory, all while professing her fidelity to Freud. In this way, psychoanalysis as a discipline appears to be more seamless than it is. I see it, rather, as resembling a postmodern work of art and, as such, a vital work in progress.

Barker, Francis. *The Tremulous Private Body*. Methuen, 1984.

Bates, Catherine. *Masculinity, Gender and Identity in the English Renaissance Lyric*. Cambridge UP, 2007.

Belsey, Catherine. *The Subject of Tragedy: Identity and Difference in Renaissance Drama*. Routledge, 1991.

Bloom, Harold. *Shakespeare: The Invention of the Human*. Riverhead Books, 1993.

Bradley, A. C. *Shakespearean Tragedy: Lectures on Hamlet, Othello, King Lear, Macbeth*. Macmillan, 1904.

Burckhardt, Jacob. *The Civilization of the Renaissance in Italy*. Translated by S. G. C. Middlemore. Penguin Books, 1990.

Cohen, Paula Marantz. "Our Lives in Literature." *Psychoanalytic Inquiry*, vol. 43, no. 5, 2023, pp. 342–46.

Davis, Natilie Zemon. *The Return of Martin Guerre*. Harvard UP, 1983.

Dollimore, Jonathan. *Radical Tragedy: Religion, Ideology and Power in the Drama of Shakespeare and his Contemporaries*. Harvester, 1984.

Fineman, Joel. *The Subjectivity Effect in the Western Literary Tradition: Essays Toward the Release of Shakespeare's Will*. MIT Press, 1991.

Fonagy, Peter, and Gyorgy Gergely, Elliot Jurist, and Mary Target. *Affect Regulation, Mentalization, and the Development of Self*. Other Press, 2002.

Freud, Sigmund. *The Revised Standard Edition of the Complete Psychological Works of Sigmund Freud*, edited and translated by James Strachey, revised by Mark Solms. 24 vols. Rowman & Littlefield Publishers, 2024. (In-text references provide *RSE* page numbers immediately after *SE* page numbers).

———. *Civilization and its Discontents* (1930). The *Standard Edition of the Complete Psychological Works of Sigmund Freud*, edited and translated by James Strachey, vol. 21, Hogarth Press, 1961, pp. 64–133/*RSE* vol. 21, pp. 59–131.

Gay, Peter. *Freud: A Life for Our Time*. Norton, 1988.

Gohlke, Madelon. "'All that is spoke is marred:' Language and Consciousness in *Othello*." *Women's Studies: An Interdisciplinary Journal*, vol. 9, no. 2, 1982, pp. 157–76.

Goulemot, Jean-Marie. "Literary Practices: Publicizing the Private." *A History of Private Life: Passions of the Renaissance*. Vol. 3, edited by Roger Chartier, translated by Arthur Goldhammer, Harvard UP, 1989, pp. 363–95.

Greenblatt, Stephen. "Psychoanalysis and Renaissance Culture." *Literary Theory/ Renaissance Texts*, edited by Patricia Parker and David Quint, Johns Hopkins UP, 1986, pp. 210–24.

Hillman, David. "Freud." *Marx and Freud: Great Shakespeareans*. Vol. 10, edited by Crystal Bartolovich, David A. Hillman, and Jean E. Howard, Continuum Publishing Group, 2012, pp. 99–176.

Jones, Ernest. *The Life and Work of Sigmund Freud*. 3 vols. Basic Books, 1953–1957.

Klein, Melanie. *Envy and Gratitude and Other Works, 1946–1963*. Delacorte, 1965.

Lacan, Jacques. "The Mirror Stage." *Écrits: A Selection*. Translated by Alan Sheridan. Tavistock, 1977, pp. 1–7.
Marshall, Cynthia. *The Shattering of the Self: Violence, Subjectivity, and Early Modern Texts*. Johns Hopkins UP, 2002.
Maus, Katharine. *Inwardness and Theater in the English Renaissance*. U of Chicago P, 1995.
Mazzotta, Giuseppe. "The *Canzoniere* and the Language of the Self." *Petrarch: Modern Critical Views*, edited by Harold Bloom, Chelsea House Publishers, 1989, pp. 57–78.
Menzer, Paul. "Something Wanting: The Actor, the Critic, and Histrionic Skill," *Shakespeare Studies* vol. 43, 2015, pp. 78–87.
Nicholson, Catherine. *Uncommon Tongues: Eloquence and Eccentricity in the English Renaissance*. U of Pennsylvania P, 2014.
Paster, Gail Kern. "*Romeo and Juliet*: A Modern Perspective." *Romeo and Juliet*. Folger Shakespeare Library, edited by Barbara A. Mowat and Paul Werstine, Simon and Shuster, 1992, pp. 257–69.
Pivnick, Billie. "Wriggles, Squiggles and Words: From Expression to Meaning in Early Childhood and Psychotherapy." *Therapeutic Presence: Bridging Expression and Form*, edited by A. Robbins, Jessica Kingsley Publishers, 1998, pp. 39–83.
Pye, Christopher. *The Vanishing: Shakespeare, the Subject, and Early Modern Culture*. Duke UP, 2002.
Romeo and Juliet (a). Directed by Baz Luhrman. Performed by Leonardo DiCaprio and Claire Danes. Warner Brothers, 1996.
Romeo and Juliet (b). Directed by Franco Zeffirelli. Performed by Olivia Hussey and Leonard Whiting. Paramount, 1968.
Rudnytsky, Peter. *Freud and Oedipus*. Columbia UP, 1987.
Scaglione, Aldo. "Classical Heritage and Petrarchan Self-Consciousness in the Literary Emergence of the Interior 'I.'" *Petrarch, Modern Critical Views*, edited by Harold Bloom, Chelsea House Publishers, 1989, pp. 125–37.
Scholes, Robert and Robert Kellogg. *The Nature of Narrative*. Oxford UP, 1968.
Shakespeare, William. *The Riverside Shakespeare*. Edited by G. Blakemore Evans, et al. Houghton Mifflin, 1997.
Sprengnether, Madelon. *The Spectral Mother: Freud, Feminism, and Psychoanalysis*. Cornell UP, 1990.
Watt, Ian. *The Rise of the Novel: Studies in Defoe, Richardson and Fielding*. U of California P, 1957.
Whitebook, Joel. *Freud: An Intellectual Biography*. Cambridge UP, 2017.
Winnicott, D. W. "Transitional Objects and Transitional Phenomena—A Study of the First Not-Me Possession." *International Journal of Psychoanalysis*, vol. 34, 1953, pp. 89–97.
Young, Sandra. "Recognizing Hamlet." *Shakespeare in Southern Africa*, vol. 26, 2014, pp. 13–26.

CHAPTER 5

Wilfred R. Bion and the Psychoanalytic Study of Thinking in *Measure for Measure*

Heather Hirschfeld

In his seminal 1962 essay "The Psycho-Analytic Study of Thinking," Wilfred Bion inverts a common-sense notion that thinking precedes, and then produces, thoughts. Rather, Bion proposes, "thinking has to be called into existence to cope with thoughts [...] thinking is a development forced on the psyche by the pressure of thoughts and not the other way round" (302). His seemingly counter-intuitive statement has deep roots in Freud's concepts of primary and secondary processes; it also has instructive resonances with contemporary neuroscientific and neuropsychoanalytic models of cognition. And, as I suggest in this chapter, it has interpretive possibilities for studying the early modern stage and its preoccupation, in Helen Hackett's words, with "representing the inner states and thought-processes of fictional characters" (11). In what follows, I consider some of the contours and implications of Bion's theories of thinking for *Measure for Measure*, a play that, as Mary Thomas Crane has written, "describes to us what it felt like to think [...] from within an early modern body" ("Male Pregnancy" 292). I give special consideration to

H. Hirschfeld (✉)
University of Tennessee, Knoxville, TN, USA
e-mail: hhirschf@utk.edu

J. W. Stone, C. Bates (eds.), *Shakespeare and Psychoanalysis*, Palgrave Shakespeare Studies,
https://doi.org/10.1007/978-3-032-07897-1_5

Bion's emphasis on psychic and bodily frustrations and their relationship to what he calls "disorders of thought" (*Elements of Psychoanalysis* 30), disturbances, confusions, and difficulties in thinking that resonate with the political and theological tensions central to a play organized around the paradoxical principle of "measure for measure." Looking at the play's scenes of especially intense cognitive pressure—Angelo's "indecent proposal" to Isabella, the Duke's bed-trick, and the trial scene—I suggest the ways in which Bion's formulations offer a unique psychoanalytic foundation for assessing one of the "problems" of this heralded "problem play": its attack on its characters' thinking.

The Psychoanalytic Study of Thinking

In its brief ten pages, "The Psycho-Analytic Study of Thinking" crystallizes Bion's "life work as a [...] formulation of a theory of thinking" (Ogden 11). The chapter takes direction from Freud's "Formulations on the Two Principles of Mental Functioning," translating into Bion's own terms the analysts' shared estimation of the power of the pleasure and reality principles in the regulation of psychic—and somatic—life. Foreshadowed as early as Freud's 1896 *Project for a Scientific Psychology*, the pleasure principle assumes that bodily and mental states of tension—hunger, pain, sexual or sensual excitement—can be experienced as unpleasurable, requiring immediate satisfaction either by external intervention or solipsistic hallucination. The reality principle, in contrast, assumes that these states of tension can be accommodated, so that satisfaction is deferred in a way that acknowledges or accedes to "the conditions imposed by the outside world" (Laplanche and Pontalis 379). Thinking, according to Freud, is one of the pre-eminent means of such accommodation, a way out of hallucinated enjoyment and thus a way into contact with things and people outside of the self. As he writes in "Formulations," thinking is "endowed with characteristics which ma[ke] it possible for the mental apparatus to tolerate an increased tension of stimulus while the process of discharge [is] postponed" (221/218). Indeed, thinking becomes action itself; it is, as Freud says, "essentially an experimental kind of acting" (221/218).

Bion extends Freud's formula, embracing its implicit estimation of thinking as essential to human contact with reality. He introduces specifically the idea of the *frustration of satisfaction* as a key element in the subject's negotiation of reality. Influenced by Melanie Klein, with whom he had been in analysis, he takes the hungry infant as both the developmental origin and as the atemporal, a-teleological model of all thinking.[1] He posits that the infant has an inborn expectation or "pre-conception" of nourishment, a kind of universal grammar of the breast. That expectation, when fulfilled, reinforces the infant's sense of his own inner liveliness as well as the objective, separate reality of the outside world and its objects. But Bion is also concerned with occasions when "no breast [is] available to satisfy" the expectation—or, more precisely, when the expectation of a breast is realized as an absent breast or "no-breast." According to Bion, this privation, this "no-breast," can be tolerated by the infant when it is processed *as a thought*: "if the capacity for toleration of frustration is sufficient the 'no-breast' inside becomes a thought, and an apparatus for 'thinking' it develops" ("Psycho-Analytic Study" 303). In other words, thinking arises in response to a thought, where that thought is the tolerated absence of a needed or desired presence. Or, as Anne Reiner puts it, thinking arises in response to the "presence of absence" (18). Mental accommodation of that present absence, she explains, "serves as the foundation of thought and the mind that can think it" (18). This thinking in turn becomes a means by which dissatisfaction is accommodated in a reinforcing—even pleasurable—loop. As Bion says, "[A] capacity for tolerating frustration thus enables the psyche to develop th[inking] as a means by which the frustration that is tolerated is itself made more tolerable" ("Psycho-Analytic Study" 303).

But if the capacity to tolerate frustration is inadequate, the "no-breast" becomes a bad internal object, unavailable for or hostile to mental processing. The infant rejects or evacuates it in a manner which Bion, looking back to Klein, labels "projective identification." In Bion's version of projective identification, unbearable elements of the psyche are ejected and cast into others, thereby *evading* the frustration and, ultimately, reality itself. The psyche thus troubled operates "on the principle that evacuation of a bad [no-]breast is synonymous with obtaining sustenance from a good breast." But the consequence of such ejection, as Bion explains, is the diminishment of the psyche and the threat of persecutory return. All incipient thoughts are "treated as if they were indistinguishable from bad

[1]Bion explicitly avoids a strictly developmental model as limiting: "I do not suggest that promotion of development provides a criterion without reservation; psychoanalytic theory and practice, in cases where thought shows serious disturbance, indicate the need for a reformulation of ideas about the origin and nature of thoughts and a parallel reformulation of ideas about the mechanisms by which 'thinking' thoughts is achieved" (*Learning from Experience* 265–66).

internal objects; the appropriate machinery is felt to be, not an apparatus for thinking the thoughts, but an apparatus for ridding the psyche of accumulations of bad internal objects" ("Psycho-Analytic Study" 303–304). In the most extreme cases, Bion proposes, the apparatus itself comes under attack, and "the possibility of the patient's conscious contact either with [themselves] or another as live objects" is "destroyed" (*Learning from Experience* 276). The experience can be consciously or unconsciously terrifying: "in the patient's phantasy the expelled particles of ego lead an independent and uncontrolled existence, either contained by or containing the external objects; they continue to exercise their functions as if the ordeal to which they have been subjected had served only to increase their number and provoke their hostility to the psyche that ejected them" (*Second Thoughts* 47).

Bion considers these opposing but related scenarios—either the modification or the evasion of frustration through thinking or projection, respectively—a recurrent feature of human mental life, as repetitions of a person's earliest experiences in the context of contemporary situations and demands. To account for them structurally and dynamically, he theorized a cognitive architecture with its own unique vocabulary, positing a mental or neural process (alpha-function) that operates both consciously and unconsciously on sense-impressions and emotions. If "successful," alpha-function converts these impressions into thoughts (alpha-elements) available for symbolic linking with other thoughts, a capacity Bion defines as the "ability to bring together two objects so that their resemblance is made manifest, yet their difference [is] left unimpaired" (*Second Thoughts* 52). If alpha-function is "disturbed," it converts them into bad objects (beta-elements) that must be ejected or "manipulated" (*Learning from Experience* 274). And, Bion warns, such frustrated impressions—"beta-elements"—"can be evacuated […] as if to substitute" for the words and ideas that constitute thinking. In such a case, what looks or feels like thinking is a masquerade: "Whatever substitute they [patients suffering from such disturbances] find for thought," Bion warns of certain kinds of patients, "is not to be classified as thought" (*Attention and Interpretation* 11–12).

While idiosyncratic, Bion's models resonate presciently with recent neuroscientific approaches that have mapped a variety of "bridges between psychoanalysis and neuroscience," particularly in terms of the non-conscious status of much human thought and cognition (Cieri and

Esposito 1).[2] At the same time, Bion's theories have also had tangible clinical results, giving priority to digesting or processing unprocessed ("unthought") thoughts and recalibrating understandings of therapeutic intersubjectivity. As Christopher Bollas says, Bion's insights have promoted the analyst's responsibility to help patients "live through for the first time elements of [their] psychic life that have not been previously thought" (278). And literary scholars such as Josie Billington have identified in Bion's work the terms with which to understand the "deeply (ontologically and emotionally) engaged" experience of readers (174). For Billington, literature—particularly the close reading of literature in groups—becomes the source and the scene to ameliorate the Bionian recognition that "thinking one's thoughts [...] could be almost impossibly hard to achieve" (177).

Bion's theories place the ability to think—the toleration of frustration and the accommodation of reality by linking images and thoughts and symbolizing objects and feeling-states—at the foundation of human flourishing. And they place the disturbances of that ability—the evasion of frustration and reality by hallucination, projection of intolerable images, and attacks on symbolization—at the foundation of human suffering. They thus provide a unique psychoanalytic vantage point on an early modern text such as *Measure for Measure*, not only because it is a "preeminently cognitive play" (Crane, "Male Pregnancy" 270), but also because the political and theological predicaments embedded in its plot—about sin, crime, contrition, and punishment according to the letter of the law—are preeminent occasions for the kinds of crises of thinking Bion anticipates. In addressing *Measure for Measure* as a play of disorders of thought, this chapter shares some thematic and methodological ground with cognitive literary criticism and its focus on "how both the architecture and the contents of the human brain/mind—both in terms of its on-line processing of information and its evolutionary history—may contribute structurally to the writing, reading, and interpretation of texts" (Hart, "Epistemology"

[2] This essay summarizes recent advances in neuroscience and their connections to psychoanalysis; it also focuses on Bion's unique contributions and their connections to contemporary understandings of the brain. The literature on neuropsychoanalysis and on avenues for productive engagement between neuroscience and psychoanalysis is now vast. Kandel's *Psychiatry, Psychoanalysis and the New Biology of Mind* and Solms's *The Feeling Brain* are useful pathways into the scholarship. It is critical to note, as Solms and Kandel do, that Freud's earliest commitments were to neurophysiological psychology.

319).[3] Of course, the "celebration of cerebral experience" (Sagaser 1) as a theme of sixteenth- and seventeenth-century literature has long been a scholarly concern, with some of its most formidable phenomenological and historicist critics studying it in terms of the problem of other minds.[4] Cognitive literary studies, however, have reoriented these approaches from the perspective of contemporary neuroscience, evolutionary psychology, and cognitive linguistics, often treating literature as what Terence Cave calls a special kind of "cognitive artefact" (2) whose historical or sociological effects are enabled by bedrock biological connections of body, brain, and world. For the early modern period, leading scholars such as Mary Thomas Crane and Evelyn Tribble, for instance, have investigated the somatic bases of early modern "cerebral experience," foregrounding the role of embodied—and often non-conscious—cognitive processes in the production, reception, and content of the drama.[5] F. Elizabeth Hart, combining historical with cognitive studies of literacy, has suggested that early modern print technology heralded a "massive shift in people's cognitive abilities," leading to increased "cultural attention on the mind and on the specialized worlds that minds create" ("1500–1620" 105). Focusing on Shakespeare's *Othello*, Paul Cefalu has discussed Iago's "mind-reading" of others as a form of mentalizing meant both to alleviate his constitutional discontentment and to provide him with a missing "self-narrative" (265, 266). And Miranda Anderson's comprehensive *The Renaissance Extended Mind* surveys a wide range of developments in recent cognitive science (including the embodied or extended mind, mirror neurons, and neural plasticity) to suggest the ways in which they "parallel" Renaissance philosophical, medical, and literary discourses.

Cefalu and Anderson both put psychoanalytic theory in productive dialogue with cognitive studies. Cefalu connects the two by suggesting that, in the case of *Othello*, psychoanalysis adds diagnostic precision to the cognitive account of Iago's mentalizing strategies, including the most malevolent ones. Cognitivist theory of mind, he writes, "helps us to see that Iago's obsessive mind reading is a symptom of some other cognitive misfire," but Iago's obsessions, he clarifies, are actually "better approached

[3]The past thirty years has seen a remarkable increase of this methodology, and the literature is vast. For an overview and bibliography of cognitive studies and Shakespeare, see Kaethler. James Newlin and James W. Stone also assess the state of the fields in their "Introduction," *New Psychoanalytic Readings of Shakespeare*, esp. p. 6.

[4]Respectively, Cavell and Maus.

[5]See Crane, *Shakespeare's Brain*, and Tribble, *Cognition in the Globe*.

from a psychoanalytic vantage point" (287), specifically that of compulsive symptomatology. And Anderson sees Freud and the Freudian heritage (specifically Jacques Lacan and Judith Butler) as congruent in important ways with key principles and implications of extended mind, including their mutual attention to the "bodily ego" and the decentering of the unified "self" (41). For Anderson, psychoanalytic theory also offers a corrective to the implicit optimism of much cognitive theory, as it "uncover[s] the dark side" (41) of human modes of thinking, learning, and knowing.[6]

I pursue similar but distinct approaches here, identifying from a Bionian perspective the "dark side" of *Measure for Measure*'s scenes of cognition. I suggest that the situation of Shakespeare's play—in which the Viennese ruler leaves his dukedom to spy on his citizens, disguising himself as a friar and leaving a puritanical deputy-turned-would-be-rapist to enforce the city's neglected laws—precipitates the frustrating "present absence" experiences that Bion identifies at the root of all mental life. As Shakespeare dramatizes them, they include explicit demands on the characters to think. But they result instead in attacks on or manipulations of cognitive processes, attacks which resonate with Bion's classification of "disorders of thought," and which take on an especially persecutory coloration. This result, I suggest, represents Shakespeare's staging of some of the potential psychic responses to the play's unabashedly political, theological, and theatrical "problems" or predicaments.

Evading Thought

Measure for Measure begins with a demand to think. Having praised his counselor Escalus for his knowledge of Vienna's laws and institutions—"your own science / Exceeds [...] all advice / My strength can give you" (1.1.5–7)—the Duke of Vienna introduces to him his plan to leave the city and install Angelo as his deputy.[7] "What figure of us *think* you he will bear?" the Duke asks, continuing:

[6] Anderson's chapter "Extending Literary Theory and the Psychoanalytic Tradition" considers how Sigmund Freud, Jacques Lacan, and Judith Butler each theorize the mind, body, and the thinking subject in ways that connect with contemporary cognitive theory, particularly extended mind. At the same time, she remains sharply critical of the Freudian developmental model of the pre- and Oedipal complex (see esp. p. 50).

[7] Shakespeare, *Measure for Measure*, ed. Braunmuller and Watson. All subsequent quotations from this edition.

> For you must know, we have with special soul
> Elected him *our absence* to supply;
> Lent him our terror, dressed him with our love
> And given his deputation all the organs
> Of our own power. What *think* you of it? (1.1.17–21; my emphasis)

This is the play's inaugural Bionian scene: a present absence is thrust upon a character, and he is commanded to think about it. It locates the origin of all the play's frustrations ("our absence") and stipulates the need to accommodate them through thinking. Only this scenario exceeds the Bionian formula, as it provides a replacement or proxy for the missing object. The proxy only reinforces the loss, as the Duke's language teasingly admits: the deputy, in his difference from his predecessor, serves as a constant reminder of him, literally "supplying" his absence and thereby maintaining its active, felt presence.[8] Indeed, the background hum of the play, with its almost constant comparisons between the two leaders and its appeals to or reminiscences of the Duke, stages over and over the dynamic of loss and replacement.

Angelo makes clear that he is ill-equipped to tolerate this dynamic and the thinking it requires. "Let there be some more test made of my metal / Before so noble and so great a figure / Be stamped upon it," the deputy asks when the Duke tells him that he should be "at full ourself" (1.1.43). The Duke diagnoses Angelo's deferral as an "evasion"—"No more evasion. / We have with a leavened and prepared choice / Proceeded to you" (1.1.49–51)—but this may be the last time that Angelo does *not* evade, in the Bionian sense, the thoughts and frustrations thrust upon him. That evasion begins off-stage, with his speedy enforcement of laws against fornication. We learn in the following scene that he has ordered the arrest and execution of Claudio, actions explained by the other characters as the "fault and glimpse of newness," a plan to make of Claudio "an example" (1.2.153). The orders run counter to the self-critical thought-processes Escalus prescribes for an equitable judge:[9]

> Let but your honour know,

[8] For the way in which the play "not only explores the capacity of the substitute to stand in for the original but also nurtures a highly self-reflexive awareness of the nature of representation and the problem of indirect knowledge," see Diehl 399.

[9] For the status and administration of equity in early modern English law and its role in the play, see Shuger, esp. 102–33.

Whom I believe to be most strait in virtue,
That in the working of your own affections,
Had time cohered with place, or place with wishing,
Or that the resolute acting of your blood
Could have attained th'effect of your own purpose,
Whether you had not sometime in your life
Erred in this point which now you censure him
And pulled the law upon you. (2.1.11–16)

But by-passing the "working of your own affections" is precisely the point of Angelo's resuscitation and prosecution of the Duke's old laws. As he explains:

'Tis one thing to be tempted, Escalus.
Another thing to fall. I not deny
The jury passing on the prisoner's life
May in the sworn twelve have a thief or two
Guiltier than him they try: what's open made to justice,
That justice seizes. What knows the laws
That thieves do pass on thieves? (2.1.17–23)

Angelo's rigidity—"You may not so extenuate his offence / For I have had such faults, but rather tell me / When I that censure him do so offend, / Let mine own judgement pattern out my death, / And nothing come in partial" (2.1.27–31)—has been read in terms of the literalism as well as hubris of a protestant hermeneutic that embraces the biblical talion.[10] I am suggesting that we read that literalism as a thought disorder. Meredith Skura gestures toward such a reading when she points out that "Angelo's lawfulness is somewhat odd. Not only does he enforce the laws without feeling (he's never been tempted himself and has no sympathy with sinners) but also without thought" (42). But Angelo's language indicates more than the sheer passive thoughtlessness Skura implies. Instead, it demonstrates a Bionian "disorder of thought," a mental alternative to thinking because thinking is impossible. "The jewel that we find," he tells Escalus, "we stoop and take't / Because we see it, but what we do not see / We tread upon and *never think of it*" (2.1.24–26; my emphasis). Angelo's surprising comparison—crime is a gemstone that is either seen and seized

[10] For the play as Shakespeare's "ironic critique of the fundamentalist reading practices" associated with the "rise of Protestant legalism" at the turn of the century, see Fulton 119.

or missed and trampled—suggests that "justice" thinks or considers the former and not the latter. But the analogy only reinforces his "never thinking" for both sides of the equation. For Angelo, if a crime is visible, it is immediately punished; if invisible, it is simply not a cognitive burden. Either way, the terms of Angelo's "justice" take the form of not thinking about others' or one's own crimes or sins.

Angelo repeats this legalism in his encounter in the next scene with Isabella, Claudio's sister who has reluctantly left her convent to plead for mercy on behalf of her brother. Her pleas depend on the demand that he think. "O, *think* on that" (my emphasis), she begs, asking Angelo to imagine his fate at the hands of divine justice. Angelo is as implacable as before with Escalus. "Be you content, fair maid, / It is the law, not I, condemn your brother," he tells her. "Were he my kinsman, brother, or my son, / It should be thus with him: he must die tomorrow" (2.2.83–86). She asks him to think again—"Good, good my lord, *bethink* you; / Who is it that hath died for this offence?" (2.2.91–92; my emphasis)—and the repetitions with which he responds suggest his recourse to the law functions not as Isabella hopes but as an *evasion* of thinking. Indeed, Angelo depicts the law as a kind of zombie, not dead but not quite conscious: "The law hath not been dead, though it hath slept" (2.2.94). The image reflects his own internal experience, what Bion describes as the "destr[uction of] the possibility of the patient's conscious contact either with himself or another as live objects" (*Learning from Experience* 276). So when Isabella encourages devotional self-exploration and acknowledgment of his own "natural guiltiness"—"Go to your bosom, / Knock there," she tells him—Angelo is thoroughly overwhelmed, both by her suggestion and his own response to it (2.2.139–40). "She speaks, and 'tis with such sense / That my sense breeds with it" (2.2.144–45), he notes in an aside, with a pun that pinpoints the "relevant ironies" (Empson 270) of the sexual excitation her rationality has provoked.

Projecting Thought

A significant strand of criticism has explained this breeding sensuality, and Angelo's torment at it, as the inevitable result or "return" of his puritanical repression. The play is at pains to remark this repression in its own, premodern terms: "Lord Angelo is precise," the Duke warns in act 1, "Stands at a guard with envy, scarce confesses / That his blood flows, or that his appetite / Is more to bread than stone" (1.3.50–53); Lucio, a scene later, claims he is "a man whose blood / Is very snowbroth" (1.4.58). In his discussion of the play as a critique of the Protestant "reformation of manners," the historian Peter Lake suggests that "[w]e are being brought up hard against the impossibility of the sort of distanced, antiseptic, closed control aspired to by the likes of Angelo [...]. Any attempt to transcend, ignore or repress an insistently fleshly human nature, [...] will always end up in disaster" (650). Musa Gurnis explains his response in terms of what she calls "the problematic of predestinarian spiritual assessment" (143): that is, once the "precise deputy" knocks on his bosom and discovers forbidden sexual desire, he assumes his unforgiveable sinfulness and operates as such, giving his "sensual race the rein" (2.4.159–60). And Mary Thomas Crane, in a learned cognitivist account, understands Angelo's response to Isabella not in terms of Protestant morality but as an experience of human cognition shaped by early modern humoral theory. As Crane explains, the play presupposes the interactivity of mind, body, and environment in the (re)production of both children and thoughts. "Bodies are penetrated by the external world and produce something—offspring, ideas, language—as a result of that penetration" ("Male Pregnancy" 276). She links this view to the characters' own perception, established from early cognitive experience, of corporeal and mental permeability and generativity. So, when Angelo is aroused by Isabella, he experiences this unexpected, unwanted desire as something from the outside, "implanted by [her] words" (284). Pressed in this way, "Angelo seems to cope with his ambivalent sexual feelings by employing metaphors of pregnancy to suggest that those feelings are alien to him" (285).

But metaphors do not solve Angelo's predicament; in fact, they seem only to exacerbate it. For what has been implanted in Angelo is not only a psychically intolerable desire but a psychically intolerable frustration. The Duke's departure created the conditions for this frustration, which now takes shape in the more proximate, intimate form of Isabella. Her status as a seventeenth-century novice gives historical, theological texture to her unavailability, a kind of "no-Isabella," which she emphasizes when she offers up to him "true prayers / That shall be up at heaven and enter there / Ere sunrise—prayers from preserved souls, / From fasting maids, whose minds are dedicate / To nothing temporal" (2.2.154–58). So, when Angelo promises, in return, to do precisely what she has asked for: "I will bethink me: come again tomorrow," such "bethinking" recoils on him (2.2.146). As he admits, thinking for him incites the merciless desire it is meant to make tolerable, one that throttles him with a series of questions and incriminations. If Angelo's earlier legalism represented one kind of evasion of thinking, he is caught here, in soliloquy, in another version, one that is punitive, persecutory of its own arousal. Intended by Isabella to make him more equitable, the consideration of his own "desire [...] for those things / That make her good" makes him more severe:

> What's this? What's this? Is this her fault or mine?
> The tempter, or the tempted, who sins most, ha?
> Not she, nor doth she tempt, but it is I
> That, lying by the violet in the sun,
> Do as the carrion does, not as the flower,
> Corrupt with virtuous season.
> ....
> O cunning enemy that, to catch a saint,
> With saints dost bait thy hook. (2.2.165–89)

Huston Diehl identifies Angelo's soliloquy as a form of idolatry: he "substitutes the woman who reflects divinity for God himself" (400). And his idolatry, insofar as it "fouls Isabella" (400) involves projective identification, that hallmark for Bion of disordered thought, according to which frustration is evacuated, thrown back toward its supposed source. As Angelo asks himself, "Having waste ground enough, / Shall we desire to raze the sanctuary / And pitch our evils there?" (2.2.173–75). The answer is yes, and those evils continue to circulate in his next scene, which opens with his second soliloquy. If such "self-speech" is conventionally understood to be a "vehicle of profound introspection" that makes "the generative process of cognition audible" (Corcoran 6, 86), in this instance it makes *problems* of cognition audible:

> When I would pray and think, I think and pray
> To several subjects. Heaven hath my empty words,
> Whilst my invention, hearing not my tongue,
> Anchors on Isabel. God in my mouth,
> As if I did but only chew His name,
> And in my heart the strong and swelling evil
> Of my conception. (2.4.1–7)

His language, as Jay Zysk has discussed effectively, rehearses the hermeneutic poles of Reformation eucharistic controversy, as Angelo identifies his difficulties here in a way that simultaneously endorses the real presence of Catholic belief and demystifies—degrades—that belief. Here this doctrinal confusion expresses an internal, psychic one in which Angelo's inability to cope with the frustrations Isabella presents disrupts or dismantles his very thinking.

That disruption gets pushed onto or into Isabella, in the indecent proposal that if she sleeps with him, he will spare her brother. The proposal is guided by a perverse literalism, as it would concretize the comparison between Angelo and Claudio that Isabella and Escalus have been urging. That is, if Isabella sleeps with him, Angelo will be guilty precisely of Claudio's crime. The play's editor Robert Watson calls the plan a "plausible syllogism" (10) in that it not only observes this principle of "measure for measure" but also relies on an implicit equation of sex and death. But it also serves another kind of logic, the logic of projection. It is a way for Angelo to evacuate unaccommodated thoughts as "bad objects," ejecting them outward to be absorbed and processed by Isabella. Angelo's chaotic syntax gives this evacuation grammatical form:

> Admit no other way to save his life—
> As I subscribe not that, nor any other—
> But, in the loss of question, that you, his sister,
> Finding yourself desired of such a person
> Whose credit with the judge, or own great place,
> Could fetch your brother from the manacles
> Of the all-binding law, and that there were
> No earthly mean to save him but that either
> You must lay down the treasures of your body
> To this supposed, or else to let him suffer,
> What would you do? (2.4.87–97)

And when Isabella refuses, threatening to "proclaim thee" to the world, Angelo turns the full force of his projection into threats of humiliation, rape, and torture:

> Who will believe thee, Isabel?
> My unsoiled name, th'austereness of my life,
> Will so your accusation overweigh
> That you shall stifle in your own report
> And smell of calumny.
> ....

Fit thy consent to my sharp appetite,
Lay by all nicety and prolixious blushes
That banish what they sue for, redeem thy brother
By yielding up thy body to my will [...]. (2.4.151, 154–64)

Angelo's aggression is the most frightening aspect of his disordered thinking. But the signature symptom is the indecent proposal itself, with its projection of thwarted desire back onto Isabella. The proposed exchange of her virginity for Claudio's life will make Isabella—caught between her body and her brother—feel as disastrously thwarted, endangered, and disordered in her thinking as Angelo does. Her exclamation, "More than our brother is our chastity" (2.4.185), so problematic in its self-conceit and lack of charity, is voiced from the same place as the deputy's own evacuated equivalences. And her response in the next scene to Claudio, when he urges her to give way to Angelo, reflects a projected fury in excess of such decisiveness:

O, you beast,
O faithless coward, O dishonest wretch,
Wilt thou be made a man out of my vice?
Is't not a kind of incest to take life
From thine own sister's shame? What should I *think*? (3.1.141–45; my emphasis)

Isabella is tumbled back into the same state of troubled thought that afflicted Angelo: "What should I think?" Angelo's proposal—the oxymoronic demand to consent to one's own rape—forces upon her a kind of "no-choice," but Claudio's encouragement of it becomes her truly intolerable frustration. As Barbara Baines suggests, "Isabella's power, place, and value in society are so determined by her chastity that its forfeiture would constitute for her a form of social and psychological suicide" (288). That the forfeiture would be endorsed by the person she most expects to reject it—this is Isabella's unbearable present absence, a kind of "no Claudio" that she cannot think. Instead, her rage sounds like Angelo's and her pledge to pray for her brother's death turns her into a version of a merciless executioner:

Take my defiance,
Die, perish. Might but my bending down
Reprieve thee from thy fate, it should proceed.
I'll pray a thousand prayers for thy death,
No word to save thee. (3.1.148–52)

Manipulating Thought

Isabella's projected fury represents a complicated form of feminist resistance, what Julia Lupton, in a powerful reading, has labeled as a "recommitment to virginity" that represents the exceptional "sovereign decision" of a saint (143). But in the bed-trick, the exchange of Mariana for Isabella that the Duke proposes to solve the unfolding crisis, it is authorized, paternalized, and institutionalized. The bed-trick—the "sexual substitution of at least one partner without the other partner's knowledge"—was an established literary and dramatic convention that offered, according to Marliss Desens's thorough survey, opportunities for audiences "to deal with emotionally intense issues in some safety" (39, 14). It served, she explains, as a "useful device" (17) to allow spectators to "explor[e] marital relations," "revealing severe disruption[s] in the [power] relations between husband and wife or between potential marital partners" (61). Shakespeare, in particular, exploited the convention to investigate "the role of desire within society, and the conflict between its disruptiveness and safe containment in marriage" (Briggs 297). And in the urgent contexts of *Measure for Measure*, scholars agree, he stretched the device to show the intractable power imbalance between the men and women of the play: "for both [Isabella and Marianna], then, the bed-trick is their only option. For Isabella, it allows her to save her brother's life and to avoid Angelo's intended rape. For Marianna, it allows her to regain the reputation and social status that Angelo's rejection has lost her. However, in using the bed-trick [...] the two women are acting out the fantasy of sexual entrapment that patriarchal societies ascribe to women and that those societies fear" (Desens 83). Or, in Janet Adelman's psychoanalytically informed account, the bed-trick provides a way "to save [...] Angelo from [his] own fantasy" of despoiling a virgin (77).

But what for Shakespeare and his audience is a theatrical convention to generate thought is for the Duke an extemporized plan that shuts thought down. The Duke has always kept his intentions, and thus his control over the unfolding events of the play, mysterious both to his fellow characters and to the audience. Ivo Kamps suggests that early modern audiences and characters would have appreciated the improvisational nature of the Duke's activities as a feature of the "comforting fantasy [of a] a figure who [...] reforms society in pursuit of order and justice" (259). But Angelo's indecent proposal serves as a frustration that imperils even the Duke. It is not only that he did not predict this turn of events. It is that, in the costume of a friar, he faces the "present absence" that is his own abdication—he is a "no Duke" to himself. The myriad details of the bed-trick make his disordered thinking audible, first in its elaborate rationale—"I do make myself believe that you may most uprighteously do a poor wronged lady a merited benefit, redeem your brother from the angry law, and much please the absent duke" (3.1.203–207)—and then in its extensive logistics. "Go you to Angelo," he instructs Isabella:

> answer his requiring with a plausible obedience, agree with his demands to the point, only refer yourself to this advantage: first, that your stay with him may not be long; that the time may have all shadow and silence in it; and the place answer to convenience. This being granted in course, and now follows all: we shall advise this wronged maid to stead up your appointment, go in your place. (3.1.245–52)

These details, which link ideas, people, times, places, seem to signal the kind of thinking heralded by Bion. But, as he himself reminds us, what looks like thinking may not be so: "what may appear to the observer as thoughts, visual images, and verbalizations" may be the "debris, remnants, or scraps of imitated speech and histrionic synthetic emotion" that characterizes attacks on thinking (*Attention and Interpretation* 12–13). "Whatever substitute [they] find for thought," Bion warns of certain kinds of patients, "is not to be classified as thought" (11–12). The previous act had featured the thwarted, persecutory, violent disordered thought of projection. The bed-trick is a variation on this disorder, a "substitute" that we should not "classify as thought."

If the Duke "finds" the bed-trick as a "substitute" for thinking, in a kind of Bionian *mise en abŷme*, that substitute is constituted by substitution itself. In its radical dependence on the interchangeability of the two women, the bed-trick defaults to a logic of exchange that preempts thinking as a response to the frustration of Angelo's proposal. This pre-emption, even more than the Duke-as-friar's imprimatur, has special appeal to the distraught Isabella. "What *think* you of it?" the Duke asks her (3.1.259; my emphasis). But the point of the trick is that she does not have to "think of" it at all. Her instantaneous, fulsome agreement—"the image of it gives me content already, and I trust it will grow to a most prosperous perfection" (3.1.261–62)—signals an almost hallucinatory participation with the Duke in a shared literalism and its corresponding evasion of reality. The convention of the bed-trick, in other words, that workhorse of Elizabethan and Jacobean sex-plots, becomes in *Measure for Measure* the purest expression of disordered thinking. It also becomes the purest revelation that the play's underlying substitutive economy—its governing principle of measure for measure—supports the evasion, offering *a way out of thinking itself.* Act 4, which brings the trick to fruition, embodies this "way out," with its frantic substitution of heads (Barnardine for Claudio, and then Ragozine for Barnardine for Claudio), and its equally frantic arrangement of logistics for the Duke's return.

(Dis)ordering Thought

Those frantic substitutions and arrangements continue through the Duke's return in act 5, in the hectic exits and entrances of the Duke, Friar Peter, Isabella, and the veiled Mariana, and in the lies told to and delivered by Isabella. So, although the Duke's return and trial scene are meant to restore order to Vienna—they are the longed for "climax," Kamps says, in which the Duke reappears in a scene of "revelation and judgment [that] resembles [...] the second coming and final judgment" (265)—they do not restore ordered thinking. In fact, the Duke's restoration of order depends upon the disclosure and maintenance of disordered or disabled thought. Nowhere is this better articulated than Mariana's central revelation that she, not Isabella, slept with Angelo: "[...] that is Angelo, / Who *thinks* he knows that he ne'er knew my body, / But knows, he *thinks*, that he knows Isabel's" (5.1.199–201; my emphasis). The puzzle is solved, of course, when Mariana removes her veil and Angelo learns he has slept with her, not Isabella. But that dénouement is underwritten by a confusion and destabilization of thought that continues to haunt the ending. We hear that haunting most clearly in Angelo's death wish, his response to Mariana's revelation as well as the one that the friar is the Duke. As he admits:

> O my dread lord,
> I should be guiltier than my guiltiness
> To *think* I can be undiscernible,
> When I perceive your Grace, like power divine,
> Hath looked upon my passes. Then, good prince,
> No longer session hold upon my shame,
> But let my trial be mine own confession.
> Immediate sentence then and sequent death
> Is all the grace I beg. (5.1.364–72; my emphasis)

He learns, to his shame, that he cannot think, and, in his shame, he wants to stop thinking altogether.

Indeed, Angelo's final death wish may be considered the Duke's own starting wish, the drive behind his departure, the drive to disorder or arrest his subjects' thinking. Critics have long noted that the Duke raises and quells politically and theologically charged emotions—anxiety, despair, humiliation—through his sudden removal; his manipulation of Claudio's (non-)death; his organization of the bed plot; and his brutal, punitive exposure of what were meant to be private exchanges or confessions.[11] Bion's theories suggest that these same causes lie behind the play's moments of problematic *thinking* as well as feeling. As we have seen, Bion understands human thinking as a response to thoughts, thoughts being the register of frustrated satisfaction, of "the presence of absence." If the psyche can tolerate this present absence, it develops the capacity for thinking that thought. If the psyche cannot bear the frustration, it cannot develop this capacity and instead projects or evacuates the "bad object" outward. According to this model, the Duke's departure initiated a sequence of frustrations that, unable to be tolerated and "thought through," were evaded or projected in the characters' persecutory legal rigor or substitutive indecency. The Duke's return would thus seem to herald the restoration of the "present absence," and thus the possibility of tolerable, thinkable frustrations. But the breach opened up by his departure cannot be repaired in this way. For the Duke who comes back to Vienna is not the same Duke who left it. Whether he has become, as he has for Angelo, an all-seeing, all-knowing divinity, or, as he has for Lucio, a figure whose reappearance may now "prove worse than hanging" (5.1.358), or, as he has for Mariana, a former friar who would "mock me with a husband" (415), the reintroduced Duke is another frustrating object, a perpetual reminder of the Duke who left and of the crises of thinking unleashed in his wake. It is possible to hear this conundrum in Isabella's forced defense of Angelo, which she can only "partly" think:

> I *partly think*
> A due sincerity governed his deeds
> ....
> For Angelo,
> His act did not o'ertake his bad intent,
> And must be buried but as an intent

[11] Consider, for instance, Sarah Beckwith: "The Duke [...] is the instigator and conduit of a technique whereby all that has been uttered to him in the privacy of the confessional is produced in a public judgment" (198).

> That perished by the way. *Thoughts are no subjects,*
> *Intents but merely thoughts.* (5.1.443–52; my emphasis)

Isabella's lines have been scrutinized for their intersection with early modern English common and ecclesiastical laws distinguishing between act and intention. Julia Briggs, for instance, explains Isabella's common-law distinction between intention and action in terms of Edmund Plowden's commentaries on Hales and Petit (1562), in which the jurist clarifies that "'For the Imagination of the mind to do Wrong, without an Act done, is not punishable in our law.'" As Briggs explains, "Isabella characterises the freedom of thoughts or 'intents' in two different ways: thoughts are no subjects—that is to say, they are lawless, insubordinate, potentially transgressive; and they are no subjects in the further sense that, unlike individuals or bodies, they are not the subjects of the state nor subject to its laws" (311).[12] In this reading, Isabella's formula grants free range to mental life as a private, symbolic realm distinct from that of action, a psychically generous approach from a character who once requested "a more strict restraint" from her convent. Or, as Debora Shuger clarifies, she simply untangles civil and ecclesiastical law that the Duke has tangled, preserving for the latter the adjudication of the forum of the conscience: "While Isabella's claim in the final scene that 'thoughts are no subjects' invokes the traditional division of spiritual from temporal jurisdiction, the Friar-Duke has been taking cognizance of his subjects' thoughts throughout the play" (108). Either way, in Bionian terms, she is still under the influence of the "thought disorders" from which the play can only pretend to emerge. For she cannot conceive of *thinking* the thoughts she pleads for. Thoughts, as she says, in the last words she will speak, are inert substantives to her, best to be buried. For Bion, buried thoughts are evaded thoughts, with the consequences we have seen. Shakespeare's play has given us both versions. But its most frightening version emerges at the play's bitter end, in Isabella's silence in the face of the Duke's marriage proposal, an equally obscene, if licensed, version of Angelo's earlier offer. Is this thinking's silence, or its incapacitation? Versions of this question have been posed in criticism and in performance. Bion might insist we

[12] Briggs notes the essential irony that these definitions are accompanied by "the uncomfortable suspicion that it is only Angelo's desiring thoughts [...] that enable him to act out the sexual consummation with Mariana at all" (311).

cannot know the answer; we can only think it for Isabella, precisely because she may be unable to herself.

Acknowledgement The author would like to thank Catherine Bates, James Newlin, James Stone, Anthony Welch, and the members of the Wednesday night Appalachian Psychoanalytic Society reading group.

Works Cited

Adelman, Janet. *Suffocating Mothers: Fantasies of Maternal Origin in Shakespeare's Plays:* Hamlet *to* The Tempest. Routledge, 1992.

Anderson, Miranda. *The Renaissance Extended Mind.* Palgrave Macmillan, 2015.

Baines, Barbara J. "Assaying the Power of Chastity in *Measure for Measure.*" *Studies in English Literature, 1500–1900*, vol. 30, no. 2, 1990, pp. 283–301.

Beckwith, Sarah. "Medieval Penance, Reformation Repentance and *Measure for Measure.*" *Reading the Medieval in Early Modern England*, edited by Gordon McMullan et al., Cambridge UP, 2007, pp. 193–204.

Billington, Josie. "The Uses of Psychoanalysis in Contemporary Reading Groups." *The Cambridge Companion to Literature and Psychoanalysis*, edited by Vera J. Camden, Cambridge UP, 2022, pp. 168–85.

Bion, Wilfred R. "Attacks on Linking." *Psychoanalytic Quarterly*, vol. 82, no. 2, 2013, pp. 285–300 (originally published in the *International Journal of Psycho-analysis*, vol. 40, 1959, pp. 285–300).

———. *Attention and Interpretation: A Scientific Approach to Insight into Psycho-Analysis and Groups. The Complete Works of W. R. Bion*, edited by Chris Mawson, Routledge, 2021, vol. 6, pp. 211–330.

———. *Elements of Psychoanalysis.* Karnac Books, 1984.

———. *Learning from Experience. Complete Works*, vol. 4, pp. 247–360.

———. "The Psycho-Analytic Study of Thinking." *Psychoanalytic Quarterly*, vol. 82, no. 2, 2013, pp. 301–10 (originally published in the *International Journal of Psycho-analysis*, vol. 43, 1962, pp. 306–10).

———. *Second Thoughts: Selected Papers in Psychoanalysis. Complete Works*, vol. 6, pp. 45–202.

Bollas, Christopher. *The Shadow of the Object: Psychoanalysis of the Unthought Known.* Columbia UP, 1987.

Briggs, Julia. "Shakespeare's Bed-Tricks." *Essays in Criticism*, vol. 44, no. 4, 1994, pp. 293–314.

Cave, Terence. *Thinking with Literature: Towards a Cognitive Criticism.* Oxford UP, 2016.

Cavell, Stanley. *Disowning Knowledge in Six Plays of Shakespeare.* Cambridge UP, 1987.

Cefalu, Paul. "The Burdens of Mind Reading in Shakespeare's *Othello*: A Cognitive and Psychoanalytic Approach to Iago's Theory of Mind." *Shakespeare Quarterly*, vol. 64, no. 3, 2013, pp. 265–94.

Cieri, Filippo, and Roberto Esposito. "Psychoanalysis and Neuroscience: The Bridge Between Mind and Brain." *Frontiers in Psychology*, vol. 10, 2019, pp. 1–15.

Corcoran, Neil. *Reading Shakespeare's Soliloquies: Text, Theatre, Film*. Bloomsbury, 2018.

Crane, Mary Thomas. "Male Pregnancy and Cognitive Permeability in Shakespeare's *Measure for Measure*." *Shakespeare Quarterly*, vol. 49, no. 3, 1998, pp. 269–92.

———. *Shakespeare's Brain: Reading with Cognitive Theory*. Princeton UP, 2001.

Desens, Marliss. *The Bed-Trick in English Renaissance Drama: Explorations in Gender, Sexuality, and Power*. U of Delaware P, 1994.

Diehl, Huston. "'Infinite Space': Representation and Reformation in *Measure for Measure*." *Shakespeare Quarterly*, vol. 49, no. 4, 1998, pp. 393–410.

Empson, William. *The Structure of Complex Words*. Chatto and Windus, 1951.

Freud, Sigmund. *The Revised Standard Edition of the Complete Psychological Works of Sigmund Freud*, edited and translated by James Strachey, revised by Mark Solms. 24 vols. Rowman & Littlefield Publishers, 2024. (In-text references provide *RSE* page numbers immediately after *SE* page numbers).

———. "Formulations on the Two Principles of Mental Functioning." *The Standard Edition of the Complete Psychological Works of Sigmund Freud*, edited and translated by James Strachey, vol.12, Hogarth Press, 1958, pp. 213–26/*RSE* vol. 12, pp. 213–22.

Fulton, Thomas. "Shakespeare's Everyman: *Measure for Measure* and English Fundamentalism." *Journal of Medieval and Early Modern Studies*, vol. 40, no. 1, 2010, pp. 119–47.

Gurnis, Musa. *Mixed Faith and Shared Feeling: Theater in Post-Reformation London*. U of Pennsylvania P, 2019.

Hackett, Helen. *The Elizabethan Mind: Searching for the Self in an Age of Uncertainty*. Yale UP, 2022.

Hart, F. Elizabeth. "The Epistemology of Cognitive Literary Studies." *Philosophy and Literature*, vol. 25, no. 2, 2001, pp. 314–34.

———. "1500–1620: Reading, Consciousness, and Romance in the Sixteenth Century." *The Emergence of Mind: Representations of Consciousness in Narrative Discourse in English*, edited by David Herman, U of Nebraska P, 2011, pp. 103–31.

Kaethler, Mark. "Shakespeare and Cognition: Scientism, Theory, and 4E." *Literature Compass*, vol. 17, no. 3–4, 2020, unpaginated.

Kamps, Ivo. "Ruling Fantasies and the Fantasies of Rule: The Phoenix and *Measure for Measure*." *Studies in Philology*, vol. 92, no. 2, 1995, pp. 248–73.

Kandel, Eric. *Psychiatry, Psychoanalysis and the New Biology of Mind*. American Psychiatric Publishers, 2005.

Laplanche, J., and J.-B. Pontalis, *The Language of Psychoanalysis*. Translated by Donald Nicholson-Smith, W. W. Norton and Co., 1973.

Lake, Peter. *The Anti-Christ's Lewd Hat: Protestants, Papists and Players in Post-Reformation England*. Yale UP, 2002.

Lupton, Julia Reinhard. *Citizen-Saints: Shakespeare and Political Theology*. U of Chicago P, 2005.

Maus, Katharine. *Inwardness and Theater in the English Renaissance*. U of Chicago P, 1995.

Newlin, James, and James W. Stone. "Introduction." *New Psychoanalytic Readings of Shakespeare: Cool Minds and Seething Brains*, edited by James Newlin and James W. Stone, Routledge, 2024, pp. 1–15.

Ogden, Thomas. *Rediscovering Psychoanalysis: Thinking and Dreaming, Learning and Forgetting*. Karnac Books, 2009.

Reiner, Annie. *W. R. Bion's Theories of Mind: A Contemporary Introduction*. Routledge, 2023.

Sagaser, Elizabeth Harris. "Shakespeare's Sweet Leaves: Mourning, Pleasure, and the Triumph of Thought in the Renaissance Love Lyric." *ELH*, vol. 61, no. 1, 1994, pp. 1–26.

Shakespeare, William. *Measure for Measure*. Edited by A. R. Braunmuller and Robert Watson. Bloomsbury, 2020.

Shuger, Debora. *Political Theologies in Shakespeare's England: The Sacred and the State in Measure for Measure*. Palgrave, 2001.

Skura, Meredith. "New Interpretations for Interpretation in *Measure for Measure*." *Boundary 2: An International Journal of Literature and Culture*, vol. 7, no. 2, 1979, pp. 39–60.

Solms, Eric. *The Feeling Brain: Selected Papers on Neuropsychoanalysis*. Karnac Books, 2015.

Tribble, Evelyn. *Cognition in the Globe: Attention and Memory in Shakespeare's Theatre*. Palgrave Macmillan, 2011.

Zysk, Jay. "John 6, *Measure for Measure*, and the Complexities of the Literal Sense." *The Bible on the Shakespearean Stage: Cultures of Interpretation in Reformation England*, edited by Thomas Fulton et al., Cambridge UP, 2018, pp. 51–68.

CHAPTER 6

~~Coriolanus~~

David Hillman and Adelais Mills

The *Tranche* of Psychoanalysis

"Qui paiera à qui la tranche de Freud?" asks Jacques Derrida in *Du Tout* (1980)—"Who will pay whom for Freud's tranche?" (*The Post Card* 520). *Du Tout* records a conversation between Derrida and the psychoanalyst René Major. Invited to speak before assembled analysts at the "Colloques Confrontation," Derrida uses this dialogue to elaborate the lexical and syntactic possibilities of a "small phrase":

> Here then is this small phrase, it is made to disappoint, I say it slowly, without any punctuation for the moment—its punctuation is in fact mobile, multiple, and essentially labile—I read it then without any punctuation for the moment as if there were a dash of equal length between each word, here it is: CE-N'EST-PAS-DU-TOUT-UNE-TRANCHE. (502–503)

In French, *une tranche* is the word for a slice, from the verb *trancher*, to slice. In psychoanalytic slang, *une tranche* is also the time one spends with an analyst, while the expression *du tout* can mean either "of the whole" or

D. Hillman (✉) • A. Mills
Cambridge, UK
e-mail: dah54@cam.ac.uk; adm76@cam.ac.uk

J. W. Stone, C. Bates (eds.), *Shakespeare and Psychoanalysis*, Palgrave Shakespeare Studies,
https://doi.org/10.1007/978-3-032-07897-1_6

"at all." So the sentence may be heard in the following ways: "This is not a 'slice' of the whole," or 'This is not at all a 'slice'." The verb *trancher* can also mean "to decide on a question" or "to resolve a question." A slice of irony, then.

Derrida's phrase, in its "mobile, multiple, and essentially labile" resonances, bears the mark of an interpretation. He offers it in response to a peculiar practice that had emerged among the factions of French psychoanalysis. Known as "*la tranche*," this practice involved a recently qualified analyst—having completed training within one school—undertaking a subsequent analysis with a member of a different organization. The practice was striking, given that each of France's psychoanalytic factions laid an exclusive claim to the name of psychoanalysis proper, refusing to recognize the legitimacy of rival groups. Each faction could well have adopted the maxim "This is not a 'slice' of the whole," for each considered itself not merely a part of French psychoanalysis but *the* whole. Here, the practice of *tranching* begins to take on the look of a symptom.

To engage in a supplementary *tranche* with an analyst of a different formation is to go to an analyst who, according to the orthodoxy of each, is not an analyst *du tout*. Yet the act of engaging in a "*tranche*" across mutually exclusive institutional formations inscribes a different topology, undermining the clear-cut boundary delineating for each analytic band the interior and exterior of psychoanalysis. Derrida's own presence at the "Colloques Confrontation" as a non-analyst recapitulates this dynamic, as does his interpretation of the *tranching* symptom. Is the cut between the analytic and the non-analytic, the analyst and the non-analyst, truly so clear? Later, Derrida will share with the audience an anecdote from a recent visit of his to an American university. At a party, a woman approaches him with a question: is it not true that he, Derrida, is the analyst of Rudolph Lowenstein? If it were, it would make Derrida the analyst of Lacan's analyst.

In analytic fashion, then, not by suggestion or force, but by leading the other to recognize the absurd consequences of their opinions (consequences containing symptoms), Derrida's phrase confronts the audience with what he takes to be the inner logic of the *tranche*: the recourse to what is beyond the bounds of the analytic as its necessary supplement.

This leads us to Derrida's closing question regarding Freud's "unanalyzed remainder"[1] (*The Post Card* 519): "*Qui paiera á qui la tranche de Freud?*" To whom will Freud go for his *tranche?*

Literature and Psychoanalysis

Literature—perhaps Shakespeare especially—has always had a claim to know something about the unanalyzed of Freud. It is among the most important of the materials from which Freud constructed his science. Like the ego and its identifications, psychoanalysis is in part a precipitate of the literary: its texts a tissue of quotation, echo, and allusion; its interpretive procedures removed from the domain of hermeneutics; at times, the unconscious can seem less a psychical space than a set of rhetorical operations by which mental representations are modified (metaphor, metonymy, condensation). More specifically, we can recall that Freud knew Shakespeare's works intimately and referred to them constantly in his writing. Shakespeare was Freud's favorite author throughout his life. From childhood, he could recite large swathes of the dramatist's works by heart (and in English; see Gay 166), while within the inner circle of Freud's colleagues, "Shakespeare was the most frequent topic of our discussions when they turned to literature" (Sachs 108n.7). Harold Bloom's suggestion, therefore, that not only is Shakespeare "everywhere in Freud" but that he is "far more present when unmentioned than when he is cited" seems entirely plausible (*Western Canon* 391).[2] Shakespeare often seems to interpret Freud, especially in those moments when his influence is subtly present but unmentioned. Freud recognizes this himself in *The Interpretation of Dreams* when he reflects on the text of his "beautiful" *non vixit* dream. Here he is struck by how the contradictory structure of the words in the dream captures the conflicting ideas within the dream itself, which expresses two opposing attitudes toward the same person, both equally valid, yet neither overcoming the other. Freud relates how

[1] "This unanalyzed will be, will have been that upon which and around which the analytic movement will have been constructed and mobilized: everything will have been constructed and calculated so that this unanalyzed might be inherited, protected, transmitted intact, suitably bequeathed, consolidated, encysted, encrypted. It is what gives its structure to the movement and to its architecture" (*The Post Card* 519–20).

[2] The argument about Freud's anxiety of influence is made throughout the chapter on Freud in this work, entitled "Freud: A Shakespearean Reading" (371–94).

the language used in the dream—"As [my friend P] had deserved well of science I built him a memorial; but as he was guilty of an evil wish … I annihilated him"—echoes the "special cadence" of "Brutus's speech of self-justification in Shakespeare's *Julius Caesar*: 'As Caesar loved me, I weep for him; as he was fortunate, I rejoice at it; as he was valiant, I honour him; but, as he was ambitious, I slew him'" (*Interpretation of Dreams* 423–24/378). Freud gradually tunes in to the underlying sound patterns shaping the dream's content, eventually arriving at what he is certain must be the Shakespearean origin of the rhythm of the dream's speech: "Were not the formal structure of these sentences and their antithetical meaning precisely the same as in the dream-thought I had uncovered? Thus I had been playing the part of Brutus in the dream" (424/378).[3] The complexity of Freud's wish—both to honor and to destroy his friend—thus draws on Shakespeare, particularly Brutus's speech justifying Caesar's murder.

It is even likely that Freud drew insights about the significance of the omitted name *from* Shakespeare, maybe even from *Coriolanus*. Consider the telling incident where the protagonist cannot recall the name of the impoverished man in Corioles who gave him succor in his time of need, exclaiming, "By Jupiter, forgot!" (1.10.90). Freud devotes an entire section in *The Psychopathology of Everyday Life* to moments of forgetting such as these (see 15–42/14–37). His analysis teaches us that such moments can be profoundly revealing; *Coriolanus* vouches for this. The incident illuminates more than just Coriolanus's disdain for those of lower social standing; it highlights the protagonist's attempt to hide his own vulnerability, his unavoidable indebtedness to others. In some ways, then, it is apt that, in his extended writing on the omission of names, Freud makes no mention of *Coriolanus*. But this is just one of many instances in Freud's work where the absence of *Coriolanus* feels significant, like a break in the chain of associations or logical threads connecting what is conscious to that which is unconscious. As far as we can establish, Freud, in fact, never directly references *Coriolanus*—this despite his deep familiarity with the playwright's entire corpus and despite the play's huge popularity during the 1910s, 1920s, and 1930s, when Freud produced so much of his decisive work. Throughout the period, and especially in the German-speaking

[3]The reference is to *Julius Caesar*, 3.2.21–23. Freud goes on: "Strange to say, I really did once play the part of Brutus. I once acted in the scene between Brutus and Caesar from Schiller [*Die Räuber*]" (424/378; see also 483/431–32 for another reference to Freud playing Brutus as a boy).

world, the play was performed countless times. Martin Brunkhorst records a hundred performances in Germany alone in each of the three decades between 1910 and 1940. Hans Rothe, whose important translation came out in 1932, was, like Freud a few years later, forced into exile by the emergent Nazi government. If, in these years, the play could have seemed to lend itself to proto-fascist interpretations, we might understand Freud's avoidance of it as a political act (indeed the play was blacklisted and not performed in Germany for the best part of a decade after the Second World War). More broadly, we could read the avoidance as Freud steering clear of what is unquestionably Shakespeare's most overtly political play.

But it may be that what put him off integrating *Coriolanus* into his thinking, more than anything else, might have been the strange combination of the opaque and the blindingly obvious in its protagonist's psyche. From the beginning—"he did it to please his mother" (1.1.35–36)—to the end of the play—"There's no man in the world more bound to's mother" (5.3.159–60)—we are explicitly informed of Coriolanus's central motivation. As Shuli Barzilai writes, "explanations of his relentless aggression are not hidden in some corner of the play … the riddle of Coriolanus's zeal is posed and a solution offered at the very outset" (233). Yet readers and audiences of the play have often felt as if "there is no inwardness in the depiction of Coriolanus," to quote Tony Tanner; the protagonist, he adds, "is all outside, all deed, all sword" (665). It is as if everything pertaining to the psychic life in the play takes place on the surface, rendering it a horizontal plane of being and delegating all verticality exterior, a matter of standing or kneeling or being trod upon, of being "heightened" or "stooping" (5.6.21–27). "Not to be other than one thing" (4.7.42)—Aufidius's sharp characterization of Coriolanus—is a profoundly un-Freudian description of psychic life.[4] *Coriolanus* may seem to blunt the tools that psychoanalysis uses: it does not seem to be operating by the mechanisms of repression (condensation, displacement).

But given the many ways, outlined below, in which *Coriolanus* seems to speak to some of Freud's most central concerns, its absence, at various points in his writings, feels so pronounced that it seems to reveal something about Freud's blind spots—as if the repression of *Coriolanus* might be homologous to what is repressed in the analyst's thought. Many of the play's central conflicts, themes, and issues closely align with topics Freud

[4]Compare Plutarch's description of Coriolanus as "simple in his nature and straight forward" (4.221).

left relatively under-explored or untouched, such as the tension between the demands of the group and those of the individual, or between the aggressive drive and the bonds of love, or (not, as we shall see, unrelatedly) the child's relationship with the mother and the mother's with the child.

This chapter makes two interconnected arguments. The first is that literature has a unique claim to bearing on Freud's psychoanalysis as the "other scene" of the unconscious bears upon conscious thought. It is the envelope of this body of work, even as this corpus seeks, in turn, to envelop some of literature's most renowned writers, texts, and characters, weaving hypotheses about the psychic origins of creativity and the unconscious motives influencing both creators and their creations. Lacan's word *extimité* captures this movement whereby what is most intimate to the structure of psychoanalysis possesses at the same time a quality of exteriority. From beyond the boundaries of his writings, literature offers interpretations of what Freud's structure omits. The second argument is that the absence of *Coriolanus* in Freud's work represents a repression of the play, and that the play itself can offer an interpretation of this repression.

Mothers and ~~Fathers~~

It makes sense to begin by asking why Freud might have been interested in *Coriolanus.* Why do we find the absence of the play surprising? Once one has begun to read Freud with *Coriolanus* in mind, it is quite remarkable how many of the pathways of Freud's thought—like the proverbial roads that lead to Rome—seem to converge on, yet come to a halt before, *Coriolanus.* It is well known that Rome had a powerful, perhaps even central, place in Freud's psyche; and, since modernity's version of Rome is one that is in good measure mediated *through* Shakespeare, Shakespeare's Rome is likely one of the unspoken layers which Freud is addressing. The city is in fact, in *Civilization and its Discontents*—a work whose intersections with *Coriolanus* will emerge at several points of this chapter—the model of psychic space par excellence. In this text, Freud constructs his famous analogy between mental space and a fantastical Rome with each of its topological states simultaneously in play. The analyst imagines a palimpsest of the eternal city in which long-vanished structures occupy the same ground as the buildings of the present day; a space at such a pitch of compression because "nothing that has once come into existence will have passed away" (70/64). But this topographical layering, which Freud found so helpful in visualizing the layering of the psyche, of necessity meant that not only desired but also disavowed or unwanted elements of the past remained present. During Freud's first visit to Rome, in 1901, the analyst divided the eternal city into three primary layers. He enjoyed the "likable," late nineteenth-century "Italian" city, and he adored wandering around the ancient ruins upon which it was built; but he found "difficult to tolerate" the remnants of medieval Rome, with its constant reminders of "my own misery" (Masson 449)—that is, his own history as a Jew, victimized by Christians. The city gave rise to complex feelings in the analyst, a persistent ambiguity or ambivalence, and accordingly Rome, with its preservation of "everything" (*Civilization and its Discontents* 69, 71/64, 65), including those things that were intractable and ineradicable and unwanted, became the source of conflict in Freud.

During the first half of his life, and despite a repeatedly avowed yearning to visit the city, the analyst was famously unable to set foot in Rome. He longed to see it, to cross into it, but psychically a boundary had been erected around the city. Perhaps it is not a coincidence then that Freud also could not reach the last in the series of Shakespeare's Roman works—almost as though the deferral of his arrival were repeated in the deferral of arriving at *Coriolanus*, the one Roman play in which, in the play's final act, the city itself is threatened with conquest by the impending arrival of a treacherous son. This dynamic of approach and retreat—with the city, with the play—is repeated in the passage from *Civilization* which sets up a parallel between the topology of Rome and that of the mind. The passage that compares the palimpsests of Rome's topography and of the mind ends with the thought that his "phantasy" merely demonstrates "how far we are from mastering the characteristics of mental life by representing them in pictorial terms" (71/65). It is as if Freud were drawing an implicit analogy between psychic and physical difficulties in approaching Rome, or in what "Rome" signifies to him. In both cases, there is a movement toward something desired (Rome, a graspable visualization of the psyche), followed by an abruption—the forward impetus cut short by an inhibition or by a sense of impossibility. Some threshold is reached, the imagined crossing of which generates, perhaps, an intolerable anxiety and a consequent withdrawal from an encounter with this limit. Already, we are hardly able to miss the parallels with *Coriolanus*, whose protagonist's march on Rome is similarly brought to an abrupt conclusion by deeply felt inhibitions.

Freud's conflicted relationship to Rome was especially acute during the period in which he worked on *The Interpretation of Dreams*. In this work of self-analysis, buoyed along by Freud's exchanges with Wilhelm Fliess, the analyst's long-standing desire for Rome intensified, but so too did his aversion. Clinically speaking, Freud's self-analysis can be seen to produce a heavily over-determined symptom.[5] In *The Interpretation* and in letters to Fliess, Freud recounted incidents from his unsuccessful attempts on the city; he wrote of dreams about his desire to reach Rome, his sadness in failing to do so and the fear which held him back. *The Interpretation* includes several dreams which bring him close to the city without being able to reach it. In one, Freud is looking out of the window of a train by the Tiber, only to have the train pull away before he could emerge and set foot on Roman soil (see *Interpretation* 194/171). In this dream, the Rome dread appears as a localized form of the more atopic anxiety around traveling by train—an anxiety that took various forms for Freud over the years, including obsessive thoughts of train accidents and of missing trains he wished to travel on. In a well-known letter (dated 3 October 1897), a part of his correspondence with Fliess, Freud touches on his anxiety about trains, recalling a brief memory that has garnered significant critical attention. As far as we can tell, though, this recollection has not been linked to his feelings about Rome. In the letter, Freud describes an early memory from a railway journey from Leipzig to Vienna, which he dates to when he was around two or two and a half years old (though some commentators argue that Freud would have been closer to four at the time). On this trip, Freud explains to Fliess, repeatedly substituting Latin words for terms with which he appears to feel uncomfortable, the young boy Freud "must have spent the night together" with his mother, "and there must have been an opportunity of seeing her *nudam* [naked]." For Freud, this trip marks the beginning of his Oedipal period, for it was on this journey that "my libido toward *matrem* [mother] was awakened" (Masson 268). The memory appears to stage the crossing of a boundary or prohibition. Freud's travel anxiety and specifically his anxiety about traveling to Rome repeatedly bring him back to this boundary and the phantasy—or indeed, memory—of crossing it. His use of Latin to encode his mother's nakedness creates a further link between Rome as the place of repressed

[5] It is in the wake of this self-analysis and the completion of the *Interpretation* (published in 1900) that Freud is able finally to enter Rome (1901).

material—Latin here deployed as an act of partial repression—and a signifier under which Freud's Oedipus complex goes.

So one obvious reason Freud might have been drawn to, and away from, *Coriolanus* is the play's focus on the maternal caste of Rome, and hence on the son's Oedipal attachment to the mother.[6] In Delmore Schwartz's poem *Coriolanus and His Mother: The Dream of One Performance*, the Ghost of Sigmund Freud appears and

> Mutters beside me in the haunted night,
> "This is the origin, this, this is the place,
> Mother in love with son and son with her,
> And his aloneness in the womb began." (lines 186–89, p. 86)

Schwartz's poem underlines the thought that the attachment Shakespeare's protagonist has to his mother was profoundly germane to Freud's thinking, and indeed could no more have escaped the analyst's attention than the character can escape his mother's sway: at the play's heart is an overwhelming maternal presence which both makes and destroys Coriolanus: the contraction of "his" to "'s" in Volumnia's "There's no man in the world more bound to's mother" (5.3.159–60) brings out acutely the "smothering" aspect of "mother." A second hypothesis would note Freud's repeated reduction of the idealization of "the mother's relation to her male child"—"the single exception," as he wrote, to the general rule that "[a]ggressiveness … forms the basis of every relation of affection and love among people" (*Civilization and Its Discontents* 113/101–102). The suggestion here is that the analyst's repression of *Coriolanus* may have had something to do with the way engagement with this play inevitably evokes the fear of both maternal deprivation and maternal engulfment—and a concomitant aggressivity in mother-son relations. Volumnia is imagined in the play as having formed her son as a distinctly phallic object; and her son's threatened destruction of Rome is (as Janet Adelman has convincingly argued) in fantasy a vengeful attack on the

[6]See especially Janet Adelman 130–64, esp. 146–64. For both mother and son, writes Adelman, masculine identity "depends on [the] transformation of … vulnerability [the oral neediness of the infant's feeding mouth] into an instrument of attack [the phallic aggression of the honorable warrior's bleeding wound]" (149). See also Stanley Cavell on the maternal Rome (151). Martin Bergmann argues that, unlike in the original, where "the character of Martius is his very own," in Shakespeare's version of Plutarch's story "[the protagonist's] violent life is a response to his mother's unconscious wish to destroy him" (147).

maternal body: aggressivity, then, both ways—something from which Freud—whose idealization of his own mother is well-established—may well have wished to turn away.

The symbolic maternal conquest of Coriolanus's attack on Rome is diverted in Freud's thinking toward patricidal matters. In his writings on Shakespeare, Freud's powers of analysis are explicitly drawn in the direction of exploring the son's relationship to the father—real, imaginary, and symbolic—and the coordinates of his own masculine identifications.[7] The father is, of course, a figure almost entirely absent from *Coriolanus* (indeed, the absence of a symbolic father in the play is concomitant with the violent contestation of the identity of the city itself in the absence of an authority-figure at its center). In this absence, the overwhelming presence of the mother takes center stage, an unrestrained, unprohibited maternal figure. This may be what Freud's memory of his mother on the train represents, and what his recurring anxiety about trains and Rome continually negotiates. Freud instead focused his interest upon the almost entirely masculine world of Shakespeare's earlier Roman play, *Julius Caesar*, above all upon that play's protagonist, Brutus, who, in killing his adoptive father, is for Freud a paradigmatic model of filial ambivalence.[8] In *The Interpretation of Dreams*, Freud weaves *Julius Caesar* into the narrative of his own life at several points. He recalls his younger brother, Julius, who died when Freud was two years old—the same age he associates with his memory of seeing his mother naked on the train to Vienna. Freud's experience playing Brutus to his nephew John's Caesar in Schiller's *Die Räuber* also resurfaces in his "non vixit" dream, where he reflects on Brutus's funeral oration as a way of processing his ambivalence toward an admired man.[9]

[7]Peter Homans writes about Rome having a (repressed) "maternal presence" (96) for Freud (because of its associations with his Catholic nursemaid).

[8]See, e.g., *The Interpretation of Dreams*, 423–24/378; *The Psychopathology of Everyday Life*, 117n.3/102n; and *Jokes and their Relation to the Unconscious*, 73/64. For a full list of Freud's references to *Julius Caesar* (and, indeed, to Shakespeare's plays more generally), see the Appendix at the end of this volume.

[9]"John Freud was the son of Emanuel Freud, the eldest son of Freud's father. According to Jones, John was Freud's "inseparable playmate" during early childhood. Jones also quotes Freud recalling John as an early influence on his fascination with martial heroes Hannibal and Masséna: "Perhaps the development of this martial ideal may be traced yet farther back, to the first three years of my childhood, to wishes which my alternately friendly and hostile relations with a boy a year older than myself must have evoked in the weaker of the two playmates" (*Sigmund Freud: Life and Work: Vol 1: The Young Freud 1856–1900* 8).

Julius Caesar again likely influenced Freud's thinking in *Totem and Taboo*, particularly regarding the primal horde of brothers and the killing of the father figure. Brutus, who kills his adoptive father, becomes the exemplary figure for Freud.[10] Again, it is notable that *Coriolanus*, whose ending might have been evocative in terms of the ur-scene (of a band of brothers murdering a male leader) which Freud describes in *Totem and Taboo*, does not seem to enter into Freud's thinking. Filial ambivalence surpasses not only maternal but also fraternal ambivalence.

Here we could consider Freud's projection of an image of his own real father as painfully weak and his concomitant wish for a more potent father. In *The Interpretation of Dreams*, Freud recounts an episode from his childhood where his father told him of having been insulted by a group of Christians and of his most Christian response—turning the other cheek. Freud had resented his father's "unheroic conduct" (197/174). He remembered having wished that his father had enjoined him, as Hannibal's father had, "to take vengeance on the Romans" (197/174). Freud conceived of Hannibal as a symbol of semitic heroic resistance, and, Freud reported, ever since the time his father had told him the story, Hannibal had had a place in his fantasies, part imaginary father, part ideal ego.[11] In a letter to Fliess dated 3 December 1897, Freud interprets his Roman symptom in the light of his "deeply neurotic" identification with Hannibal, Rome's supreme enemy (Masson 285). During one approach to Rome, Freud came as far as Lake Trasimeno—just fifty or so miles from the city—only to turn back. As Freud knew, the lake was the scene of a significant battle in the Punic Wars, in which Hannibal's troops destroyed a substantial part of the Roman army. On

[10] Bloom regarded *Totem and Taboo* as essentially a rewriting of Shakespeare's *Julius Caesar* (*The Invention of the Human* 108).

[11] Hannibal, and Rome, return (like the repressed) at the opening of *Civilization and Its Discontents*, which begins by discussing the "oceanic feeling," a concept Freud says he owes to "a friend" (64/59); this "friend" is Romain Rolland, though Freud does not name him (the given name is of course evocative of Rome). Freud says in the following paragraph that "I cannot discover this 'oceanic' feeling in myself" (65/60), and he tries to pin down "the ideational content" (65/60) of the feeling by quoting "the consolation offered by an original and somewhat eccentric dramatist to his hero who is facing a self-inflicted death: 'We cannot fall out of this world'" (65/60). The hero in question (also unnamed by Freud) is Hannibal in Christian Dietrich Grabbe's tragedy, *Hannibal* (1835).

the verge of marching into Rome, Hannibal, like Freud, turned back. "I had actually been following in Hannibal's footsteps," he wrote (*Interpretation* 196/173). But here again, we might wonder at the absence of any mention of Coriolanus—one of Shakespeare's greatest martial heroes, so nearly Rome's ultimate nemesis, who just as famously got to the verge, "within fortie furlonge" of Rome, as Thomas North put it in his translation of Plutarch's *Lives* (see Bullough 5.533)—in Freud's work: if Hannibal, why not Coriolanus?

Freud repeatedly identified himself with conquistadors and great military leaders—with Julius Caesar, with Napoleon, but above all with Hannibal, Rome's supreme enemy. The kind of hero-worship (of a military leader) which Freud demonstrates vis-à-vis these military figures is evoked in *Coriolanus*, where the protagonist is treated in this way by both the Romans (in 1.7) and the Volscians: "He is their god. He leads them like a thing / Made by some other deity than nature, / That shapes man better, and they follow him … with no less confidence / Than boys pursuing summer butterflies" (4.6.94–98). In both cases, the hero-worship turns into loathing as soon as peace returns, and the war-hero is no longer needed; might this dynamic have played into Freud's "avoidance" of the play? "Boys pursuing summer butterflies" like "butchers killing flies" (4.6.99) is hardly an unequivocally positive image, and Freud might also not have wanted to see—at least during the early phases of his analytic career—how what he regarded as "martial heroism" may be understood as a manifestation of what he later came to see as the death drive. Martius is described as being, from childhood onward (and under the tutelage of his mother), a killing machine, whose relentlessness is eventually turned back on himself: "Death, that dark spirit, in's nervy arm doth lie" (2.1.156), as his mother declares. This renders him both heroic, from a military point of view, and pathological. Freud writes of the death instinct emerging at its purest, "in the blindest fury of destructiveness" where "the satisfaction of the instinct is accompanied by an extraordinarily high degree of narcissistic enjoyment, owing to its presenting the ego with a fulfilment of the latter's old wishes for omnipotence" (*Civilization and Its Discontents*

121/109).[12] Who better than Coriolanus to exemplify this?[13] What we find in *Coriolanus* is a character who manifests supremely what, in *Civilization and Its Discontents*, Freud terms "the human love of aggression" (113/101).

Butterflies, Caterpillars, and Wolves

Freud was already edging toward seeing this love of aggression, or the aggressive orientation of love, in his early case histories, and one of these in particular—*From the History of an Infantile Neurosis* (often referred to as "The Wolfman")—seems to us to be of evident relevance to *Coriolanus*. It is, firstly, in its incidental details that the case history uncannily evokes the play. Three elements from the analytic case can be juxtaposed fascinatingly with *Coriolanus*. First, we note the memory Freud's patient describes early in his analysis:

> Once he was running after a beautiful big butterfly, with striped yellow wings which ended in points, in the hope of catching it. (It was no doubt a "swallow-tail".) He was suddenly seized with a terrible fear of the creature, and, screaming, gave up the chase. He also felt fear and loathing of beetles

[12]Freud wrote the important essay *On Narcissism: An Introduction* in Rome (and of course the term "narcissism" is primarily derived from one of the greatest of Roman poets, Ovid). We are hardly the first to indicate the relevance of narcissism to *Coriolanus*. Cavell, for example, indicates his sense of "the thoroughness with which Narcissus's fate is mirrored in the figure of Coriolanus" (144). So we can surely point to the dovetailing of Shakespeare's protagonist with ideas expressed in *On Narcissism: An Introduction*—ideas such as the transformation of eroticism into aggressivity as a result of a disturbed sense of identity—almost self-evidently Coriolanus's case—or the picture of "a son's over-attachment to a narcissistic mother [which] often results in a flight from femininity and compensatory attraction to another male who is really a surrogate for himself, especially if the father is ineffectual or absent" (Parker 57). Here again we might have expected Freud to bring to mind Coriolanus, whose relation to Aufidius (clearly "a surrogate for himself") is seemingly far more intense than his relation to his wife, or even his son—though in the end it proves less intense than his "over-attachment to a narcissistic mother." Here we surely have a prime example of Freud's narcissistic type, who is "plainly seeking *themselves* as a love object, and exhibiting a type of object-choice that must be termed 'narcissistic'" (Freud, *On Narcissism* 88/76). Coriolanus's narcissism expresses itself partly in just this way, and partly in his emphatic claim to be *sui generis*. A hypothesis here might move in the direction of Freud's avoidance of identification with a character who both draws on his own interest in martial heroism and is manifestly narcissistic. A second hypothesis might work along the lines of Freud's defense against his own homosexual impulses.

[13]Barzilai reads the play as a demonstration *avant la lettre* of the repetition compulsion.

> and caterpillars. Yet he could also remember that at this very time he used to torment beetles and cut caterpillars to pieces. (16/14–15)

The parallels and differences between this scene and the scene Valeria (a friend of Coriolanus's mother and wife) describes early in the play are noteworthy:

> O'my word, the father's son! I'll swear 'tis a very pretty boy. O'my troth, I looked upon him o'Wednesday half an hour together. 'Has such a confirmed countenance! I saw him run after a gilded butterfly, and when he caught it, he let it go again, and after it again, and over and over he comes, and up again, catched it again. Or whether his fall enraged him, or how 'twas, he did so set his teeth and tear it. O, I warrant how he mammocked it! (1.3.60–68)

If Freud recalls the scene from *Coriolanus*, he gives no hint of it. In both scenes "the human love of aggression" seems writ large. Some of the details are strikingly similar: the young boy giving chase; the gilded and the yellow-winged butterfly; the "mammock[ing]"[14] or tearing to pieces; the implicit oral component (little Martius "did set his teeth and tear it"; "It was no doubt a 'swallow-tail'"); the ambivalence, expressed in Coriolanus's son by the rhythm of catch-and-release—so reminiscent of the *fort-da* game Freud was to describe in *Beyond the Pleasure Principle*—and in the Wolfman by giving up the chase before eventually "torment[ing]" the little creatures. (The structure of approach and relinquishment/resistance is shared by the boys' relation to the butterfly and Freud's movement toward Rome.) In the Wolfman's case the dismembering is, tellingly, of the more phallic caterpillar (or of the *schwanz* [tail or penis] of the *schwalbenschwanz* [swallow-tail]) rather than of the more feminized butterfly. In *Coriolanus*, Menenius uses just this supposed "differency" to delineate Coriolanus's transformation "from man to dragon": "There is differency between a grub and a butterfly, yet your butterfly was a grub. This Martius is grown from man to dragon. He has wings; he's more than a creeping thing" (5.4.11–14). Of course, we have just seen (in the previous scene, the scene of Coriolanus's abandonment of the attack on Rome in the face of his mother's representations) how un-dragonish Coriolanus

[14]This is Shakespeare's only use of the word "mammock" which, like the nearly contemporaneous "Mamillius," is so clearly evocative of the mother, hence undermining Valeria's "the father's son," which works to exclude the maternal.

is—how he is, just as he always was, his mother's creation. So Menenius's distinction between grubs and butterflies (between phallic and female creatures)—like the Wolfman's between caterpillars and butterflies—is implicitly destabilized.

In both *Coriolanus* and the *History of an Infantile Neurosis*, there is an oscillation between desire (expressed in the butterfly scene as oral voraciousness) and dread (which develops for the Wolfman into a phobia of animals—and in Coriolanus into a loathing of what the plebeians represent for him—bodily disintegration). The *History of an Infantile Neurosis* is most particularly related to Freud's elaboration of castration anxiety. Freud interprets the V-shape made by the antennae of the butterfly as a "crude" representation of the position of a woman's legs during intercourse:

> Many months later, in quite another connection, the patient remarked that the opening and shutting of the butterfly's wings while it was settled on the flower had given him an uncanny feeling. It had looked, so he said, like a woman opening her legs, and the legs then made the shape of a Roman V … the crude hypothesis that it had been this girl whom, when he was a small child, he had first seen making the movements with her legs which he had fixed in his mind with the Roman V—movements which allow access to the genitals. (90–91/80–81)

Strangely enough, Freud's repetition of the term "*Roman* V" (rather than, say, "the letter V") brings into focus the fact that all three female characters in Shakespeare's late Roman play have names beginning with "V": Volumnia, Virgilia, Valeria. (Incidentally, apart from this triumvirate of women there are no other female characters with "V" names in any of Shakespeare's other Roman plays.) Freud reads the "V" as referring partly (in its shape) to a woman's legs, and partly (in its signification as a Roman numeral) to the hour of the day (5:00 pm) when the Wolfman presumptively witnessed the primal scene; in both cases, the "V" points ineluctably, says Freud, to castration. The spacing of the letter confirms what the Wolfman's "observation of his parents' intercourse" has revealed: "the conviction of the reality of castration" (45/40). But Freud's emphasis on the "Romanness" of the letter has not garnered attention: this is not just a "V," it is (he repeats twice) a "*Roman* V." In the light of the preceding material about Freud's Rome, we can add to his interpretation (which is of course always a joint creation of analyst and patient) a thought about the maternal connotations of that forbidden/repressed "Roman" space.

One thing Freud's reading of the "Roman V" might add to our understanding of *Coriolanus* is a sense of the play's geometry, so to speak. After ceding to his mother's request, Coriolanus turns to Aufidius and says: "I'll not to Rome; I'll back with you and pray you / Stand to me in this cause" (5.3.199–200). "Stand to me" seems to mean in this context "support me." It is certainly available to set (geometrically, so to speak) beside that final, chilling-comic stage direction, "*Aufidius stands on him*" (5.6.131). But, perhaps just as significantly, it seems to be almost the only place in the play where Coriolanus becomes (to use Freud's terminology) anaclitic: asking for, needing, another to lean against—to "stand *to*" him (like the two segments of the "V")—rather than standing phallically alone (like a single line or sword or penis). And the movement from "stand to me" to an intuition of his coming downfall is precipitous, as if Coriolanus feels that the only alternative to absolute erection or uprightness is proneness, so that as soon as he leans (upon another) he knows that he's headed for the soles of Aufidius's feet ("cause"—in "this cause"—being etymologically derived from the Latin *casus*, "a falling"). As if the alternative to constant (phallic) activity is utter (feminized) passivity (hence he disavows his active role in the decision to turn back from Rome and bestows the decisive action upon Volumnia: "O mother, mother! / What have *you done?*" (5.3.183–84)). From this perspective, we could think of the play's interest in the "Roman V" as not merely indicating castration (through the absence of anything protruding from between the legs of the "V") but also, perhaps, suggestive of anaclitic relatedness, a kind of hieroglyph of two "I"s leaning against each other to form a "V."

So perhaps it is not entirely beside the point that the final castrative movement in Coriolanus's tragedy takes place in "Act V." "Cut me to pieces, Volsces men and lads; / Stain all your edges on me" (5.6.112–13) is Coriolanus's plea just before his death at the hands of those Volsces (the other standout "V" in the play)—who (says Aufidius) will "rejoice / That he is thus cut off" (5.6.138–39). The "cut[ting] off" of Caius Martius Coriolanus (epitomized in Aufidius's lopping of his honorific title "Coriolanus" in the same scene—"Ay, Martius, Caius Martius" (5.6.90)—is an apt conclusion for a character who has fought so hard to "stand alone"—upright, singular, phallic, at one with his sword—a character who has insisted, with his every word and act that there is, at least for him, no castration, that "CE-N'EST-PAS-DU-TOUT-UNE-TRANCHE!"

Castration Complexities

Of course, the animal most associated with classical Rome is not the butterfly but the wolf—an animal usually imagined in fairy tales as male, but, in relation to Rome, identified as the she-wolf who mythically suckled Romulus and Remus. Here again we find fascinating reverberations between the play and the case history. Freud interprets his patient's fantasies of being eaten by a wolf as expressions of the early oral organization of the libido alongside its sadomasochistic coordinates[15]—elements quite clearly at play in *Coriolanus*, where the wolf is a recurrent image, most notably in the exchange between Menenius and Sicinius (one of the people's tribunes) at the beginning of act two:

> MENENIUS: Pray you, who does the wolf love?
> SICINIUS: The lamb. (2.1.7–8)[16]

The exchange between Menenius and Sicinius distils the interpretive tussle in the play between the two sides (plebeians and patricians), each wishing to portray themselves as lamb-like to wolfish other. Stanley Cavell takes the exchange between Menenius and Sicinius as allowing us to see how "devouring can be an expression of love" (153). Here again, Freud might have found some interest in Shakespeare's play. In *Coriolanus*, at the point of standing for the senate, the protagonist disdains to wear "this wolvish toge" (2.3.111): he refuses, that is, to see himself as someone in disguise, to represent himself as a wolf in sheep's clothing. The Folio's "Wooluish" brings out the "wool" in "wolf"—which is to say, the textual crux fleetingly evokes the oscillation or ambiguity in sadomasochism. In *The History of an Infantile Neurosis*, the analysand also reveals a certain oscillation between wolves and sheep, first indicating that "The wolves were quite white, and looked more like foxes or sheep-dogs" (29/26), and then adding: "Why were the wolves white? This made him think of the sheep" (30/27). Identification and phobia, oral desire for the other and the desire to destroy, are hard to disentangle.

The profusion of animals in this reconstruction of infantile phobia points us to the intricated web of stories, encountered by a child of four

[15] Tregear suggests "reading [Coriolanus's] penchant for self-sabotage as a form of defence, or a case of what Sigmund Freud calls 'moral masochism'" (forthcoming).

[16] Compare Cominius's later comment that "the people / Deserve such pity of him as the wolf / Does of the shepherds" (4.6.114–16).

and a half or five, that analyst and patient together peel apart over the course of the treatment. At the center of this case is a motif—white wolves in a walnut tree—whose branching associations quickly pitch us into the texts of fairy tales. The first is to the Wolfman's memory of being terrorized as a child of five by his older sister brandishing a picture in an illustrated book of fairytales showing "a wolf standing upright and striding along" (16/14). "Whenever he caught sight of this picture he began to scream like a lunatic that he was afraid of the wolf coming and eating him up" (16/14). The position of the older sister as facilitator of the child's exposure to this terrifying scene appears to index her role in his seduction, for this scene of the sister and the picture book gives way in the course of the analysis to the Wolfman's recollection of an earlier time when his sister had "taken hold of his penis and played with it" (20/18) accompanying the act with words about the upending sexuality of his nanny, who, according to the sister, "used to do the same thing with all kinds of people—for instance, with the gardener: she [Nanya] used to stand him on his head, and then take hold of his genitals" (20/18). Inverted in the phobic scene of the upright, gobbling wolf of fable is the long-forgotten trace of something passive, something with the "upside" facing "down."

Freud notes that, during the course of his analysis, the Wolfman spends time attempting to locate in antiquary shops the picture book from which the image of the upright wolf originated. While the Wolfman initially associates the illustration to the story of "Little Red Riding Hood," his later recovery of the book confirms what Freud has come to suspect: its derivation from "The Wolf and the Seven Kids." It is by piecing together the problems articulated in "Reynard the Fox"—"how the wolf wanted to go fishing in the winter, and used his tail as a bait, and how in that way his tail was broken off in the ice" (25/22)—in the story told by the Wolfman's grandfather (of the wolf who loses his tail to the tailor) and in "The Seven Little Kids" that Freud and the Wolfman arrive at the reconstruction of the primal scene, and the unconscious conflict inferred to underpin all the Wolfman's later symptom formations. The analysis reveals how the unconscious relies on a literary assemblage—a palimpsest of allusions, borrowed elements, and symbolic representations—to speak. By examining this web of literary references, Freud is able to formulate a hypothesis about the long-buried problem at the heart of the Wolfman's love relations: to be loved by the father and become a woman (a desire shaped by the equation of womanhood with castration), or to relinquish the father in favor of one's own masculinity? Here, the unconscious becomes a vanishing point on the horizon of literary allusion, readable only through the stories it elects to give form to its conflicts. Through the motifs of the wolf and the loss of an appendage, Freud traces the vicissitudes of a current of wishes attendant on the father: the Wolfman's desires to emulate the father, to be the father's sexual partner, to take up the mother's role and thus become the father's object of desire, and the accompanying fears triggered by the boy's discovery of a woman's sexual difference. The case makes strikingly clear the role of literature as the "other scene" of the unconscious with certain texts emerging as repositories of problem-situations on which the unconscious can lean to point the way back to these structural conflicts.

Our suggestion in these final paragraphs is that *Coriolanus* might be seen as a similar repository for questions and problems buried for Freud; a literary "other scene" where an unanalyzed remainder plays out. Just as Derrida's phrase "CE-N'EST-PAS-DU-TOUT-UNE-TRANCHE" unsettles clear boundaries, a line from *Coriolanus* might similarly serve as a mobile, equivocal phrase that speaks to Freud from "inside out." Coriolanus's famous moment of capitulation to his mother—"O mother, mother! / What have you done?" (5.3.183–84)—is both a cry of loss and a declaration of submission, embodying the moment where castration does not resolve the Oedipal crisis but rather deepens the attachment to the maternal figure. What we find in *Coriolanus*, then, is not a trajectory from Oedipus to castration but a looping return, a recursive structure where renunciation fails to sever the incestuous tie. The play, in this way, destabilizes Freud's pathway for the male Oedipal child, revealing the very fissures in the analytic structure he sought to construct. In part this is because the Oedipus of Coriolanus is not at all a triangular structure. It is a "V"—a mother and a son—missing the third strut that would mediate the relationship between them. In the absence of this intervention, the wager that Freud posits as the passage out of Oedipus for the male child does not operate. In 1924, Freud published "The Dissolution of the Oedipus Complex." In this, Freud had described the castration complex as the force that destroys the Oedipus complex for a boy: when the narcissistic value of what one values most is weighed against the incestuous desire for the parent, the wish to preserve the former facilitates the turn away from the incestuous object. For Coriolanus what we see however is that there is no possibility of turning from the mother. Aufidius drives this home when he describes Coriolanus as "thou boy of tears" (5.6.103). This may well be because the castration complex depends upon the very intervention that is impossible in the "V"-like geometry between

Coriolanus and Volumnia. Whereas the Wolfman invents the fearsome wolf to come between him and his wished-for parent, a figure which demands he renounce his father as love object or lose his sex, there is no commensurate separative figure for Coriolanus. The very person who demands that he renounce his attack on Rome is his own mother; and in exchange for this renunciation, he once again becomes her instrument. One could see Coriolanus's decision to approach Aufidius here as the most desperate search for a wolf-like figure that could present him with the castration he so misses; an election comparable perhaps to the ideally martial father-substitutes that Freud chose for himself. But this castration for Coriolanus can only now come in the most physically rending of forms as though the only way left to separate from his mother's body was to be separated from the body itself. *Coriolanus* leaves us in the wake of an inability to traverse the Oedipal trajectory Freud traced, exposing the unexamined residue of his theory as that which awaited him on a train to Rome: the mother from whom one can never turn away, only go toward.

Acknowledgement The authors thank Catherine Bates, Bernard Burgoyne, Maud Ellmann, the late Mike Schoenfeldt, James W. Stone, and Ted Tregear for their thoughtful comments on drafts of this chapter.

Works Cited

Adelman, Janet. *Suffocating Mothers: Fantasies of Maternal Origin in Shakespeare's Plays,* Hamlet *to* The Tempest. Routledge, 1992.

Barzilai, Shuli. "*Coriolanus* and the Compulsion to Repeat." *Strands Afar Remote: Israeli Perspectives on Shakespeare*, edited by Avraham Oz, Associated UP, 1998, pp. 232–54.

Bergmann, Martin S. *The Unconscious in Shakespeare's Plays.* Routledge, 2019.

Bloom, Harold. *Shakespeare: The Invention of the Human.* Riverhead Books, 1998.

———. *The Western Canon.* Penguin, 1994.

Brunkhorst, Martin. *Shakespeares* Coriolanus *in Deutscher Bearbeitun.* De Gruyter, 1973.

Bullough, Geoffrey, editor. *Narrative and Dramatic Sources of Shakespeare.* 8 vols. Columbia UP, 1957–1975.

Cavell, Stanley. *Disowning Knowledge in Seven Plays of Shakespeare.* Cambridge UP, 2008.

Derrida, Jacques. *Disseminations.* Translated by Barbara Johnson, U of Chicago P, 1981.

———. *The Post Card: From Socrates to Freud and Beyond*. Translated by Alan Bass, U of Chicago P, 1987.

Freud, Sigmund. *The Revised Standard Edition of the Complete Psychological Works of Sigmund Freud*, edited and translated by James Strachey, revised by Mark Solms. 24 vols. Rowman & Littlefield Publishers, 2024. (In-text references provide *RSE* page numbers immediately after *SE* page numbers).

———. *Civilization and its Discontents* (1930). *The Standard Edition of the Complete Psychological Works of Sigmund Freud*, edited and translated by James Strachey, vol. 21, Hogarth Press, 1961, pp. 57–145/*RSE* vol. 21, pp. 55–134.

———. *From the History of an Infantile Neurosis* ("The Wolfman") (1925). *SE* vol. 17, 1955, pp. 1–122/*RSE* vol. 17, pp 1–112.

———. *The Interpretation of Dreams* (1900). *SE* vols. 4 and 5, 1953/*RSE* vols. 4 and 5.

———. *Jokes and their Relation to the Unconscious* (1905). *SE* vol. 8, 1960/*RSE* vol. 8.

———. *On Narcissism: An Introduction* (1914). *SE* vol. 14, 1957, pp. 67–102/*RSE* vol. 14, pp. 61–89.

———. *The Psychopathology of Everyday Life* (1901). *SE* vol. 6, 1966/*RSE* vol. 6.

Gay, Peter. *Freud: A Life for our Times*. Norton, 1988.

Homans, Peter. *The Ability to Mourn: Disillusionment and the Social Origins of Psychoanalysis*. U of Chicago P, 1989.

Jones, Ernest. *Sigmund Freud: Life and Work: Vol 1: The Young Freud 1856–1900*. Basic Books, 1953.

Lacan, Jacques. *The Seminar. Book VII. The Ethics of Psychoanalysis, 1959–60*. Translated by Dennis Porter, Routledge, 1992.

Masson, Jeffrey Moussaieff, translator and editor. *The Complete Letters of Sigmund Freud to Wilhelm Fliess, 1887–1904*. Belknap Press, 1985.

Plutarch. *Lives*. Translated by Bernadotte Perrin. 11 vols. Harvard UP, 1914–1926.

Sachs, Hans. *Freud: Master and Friend*. Harvard UP, 1944.

Schwartz, Delmore. "Act One: 'O Me! Make You a Sword of Me!'" *Summer Knowledge: New and Selected Poems*. Garden City, 1967.

Shakespeare, William. *Coriolanus*. Edited by R. B. Parker, Oxford UP, 1994.

Spevack, Martin, editor, revised by Jeremy Lopez. *Julius Caesar*. Cambridge UP, 2004.

Tanner, Tony. *Prefaces to Shakespeare*. Harvard UP, 2010.

Tregear, Ted, editor. *Coriolanus*. Oxford UP, forthcoming.

PART II

Psychoanalysis and Shakespeare

CHAPTER 7

The Imaginary and the Symbolic in Shakespeare's *Venus and Adonis*

Catherine Bates

The story of Venus and Adonis, as it appears in Shakespeare's poem and in earlier mytho-poetic versions, involves three parties—a goddess, a youth, and a boar—the third of which intrudes upon the relationship between the other two (in Shakespeare, that relationship is more verbalized than realized, for reasons we shall explore further below). It is significant that the parties in question belong to three quite different orders or "layers" of existence—divine, human, and animal—and equally significant that the first two of these have speech while the third does not.[1] In the relationship

[1] Barkan describes Ovid's *Metamorphoses*, Shakespeare's main source for the Venus and Adonis story, as follows: "The universe is structured in layers—in this case, divine, human, and animal—and metamorphosis is the vehicle whereby individuals are transported among the layers" (2). The three different levels are well populated in Shakespeare's poem, though unevenly so. Thus, Venus can count Titan (the sun god), Mars, Jove, Cupid, and Diana/Cynthia (the moon goddess) among her kind; Adonis, his male hunting companions; but both are massively outnumbered by the animals which the boar can count among his. These animals appear either "in person" in the poem (Adonis's hunting hounds, his horse, a

C. Bates (✉)
University of Warwick, Coventry, UK
e-mail: c.t.bates@warwick.ac.uk

J. W. Stone, C. Bates (eds.), *Shakespeare and Psychoanalysis*, Palgrave Shakespeare Studies,
https://doi.org/10.1007/978-3-032-07897-1_7

between immortal goddess and vulnerable human youth, it is not difficult to trace a mystification of the symbiotic, preoedipal mother/child dyad, something Shakespeare does little to deny, presenting a sexual relation between partners of exaggeratedly unequal age, size, and agency which, as Jonathan Bate writes, is bound at some level "to replicate the archetypal relationship based on an unequal power-structure, incest between a parent and a child" (64).[2] The boar, meanwhile, is positioned as a fatal force which comes from without: the third term—rival, conqueror, and unassailable usurper—which threatens to split apart this idyll of the loving or would-be loving couple and destroy it for good.[3] In the relationship between the boar and the goddess and boy, therefore, it is not difficult to trace a mystification of the Phallus, something, again, that Shakespeare does little to deny, presenting the boar as the justifiable object of Venus's jealousy and suspicion.[4] In Venus's typically expansive descriptions, every aspect of the boar's body—its "bristly pikes" (line 620), its "eyes like glow-worms" (line 621), its snout that "digs" (line 622) and "roots" (line 636) and is like an "urchin" or hedgehog (line 1105), its "short thick neck" (line 627), not to mention its terrible tusks, those "sharp fangs"

"breeding jennet" or mare), or in metaphors, comparisons, references, inset descriptions, and so on, and include many different types of bird (doves, an eagle, a trapped bird, a dive-dapper, an owl, a vulture, a wild bird, a lark, falcons), mammals (deer, dogs, a wolf, sheep, a hare, a fox, a roe, rabbits, a doe and her fawn, a bear, a lion, a hedgehog), reptiles (a serpent, an adder), invertebrates (glow-worms, caterpillars, a snail), and fish. The unspeaking population of the poem undoubtedly has a numerical advantage over the speaking one. See also note 11 below.

[2] Shakespeare's narrator compares Adonis to "the froward infant still'd with dandling" (line 562) and Venus to "a milch doe, whose swelling dugs do ache, / Hasting to feed her fawn hid in some brake" (lines 875–76), while Adonis repeatedly refers to his own immaturity and "little heart" (line 783), comparing himself to a "bud" (line 416) and unripe fruit (see lines 524–28).

[3] As Weaver notes, the fact the myth recounts "a triangular love affair" (70) obtains even in those versions which exclude the boar. For example, in Aphthonius's *Progymnasmata* (a fourth-century rhetorical handbook, translated into Latin in the late fifteenth century and a highly influential textbook in the early modern grammar school), it is Venus's jealous lover Mars who kills Adonis (see Kennedy 97). In other variations on this version of events, Mars takes the shape of the boar to eliminate his rival (see Hulse 157).

[4] Venus's foreboding that "Jealousy, that sour unwelcome guest, / Should by his stealing in disturb the feast" (lines 449–50) comes to fruition when she identifies the boar as the feared intruder: "disturbing Jealousy" (line 649), "This sour informer" (line 655), "dissentious Jealousy" (line 657). The animal's killing of Adonis is described by the narrator as "The foul boar's conquest on her dear delight" (line 1030).

(line 663)—conjures the Phallus in all its mystified enormity (see Lacan, *Écrits* 685–95).

As the agent of a catastrophic separation, an irreversible breach which wreaks irreparable damage and permanent change upon the human subject, the boar is a mytheme which sinks its roots deep in Western mythology. Human encounters with this animal—a single, wild, male beast armed (literally) to the teeth which could be attacked only at close range and with mighty javelins or spears (arrows were quite insufficient)—have, from ancient times, signified the ultimate initiation rite from which humans (usually, though not always, male ones) emerge variously wounded, scarred, killed, or metamorphosed, but one way or another transformed (see Bates 1–43).[5] Through medieval and Renaissance texts, too, including other works by Shakespeare, this animal marks its distinctive passage as "[t]he wretched, bloody, and usurping boar" which ravages youth, beauty, love, marriage, fertility, prosperity, and lays all to waste.[6] To this extent,

[5] Odysseus receives his identifying scar from a boar-hunt undertaken in his youth (the story is told in Book 19 of the *Odyssey*). Wounded above the knee, Odysseus emerges from this *rite de passage* to bear forever after the identifying mark of a "castrated" humanity. Gored likewise in the thigh, Adonis does not live to bear a scar but is effectively transformed into one: into a flower which, in Shakespeare's poem, is "purple [...] check'red with white" (line 1168) to figure the bloodied, spumy, and spermy snout of the boar which inflicted the wound, its "frothy mouth bepainted all with red, / Like milk and blood being mingled both together" (lines 901–02). As Phallus, of course, the boar is agent of castration. On female engagements with the boar, see the interesting story of Atalanta, the first part of which is told in Book 8 of the *Metamorphoses*: beloved of Meleager, prince of Calydon, Atalanta joins his otherwise all-male hunting party to pursue a monstrous boar; she wounds but does not kill the beast (being armed only with arrows), which is finally finished off by Meleager, who then offers her the spoils (the beast's skin and head) in tribute. The second part of Atalanta's story (her relationship with Hippomenes and subsequent metamorphosis into a lioness) is told in Book 10 of the *Metamorphoses*, where it appears as an inset narrative told by Venus to Adonis to warn him against hunting the boar: a beast which, as a result, must now be seen as a mythic relation of the fearful Calydonian boar. As a female subject, Atalanta's body already bears castration's "scar."

[6] *Richard III*, 5.2.7 (the boar also served as the heraldic badge of the usurping king); see also *Titus Andronicus*, 4.2.138, in which Aaron (having sired an illegitimate child on the Empress Tamora) compares himself to "The chafed boar"; *A Midsummer Night's Dream*, 2.2.32, in which Oberon vindictively wishes that a "boar with bristled hair" might be one of the prospective lovers of the bewitched Titania; and *Cymbeline*, 2.5.16, in which the jealous Posthumous, imagining Iachimo committing adultery with his wife, compares him to "a full-acorn'd boar." The most extensive mythic analysis of the boar-motif in Shakespeare's work remains that by Ted Hughes. The motif similarly appears in medieval texts such as Gottfried von Strassburg's *Tristan*, Giovanni Boccaccio's *Filostrato*, and Geoffrey Chaucer's *Troilus*

the boar has affinities with another suggestively phallic beast that intervenes catastrophically to separate humans from their otherwise innocent and happy communion with the divine. Shakespeare's Venus seems aware of the connection from the beginning of the poem, when she invites Adonis to join her in the idyllic floral space "where never serpent hisses" (line 17), and later, when she hears the dreaded sounds which tell her that the boar hunt is underway, "Whereat she starts like one that spies an adder / Wreath'd up in fatal folds just in his way, / The fear whereof doth make him shake and shudder" (lines 878–80).[7] The garden already harbors the agent of its own destruction, as the ontogenetic prehistory of the individual—his or her transition from the speechlessness and sexlessness of the *infans* to a postlapsarian state as the subject of language and desire—gets told as the phylogenetic prehistory of the species: a culture's story about the genesis of the human condition.

The Venus and Adonis story, then, seems to map rather neatly onto Lacan's retelling of the same mythology in terms of a transition from the Imaginary to the Symbolic: a shift—no less consequence-laden—which marks the subject's entry into absence and difference, language and desire, and thence into all the effects of oedipalization: the gender binary, the incest taboo, the *Nom/Non du Père*, law, ethics, guilt, shame, repression, sublimation, and the rest.[8] Shakespeare's version of the story has attracted a number of readings over the years in which aspects of the poem's congruence with Lacanian or Lacanian-oriented theory—the infantile state of symbiotic fusion, the role of the Phallus in producing a "castrated" subjectivity, the insatiability of desire, the no less endless quest of signifier for signified, the illusoriness of the Imaginary, and so forth—have been

and Criseyde. For Hatto, the ravaging beast in Shakespeare's *Venus and Adonis* "is taken from the symbolical treatment of the third character in the unusual triangular situation, where his terrible majesty, gaining strength in turn from the Classical, Medieval, Renaissance and living species of the Boar, achieves his apotheosis" (361).

[7] On the Renaissance belief that "Adon" and "Eden" might be etymologically related, see Hamilton under "Adonis, gardens of."

[8] Lacan evolved his structure of the Imaginary, Symbolic, and Real over the course of his long career, and as a result there is no single essay which provides a precise summary of his thinking on the subject. Important discussions of aspects of the three orders occur in his *Écrits* 11, 25, 31, 52, 53, 68–70, 149, 276, 349–50, 383–99, 437, 463–4, 546, 550, 554, 647–9, 670, 720, 728. Helpful summaries can be found in Lacan, *Four Fundamental Concepts* 279–80, and Bowie, esp. chapter 4.

touched on and explored.[9] There remains much to be developed, however, and many ways in which such an approach can enable a richer appreciation and deeper understanding of Shakespeare's poem. This chapter considers, therefore, the way the Venus and Adonis story might have presented Shakespeare with an opportunity to explore two radically different linguistic registers (named here as the Imaginary and the Symbolic), allowing him to weigh up and play off one against another, and thus presenting him—still, at that point in 1593, at an early stage in his writing career—with different options, modes, and possibilities for his craft.

The relation between these two registers is not a straightforward one, for although logically and chronologically prior to the Symbolic, the Imaginary is nonetheless a construction of it. The intrusion of the Phallus propels the *infans* from its state of undifferentiated fusion within the mother/child dyad and introduces it to difference. With that break comes the first glimmering that there is a mother and a child: a separation experienced as both new and traumatic, for it mobilizes the beginnings of desire (the first attempt to bridge the gap which has opened up) and the beginnings of language (the first attempt to fill that gap with words). It is only after the event, therefore, that the newly fledged human subject is in a position to conceive of a beforetime—of something different from its now permanently differentiated state—an experience anciently articulated as an ejection from the garden, a paradise irretrievably lost. The Imaginary is necessarily recursive, in other words—a secondary formation which, as in a kind of *Nachträglichkeit* or *après-coup*, succeeds the Symbolic—and with it comes the whole order of art: of all that can be imagined, narrated, and believed.[10] Yet art's fictions, its ideal and fantasized worlds, are a by-product, an effect, of that primary loss—are brought into being and eternally fueled by an abyssal emptiness which is never to be filled—and to that

[9] See, e.g., Belsey, Halpern, Schiffer, Stanivukovic, Kuchar, Shohet, and Enterline, "Psychoanalytic Criticisms," revised and extended in Enterline, *Shakespeare's Schoolroom* 62–94. Although Ellis, *Sexuality and Citizenship* ostensibly presents a Lacanian reading of the poem, his account is in fact superimposed with a normalizing narrative—modeled on object-relations theory—which promotes a "proper" (85) and "phallic masculinity" (89) which condemns "those forms of desire that challenge the autonomy or integrity of the masculine subject" (65): views which are entirely antithetical to Lacan. Sheidley discusses the absent phallus as standing at "the arithmetical, structural, and dramatic center of the poem" (10), but without recourse to Lacanian theory.

[10] For Lacan's use of the Freudian terms, *nachträglich* and *Nachträglichkeit*, see *Écrits* 256, 532, 684, 685, 839.

extent are indeed "imaginary," illusory.[11] As presented in *Venus and Adonis*, this etiology of the inevitably fallen, "castrated," desiring, speaking human being, I suggest, presented the writing subject that was Shakespeare with some stark choices about his medium: the creative power and infinite potentiality of language, on the one hand, its hollowness and ghostliness, on the other.

❦

To gauge the strengths and subtleties of Shakespeare's poem—the departures and modifications which make his rendering of this primary myth distinctive—it is useful to begin with earlier versions of the story, above all that of Ovid. As he tells the tale in Book 10 of the *Metamorphoses* (in fact, a tale within a tale, as narrated by Orpheus), Ovid makes no bones about the fact that Venus and Adonis form a version of the original incestuous couple, that of mother and child. When Adonis was born (himself the issue of an incestuous union between father and daughter), he was so beautiful as to resemble Cupid himself—or at least painted versions of the *putto*—so much so that you could either give him a quiver of arrows or take it from Cupid and it would make no difference.[12] Adonis grows, in the flash of narrative time, into no less beautiful a youth, yet since Venus's love for him involves moving from one order or "layer" of existence to another—divine to human—it requires special assistance to do so, and this is provided by none other than Cupid, one son effectively enabling her

[11] Inaccessible to language, Lacan's elusive third register of the Real remains unavailable to speaking beings (to Venus and Adonis in Shakespeare's poem), but the same need not apply to the animal kingdom or to the myriad beings within the poem (including the boar) which operate perfectly well—perfectly "naturally"—without speech. That these non-speaking beings should so outnumber those who speak in the poem (see note 1 above) might be Shakespeare's way of suggesting the presence of that which cannot be represented. It is not the animals themselves which cannot be represented but rather their view of the world which is unmediated by language. Critics who identify the third party in this story of triangulated desire as the poem's *narrator* (as opposed to the boar), and credit him with "control" over (Lanham 90) or "mastery" of (Cousins 15) his material, thereby overvalue the power of language and miss the importance of that which eludes representation. On the masterly "Ovidian narrator" appearing in English epyillia more generally, see Ellis, "Imagining Heterosexuality" 54.

[12] "qualia namque / corpora nudorum tabula pinguntur Amorum, / talis erat, sed, ne faciat discrimina cultus, / aut huic adde leves, aut illis deme pharetras [for he looked like one of the naked loves portrayed on canvas. But, that dress may make no distinction, you should either give him a light quiver or take it away from them]" (10.515–18).

union with another: "For while the goddess' son, with quiver on shoulder, was kissing his mother, he chanced unwittingly to graze her breast with a projecting arrow. The wounded goddess pushed her son away; but the scratch had gone deeper than she thought, and she herself was at first deceived. Now, smitten with the beauty of a mortal, she cares no more for the borders of Cythera."[13] The fact that Adonis's mother, Myrrha—named after the myrrh tree (*murra*) whose bitter gum was used to make a highly aromatic incense or perfume used largely for embalming corpses—shares an etymological link with the myrtle bush (*myrtus*)—sacred to Venus and an ancient euphemism for the female genitals—hints at a link between the two incestuous mothers.[14] The god/goddess who intervenes to metamorphose Myrrha on the birth of her son pointedly goes unnamed, but, given this association between the bitter-sweet myrrh and the "double-hued myrtle," we might suspect that it was Venus.[15] After all, Venus had intervened directly to bring Pygmalion's statue to life—Myrrha being the grandchild, and Adonis the (great-)grandchild, of that dubious union between a human being and his fetish object—so whether or not the goddess was instrumental in the beautiful boy's birth, she certainly had a high degree of involvement with him from the start.[16] One might say that the story comes full circle when Venus breathes life into Pygmalion's ivory

[13] "namque pharetratus dum dat puer oscula matri, / inscius exstanti destrinxit harundine pectus; / laesa manu natum dea reppulit: altius actum / vulnus erat specie primoque fefellerat ipsam. / capta viri forma non iam Cythereia curat / litora" (10.525–30). In his own version of the story, *Stanze nella favola d'Adone* (1545), Ludovico Dolce makes the connection explicit, noting that Adonis looks like Cupid's twin. As Mortimer notes, "That the lover of Venus should be the double of her son and that his beauty should have such a distinctly homoerotic appeal is enough to remind us of the ill-fated incestuous and homosexual passions that play such a large part in the *Metamorphoses*" (175).

[14] See Angello 5–6. See also note 35 below.

[15] The "double-hued myrtle [bicolor myrtus]" (10.98) is one of the trees so moved by Orpheus's song at the beginning of Book 10 (see note 20 below), in which case a version of Venus in her arboreal form is in effect listening to the telling of her own story. On the god/goddess which comes to Myrrha's aid going unnamed, see: "Some god did listen to her prayer; her last petition had its answering gods [numen confessis aliquod patet: ultima certe / vota suos habuere deos]" (10.488–89).

[16] Of course, Adonis could also be said to be the grandchild (rather than great-grandchild) of Pygmalion since his father is also the father of his mother/sister, Myrrha. For Venus's positive response to Pygmalion's prayer that his ivory statue come to life, see *Metamorphoses* 10.277–79.

statue only for Adonis to lose his on the ivory tusks of the boar.[17] When Adonis finally exits this intensely endogamous and multi-generational relationship—meeting castration and death on the tusks of the boar—these intertwined themes of maternity, metamorphosis, vegetal symbolism, and fragrance come together when Venus, in turn, sprinkles the dead boy's blood with "sweet-scented nectar [*nectare odorato*]" (10.732) and transforms him into an anemone or "wind-flower" (from Greek ἄνεμος, wind).[18]

Ovid stresses the fragility of the speaking subject which emerges from the incestuous dyad of the Imaginary into the cold, harsh world of the Symbolic, describing this flower as "short-lived [...] for the winds from which it takes its name shake off the flower so delicately clinging and doomed too easily to fall."[19] In fact, he does not even name the delicate bloom—capable of being de-petaled by the merest breath of wind—referring to it only periphrastically by the destructive winds from which it takes its name, as if it has already been blasted to leave only an empty signifier or *nomina* of itself. Indeed, Book 10 as a whole—and with it the Venus and Adonis story and Orpheus's song in its entirety—closes on that word *venti* (winds), as if all we are left with at the end is empty air, though perhaps with the faintest whiff of perfume on it as it inexorably fades away. The framing of the Venus and Adonis story by that of its narrator, moreover, only adds to this theme. For Orpheus becomes a poet in the first place on the loss of his wife-to-be, Eurydice, who is bitten by a serpent in a garden before their wedding can be consummated. Descending into the Underworld, Orpheus's poetry so charms the shades below that they permit him to take her back to earth, on condition that he does not look back. This, of course, he does, thereby losing her forever—"but, unhappy one, he clasped nothing but the yielding air [*cedentes auras*]" (10.59)—and, utterly bereft, he resolves thereafter to fill that void with verse. Orpheus's narratives proceed to fill the rest of Book 10 and culminate in

[17] Critics sometimes assume that Pygmalion's statue is sculpted from marble or stone, but Ovid is quite clear that it is ivory (*ebur*): see 10.248, 255, 275, 276, 283.

[18] In this, Venus follows Persephone who transformed the nymph Menthe into the sweet-smelling herb, mint: "Or was it once allowed to thee, Persephone, to change a maiden's form to fragrant mint, and shall the change of my hero, offspring of Cinyras, be grudged to me? [an tibi quondam / femineos artus in olentes vertere mentas, / Persephone, licuit: nobis Cinyreius heros / invidiae mutatus erit?]" (10.728–31).

[19] [est tamen usus in illo; / namque male haerentem et nimia levitate caducum / excutunt idem, qui praestant nomina, venti] (10.737–39).

the story of Venus and Adonis which is, essentially, a reprise of his own: the fatal intrusion of a phallic beast into the garden of the idyllic, presexual mother/child dyad, the impossibility of not looking back (creating the Imaginary), the determination to fill that yielding air with words, and the sheer airiness and ghostliness of the result. The tale of Venus and Adonis is the last story Orpheus tells before he dies, savagely murdered by the Maenads at the beginning of Book 11, as a result of which his "soul, breathed out, went faring forth in air [*in ventos anima exhalata recessit*]" (11.43).

Alongside this emphasis on the fragility of the speaking subject, however, Ovid also stresses the surprising durability, if not of the subject, then of the airy words he or she speaks: the unexpected strength and power of this language which the speaking subject inherits as a consolation for his or her loss. Orpheus may lose Eurydice to the yielding air, but before he yields up his own breath to that air, he sings songs and tells stories that have the power to uproot trees—now drawn irresistibly toward him—to make stones sit up and listen, the wild beasts to respond.[20] The story of Venus and Adonis might be the last tale he tells, but it is as if he does so in order to pass the baton on. For the story ends with Venus's declaration that, for all its fragility, the wind-flower into which Adonis has been changed will nonetheless endure as a perpetual memorial of her grief: "My grief, Adonis, shall have an enduring monument [*monimenta*], and each passing year in memory of your death shall give an imitation of my grief" (10.725–27).[21] Adonis effectively becomes immortalized in this flower which reblooms each year, its renewed perfume—no matter how delicate—effectively trumping the winds which threaten to destroy it, and thus perpetuating the beautiful air that came out of Orpheus's mouth when he spoke and sang. Adonis and Eurydice both die twice, yet both live on in the breath of those who remember and speak of them. And that, of course, includes Ovid himself, who, in turn, passes the baton on to his own readers, both contemporaries and those who with luck might read and speak his stories down the ages. In his nesting of storytellers (the story of Venus and Adonis as told by Orpheus as told by Ovid), the poet invests nothing less than his own poetry and his own poetic voice in the fragrant,

[20] For the catalogue of the trees which gather round, see 10.86–105; for the listening rocks and attendant beasts, see 11.42.

[21] Rather as myrrh, perhaps, was used in embalming; not, admittedly, to keep bodies alive but at least to ensure that they remained uncorrupted.

harmonious, moving, and death-defying breath of story, poetry, and song. It is the same wind, breath, air, spirit, or *pneuma* which he invokes at both the beginning of the *Metamorphoses*, when he asks the gods in the opening lines to "breathe on [*adspirate*] these my undertakings" (1.3), and the end, when he declares in the closing lines that his name and his poem will endure forever on the breath of those who read his verse in times to come: for "I shall be read by the tongues of men [*ore legar populi*]" (15.878).[22] By acknowledging the fugitive and fragile aspects of art in the death of Orpheus and the delicacy of the windflower, Ovid hedges his bets. He avoids asserting any callow exceptionalism for his own art by assuming nothing, allowing for different outcomes, accepting that his name and work may or may not survive. But by suggesting that, so long as there are speaking beings on earth, their breath and the stories carried on it might continue and survive through time, he holds out the possibility—the paradoxical miracle—that something as insubstantial as the breath might outlast monuments of stone or brass, if not whole empires. The fact that we are still reading and talking about his poem two millennia later suggests that the gamble paid off.

To this extent, the durability of art—the realm of the Imaginary—seems to go some way toward mitigating the horrors of the Symbolic and the finality and disaster it spells for human beings: the severity of the fall into separation, loss, absence, difference, "castration," and ultimately death. If Ovid balances the fragility of art against its durability, hoping for the best, there was at the same time another older and parallel tradition in which the Venus and Adonis story served to mobilize an even more hopeful, optimistic outcome: a still greater mitigation of loss. As told by the Hellenistic poets, this version focuses on the infancy of Adonis in a way that Ovid does not, drawing on the tradition that, after his birth, the baby was co-fostered by Aphrodite/Venus in the summer months, and Persephone, goddess of the underworld, in the winter.[23] These poems thus put a greater emphasis on—one might say faith in—the regenerative aspects of the story in which the death of Adonis is redeemed by his annual

[22] For a thorough discussion of Ovid's two representations of this breath or wind as alienated, on the one hand, and immortal, on the other, see Enterline, *Rhetoric of the Body* 49–55.

[23] Although Ovid passes over Adonis's early years, his concessions to the Hellenistic tradition appear in the hints of Venus's maternal involvement in the child's conception and birth, and in her transforming his dead body into an annually reblooming flower (as Persephone had done with the nymph Menthe, see note 18 above).

rebirth in floral form.[24] Apotheosized on the model of pagan sun-gods who die to rise again, Adonis became titular god of the Adonia: the pagan vegetation myth, fertility ritual, and largely female cult in which women would grow "gardens of Adonis" by planting delicate, short-lived herbs in shallow pots or potsherds, deliberately leaving them out to wilt and wither in the late summer heat—and be extravagantly mourned—in the knowledge that they would revive the following spring.

In these versions of the myth, the emphasis shifts from loss to recovery as the terrible effects of the entry into the Symbolic, the ejection from the garden, are mitigated by its seasonal renewal. The diminution if not denial of the part the Phallus plays in shattering the idyll once and for all, with no possibility of reversal, regeneration, or redemption thereafter, is most visible in the anonymous poem, "Adonis Dead."[25] Here, a repentant boar, brought in fetters to answer to the vengeful Aphrodite/Venus, explains that he was so driven by desire for Adonis's statue-like beauty that he simply meant to kiss his naked thigh, in no way intending to kill him. In sorrow for what he has done, the boar begs the goddess to chastise him—"take these tusks and cut them off and punish them"—and, when she relents and forgives his crime, the boar thenceforth follows the goddess demurely, gives up hunting for good, and burns the offending tusks himself.[26] In this fantasy of the domestication, penitence, and self-castration of the beast, one could scarcely imagine a more transparent or wishful denial of the Phallus, the fact that the boar *speaks* being not the least sign of his diminution.[27] The monster has become Disneyfied, a mere pet. Although too

[24] These poets and poems include Theocritus (born after 260 BCE), specifically, his *Idyll* 15; Bion of Smyrna (120–50 BCE), specifically "The Lament for Adonis," a dirge for the dead god; Moschus (flourished 150 BCE), specifically his "Lament for Bion," which echoes the latter; and the anonymous "Adonis Dead," closely related to Bion's "Lament." For texts and commentary, see Hopkinson.

[25] "Adonis Dead" is composed in a meter associated with the *Anacreontea*, a collection of poems ranging from around the second century BCE to the sixth century CE. The date of its composition is unknown.

[26] "Deal harshly with me; take these tusks and cut them off and punish them, Cypris: why should I have tusks that are so extremely passionate? [...] After that he followed her and no longer went into the forest; approaching the fire, he burned his tusks [τούτους λαβοῦσα τέμνε, / τούτους κόλαζε, Κύπρι· / τί γὰρ φέρω περισσῶς / ἐρωτικοὺς ὀδόντας [...] ἐκ τῶδ' ἐπηκολούθει, / κὰς ὕλαν οὐκ ἔβαινε, / καὶ τῷ πυρὶ προσελθών / ἔκαιε τοὺς ὀδόντας]," "Adonis Dead," lines 33–36.

[27] As Caruso comments, the boar in this poem has "altogether lost its menacing outlook" as the tragedy is "reduced to the dimension of an unwanted accident" and the culprit identi-

complex to explore in any detail here, Edmund Spenser's variation on the myth in the Garden of Adonis episode of *The Faerie Queene* (1590) also seems drawn to these regenerative and redemptive aspects of the story:

> There now he liueth in eternall blis,
> Ioying his goddesse, and of her enioyd:
> Ne feareth he henceforth that foe of his,
> Which with his cruell tuske him deadly cloyd:
> For that wilde Bore, the which him once annoyd,
> She firmely hath emprisoned for ay,
> That her sweet loue his malice mote auoyd,
> In a strong rocky Caue, which is they say,
> Hewen vnderneath that Mount, that none him losen may. (3.6.48)

With the boar safely captive and contained (in the *mons veneris* of the phallic mother, no less), the illusions of wholeness and oneness—the idyll of the mother/child dyad—can go on forever, spared the depredations of the Phallus in the same way that death, too, can be endlessly redeemed and regenerated by the cycle of life. Even Cupid is on board: by acting out his own version of tusk-burning "and laying his sad dartes / Asyde," he "with faire *Adonis* playes his wanton partes" (3.6.49, lines 8–9) in incestuous, homosocial, and fraternal safety.

❦

By comparison with these versions of the myth, which in varying degrees work to mitigate the disaster of humanity's imperfect, unhappy condition, Shakespeare's poem seems determined to explore the full impact of the Phallus—its role in catapulting the human subject into the eternal dissatisfactions of the Symbolic—unvarnished and with no holds barred. Shakespeare does this by introducing a major change to the story, for which there seems no precedent, namely, to present Adonis as *resistant* to Venus's desire. This alteration makes a significant difference, and its repercussions will occupy the remainder of this chapter. One of its first effects is to complicate the straightforwardly linear narrative of previous versions

fied as "a 'humanized' beast" (34). This and the other "Adonian" poems mentioned in note 24 above were among those published in the *Corpus Theocriteum* (1495), making them available to humanist poets, first in Italy and then in France, as the sixteenth century progressed (for a tentative list of those who wrote on the Adonian theme, see Caruso 29). In his "L'Adone" (1545), the Italian poet, Giovanni Tarcagnota, came the closest to imitating the light if not frivolous tone of "Adonis Dead" (see also Mortimer 176–78).

which (when not denying the Phallus altogether as in *The Faerie Queene*) generally move chronologically from the relationship of the incestuous couple to its destruction by the boar: from love to lament.[28] In Shakespeare's version, by contrast, the "love" never takes place because Adonis seems to be under the influence of the incest taboo *already*. He is embarrassed, if not horrified, by Venus's advances from the outset and determined to remove from her at the earliest possible opportunity, as if his entry into the Symbolic had already occurred and he had gone through the process of oedipalization, with its threat of castration, before he meets the boar. By introducing this fold or wrinkle in narrative time, *Venus and Adonis* is thus truer to the retrospective structure noted above, whereby, although logically and chronologically its precursor, the Imaginary is nonetheless a recursive construction of the Symbolic. In this respect, Shakespeare's poem is also truer to human experience, for the speaking, desiring subject does not, of course, spring fully formed on the first entry of the *infans* into oedipalization. While the first glimmerings of a separateness between mother and child occur very early, within the first few months, there follows the long slow process of language acquisition, and the longer, slower process—extended by the uniquely bi-phasal model of human sexuality—whereby it is only at and after puberty that the subject is able to look back over what Freud calls a "latency period" of several years ("Three Essays" 175–79/157–59) to what now seems the "prehistoric epoch" of infancy (176/156), and to see the polymorphous perversity of infantile sexuality for what it was.[29] Only then, courtesy of the Symbolic, does the subject experience the shattering impact and the full social and cultural implications of the incest taboo, the law and its punitive "castration": his or her socially approved gender identity and sexual orientation going forward, the demands of exogamy, the knowledge that the preoedipal paradise (only now capable of construction) can never be regained, and that a life of inexpiable crime, sin, and guilt, of permanent subjection to the unreliability of meaning and the insatiability of desire, is what awaits.

[28] As Mortimer notes, when Shakespeare presents Venus and Adonis in conflict rather than in love, he makes a "fundamental modification" to the previously dominant two-part structure of the story (195).

[29] On the "latency period," see also "Three Essays" 188n/167n, 200/177, 208/184, 222/196, 226n/199n, 232–33/205–06, 238/211, 240/212; and "The Dissolution of the Oedipus Complex" 173/167, 177–78/171, 179/173.

In Ovid's—or rather Orpheus's—swift telling of the story, Adonis's development from baby (*infans*) to youth (*iuvenis*) to man (*vir*) occupies no more than two lines, and Adonis is clearly a *vir* when he makes love to Venus and when he hunts the boar.[30] In Shakespeare's greatly expanded version of the story, by contrast, Adonis is referred to as an "infant" twice (lines 562, 942) and a "boy" nine times (lines 32, 95, 155, 344, 403, 467, 583, 613, 1165). He is never referred to as a "man" except to indicate something he is not: Venus describes him as "more lovely than a man" (line 9), as a "Thing like a man, but of no woman bred! / Thou art no man, though of a man's complexion" (lines 214–15), and she hypothesizes what would happen if "thou were as I am, and I a man" (line 369). By comparison with Ovid, then, Shakespeare seems more interested in process—in the complicated twists and turns by means of which the mature speaking, desiring subject as *vir* comes into being—and especially in the liminal period of puberty during which the complex back-and-forth relation between Imaginary and Symbolic comes to be sealed.[31] Indeed, Shakespeare seems careful to specify that Adonis is at the stage of early puberty, old enough dimly to recall the incestuous couplings of infancy and to want to run a mile when these reappear in the form of Venus's unwelcome approaches, but not old enough to know that what seems like a blessed escape from such horrors—the hunt—is no such thing.[32]

"Hunting he lov'd, but love he laugh'd to scorn" (line 4), we are told at the beginning of the poem, and yet by seeking to fly from such dubiously incestuous sexual relations as fast as he can, Adonis ends up flying straight into them, for by substituting love for the goddess with love for the all-male hunt, he simply substitutes one kind of tabooed sameness (familial) for another (homosocial). It is no accident that the same word "venery" applies to both activities, for symbolically they are to all intents

[30] Adonis, "lately born, then a most lovely baby-boy, is now a youth, now man [nuper erat genitus, modo formosissimus infans, / iam iuvenis, iam vir, iam se formosior ipso est]" (10.522–23).

[31] As Enterline suggests, Shakespeare's poem "give[s] the lie to simple taxonomies that separate pre- from post-oedipal narratives or hetero- from homo-erotic desires" (*Shakespeare's Schoolroom*, 68). Enterline draws here on Jean Laplanche's revision of the concept of *Nachträglichkeit*, in which the *infans* experiences the intrusion of unconscious adult fantasy as an enigmatic message which remains indecipherable until a later point in its sexual development.

[32] In his own reading of Venus's advances in the poem, Lewis inadvertently situates himself at the same developmental stage: "Certain horrible interviews with voluminous female relatives in one's early childhood inevitably recur to the mind" (498).

and purposes the same, as the well-established motif of the *chasse d'amour* with its convenient English puns (hart/heart, deer/dear, chased/chaste, and so on) had long since exploited. For Adonis to rush off with his male "friends" (lines 588, 718) to pursue a (as it happens, monstrously virile) male predator/prey and stick his javelin into it—"He ran upon the boar with his sharp spear" (line 1112)—is simply a roundabout way of Adonis sticking his bodily equivalent into Venus (the one thing she wants).[33] In Ovid's version, Cupid had already started the ball rolling, so to speak, by sticking his arrow into Venus, and, as if led by example, Adonis is so unphased by indulging in dubiously incestuous sexual relations with the goddess himself that the two of them go off "hunting" together (chasing "soft," unthreatening creatures like hares or hinds). In Shakespeare's version, however, Adonis is like a boy in the lower forms at school who has yet to read his Ovid, Virgil, or Seneca, and is yet to realize that hunting *is* loving, not its opposite, with predictably disastrous results. Having failed to learn from the examples of literature, Shakespeare's Adonis falls victim not only to the boar but to the mythic cliché of the hunter hunted.[34] Although his death looks like an accident, it is in fact no accident at all that Adonis should meet his end in "a myrtle grove" (line 865)—ancient symbol of the female genitals—and there experience "castration."[35] Sexual

[33] Although not a psychoanalytic reading, Williams suggests that the poem depicts a sexual awakening on Adonis's part. As Venus correctly points out, however, at this point in the poem Adonis still "know'st not what it is / With javelin's point a churlish swine to gore" (lines 615–16).

[34] A more literate Adonis would have had plenty of examples from which to learn. The youths Cyparissus and Hyacinthus (whose stories are also told by Orpheus in Book 10 of the *Metamorphoses*), both love hunting and are both beloved by Apollo, the former accidently killing the god's pet stag and resolving to die, the latter accidentally killed by the god's discus while sporting with him. Narcissus (whose story is told in in Book 3 of the *Metamorphoses*) chooses the hunt over love, never to exit from the closed loop of sameness, becoming enthralled with his own image (i.e., locked within the Imaginary, stuck at the mirror stage). In Book 4 of the *Aeneid*, Dido consummates her illicit love for Aeneas during a hunt and suffers from her desire like a hind struck by an arrow. In Seneca's *Phaedra*, the young, chaste Hippolytus is devoted to the hunt yet punished for committing/refusing to commit incest with his eponymous stepmother. For a discussion of the mythic connections between hunting, love, tabooed sameness, and punishment, see Bates 17–19; and on Cupid shooting arrows into the lover as an archetypal image of the hunter hunted—as, projected and externalized, the subject's desire simply boomerangs back to wound itself—see 42–43.

[35] The famous Greek drinking song which boasted that the speaker would "carry my sword in a myrtle branch [ἐν μύρτου κλαδί]" (i.e., penetrate women) is cited in Aristophanes, *Lysistrata*, line 632 (see Aristophanes 354–55); and in Athenaeus, *Deipnosophistae*, Book 15: "I will bear my sword in a myrtle branch [ἐν μύρτου κλαδὶ τὸ ξίφος φορήσω]" (see Athenaeus vol. 8, pp. 164–65). See also Angello 4–6.

"awakening" is not sex for the first time but the retrospective knowledge that the sexual act recalls an earlier, prehistoric relation—the mother/child dyad—now branded incestuous and guilty. Shakespeare's poem catches Adonis at exactly the stage when this realization begins to dawn. Oedipus had plucked out his eyeballs at a similar stage. Adonis loses his testicles.[36]

That Adonis is presented as a newly pubertal boy—a *iuvenis* rather than a *vir*—is equally evident in the reproachful speech he makes to Venus on the difference between love and lust:

> Call it not love, for Love to heaven is fled,
> Since sweating Lust on earth usurp'd his name,
> Under whose simple semblance he hath fed
> Upon fresh beauty, blotting it with blame;
> Which the hot tyrant stains, and soon bereaves,
> As caterpillars do the tender leaves.
>
> Love comforteth like sunshine after rain,
> But Lust's effect is tempest after sun;
> Love's gentle spring doth always fresh remain,
> Lust's winter comes ere summer half be done;
> Love surfeits not, Lust like a glutton dies;
> Love is all truth, Lust full of forged lies. (lines 793–804)

Critics agree on the immaturity of this speech, variously describing it as "rigid" and "inadequate" (Sheidley 15), as "shallow, copy-book wisdom" that is "parrotlike" (Lanham 88), characterized by "smugness" (Dubrow 45), delivered by one "so young that he knows nothing of love" (Belsey 265), "clipped and rigorous" (Mortimer 31), "banal, priggishly idealistic" (Ellis, *Sexuality and Citizenship* 91), and an example of "all-too-simple dualism" (Mukherji 402). Callow it may be, yet Adonis's distinction does contain an element of truth. For, however schematically, one might map the "love" and "lust" so differentiated onto the Imaginary and the Symbolic, respectively. Thus, "love," as Adonis here describes it, is a figuration of the preoedipal state: a none-too-original imagining of that state as the blissful beforetime, as nice weather in a lovely garden, as an Eden, a golden world, an ideal of fullness and wholeness, a land of milk and honey

[36] In his translation of the *Metamorphoses* (1567), Arthur Golding makes this quite explicit, describing how the boar pursued Adonis, "And hiding in his cods [testicles] his tusks as far as he could thrust, / He laid him all along for dead upon the yellow dust" (10.839–40).

that recalls the body of the phallic mother and enjoyment of which, having been gratefully desexualized, is now rebranded as innocent and true.[37] Except the imagining—and poetic making—of this idyll is only possible because it has been irretrievably lost. It is a recursive construction visible only from the other side of the garden gate and from the viewpoint of a world which—because governed by difference—*is* radically different: postlapsarian, fully oedipalized, and "usurp'd" (a key word) by the boar-like lust.[38] Thus "lust" as Adonis here describes it is a figuration of that fallen, brazen world: criminal, polluting, hot, hungry, empty, dead, and full of lies, it is the cursed love of having (*amor sceleratus habendi*) with which Ovid characterizes his Iron Age in the *Metamorphoses* (1.131) and which Shakespeare describes elsewhere as "Past reason hunted [...] Past reason hated" (sonnet 129, lines 6, 7).[39] Preoedipal "love" can only be imagined from the place of oedipalized "lust" and is thus the ghostly product of it (ghostly because literary, poetic, imagined, represented). Adonis is right to sense an absolute difference between the Imaginary and Symbolic registers: his immaturity (unmistakable in the tone of his pert little speech) shows in his inability to grasp this point, or to see and accept the inextricable relation between the two.

At this stage in the poem, then, Adonis is not yet fully oedipalized. His resistance to Venus might make it look as if he is under the influence of the incest taboo, but this is belied by the fact that he flies straight from one kind of "incestuous" sameness into another. His characterizations of "lust" suggest an intuition on his part that there is something terrible coming, but he remains blissfully unaware that he is heading straight for it. The effect (and probably the purpose) of Shakespeare's signature

[37] This is precisely the fantasy which Venus had earlier offered to Adonis in the form of her body as a "park" on which the "deer" (line 231) infant is free to drink and graze. One recalls the "swelling dugs" of the "milch doe" to which she is later compared (line 875). One might also, perhaps, situate here the epigraph from Ovid's *Amores*, 1.15.35–36, which Shakespeare cites at the beginning of his poem—"Vilia miretur vulgus; mihi flavus Apollo / Pocula Castalia plena ministret aqua [for me may golden Apollo minister full cups from the Castalian fount]"—a fantasy of poetry as satisfyingly "full" if not overflowing. In the next line, Ovid imagines donning a poet's crown of myrtle (evergreen, like Apollo's poetry) and goes on to claim that he, too, will "live on, and the great part of me survive my death" [vivam, parsque mei multa superstes erit] (42).

[38] On the significance of the word, see Hatto 360.

[39] Although it barely touches on *Venus and Adonis*, the Lacanian reading of Shakespeare's sonnets in Fineman might be apposite here, tracing as it does the path from a poetics of the same in the sonnets to the Young Man to a poetics of difference in those to the Dark Lady.

departure from Ovid—his juvenilizing of Adonis—is, I would argue, precisely to stress the seriousness of the real thing when, all too soon, it occurs. Where previous versions of the story had moved more or less chronologically from love to lament, here the story moves rather from one kind of lament to another: from Venus's complaint that she lacks her desire to her complaint that she has lost her desire.[40] As if dissatisfied with previous versions of the story, Shakespeare seems determined to dramatize oedipalization and its discontents in all their horror as an experience violent, initiatory, transformative, irreparable, and irreversible. The boar roars into the story and changes everything forever. The mangled, castrated body. The blood on the grass. The sense of shock. The sudden sickening lurch from comic to tragic. It is these which do justice to the full impact of the Phallus upon the preoedipal couple, the threat of castration, and the subject's decisive entry into the Symbolic.

The tension between a linear, "biographical" story which unfolds in narrative time and the retrospective construction of that story only after the event (what I describe above as a fold or wrinkle in narrative time) is evident not only in the content of Adonis's speech, moreover, but also in its circumstance. "Love to heaven is fled" (line 793), the teenager crassly declares, yet "Love" is the very figure he is addressing, standing right in front of him. The fact that Venus is absent and present at the same time is testimony to Adonis's tortuous passage through the long process of oedipalization. While the preoedipal mother "is fled" to the extent that the *infans* has long since exited the mother/child dyad, she is all too present to the embarrassed *iuvenis* who is just waking up to the sexual nature of that relation (incestuous, polymorphously perverse) and doing all he can to deny it: no sooner has he ended this speech than Adonis finally wriggles free from the goddess and "Leaves Love upon her back, deeply distress'd" (line 814). There is no escape, however (trying to escape only leads Adonis the more surely to his destined destination), for mother and child have long been separate entities and it is only a matter of time before full oedipalization and its attendant "castration" come into play (only then does Adonis discover to his cost that leaving Venus was only a roundabout way of loving Venus). The process cannot be stalled or reversed, and the

[40] These two forms of complaint comprise Francis Petrarch's *Canzoniere*, the foundational text of early modern lyric. In the first part of the sonnet sequence (*in vita*), the beloved Laura is alive but alas unresponsive to the lover's desire; in the second part (*in morte*), she has alas departed this world, and the lover mourns her death.

iuvenis is on his way to becoming a desiring, speaking subject, a *vir*, whether he likes it or not: there would be no story to tell, otherwise.

"Leave me, and then the story aptly ends" (line 716), Adonis had brusquely told Venus shortly before he embarks on his speech; but leaving "love" *is* the story, the slow process by which the subject separates from the mother/child dyad to become a speaking being equipped with a history, a prehistory, and the words with which to tell it. As Shakespeare distinctively narrates it, this story both is happening and has already happened: it is unfolding in the narrative present as Adonis experiences it in time, but it is also predetermined, is only going to end in one way, and is seen, constructed, shaped, and narrated from the perspective of that end from the very start (something of which Adonis remains unaware). It has often been noted that the poem begins with a lover leaving—"Even as the sun with purple-color'd face / Had ta'en his last leave of the weeping morn" (lines 1–2)—the theme of a loving couple, their separation, and the subsequent tears being proleptically announced in the opening lines and thereby "establishing the poem's pattern of endless seeking," as Gary Kuchar writes, "a pattern which fails to cease even at Adonis's death" (5).[41] It is not an accident that "love" and "leave" are etymologically related, for it is only once love has left or been left that it can be known.[42] In terms of linear, "biographical" time, of course, Venus does flee to heaven at the end of the poem—"away she hies [...] through the empty skies" (lines 1189, 1191)—but in a sense "Love" has never been anywhere else: the phallic mother, that storied, poeticized, mythicized construct of the Imaginary, has always been a *dea abscondita*, absent, lost, otherwhere, in "heaven" because not of this earth.

The fold or wrinkle in time, which is distinctive to Shakespeare's telling of the story, can also finally be seen in Venus's prognostication of what is set to follow from Adonis's death: "Since thou art dead, lo here I prophesy, / Sorrow on love hereafter shall attend" (lines 1135–36). As almost

[41] Sheidley concurs, noting that "Shakespeare's poem [...] contains numerous foreshadowings of disaster from the outset" (5); as does Mortimer, "All the details combine to make the first stanza prefigure the whole poem" (38), a point, he notes, also stressed by Samuel Taylor Coleridge.

[42] On the rich and complex semantic field of these words, see *OED*: leave v^1 develops two parallel stems from early Old English læfan: "I. Senses including the idea of something or someone remaining" and "II. Senses involving simply departing or relinquishing"; from the same root comes leave n^1, "Permission asked for or granted to do something," which is also cognate with love n^1.

every critic notes, Venus's curse on love—her promise that forever after "Perverse it shall be" (line 1157)—describes as a future condition pretty much what love has been throughout the poem: it has never been anything other than unsatisfactory (it has in fact been "lust" all along, not "love").[43] Venus's words are both metaleptic and proleptic since she describes what she and Adonis have just experienced of love's problems and frustrations as well as what all lovers will encounter in future. This clash of perspectives is endemic to those myths which combine the ontogenetic prehistory of the subject with the phylogenetic prehistory of the species, each individual experiencing—as if for the first time, as if this time things might turn out differently—the same predetermined and definitively human story. While earlier versions of the myth take heart from the fact that either the generation of art down the generations is a consolation for loss (the Imaginary mitigating the Symbolic that way) or—in the more "redemptive" Hellenistic and Spenserian renderings—that life is constantly replenished and the story thus able to be retold from the beginning with every new individual born, Shakespeare's telling, by contrast, takes a distinctly more gloomy, tragic outlook. For him, things will never turn out differently since the story is predetermined for individual and species alike—a cursed state, indeed, so what kind of consolation is that?—giving rise to those other eternal questions that we have been exploring here: how did the hissing serpent or the usurping boar get to be in the garden in the first place; what is the origin of evil; what cause moved our grandparents in that happy state, favored of heaven so highly, to fall off from their creator, and transgress his will?

This is important because it helps explain why Shakespeare's signature change to the story—the resistance of Adonis—makes no difference to the outcome. Critics who try to moralize the story are confused by the fact Adonis ends up being "punished" whether he has sexual relations with Venus (as in all previous versions) or not (as in Shakespeare).[44] Without Shakespeare's distinctive intervention, it would have been less obvious why this issue turns out to be quite immaterial, for if the *infans* is to

[43] Berry speaks for many when he writes that "[t]he catalogue of sorrows she describes—of inconstancy, deception, madness, jealousy, war—is not called into being by Venus but called into consciousness. The sorrows of love are not new to the poem" (57).

[44] As Bate argues, Eros proves to be "a contrary little bastard" (49) and the theme of the story in both Ovid and Shakespeare seems to be that "whichever way you turn love will destroy you. It is essentially something out of your control, a force that drives you rather than vice versa" (58).

become a speaking, desiring being, such "punishment" is quite unavoidable: as a condition of that metamorphosis, "castration" is going to happen anyway, and the story is proof that it has already occurred.[45] Shakespeare's Adonis resists because the poet homes in on the period in personal, "biographical" time when the pubertal *iuvenis* is closer to the catastrophic impact of that event. But the oedipal "crime" was committed long ago within the incestuous mother/child dyad and long before it was known and subsequently "criminalized" by the law, judgment, morality, taboo, and punishment which the Phallus brings in its wake, as it hurls individual and species into the Symbolic, destroying and creating that Edenic idyll, the Imaginary, in one fell swoop.

❦

Shakespeare's unique decision to make Adonis resistant has another important effect on the poem, and that is to precipitate the gushing fountain of Venus's rhetoric. The goddess calls upon all the resources of oratory to woo, persuade, and seduce the coy boy back into the incestuous and polymorphously perverse relation which, in his long-forgotten but now reawakening prehistory, he had once enjoyed with her. It is thus she who imagines the Imaginary—who recalls, names, dresses, shapes, and poeticizes that long-lost idyll—verbalizing it, appropriately enough, with words at their most self-conscious, ostentatious, extravagant, and ornamental: with language in all its glory. Role reversal is the most obvious upshot of this scenario, as, in a hilarious sendup of Petrarchan tradition, Venus now assumes the part of the aggressive lover hunting for love, and Adonis that of the chaste, fugitive quarry.[46] Most critics focus on the gender swap between the two, although—with a sexually frustrated goddess and a beardless, flaccid boy—what the poem effectively gives us is two "female" bodies with nary a penis between them, so that however full-on Venus's actions or demands (plucking Adonis from his horse, tucking him under her arm, pushing him over, lying on top of him, kissing him, harassing him, assaulting him, and so on), we still find ourselves within the world of tabooed incestuous sameness. This world seems to meet the squirming Adonis whichever way he turns, in the familial sameness of the

[45] Indeed, insofar as myth tells the story—puts it into words—this will be true of all versions, the more apparently "redemptive" kind included. Shakespeare's poem effectively calls out as deluded the denial of the Phallus in the Hellenistic and Spenserian versions of the story.

[46] On Venus's sexual aggressiveness, see Wortis, and Crewe xix–liv.

mother/child couple, and in the homosocial sameness of these all-"female" bodies, or that of the all-male hunting party.

That the *iuvenis* still sees sexual sameness all around him would suggest that what is lacking here—"The warm effects which she in him finds missing / She seeks to kindle with continual kissing" (lines 605–606)—is therefore the humble *penis*, not to be confused with the mystified cultural abstraction of the Phallus which has evidently yet to make its decisive and castrating entry onto the scene.[47] Lacan would, perhaps, have especially appreciated the way in which Shakespeare describes Venus's expectation and disappointment over the penis that is missing in action (as it happens, at the exact midpoint of the poem): "All is imaginary she doth prove, / He will not manage her, although he mount her" (lines 597–98). Indeed, the suggestion that it is the penis and not the Phallus that is at issue would seem to be confirmed by the famous cameo of Adonis's horse mounting a mare, "A breeding jennet, lusty, young, and proud" (line 260), because animals—who are never in danger of becoming desiring, speaking beings—are blessedly spared the depredations of the Phallus we have been tracing here.[48] The stallion's organ is very much in evidence, even if discreetly displaced in the poem onto his "ears up-prick'd," his "hanging mane," his "compass'd [arched] crest" which "stand[s] on end," his "hot courage," his "high desire," his "melting buttock" (lines 271, 272, 276, 315), and so on. Never one to lose an opportunity, Venus uses this equine example to urge Adonis to "learn to love, the lesson is but plain" (line 407), and some critics have taken this as an invitation to "natural" lovemaking ("horseplay," one might call it), whether that is to be approved of or not. But the lesson is far from plain, and so it proves—the horses canter out of the frame together, never to be seen again, and Adonis remains entirely unmoved by Venus's instruction—for human desire passes through the artificial structures of language in a way that equine desire does not.[49]

[47] *Pace* Sheidley, who argues that the poem "obviously lacks one crucial factor which, if present, would allow Venus's hopes and those of the sympathetic reader to be fulfilled: that is, simply, an erect phallus" (9–10); and Schiffer, who regards this as "a situation that Lacan would no doubt recognize as signifying the absence of the phallus" (364).

[48] Fletcher argues that "[w]hat distinguishes humanity from the animals in *Venus and Adonis* [...] is not reasoning, or feeling, or the ability to communicate, since the animals share these characteristics. Words and the understanding of words alone distinguish us from the animals, though these are large distinctions. Words are used to lie and cheat" (10).

[49] As Enterline notes, "Venus's tantalizing 'lack' begins to get at something like what Lacan means by saying that language separates us from the unmediated world of need and engenders the unending world of desire" ("Psychoanalytic Criticisms" 468).

There is no "natural" similarity between them at all. The vicissitudes of the penis, its absence or presence, its softness or hardness—played out here as a kind of *fort/da* between Adonis and his stallion—are the stuff of high comedy.[50] The Phallus, by contrast, brings nothing but tragedy in its wake, and Shakespeare's little digression serves to emphasize the entirely different order to which it belongs when, in the form of the boar, it eventually does come crashing onto the scene.[51]

If critics tend to focus on the gender reversal occasioned by Adonis's resistance and Venus's rhetoric, another kind of reversal—that of class—has generally elicited less attention. For that we have to go back to Kenneth Burke's often overlooked reading of the poem which begins with the same premise as the present chapter, namely, that "we find three major characters in this dramatic narrative, each of them at a different qualitative stage in the hierarchy of motives: a goddess [...], a human [...], and an animal" (212–13). To this Burke adds that each of these figures "is of a different 'class'" (213), in the sense both that they are beings of a different class and that they belong to different classes of being (not unlike the different orders or "layers" of existence, divine, human, and animal, which Ovid differentiates in the *Metamorphoses*). In his broadly Marxist analysis, Burke distributes the three protagonists across different social classes, seeing Venus's divine status as a mystification of social superiority to draw out, in her desperate wooing of Adonis, the "notable inversion whereby a superior is depicted begging favors of an inferior" (216). Traditionally, the rhetoric of courtship works the other way round. The socially superior party has no need of rhetoric because they are already possessed of power: it is not necessary to cajole, persuade, or convince when you can dismiss or command (as Venus reminds Adonis, she has been capable of commanding even gods before, having "overswayed" Mars and made him "servile to my coy disdain," lines 109, 112). By contrast, for the socially inferior party to move a superior—otherwise supremely indifferent to them—he or she must make a supreme effort, do the work, undertake the labor required, use all the resources of language available in order to make

[50] As Thomas Nashe makes clear in his own contribution to the epyllion genre, "The Choice of Valentines" (composed c. 1592–93, and, like *Venus and Adonis*, also dedicated to Henry Wriothesley, Earl of Southampton), which plays off the protagonist's premature ejaculation against the steely reliability of his mistress's (naturally, unspeaking) dildo.

[51] See Shohet, who notes "the abstract qualities linking the boar not merely to the penis but to the phallus, with the full weight of cultural privilege which that term connotes" (88).

that party notice, attend, listen, respond, and ideally do as requested: the formula of every begging letter, Petrarchan poem, and prayer. For early moderns, the fantasy of such effective rhetoric was embodied in the figure of Orpheus, at least the Orpheus who was capable of moving beasts, stones, and trees.

By comparison with the gender reversal, then (which, as we have seen, changes very little in the poem), this reversal of class positions turns out to be a much bigger deal—not far off from a "revolutionary challenge" (217), as Burke remarks—for now the entire social, indeed, cosmic order is turned upside down. A goddess petitions a youth, the divine stoops to conquer the human. To appreciate the unthinkability, the sheer outrage of this, it is worth remembering the context in which *Venus and Adonis* was composed and presented to the world (as Shakespeare's first and very carefully managed appearance in print), namely, as a work deferentially dedicated by a common playwright to an earl, stratospherically his social superior, in the humble hope of preferment:

> Right Honorable, I know not how I shall offend in dedicating my unpolished lines to your Lordship, nor how the world will censure me for choosing so strong a prop to support so weak a burden, only if your Honor seem but pleased, I account myself highly praised, and vow to take advantage of all idle hours, till I have honored you with some graver labor. But if the first heir of my invention prove deformed, I shall be sorry it had so noble a godfather: and never after ear [plough] so barren a land, for fear it yield me still so bad a harvest. I leave it to your Honorable survey, and your Honor to your heart's content, which I wish may always answer your own wish, and the world's hopeful expectation.[52]

Shakespeare's dedication of *Venus and Adonis* to Henry Wriothesley is a classic example of the rhetoric of courtship (he clearly knew how to do it when he wanted). Yet in the poem which follows he unfolds a scenario in which Venus woos Adonis with the phrases and gestures of a groveling suitor—"If thou wilt deign this favor" (line 15), "Still she entreats, and prettily entreats" (line 73), "And like a lowly lover down she kneels [...] Her eyes petitioners to his eyes suing" (lines 350, 356)—for all the world as if the Earl of Southampton were going down on his bended knee to beg favors of the upstart poet. It is as if the patron were courting the client, or the Petrarchan Beloved her suitor, or God His supplicant. As if the Sonnets

[52] Spelling modernized.

were composed by the beautiful, aristocratic Young Man and addressed imploringly to the impoverished, ageing Shakespeare, not the other way round.

Not the least outrage of Shakespeare's poem is the fact that Venus uses rhetoric to persuade Adonis (indeed, a most impressive array of rhetorical devices) *and fails.*[53] As a rule, in the traditional scheme of things when an inferior party addresses a social superior their rhetoric normally fails, or at least its success can never be guaranteed. Such is the disappointing outcome of most begging letters, Petrarchan poems, and prayers, but at least it keeps the social and cosmic hierarchy intact. But even when the situation is reversed so that the direction of travel moves from high to low instead of from low to high, rhetoric proves no more successful. Shakespeare's poem gives an extended scenario in which a goddess—who has the world of mortals at her command, not to mention other gods—uncharacteristically resorts to a rhetoric wholly alien to her position, *and still fails.* Neither her superior position *nor her words* prevail. With no power to move or seduce the reluctant boy, Venus is not only humbled and demeaned: she is utterly disempowered. Her celestial ranking makes no difference to her status as a speaking being: this, it transpires, outflanks everything else. To that extent, the goddess—or any superior party, from Wriothesley right up to God—is no different from any other speaking being. That truly is a revolutionary idea, more so even than Burke's political agenda of the lower classes leveling up by bringing the upper classes down. It is so revolutionary, in fact, that I suggest the real reversal at stake in *Venus and Adonis* is not that of gender or of class but rather of the speaking subject's relation to language.[54] The speaking subject—anyone who comes into that category from God down—is not, as they might like to think, the creator or master of words, as per the Orpheus who is capable of moving beasts, stones, and trees. They are, rather, the creature of words; they are, precisely, *subject* to language, to an alien, differential system with its own set of rules over which they have no control, as per the Orpheus

[53] That Venus is in some way trapped by or the victim of her own rhetoric is a common critical theme: see, e.g., Dubrow 22, 23; Stanivukovic 293, 296–97; Kuchar; Mortimer 16, 18; Enterline, "Psychoanalytic Criticisms" 464; and Enterline, *Shakespeare's Schoolroom* 79.

[54] As Enterline notes, Lacan built his career on Freud's insight that "language exceeds and masters its speakers rather than the other way around," it being no accident that the resulting "fascination with the unexpected reversal of priority between speakers and their language [...] has drawn the attention of many psychoanalytic readers of Shakespeare's plays and poems" ("Psychoanalytic Criticisms" 453).

who dies at the hands of those who refuse to heed his words, exhaling his last breath uselessly onto the passing air.[55]

As suggested earlier, Ovid includes both versions of Orpheus in the *Metamorphoses* to keep his options open, eschewing on his part any fate-tempting exceptionalism for his own art. As a poet, he, too, could be a mere peddler of empty fictions, helpless before the liabilities of language and ultimately silenced by them, a victim of forces beyond his control. However, by situating his poem between the inspiring breath of the gods, at the beginning, and the continuing breath of the human race, at the end, Ovid seems on the whole to tilt toward a more optimistic outcome for his art and to hope for the best. As a poet, he, too, could be the master wordsmith capable of moving the immovable, the famed creator of worlds whose words, respoken and retold, are destined to be a monument for all time. What Shakespeare seems to be doing in *Venus and Adonis* is to tilt the balance firmly back in a pessimistic direction, and this is most visible in the striking change he makes to his Ovidian source. For in the *Metamorphoses*, Venus never loses the magical fiat of a god's word. Even though she has lost Adonis, she is still capable of transforming him into a flower simply by virtue of saying it: "your blood shall be changed [*mutabitur*] to a flower" (10.727) and lo! the metamorphosis occurs. As part of his ruthless disempowering of the goddess, by contrast, Shakespeare gives his Venus no such capability. Instead, Adonis simply vaporizes of his own accord in a kind of sixteenth-century equivalent of spontaneous combustion—"By this the boy that by her side lay kill'd / Was melted like a vapor from her sight" (lines 1165–66)—and a flower springs from his blood without any say-so from her. Ovid's Venus sees the annual reblooming of the flower as an enduring monument to her grief, with Adonis's breath still present in the promise of its fragrance to come year after year. Shakespeare's Venus, by contrast, ensures the flower will never rebloom. Smelling the flower and "Comparing it to her Adonis' breath" (line 1172), she promptly "crops the stalk" (line 1175), so that although the bloom is, in her own words, the "Sweet issue of a more sweet-smelling sire" (line 1178), it will no more regrow, its smell to waft on the air each spring, than

[55] On this latter aspect of Orpheus, see Nicholson 1–17.

Adonis will ever breathe again. It is as dead as any cut flower thrown onto a coffin or corpse.[56]

In the circumstances, Venus's action seems counterintuitive, bizarre. In departing from Ovid here, it is as if Shakespeare were curiously determined to stress her snuffing out not only of the air (the wind-flower winded), but of any possibility that it might return. Compare his confidence in the Sonnets that poetry, carried on the breaths of future generations, is capable of immortalizing both poetic object and poetic subject. Here are his words addressed to another beloved *iuvenis*:

> Your name from hence immortal life shall have,
> ....
> When you entombed in men's eyes shall lie;
> Your monument shall be my gentle verse,
> Which eyes not yet created shall o'er-read,
> And tongues to be your being shall rehearse,
> When all the breathers of this world are dead;
> You still shall live (such virtue hath my pen)
> Where breath most breathes, even in the mouths of men.
> (sonnet 81, lines 5, 8–14).

Contrast Venus's act of willful suffocation in which, as if casting the flower onto a hearse, she effectively prevents its story from ever being rehearsed. Indeed, the more you look at *Venus and Adonis*, the more evident it becomes that Shakespeare is subjecting Ovid's ubiquitous motif of the wind, breath, air, spirit, or *pneuma* to a major analysis if not metamorphosis. For, up until the entrance of the boar, his poem reverberates with gusts and draughts every bit as lively as those which blow through Ovid's animated universe. As one might expect, there is plenty of heavy breathing in Shakespeare's poem: Venus and Adonis may not exchange bodily fluids, but they certainly exchange breaths. Venus's "windy sighs" (line 51) fan

[56] As often noted, Shakespeare's Adonis thus effectively dies twice, once as a boy and once as a flower (though the comparison with Eurydice is generally not made). Belsey 260, and Schiffer 373, both see in this double deferral or substitution the ever-elusive *objet petit a*. Mortimer finds it "significant that Shakespeare does not identify the flower," and suggests that, by not naming it, he "may be implying that it no longer exists; its beauty, like that of Adonis, has been lost without trace" (163). For Moss, the plucking of the flower signifies the eclipsing of Ovidianism altogether: "No longer a metaphor for springtime rebirth [as, e.g., in Spenser's Garden of Adonis], Shakespeare's Adonis figures metamorphosis—a synecdoche for Ovidian imitation itself—as stillbirth" (25).

Adonis's burning cheeks, while "Panting he lies and breatheth in her face. / She feedeth on the steam as on a prey, / And calls it heavenly moisture, air of grace" (lines 62–64). She tells him she will "sigh celestial breath, whose gentle wind / Shall cool the heat of this descending sun" (lines 189–90), and that "from the stillitory of thy face excelling / Comes breath perfum'd, that breedeth love by smelling" (lines 443–44).[57] The "Free vent of words love's fire doth assuage" (line 334), but the heat only increases when those words are bottled up, so when Adonis sees Venus coming, he "begins to glow, / Even as a dying coal revives with wind" (lines 337–38). When she faints, Adonis performs mouth-to-mouth resuscitation "Till his breath breatheth life in her again" (line 474). The life-reviving power of his breath thereby reaffirmed, Venus declares, it will hereafter have universally healing properties and be a cure for all maladies—"the plague is banish'd by thy breath" (line 510)—kissing him passionately in response: "Incorporate then they seem, face grows to face; // Till breathless he disjoin'd" (lines 540–41). Nor is it only the speaking beings who are caught up in the atmospheric excitement. The animals are affected, too. Of Adonis's desirous horse we are told that "His nostrils [did] drink the air, and forth again / As from a furnace, vapors doth he send" (lines 273–74), and that he challenges the wind to a race—"To bid the wind a base he now prepares" (line 303)—so that "through his mane and tail the high wind sings, / Fanning the hairs, who wave like feather'd wings" (lines 305–06). Venus describes the animal to Adonis as "thy well-breath'd horse" (line 678), as she imagines the mounted boy coursing the hare, though the eternal hunt of love and desire is destined never to end since the hunted hare in its turn also "outruns the wind" (line 681). So far, so Ovidian.

Everything changes with the boar, however, whose invisible but brooding presence is sensed long before it physically enters onto the scene. Adonis first makes mention of his intended quarry early on—"I know not love, quoth he, nor will not know it, / Unless it be a boar, and then I chase it" (lines 409–10)—something Venus wishes she had not heard, and, when Adonis opens his mouth again to confirm his plans, the bad news it betokens is compared to a "tempest" (line 454), to "Gusts and foul flaws [sudden squalls of wind]" (line 456). That this is the beginning of the end is marked by a notable hiatus: presaging the worst, Venus pauses for a moment—"Even as the wind is hush'd before it raineth" (line 458)—before she falls in a dead faint for fear. Unwittingly, Adonis anticipates the

[57] A stillatory is a still or vessel in which distilling (alcohol, perfume) takes place.

coming change in the same terms when he later describes "Lust's effect" as "tempest after sun" (line 800), as when "winter comes ere summer half be done" (line 802). Indeed, those winds begin to blow as cold as a nuclear winter when the beast eventually enters the scene. When Adonis finally leaves her, to prepare for the hunt the following morning, Venus is as lost as a night-traveler whose light is "blown out" (line 826). Intuiting from the sight of Adonis's wounded hounds that the boar-hunt has not ended well, Venus "at these sad signs draws up her breath, / And sighing it again, exclaims on Death" (lines 929–30). Addressing Death directly, she asks, "what dost thou mean / To stifle beauty, and to steal his breath? / Who when he liv'd, his breath and beauty set / Gloss on the rose, smell to the violet" (lines 933–36). Once "friendly sighs" (line 964) which had sought to cool or dry like a summer breeze are now "like a stormy day, now wind, now rain, / Sighs dry her cheeks, tears make them wet again" (lines 965–66). On finding Adonis's mangled remains, Venus loses consciousness, her senses overwhelmed as if by an earthquake (understood in those days to be the terrible eruption of air from underground, the netherworld): "As when the wind imprison'd in the ground, / Struggling for passage, earth's foundation shakes" (lines 1046–47). The blast is of such magnitude that it quite extinguishes her own personal storm: "My sighs are blown away, my salt tears gone" (line 1071). And in the postlapsarian world now robbed of Adonis, these cold and harsh conditions are set to remain. Addressing the creatures of this poor new world, Venus prophesies that, since the sun will no longer caress Adonis's skin nor the wind play with his hair, "No sun nor wind will ever strive to kiss you [...] The sun doth scorn you, and the wind doth hiss you" (lines 1082, 1084). Cursing love, she prophesies that it, too, shall "Bud, and be blasted, in a breathing while" (line 1142), not only recalling Adonis's own schoolboy wisdom on the subject—"For I have heard it is a life in death, / That laughs and weeps, and all but with a breath" (lines 413–14)—but also fulfilling her own prophecy when, only a few lines later, she herself blasts the bud that springs from his blood, and stifles its breath forever. Crushed and strangled, the flower will "wither" (line 1182) in the "hollow cradle" (line 1185) of her breast, as "away she hies [...] through the empty skies" (lines 1189–1191), a universe evacuated, voided, silenced, stilled.[58]

[58] On the contradictory or antithetical representation of wind in *The Rape of Lucrece*, see further the chapter by James W. Stone in this volume.

❦

Venus and Adonis thus presents two quite different ways of thinking about and looking at this wind or air. On the one hand, it is the "air of grace," the living and life-giving breath which pulsates through nature, poetry, speech, and song. On the other, it is the dead and death-dealing vacuum, or the nuclear and solar winds which are inimical to all life. In between lies the fragile wind-flower—whose precious scent, if renewed in the spring, carries on it all that is sweet, beautiful, and hopeful about the air that lives on—but that is also capable of being blasted out of existence by the harsh winds that give it its name. In concluding this chapter, then, I would like to suggest that these two conceptions might map onto the Imaginary and the Symbolic, respectively. The former is a light and airy space to be filled with words, a space infinitely expandable and receptive to the best and most beautiful words of which speaking beings are capable. The latter is the yawning gap, the swallowing hole that opens up between mother and child, as abyssal, empty, and galactic as outer space. As the Imaginary emerges from the Symbolic to console and compensate the subject for its sense of unbearable loss, the two linguistic registers are quite inseparable, and their relation is the story of language. It does not seem inappropriate that, at the early stages of his writing career, a man of words might undertake a deep meditation on the origins, potentialities, and liabilities of his medium, and on what these might mean for his craft. This, I think, is what Shakespeare is doing in *Venus and Adonis*, inspired by Ovid's similar meditation in the *Metamorphoses* but boldly going further into that dark night. Richard Lanham describes *Venus and Adonis* as a masterpiece "in the old sense of the word"—a piece "made by an artist to prove he is a master" (82)—and many readers have sensed that the poem Shakespeare himself describes as "first heir of my invention" somehow contains within it the seeds of everything he was to write in the future. In the initiation of the young Adonis, as he is propelled violently into the Symbolic, Shakespeare enacts the initiation of the apprentice poet, as he takes up the mantle of language and embarks on the career of sorcerer, magus of words, and master of illusion, yet under no illusions as to the baseless fabric of those visions that are destined to melt into air, thin air, and are built on nothing but an empty, dreamless sleep. Beautiful illusions emerging from and resting on a void: on this model which is, more or less, what the human condition amounts to.

By exploring and embracing language in both its registers, Shakespeare found everything he needed. The Imaginary gave him language in the creative, copious, and compensatory aspect he figures so unforgettably in the gushing Venus. As a "genetrix of eloquence" (Lanham 84), Venus is also the archetypal "literary fat lady" (Parker): a maternal goddess who embodies *copia*—the rhetorical demand to increase and multiply—as her unstoppable, lasciviously open-ended, space-filling, air-filling torrent of words duly enlarges the matter or material in hand; indeed, "increase" (lines 169, 170, 791) is often her very theme.[59] Embodying the principle of *coniunctio*—the motto of "only connect"—Venus is patroness not only of the sexual realm but also of the literary modes she exemplifies: the pathetic fallacy (which only makes sense in a magical universe of mysterious sympathies, signatures, correspondences, analogies, and signs) and puns (which show signifiers hook up with signifieds in promiscuous abandon).[60] Venus is queen of the Imaginary and insists on living in its fantasized world: she bids Adonis to "imagine" (line 721), for example, that if he falls it is simply the earth pulling him down to kiss him. She is as expert as any poet in conjuring up a "picture" of the boar (line 662) and an "image" of the stricken Adonis (line 664), both so lifelike that she cannot but "tremble at th'imagination" (line 667). When the tragedy she here foresees actually comes to pass, she uses her "imagination" (line 975) to persuade herself that the huntsman whose cry she hears is in fact Adonis, proving he is still alive. Filling the void with words, Venus creates the illusion of presence and thus shows art to be the ultimate fetish object, acknowledging and denying absence at the same time. Indeed, she fetishizes artistic creation (*poesis*)—the made worlds, green idylls, golden ages, fictions, heterocosms, and *loci amoeni* fashioned by poets—and, within this universe of idealist poetics, a painted horse is indeed superior

[59] Although Parker does not discuss Shakespeare's poem in her book, Venus more than exemplifies the principle of "dilatoriness or dalliance" (11) which characterizes the feminized rhetorical excess which is Parker's theme. On the gendered aspect of such overproduction, see also Angello, and Brown chapter 3.

[60] See, e.g., the "solemn sympathy" (line 1057) which Venus notes when the vegetation surrounding the wounded Adonis is so drenched with his blood that it "seem'd with him to bleed" (line 1056). On Venus's patronage of this world of analogies, see Shohet 87, 90, 94; on the "recreative licence" of wordplay in the poem, see Tudeau-Clayton 12, 18, 19.

to a real one, "As if the dead the living should exceed" (line 292) and "painted grapes" (line 601) capable of deceiving birds.[61] Although she complains that Adonis is a "Well-painted idol" (line 212) rather than a living man, it is the visual aesthetics of his beauty—figured throughout as a painterly red and white—which she has admired and desired from the beginning.[62] Although she complains that Adonis is like Narcissus who "himself himself forsook, / And died to kiss his shadow in the brook" (lines 161–62), her inability to make the beautiful youth behave any differently only testifies to the power of the narcissistic imago, false and empty as the jubilations of the mirror stage, but no less compelling for that.

The Symbolic, meanwhile, gave Shakespeare language in the insatiable, hollowing, and desperate aspect he figures so unforgettably in the usurping boar. The boar, who has no words and makes only the briefest appearance in the poem, is known rather by his effects.[63] In this world, Venus's *copia* might fill the air—"all the neighbor caves, as seeming troubled, / Make verbal repetition of her moans" (lines 830–31), "Ay me! she cries, and twenty times, Woe, woe!, / And twenty echoes twenty times cry so" (lines 833–34)—but it persuades no one and changes nothing: her "copious stories [...] / End without audience, and are never done" (lines 845–46). No one heeds her words, no one is moved. Her speech does not compensate for anything, and with Adonis dead and his beauty gone, the "black chaos" which her idealizing and wish-fulfilling imaginings have been trying to fend off simply "comes again" (line 1020), as it always would.[64] Although she behaves as if her desire might be satisfied were Adonis only to respond in kind, Venus is, of course, the embodiment, the personification, of Desire—"she cannot choose but love" (line 79)—and

[61] For a reading of *Venus and Adonis* as an uncritical endorsement of such idealist poetics, see Roe 3–5, 12.

[62] Although, in the next line, Venus likewise condemns Adonis as a "Statuë contenting but the eye alone" (line 213), he is of course the (great-)grandchild of an ivory statue, and less than three stanzas later Venus invites him to enter "the circuit of this ivory pale" (line 230), that is, her white body. Not long after that, his white hand in hers is described as "ivory in an alablaster band" (line 363). In this ivory-on-ivory action, Venus's desire is perfectly capable of accommodating the kinky fetishism of Adonis's forebear, Pygmalion. That Adonis is an aesthetic object is all part of the fun.

[63] The only appearance the animal makes onto the scene is when Venus "spied the hunted boar" (line 900).

[64] As Schiffer notes, "words are a poor consolation for the loss of Adonis, even for an Adonis she never possessed" (373); like Caliban, Venus's only profit from language is to learn how to curse.

is therefore by definition destined to remain unsatisfied: "Poor queen of love, in thine own law forlorn" (line 251).[65] "She's Love, she loves, and yet she is not lov'd" (line 610) *because* she's Love, she loves, and yet ... and so, as Venus discovers, the mantra repeats on a continuous loop, *ad infinitum*. Parody or caricature she may be, but Venus is the very picture of desiring, speaking subjectivity. Her conjunctive universe, in which everything is magically connected with everything else, gives way instead to a disjunctive and radically disenchanted world, in which the specious similarities that seemed to exist between things were (with the early stirrings of modern science) beginning to be rejected as childish illusions.[66] Here pathos lies not in such supposedly "natural" sympathies but rather in the emptiness of representation, a mere ghost of the presence it can re-present and repeat any number of times but never recapture, any more than Orpheus could bring Eurydice back to life.[67] Within the fallen, boorish realm of the Symbolic, the relation between signifier and signified is characterized not by *coniunctio* or even by promiscuity but rather by absence and difference, deferral and différance, the letter not only appearing sans spirit but seeming to exercise an uncanny agency of its own.

Venus and Adonis, then, does not or not only show Shakespeare making stylistic decisions about his literary career, strategically positioning himself between the Ovidianism of Marlowe and the Virgilianism of Spenser, for example.[68] It also shows him meditating at the deepest level on the fundamental qualities of language—where it comes from, what it can do, what its limitations are—learning, as any writer must, to know, respect, and even fear his medium. In the epyllion, Shakespeare is, as he would remain, an adept in both the registers we have been discussing, for it never was a case of either/or and the unhappy fates of both Venus and Adonis in the poem show what happens if you think you can stay in one of them—in the

[65] On the insatiability of Venus's desire, see Lanham 87; Belsey 259; Schiffer 367, 369; Roe 8; and Menon 511.

[66] See Greene on this distinction between "conjunctive" and "disjunctive" literary and linguistic worlds.

[67] See Fineman: "Representation, stressing and registering itself as representation, calls up and evokes as something absent the truthful presentation it confesses truly it is not. There is therefore, as Shakespeare develops it, a structural pathos built into representation. The 're-' of representation effects the loss of presentation; it is responsible for that loss because representation is not only achieved over the dead body of the presence it repeats, but, more actively, this very repetition is what transforms such ideal presence into something of the past" (297).

[68] As suggested by Cheney chapter 3.

fantasized world of beautiful sameness—forever. Instead, Shakespeare sensibly distributes the two linguistic registers across the genres. The Imaginary belongs to the worlds of comedy, lyric, and romance, where *coniunctio* is celebrated; where the continuity of life, breath, language, and poetry are seemingly assured; where stories end in marriage and babies and still more stories; where the Young Man's beauty is due to outlast time in the Sonnets; and where the fragrance of the wind-flower is set to re-perfume the air every spring. The Symbolic belongs to the worlds of tragedy, satire, and complaint, where *coniunctio* is trashed; where marriage is shown to be incestuous, polluted, adulterated, taboo; where "love" is shown to be nothing but "lust," perjur'd, murd'rous, bloody, full of blame, savage, extreme, rude, cruel, not to trust, as in relations with the Dark Lady; where stories end with lives, whole family lines, and stories about them stopped in their tracks; and where the wind-flower withers and dies, whether deflowered by the wind or torn up and thrown onto a corpse that can no more be revived than itself. The world has room for both.[69] For the poet who (like Venus) is "of imagination all compact," whose "imagination bodies forth / The forms of things unknown," and whose pen "gives to aery nothing / A local habitation and a name" (*A Midsummer Night's Dream*, 5.1.8, 14–15, 16–17). And for the poet who (more like the boar) can write the barely verbal howl that issues from the mouth of the bare forked animal when the breath of his own beloved child is snuffed out, never to return: "She's dead as earth. Lend me a looking-glass, / If that her breath will mist or stain the stone, / Why then she lives"; "Cordelia, Cordelia, stay a little. Ha! / What is't thou sayest? / Her voice was ever soft, / Gentle, and low, an excellent thing in woman" (*King Lear*, 5.3.262–4, 272–4).[70] The material for all the poems and plays which Shakespeare would go on to write was already there, contained within *Venus and Adonis.* With that poem, Shakespeare launched his writing career with both a bang and a whimper.

Acknowledgement Awarded the Julius Silberger Prize in 2023, this chapter first appeared in *American Imago*, vol. 81, no. 4, 2024, pp. 335–66. I am grateful to the Editor for permission to reproduce a longer version of the chapter here.

[69] Answering Lanham's question, perhaps: "Why, instead of romantic comedy's redemption of love, [does Shakespeare] offer his story [of Venus and Adonis] as exemplum for the future horrors of love? Still more, why couch those horrors in cosmic terms?" (90).

[70] For Lear's "Howl, howl, howl!," see 5.3.258.

Works Cited

Angello, Lizz. "Venus's Bush(Es)." *Object Oriented Environs*, edited by Jeffrey Jerome Cohen and Julian Yates, Punctum Books, 2016, pp. 1–8.

Aristophanes. *Birds. Lysistrata. Women at the Thesmophoria*. Translated by J. Henderson, Harvard UP, 2000.

Athenaeus. *Deipnosophistae: The Learned Banqueters*. Translated by S. D. Olson, Harvard UP, 2012.

Barkan, Leonard. *The Gods Made Flesh: Metamorphosis and the Pursuit of Paganism*. Yale UP, 1986.

Bate, Jonathan. *Shakespeare and Ovid*. Clarendon P, 1993.

Bates, Catherine. *Masculinity and the Hunt: Wyatt to Spenser*. Oxford UP, 2013.

Belsey, Catherine. "Love as Trompe-l'oeil: Taxonomies of Desire in *Venus and Adonis*." *Shakespeare Quarterly*, vol. 46, no. 3, 1995, pp. 257–76.

Berry, Edward. *Shakespeare and the Hunt: A Cultural and Social Study*. Cambridge UP, 2001.

Bowie, Malcolm. *Lacan*. Fontana, 1991.

Brown, Georgia. *Redefining Elizabethan Literature*. Cambridge UP, 2004.

Burke, Kenneth. *A Rhetoric of Motives*. U of California P, 1950.

Caruso, Carlo. *Adonis: The Myth of the Dying God in the Italian Renaissance*. Bloomsbury, 2013.

Cheney, Patrick. *Shakespeare, National Poet-Playwright*. Cambridge UP, 2004.

Cousins, A. D., editor. *Shakespeare's Sonnets and Narrative Poems*. Routledge, 2000.

Crewe, Jonathan, editor. *William Shakespeare: The Narrative Poems*. Penguin, 1999.

Dubrow, Heather. *Captive Victors: Shakespeare's Narrative Poems and Sonnets*. Cornell UP, 1987.

Ellis, Jim. "Imagining Heterosexuality in the Epyllia." *Ovid and the Renaissance Body*, edited by Goran V. Stanivukovic and Valerie Traub, U of Toronto P, 2001, pp. 38–58.

———. *Sexuality and Citizenship: Metamorphosis in Elizabethan Erotic Verse*. U of Toronto P, 2003.

Enterline, Lynn. "Psychoanalytic Criticisms." *An Oxford Guide to Shakespeare*, edited by Stanley Wells and Lena Cowlin Orlin, Oxford UP, 2003, pp. 451–71.

———. *The Rhetoric of the Body from Ovid to Shakespeare*. Cambridge UP, 2000.

———. *Shakespeare's Schoolroom: Rhetoric, Discipline, Emotion*. U of Pennsylvania P, 2012.

Fineman, Joel. *Shakespeare's Perjured Eye: The Invention of Poetic Subjectivity in the Sonnets*. U of California P, 1986.

Fletcher, Loraine. "Animal Rites: A Reading of *Venus and Adonis*." *Critical Survey*, vol. 17, no. 3, 2005, pp. 1–14.

Freud, Sigmund. *The Revised Standard Edition of the Complete Psychological Works of Sigmund Freud*, edited and translated by James Strachey, revised by Mark

Solms. 24 vols. Rowman & Littlefield Publishers, 2024. (In-text references provide *RSE* page numbers immediately after *SE* page numbers).
———. "The Dissolution of the Oedipus Complex" (1924). *The Standard Edition of the Complete Psychological Works of Sigmund Freud*, edited and translated by James Strachey, vol. 19, Hogarth Press, 1961, pp. 173–79/*RSE* vol.19, pp. 165–73.
———. "Three Essays on Sexuality" (1905). *SE* vol. 7, 1953, pp. 123–245/*RSE* vol.7, pp. 111–217.
Golding, Arthur, translator. *Ovid's Metamorphoses.* Edited by Madeleine Forey, Penguin, 2002.
Greene, Thomas M., and David Quint. *Poetry, Signs, and Magic.* U of Delaware P, 2005.
Halpern, Richard. "'Pining Their Maws': Female Readers and the Erotic Ontology of the Text in Shakespeare's *Venus and Adonis.*" Venus and Adonis: *Critical Essays*, edited by Philip C. Kolin, Garland Publishing, 1997, pp. 377–88.
Hamilton, A. C., et al. *The Spenser Encyclopedia.* U of Toronto P, 1990.
Hatto, A. T. "Venus and Adonis—and the Boar." *Modern Language Review*, vol. 41, no. 4, 1946, pp. 353–61.
Hopkinson, N., editor. *Theocritus. Moschus. Bion.* Harvard UP, 2015.
Hughes, Ted. *Shakespeare and the Goddess of Complete Being.* Faber, 1992.
Hulse, Clark. *Metamorphic Verse: The Elizabethan Minor Epic.* Princeton UP, 1981.
Kennedy, G. A., editor. *Progymnasmata: Greek Textbooks of Prose Composition and Rhetoric.* Society of Biblical Literature, 2003.
Kuchar, Gary. "Narrative and the Forms of Desire in Shakespeare's *Venus and Adonis.*" *Early Modern Literary Studies: A Journal of Sixteenth- and Seventeenth-Century English Literature*, vol. 5, no. 2, 1999, unpaginated.
Lacan, Jacques. *Écrits: The First Complete Edition in English.* Translated by Bruce Fink. Norton, 2006.
———. *The Four Fundamental Concepts of Psychoanalysis*, edited by Jacques-Alain Miller, translated by Alan Sheridan, Penguin, 1994.
Lanham, Richard A. *The Motives of Eloquence: Literary Rhetoric in the Renaissance.* Yale UP, 1976.
Laplanche, Jean. *Essays on Otherness.* Translated by John Fletcher, Routledge, 1999.
Lewis, C. S. *English Literature in the Sixteenth Century, Excluding Drama.* Clarendon Press, 1954.
Menon, Madhavi. "Spurning Teleology in *Venus and Adonis.*" *GLQ: A Journal of Lesbian and Gay Studies*, vol. 11, no. 4, 2005, pp. 491–519.
Mortimer, Anthony Robert. *Variable Passions: A Reading of Shakespeare's* Venus and Adonis. AMS Press, 2000.
Moss, Daniel D. *The Ovidian Vogue: Literary Fashion and Imitative Practice in Late Elizabethan England.* U of Toronto P, 2014.

Mukherji, Subha. "Outgrowing Adonis: The Disorienting Narrative of *Venus and Adonis*." *The Oxford Handbook of Shakespeare's Poetry*, edited by Jonathan Post, Oxford UP, 2013, pp. 396–412.

Nicholson, Catherine. *Uncommon Tongues: Eloquence and Eccentricity in the English Renaissance*. U of Pennsylvania P, 2014.

Ovid. *Heroides. Amores*. Translated by G. Showerman, Harvard UP, 1914.

———. *Metamorphoses*. Translated by F. J. Miller, Harvard UP, 1916.

Parker, Patricia. *Literary Fat Ladies: Rhetoric, Gender, Property*. Methuen, 1987.

Roe, John, editor. *William Shakespeare: The Poems*. Cambridge UP, 1992.

Schiffer, James. "Shakespeare's *Venus and Adonis*: A Lacanian Tragicomedy of Desire." Venus and Adonis: *Critical Essays*, edited by Philip C. Kolin, Garland Publishing, 1997, pp. 359–76.

Shakespeare, William. *The Riverside Shakespeare*. Edited by G. Blakemore Evans, et al., Houghton Mifflin, 1997.

Sheidley, William E. "'Unless It Be a Boar': Love and Wisdom in Shakespeare's *Venus and Adonis*." *Modern Language Quarterly*, vol. 35, 1974, pp. 3–15.

Shohet, Lauren. "Shakespeare's Eager Adonis." *Studies in English Literature, 1500–1900*, vol. 42, no. 1, 2002, pp. 85–102.

Spenser, Edmund. *The Faerie Queene*. Edited by A. C. Hamilton, Pearson Longman, 2007.

Stanivukovic, Goran V. "Troping Desire in Shakespeare's *Venus and Adonis*." *Forum for Modern Language Studies*, vol. 33, no. 4, Oct. 1997, pp. 289–301.

Tudeau-Clayton, Margaret. "Stepping Out of Narrative Line: A Bit of Word, and Horse, Play in *Venus and Adonis*." *Shakespeare Survey*, vol. 53, 2000, pp. 12–24.

Weaver, William P. *Untutored Lines: The Making of the English Epyllion*. Edinburgh UP, 2012.

Williams, Gordon. "The Coming of Age of Shakespeare's Adonis." *Modern Language Review*, vol. 78, no. 4, Oct. 1983, pp. 769–76.

Wortis, Joesph. "*Venus and Adonis*: An Early Account of Sexual Harassment." Venus and Adonis: *Critical Essays*, edited by Philip C. Kolin, Garland Publishing, 1997, pp. 259–60.

CHAPTER 8

Antithetical Words, Rape, and Ekphrasis in Shakespeare's *The Rape of Lucrece*

James W. Stone

The Rape of Lucrece (1594) has proved to be a political battleground for feminist critics and their adversaries over the question of who or what (e.g., language) is the agent of rape. In this chapter I propose to look at an important and influential misogynistic "logic" which posits an antithetical language that turns every resistance to rape into an incitement to or a permission for a man to violate a woman.

In opposition to this *mise en abîme* logic in the first part of this long narrative poem, in the second half of the epyllion the ekphrastic tapestry that depicts the fall of Troy provides warnings against deceptive speech and suggests models for heroic resistance that, although ambiguous and even paradoxical, are legible and do not collapse into antithetical aporias. The narrative woven into the tapestry serves Lucrece as a spur for action, ultimately for her heroic suicide which, I argue, turns the rape inside out and reverses its polluting consequences. Lucrece's Stoicism resists the collapse of resistance (and of difference), a collapse whose support rapacious antifeminism and misogyny derive from the primal sense of antithetical words (to use Freud's terminology).

J. W. Stone (✉)
American University, Paris, France

J. W. Stone, C. Bates (eds.), *Shakespeare and Psychoanalysis*, Palgrave Shakespeare Studies,
https://doi.org/10.1007/978-3-032-07897-1_8

The "logic" of rape, or at any rate the logic that motivates the rapist, is antinomian and antithetical. The rapist takes comfort, pleasure, stimulation in the mixed signals that words vouchsafe him. For Tarquin, language that prohibits may also carry the contrary valence of permission, encouragement, excitation. Taboo is unthinkable apart from its transgression in much the same way that the sacred cannot mean apart from the profane that feeds parasitically upon it. Look at how the wind blows more ways than one in the following passage and so provides no clear moral compass for Tarquin; it is a licensing and licentious wind:

> As each unwilling portal yields him way,
> Through little vents and crannies of the place
> The wind wars with his torch to make him stay,
> And blows the smoke of it into his face,
> Extinguishing his conduct in this case.
> But his hot heart, which fond desire doth scorch,
> Puffs forth another wind that fires the torch. (lines 309–15)[1]

The narrative employs "wind" in contrary senses, inverse directions. On the one hand, the "wind" that "wars with his torch to make him stay" points toward prophylaxis, the prevention of rape. On the other hand, the narrator reverses (also in the etymological sense of the turn (*vertere*) from the end of one line of verse to the start of the next) direction in the stanza's closing couplet, re-employing the identical language and theme but in an opposing sense: Tarquin's heart kindles a second wind that fires his formerly smoke-choked torch, now turned toward a phallic valence. Wind may put out or stoke a fire, depending on its (the wind's, the fire's) intensity and vectorial momentum. The referent of "wind" at line 311 is an external breeze that blows through the portal, whereas the referent at the end of the stanza seems to be a sexual excitation. The same word is anything but the same thing, nor is the effect of this referent the same in the two cases: What blows cold from the outside in line 311 only serves to spark internal heat and rapacious desire in the somewhat paradoxical formulation in lines 314–15. The wind reverses (re-verses, re-metaphorizes) itself.

The more he is "let" or barred, the more Tarquin becomes excited for sex and for power, notably and explicitly so when a needle folded into

[1] This and all subsequent quotations from the poem are from the Arden edition, edited by Katherine Duncan-Jones and H. R. Woudhuysen.

Lucrece's prophylactic but fetishistic glove "his finger pricks" (line 319). The narrator gives voice to needle and glove in order to make manifest the moral point of the prick:

> As who should say, "This glove to wanton tricks
> Is not inured. Return again in haste;
> Thou seest our mistress' ornaments are chaste." (lines 320–22)

Lucrece's garments, like the insistent whiteness of her face, are chaste; chastity, however, only serves the more to arouse Tarquin's desire to violate and to pollute what he is forbidden to have. Such is the misogynistic logos of the "let," whose chiastic and paradoxical rhetoricity Joel Fineman anatomized in one of the best and most controversial essays on the poem. The needle-prick excites desire even as it purports to defend against it:

> But all these poor forbiddings could not stay him;
> He in the worst sense consters their denial:
> The doors, the wind, the glove that did delay him
> He takes for accidental things of trial;
> Or as those bars which stop the hourly dial,
> Who with a ling'ring stay his course doth let
> Till every minute pays the hour his debt. (lines 323–29)

The let is a hindrance or obstruction that resists the forward movement of the clock's hand yet, after a short delay, permits (lets) the hand to move forward. This "let" (which is one of the hinges of Joel Fineman's essay) exemplifies what Freud calls a "primal" word whose sense is "antithetical" (153–61/141–48); that is, it comprises in the "same" word both one sense and the opposite of this sense. As the dial's hand comes into contact with the bar, the bar both resists the hand (on the one hand) and excites the hand to push it forward (on the other hand). Resistance creates in turn a counter-resistance to itself. Resistance and obstruction work against themselves to open up, antithetically, a field for permission. The good sense of a word is undermined by the "worst sense" (in the quotation above) of the putatively same word.

> "So, so," quoth he, "these lets attend the time,
> Like little frosts that sometime threat the spring
> To add a more rejoicing to the prime,
> And give the sneaped birds more cause to sing.
> Pain pays the income of each precious thing." (lines 330–34)

Desire is excited by what opposes it, Tarquin opines. The prime pushes forward in proportion as the cold (chaste) frosts resist it. Rape presupposes a state of innocence that acts like a bar resisting the advance of the rapist. The rapist's sword-wielding hand, like the hand of a clock, presses forward inexorably to devour the putatively self-identical—the ostensibly unchanging and eternal—moment of chastity. The passing of time is premised on the let that resists/allows its passing. Temporality implicates the passing of a chastity that vaunts itself to be eternal.

The rapist's excited virility is described as a fiery and smoking torch (line 315) or, in the following passage, as a stinging serpent:

> This said, his guilty hand plucked up the latch,
> And with his knee the door he opens wide.
> The dove sleeps fast that this night-owl will catch.
> Thus treason works ere traitors be espied.
> Who sees the lurking serpent steps aside,
>   But she, sound sleeping, fearing no such thing,
>   Lies at the mercy of his mortal sting. (lines 358–64)

This portrayal of Tarquin's voyeurism is disturbing because it presumes that Lucrece's closed eyes are in (winking) collusion with the rapist's open and excited ones, the non-vigilance of the former evidently permitting latch and door to open to the advancing eyes and hands of the serpent. (Every resistance ["let"] presupposes an antithetical or opposing permission [the letting of the "let"]. For one to belabor this point is simply to imitate resistlessly the poem's belaboring of the point. But later, the poem and its reader will find traction for a genuine resistance.) The lids that cover the eyes and thus protect them from the invasive light of Tarquin's smoking torch produce also the counter-effect of the shutdown of Lucrece's faculties of resistance in sleep; her defense is simultaneously the letting down of her guard. Her ears engage in the same type of non-defense as her eyes: she sleeps so "sound" (deeply and deafly) that she hears no warning sounds. Dove-like, she sleeps so "fast" as to be slow or motionless, an easy catch for the raptor owl. Lucrece's vigilant guardians, asleep on the job, foreclose and compromise her safety.

Such, at any rate, is the tendentious male fantasy of the rapist, whose point of view predominates in this section of the poem.

The sleeping heroine is unable to find protection despite the existence of the carefully prepared panoply of defensive guards: the outer portal to her bedroom, the latch and locks, the winds that blow athwart the rapist (yet fan his desire within), the prophylactic yet fetishistic needle in the glove, the lids that guard Lucrece's eyes in sleep. As Tarquin presses forward relentlessly, pricked on "to make his stand" (line 438) sexually, every resistance that he encounters excites a counter-pulsion to violate Lucrece. The thorns set in place to defend the virginal rose from injury (line 492) are ineffectual, for they prick desire on even as they attempt to guard against the plucking of the flower that they protect.

Fort / fault / *foutre*: the fort of the chaste body is riven by faults in its walls. Or so Tarquin's excited fantasy permits itself to believe. Tarquin breaks through the genitals that are metaphorized as a fort. The pun that underlies yet undermines the "fort" illustrates and performs the double play of vigilance/betrayal that characterizes the various chaste resistances that we have analyzed so far, for the "fort" that designates the walls that guard the vagina against penetration is also a "fault" and a detouring away from the fort via the French *foutre* = copulation (Kökeritz 311n2). "Fort" is an antithetical primal word that, in pushing away Lucrece's rapacious binary opponent, draws him in. The vector turns back on itself. This uncanny anti-logic (*différance*) motivates Tarquin's apologia, in the two contrary senses of the word: confession of guilt versus self-justification:

> "Under that colour am I come to scale
> Thy never-conquered fort. The fault is thine,
> For those thine eyes betray thee unto mine." (lines 481–83)

As Tarquin has argued that Lucrece's eyes are traitors to the fort of her chastity, in that they excite his lust when open (whereas her eyes closed in sleep excite as well and betray the sleeper due to their lack of vigilance), so in putting in proximity the words "fort" and "fault" in this passage, Tarquin performs the latter's antithetical undermining and conquest of the former. "Fault" may have as referent both the woman's flawed character and her vagina, and as a sound-image (signifier) its pronunciation is identical to the French *foutre*.[2] The woman is at fault, according to Tarquin's fantasmatic logic, because from her eyes to her loins she sends

[2]For the use of "fault" as a term for the female genitalia, a word that locates a woman's lapses reductively in her vagina/vice, see Janet Adelman 252–53. Amy Greenstadt writes that Tarquin believes that Lucrece "bears the fault for the rape because her 'fault' is (literally) the opening of her eyes that lets him imaginatively enter her body" (54), as if her beauty forces Tarquin to rape her. The opening of the eyes is homologous to the opening of the sexual orifices, at least from the psychotical perspective of the rapist, quick to practice metonymic short-circuiting from one body part to another.

the mixed signal for the man to perform penetration even as she mounts resistance. Tarquin's ravenous and ravishing male fantasy seeks to fault the woman's fort. The rapist's wishful thinking is motivated by lust and consummated with a licentiously playful pun, a *jouissance* that self-servingly allies pleasure and moral judgment, transumptively collapsing the latter into the former. The wordplay on *fort/fault* manifests a scandalously marginal exemplarity—both marginal and central, subversive and normative—that instances Freud's antithetical sense of primal words. The rapist appeals to the uncannily self-dividing difference within the fort, to the way that it reveals an opening within itself, manifested as incipient faults in its walls, thus giving rise to the very transgression that the walls were putatively erected in opposition to. (This subversive logic is nonetheless consistent and compelling from the antinomian transgressor's point of view; from the victim's viewpoint, however, this contradiction-saturated logic of rape is dangerously illogical.) The erected (yet fault-riven) walls of the fort cause an erection in Tarquin that propels him to destroy the fort.

Nature's course, Tarquin observes, directs the fresh waters of streams to flow into the sea, "their salt sovereign" (line 650), paying it their tributary debt. As a defensive apology for his actions, the rapist avers that a relatively small spurt of liquid pollution may be cleansed when diffused within the much larger body of salt water, whose power to purify is the consequence of the sea's paradoxically boundless bounds. In the effort to seduce Lucrece, Tarquin's rhetorical temptation is to suggest that the moral distinction between lawful and illicit sex is dissolved in the expanse of the non-bounded aqueous ether. The limitlessness of the sea licenses any breach of moral limits at the level of local, interpersonal conduct. Lucrece abjures this argument in favor of rape by insisting on the integrity of the circumscribed and very finite microcosm of her womb. It is *not* the case that Tarquin's semen will be dispersed into the sovereign sea; rather, the ejaculant will be injected into and will contaminate Lucrece's bodily interior. The circumscribing bounds of this interior define it as a sacred space, an inner sanctum whose delimitations are subject to potential pollution and profanation when penetrated (interpolated) by external foreign matter:

> "Thou art," quoth she, "a sea, a sovereign king,
> And lo, there falls into thy boundless flood
> Black lust, dishonour, shame, misgoverning,
> Who seek to stain the ocean of thy blood.
> If all these petty ills shall change thy good,

> Thy sea within a puddle's womb is hearsed,
> And not the puddle in thy sea dispersed." (lines 652–58)

In short, Lucrece insists on the boundary between sacred and profane, the boundary delimited by a woman's body, as opposed to the apparent licensing boundlessness of the sea, which has no inside or outside and does not lend itself to being sullied by any finite pollutant (like semen). Because it is finite, bounded, fragile, the violated womb risks becoming a place of death, a hearse or casket. Tarquin's aggressive sexual drive is a death drive: for Lucrece, for Tarquin's royal family. Lucrece eschews the notion of downplaying dishonor as something small and dispersible, whether in Tarquin's "blood" (bodily fluid or offspring/bloodline) or her own. On the contrary, the stain of sexual dishonor cannot be cleansed, she insists. Blood (its mark, its stain) entrains death as inevitable consequence. Lucrece avers that Tarquin's ills, far from advancing his interests, shall be his "fouler grave" (line 661). The blood that he draws from her will destroy her and will also mark out his doom in turn; *his* chastity too will be fatally compromised. Death and the grave await both parties to dishonor, irrespective of who is innocent, who is not.

The womb as tomb is a conventional figure in English Renaissance poetry, one that deploys itself in *The Rape of Lucrece* in a cluster of macabre sub-images. The sovereign sea "hearsed" in the womb and the "grave" into which Tarquin's reputation will fall anticipate Shakespeare's use of another sepulchral enclosure a few lines later:

> The wolf hath seized his prey, the poor lamb cries,
> Till with her own white fleece her voice controlled
> *Entombs* her outcry in her lips' sweet fold.
>
> For with the nightly linen that she wears
> He pens her piteous clamours in her head. (lines 677–81; my emphasis)

Tarquin stops up Lucrece's mouth, as a precautionary foreclosure, just before he violates the rest of her body. Lucrece's mouth is stuffed with her white nightgown or bed-linen, much as Othello plugs Desdemona's orifice when he makes love to/kills her on her wedding/death bed, making of the appurtenances of the wedding chamber both the instruments (pillow or sheets) for smothering the body and the shroud (bedsheet) for burying it. Tarquin stops up Lucrece's voice of protest, recalling the cutting out of Philomela's tongue after she is raped by her brother-in-law

Tereus. Whether the lips' sweet fold has oral or vaginal referent (or at line 681 it refers to a pen for sheep[3]), the lips can be seen (and heard) in the word *entombs*, which implies the opening/closure of a grave, inside of which the voice is rendered dumb or dead. In many a pictured representation of rape, like those that form the long history of paintings or tapestries of the rape of Lucrece, the woman's vocal protest is held in suspension, mute. The stuffing of the mouth with white fleece forecloses any further verbal resistance on Lucrece's part to the violation of her body that is about to take place. The entombing of the victim's outcry within her lips' sweet fold is analogous to sonnet 86, in which the poet wonders whether his rival's verse "did my ripe thoughts in my brain inhearse, / Making their tomb the womb wherein they grew?"[4] The rival poet's superior talents abort what the poet wishes to bring forth parthenogenetically from his womb. Once she is raped, inseminated, perhaps impregnated too—an issue to which we shall return—Lucrece will regard her womb as the locus of death, as the antipodes to the life-giving force that it had been before the rape.

Hearse, grave, casket, coffers, sepulcher—these various displacements of the womb will become available to the rape victim in a still catastrophic yet potentially redemptive register after her womb has been violated. The abused womb will be restored via death—specifically by means of becoming not only the place where death lodges but also the locus for wounded honor to find refuge. Lucrece laments that her "scapes" (line 747) are open to the shaming light of day. Immediately before and during her long apostrophe to Night (lines 764 ff.), she yearns for a darkness that will "make her unseen sin remain untold" (line 753), in order that she be spared the humiliation of being witnessed. The rape that she has suffered

[3]Following Jonathan Goldberg, Miriam Jacobson sees a pun on *penes*/penis, the phallic violence of the letter that the rapist inscribes (pens) on the body of his victim (353–54). In analyzing a different passage, Greenstadt argues that "Tarquin likens the movements of the writing hand to the unruly motions of the male genitals" (47). David Willbern draws a connection through the word "pens" to several acts of writing/rape: Shakespeare's act of writing the poem, the moment that Lucrece "prepares to write, / First hovering o'er the paper with her quill" (lines 1296–97) in composing the narrative of the rape for her husband, and Tarquin's earlier "shak[ing] aloft his Roman blade" (line 550) as he threatens to rape his victim (92).

[4]John Roe points to "an antithetical tomb-womb effect" produced by the words "womb" and "hearsed" in line 657 (175n).

causes her to weep tears that "grave" (line 755) her cheeks in the way that *aquafortis* is used to engrave a metal plate with indelible traces. Engraved traces mark the rape victim out for death and the darkness of night. Here, a thousand lines before Lucrece's suicide, Shakespeare deploys proleptically the language of the tomb and of the grave. The narrator tells us that the heroine beats on her "breast" (line 759) in the hope that her heart "may find / Some purer chest to close so pure a mind" (lines 760–61). The internal rhyme on "breast" and "chest" predicts and prescribes the moment, at the end of the poem, when Lucrece will bury the knife in her breast—thus reversing by re-enacting the gesture of the original rape, as we shall see—making of her rhyming chest/breast not a symbol of violated life but instead a comforting chamber/casket in which to house the re-chastened body of the deceased. Suicidal knifing in the breast symbolically reverses the rapist's penetration of Lucrece's vagina. Lucrece's chaste "chest" is a casket, as both the New Cambridge and the Arden editors gloss the word, a sepulcher whose darkness will provide a secure resting place for militant chastity.[5] The violence and violation done to the womb look forward to a fortunate (if not altogether cheerful) teleology: the peace and restoration of the woman's honor in the tomb.

The poem refers frequently to how the rape of Lucrece risks causing irreparable damage, both prospectively and retroactively, to the reputation of her family line—to its coat of arms, its escutcheon, its mottoes and devices. Lucrece is anxious lest she become a byword for unchastity and thus damage her family name. (Immediately after her death, her husband and her father will debate about which man's honor has suffered the graver blow, to the degree that Lucrece herself drops out of the discussion entirely.) Tarquin threatens that if she refuses to have intercourse with him, he will kill Lucrece and one of her household slaves, framing them as adulterous lovers whom he caught, killed, and exposed in the act of lovemaking. He threatens further that poets will vilify Lucrece as a type for unfaithfulness, a woman who "shalt have thy trespass cited up in rhymes / And sung by children in succeeding times" (lines 524–25). A new fame, of the wrong kind, risks effacing Collatine's heraldry; the family's

[5]For more on the casket, in the context of *The Merchant of Venice*, see the chapter by Christian A. Smith in this volume and the article by James W. Stone.

long-earned reputation teeters on the abyss of being turned inside out, reduced to a cipher.[6]

How may Lucrece come to be celebrated in story and song rather than traduced in narrative as the corruptor of a long-distinguished genealogy? Lucrece laments that her name has been "sepulchred" (line 805) in Night's shade, for it has been written over with so many marks and blots that even those unable to decipher "what is writ in learned books, / Will quote my loathsome trespass in my looks" (lines 811–12). She frets lest "the branches of another root are rotted" (line 823), anxious that through her acts (including passive ones) Collatine's family tree will be undermined. The marks upon Lucrece effect an open wound upon her body and a marring of her name. Like Lavinia in *Titus Andronicus*, Lucrece's marks of shame are both corporeal and textual, amounting to the narrative of a damaged reputation (through no fault of her own), figured in terms of a script that supplements and blots what is taken to be the pure presence of an unmarked, unmarred original:

> "O unseen shame, invisible disgrace!
> O unfelt sore, crest-wounding private scar!
> Reproach is stamped in Collatinus' face,
> And Tarquin's eye may read the mot afar,
> How he in peace is wounded, not in war." (lines 827–31)

The privacy of the scar must be made public—must be published—if Lucrece hopes to succeed in restoring the family name. But to publish her shame risks damaging further the name that has stood so long for virtue. Sexual violation entrains loss of reputation, to be sure, and in Shakespeare's poem this loss is closely linked to debasement of heraldry, as the indelible scarring (marking) of the crest indicates. Duncan-Jones and Woudhuysen regard the "crest" as "an externally visible symbol for the phallus" (here

[6]Jacobson argues that "rape publishes streams of Os in its wake" (336). She explores O as the genital nothing, as multiplying placeholder, as cryptic signifier, and as the sign of signifying nothing. Images of castration pursue their course when Tarquin laments that his transgression "will live engraven in my face" (line 203) and that the herald will apply a "loathsome dash" (line 206) to his coat of arms in order "To cipher me how fondly I did dote" (line 207). Honor is both invoked in the shield (as a memory) and blotted out (castrated), for Tarquin as for Collatine.

and in line 104 of *Venus and Adonis*) (25).[7] Damage to the physical body of the married woman is damage to the reputation of her husband; genital damage to the one is by transference damage to the genitalia and to the genealogy of the other. Physical depredations result in the family motto falling into a mere "mot" for disrespectability, a nayword, a byword for ill repute. The family name is evacuated. Nullified. Castrated.

ii a

In her long, moralizing speeches in the second half of the poem, Lucrece will eschew the antithesis-saturated logic/"logic" of rape, what Joel Fineman unpacks as the irresistible pulsion of the "let" that enables and makes necessary the rapacious friction between the sexes. Many feminist critics find this logic perverse for its fatalistic insistence that since a woman is chaste and off limits ("let" in the sense of *prohibited*) she therefore provokes rape ("let" in the sense of *permits*). Lucrece champions Stoical, heroic rhetoric over against Tarquin's (and Fineman's) deconstructions of chastity, that is, the sophisticated but specious argument that the chaster a woman is, the more she invites rape. Lucrece ultimately chastises and chastens this wanton wordplay that makes a mockery of the very idea of chastity. As allegorical exemplar of Chastity, Lucrece can and does defeat Tarquin's attacks on chastity, but only, it seems, at the ultimate expense of spirit, by putting into effect the paradox that the sole means for a paragon of virtue to vindicate her chastity is to kill herself. Such reasoning is not so far from the unfeminist tag that the only chaste woman is a dead woman. This specious logic is quite familiar to students of Shakespearean misogyny, as when Othello is finally assured of Desdmona's chastity, and Leontes of Hermione's, once the repentant husband comes to mourn the loss of his wife and her chastity shortly after she dies (or seems to die, in the case of Hermione). Both men, skeptical of their wife's chastity, come to believe that the *bona fides* of the woman's chastity is secured only retrospectively, by the fact of her death.

[7] One is struck by this comment if only for the fact that Arden editors Duncan-Jones and Woudhuysen are rarely given to remarks of a psychoanalytic tenor in their edition of the narrative poems. *The Rape of Lucrece* is conventional and unsubtle in its abundant deployment of genital symbols, to the point that a commentator like me risks belaboring what this most psychoanalytically rhetorical of poems has already belabored. Jacobson sees the "crest-wounding private scar" as the genital O or cipher. The phrase alludes to Collatine's invisible cuckold's horns, his "unseen shame" and "unfelt sore," but it may "also allude to Lucrece's vagina, her secret 'nothing' invisibly bruised by rape" (355).

Lucrece regards a tapestry that narrates the end of the Trojan War. She witnesses violence without screams, a silent unfolding of images that belies the full horror of the body in pain by suppressing sound and speech. The contest between the tapestry-weaver's art and the poet's is a *paragone*. The tapestry that Lucrece sees alludes to and follows the precedent of tongue-shorn Philomela's tapestry in Ovid's *Metamorphoses*, which Philomela weaves in order to narrate the story of her rape by Tereus, her brother-in-law.[8] In the story of the fall of Troy, Lucrece the spectator sees Hecuba "behold" and "stare" (lines 1447–48) but does not hear anything as she witnesses Pyrrhus slaughter Priam. Priam's death marks the terminus of the war whose point of origin was the rape of Helen by Paris (the son of Priam and Hecuba). Rape begets murder and death during the long lapse of the Trojan War; in the teleological decennial of war, the circle closes itself off at the end as death puts paid to rape. The catastrophe of the slaughter of Priam, as portrayed in the ekphrasis (the poet's written description of the story depicted in the tapestry), is attenuated by the weaver of the tapestry; since the violence unfolds solely in images, it is in part made more endurable. Muting or entombing the voice of a victim of violence traces out the curve of a limit, an asymptote, a sublimation. Physical violence is both captured and distanced through Shakespeare's ekphrastic poesis that deploys the conventional metaphors of hearse, tomb, and womb; of the mouth's cavity, like Philomela's, sans vocalizing tongue. The violent end of Troy is a silent picture, analogous to a silent representation of a rape (Philomela's, Lucrece's, Helen's), whether shown on cloth, canvas, or wood panel, or woven into a written text, like Shakespeare's, to form a warp and woof that is vivid yet muted, immediate yet distanced.[9]

[8]Jane Newman argues that the tale of Philomela and her maenadic revenge against Tereus is mentioned but downplayed in *The Rape of Lucrece* in favor of foregrounding a heroine less inclined to take political action, whose predisposition toward self-victimization and self-sacrifice prevent her from wanting to commit violence against the perpetrator. "In the reception of Lucrece alternate forms of women's political agency not complicit in the reproduction of patriarchy have been as repressed, as silenced, as Philomela herself" (306) since the poem construes the male Brutus as the sole locus of political revenge and reform. Unlike Philomela, the more cautious Lucrece does not lose her tongue.

[9]In the critical debate over the material medium that Lucrece is looking at when she recounts the story of Troy, S. Clark Hulse believes that it is a tapestry (15). Duncan-Jones and Woudhuysen opine that the images of Troy are painted on the panels of a *cassone* (48).

Lucrece feels that only by killing herself with a knife, thus repeating the act of rape in inverted form—Tarquin held his falchion or sword to her neck when he raped her—will she be able to reverse the rape's polluting consequences. She senses herself compelled to internalize both the spirit of the law of chastity and its practical execution, the latter encompassing the act of taking punishment into her own *hand*, a word whose repetition in the poem gives point to the fact that Lucrece's hand reverses what Tarquin's hand did, answering blade for blade, cut for cut.[10] The same gesture of stabbing is not the same, for Tarquin's use of sword and penis to penetrate Lucrece cuts deeply (and castratingly, as Duncan-Jones and Woudhuysen suggest) into the family's crest, whereas Lucrece's use of the knife to spill her own blood restores lost honor, albeit at the expense of her life.[11] Reciprocity of phallic and manual penetrative gestures is a repetition that reverses: from dishonor to honor, from the rape of a woman to the eternal memory of a woman who martyrs herself for chastity.

ii b

The depiction of the end of the Trojan War marks a transition from the Symbolic to the Imaginary register, from spoken to woven text. Readers of the poem, like Lucrece but more so, are poised at varying distances, drawn out among several media. The visual scene of the tapestry represents verbal negotiations among Greeks and Trojans, all the speech framed within the poet's written language. We readers of Shakespeare's *The Rape of Lucrece* learn from our second-order distance about the eponymous heroine initially *not* seeing in the tapestry of Sinon the truth that he is a deceiver. But Lucrece's perspective evolves and adjusts itself. The painted deception that challenges (but does not defeat) Lucrece is at the level of

[10] Tarquin's hand is initially a confidently "rude ram" that seeks to batter down his victim's "ivory wall" (line 464) but comes to be so perturbed by the beating of the heart and the rising and falling of Lucrece's ventral cavity that "his hand shakes withal" (line 467). This unsteadying of his hand only serves to anger Tarquin more, motivating him "to make the breach and enter this sweet city" (line 469).

[11] Catherine Belsey opposes critics who argue that in stabbing herself Lucrece simply repeats and consummates the misogyny of Tarquin. In section IV of her essay, Belsey makes the case for Lucrece as a political heroine and as someone who dissolves the shame that the rape has cast upon her. Philippa Berry asserts that Lucrece does not simply drop out by virtue of being positioned "between men" in the homosocial nexus. Instead, Berry sees Lucrece as someone who dominates the poem, speaking more lines by far than any other character, in bold defense of a feminine version of Machiavelli's *virtù* (33–39).

the veil (the visual, the Imaginary), whereas earlier in the poem, in the face of Tarquin's spoken aggressions, Lucrece suffered the passion of a specifically linguistic duplicity, the performative hollowing out of words by means of words that sounded the same but signified antithetically. Reading the visual story depicted in tapestry gradually teaches Lucrece an unambiguous lesson and provides her a remedy, suicide. Lucrece could not have availed herself of reparative suicide in her too direct, too immediate experience of Tarquin the rapist's words and sword. Looking at a pictorial representation of a narrative allows Lucrece a safer, more reflective distance than was available in her too intense, violently immersive narrative exchange of words with Tarquin, in which the slippages within language made of her a divided and violated subject of loss.

In the long description of the fall of Troy, the gender of the viewer of the tapestry affects one's understanding of the scene. The narrator remarks that from his perspective the relationship between facial appearance and character is transparent:

> In Ajax and Ulysses, O, what art
> Of physiognomy might one behold!
> The face of either ciphered either's heart;
> Their face their manners most expressly told. (lines 1394–97)

The impersonal ("one") observer of Ajax and Ulysses finds no disjunction between face and heart; what one sees in the lines of the face provides a direct and transparent window onto the inner man, who is what he seems to be. The transition from the impersonal to the more subjective and complex perspective of Lucrece begins at line 1443 as she learns how to do character criticism, to read the lines that are "ciphered" (decipherable) in faces. Colin Burrow points out that Paulus Marsus's marginal commentary in his 1482 edition of Ovid's *Fasti* is what provided the cue for Shakespeare's decision to have Lucrece dilate upon the pictorial representation of the fall of Troy and the similarity between Sinon and Tarquin (62–63).[12] Like Paulus Marsus, Lucrece is a commentator who observes from, and makes notations in, the margins.

Relevant to the depiction of the fall of Troy in *The Rape of Lucrece* are the allusions to Ovid's tale of the rape of Philomela (*Metamorphoses* 6): the cutting out of her tongue to prevent her from revealing the identity of the

[12] The most elaborate study of Shakespeare's source texts is the text by T. W. Baldwin.

rapist, and her weaving of the story of her violation into a tapestry in order to publish her plight and to achieve ultimate vindication. Since Lucrece's observation and narration of Hecuba and Priam's fate is interlaced with references to Philomela, there is an implied analogy between murder, on the one hand, and rape, on the other hand, as acts of violation that have grave political consequences. "My tongue shall utter all" (line 1076), Lucrece avers courageously, and just three lines later the narrator addresses her as "lamenting Philomel," even though her tongue is intact. Lucrece "swears the painter did her [Philomel] wrong / To give her so much grief and not a tongue" (lines 1462–63). Although her reading and interpreting the tapestry aloud marks a difference between herself and Philomela, who weaves and depicts her woes in silence, Lucrece identifies with Philomela as rape victim.[13] Her boldness personified insists on speaking even under the most unfavorable conditions, when there is every risk that she will lose her tongue, like Philomela, or like Lavinia in *Titus Andronicus*.[14] Substituting tongue for life, Lucrece is willing to offer the ultimate sacrifice (life) to make known (to lend her tongue to) the story of her violation and the violations of her fellow allegorical sisters. The unambiguous righteousness of her speech takes as its foil the forked tongue of Tarquin's "let," illegible and antinomian. The ekphrasis in the tapestry is the antidote to the rapist's punning temporality and his linguistic duplicity.

The murderous violation of Troy at the end of the war provides an extended analogy for the rape that Lucrece has just endured. The heroine identifies with Hecuba, who is violated in losing her husband Priam to the sword of Pyrrhus.[15] The breaches of their marriages occasion the women's

[13] In chapter 5 of her book, Lynn Enterline shows how Lucrece lends a tongue (or ventriloquizes) on behalf of the raped and tongue-torn Philomela. The hindering of speech by cutting the tongue is a paradigm for what makes vicarious poetic discourse possible.

[14] See the article by Csilla Kelemen.

[15] William P. Weaver shows how Sinon and Hecuba played key roles in the sixteenth-century rhetorical education that prepared students for forensic practice. "Shakespeare makes the tapestry scene the supreme moment of Lucrece's legal preparation, for the tapestry becomes a way for Lucrece to perform the popular rhetorical exercise of *ethopoeia*, in which a student impersonated a legendary character for the sake of matching style to character, or borrowing that person's misfortune for the sake of feeling emotion" (442). Lucrece expresses her own sorrow by means of an imaginary pathetical identification with words that Hecuba could have spoken in lamenting the destruction of Troy. Enterline looks at Lucrece's imitation of classical models like Hecuba to demonstrate Shakespeare's efforts to become the English Ovid (166–70).

extended complaints.[16] Lucrece lends Hecuba her tongue (line 1465). Ventriloquizing the silent lamentation of these tapestry figures is a means for Lucrece to sublimate her own grief. Thus a polyphonic chorus, a weaving of mute tapestry and spoken complaint, holds the victimized women together in communion. Tongueless Philomela and captionless Hecuba are animated into life-like speech by the supplemental, empathetic vocal projections of the one who narrates them. The violated women depicted in the tapestry interpellate Lucrece in turn, calling her forth as a fellow subject of loss. She "feelingly weeps Troy's painted woes" (line 1492):

> So Lucrece, set a-work, sad tales doth tell
> To pencilled pensiveness and coloured sorrow;
> She lends them words, and she their looks doth borrow. (lines 1496–98)

Telling the story and projecting the voices of its principals permits Lucrece to feel the pain of others and to understand and to describe her own pain in terms of theirs. Her self-reflexivity (the reverse side of her projection) is engendered by her reflecting into herself what she sees depicted in the painted tapestry.

In contrast to the emotional bonds that allow Lucrece to effect an identification with other female victims, in Sinon she will come to see a mirror image—the register of the visual, the specular, as opposed to the register of the Symbolic (of language)—of Tarquin the destroyer. She will see Sinon's deceit in a way that she could not see or hear Tarquin's. But in her initial sight of Sinon, Lucrece is as deceived by suave looks as she was when she welcomed Tarquin as a household guest. The well-established anecdote of Sinon and the Trojan horse from ancient history is a precedent for the long tale of rape that unravels in the timeframe of Shakespeare's narrative. Exemplifying a visual complication that runs parallel to the linguistic "let" but is easier to decipher in the long run, if not initially, the image of Sinon effects a type of puzzle or snare: innocent appearance masks and belies the truth of his character. Whereas "perjured" Sinon's "enchanting story" proves to be the death of "credulous old Priam" (lines 1521–22)—as the omniscient narrator puts it, still unbeknownst to Lucrece—for Lucrece it is not the verbal narrative of Sinon but rather the physiognomy of Sinon that makes her do a double take, for at first she is dumbfounded because "the painter laboured with his skill / To hide deceit" (lines

[16] Heather Dubrow analyzes Shakespeare's indebtedness to the complaint genre.

1506–07) in the portrait. (Even the truth of painting is a lie, as Plato objected. Zeuxis's verisimilar grapes attract the birds but provide them only phantom nourishment.)[17] In the *paragone* that places visual art and verbal rhetoric in competition, the rival forms of mimesis share at least one thing in common: the deceit that veils deceit, a faining/feigning verisimilitude. The narrator advances in writing the allegorical truth that escapes Lucrece's notice initially, namely, that visual representation is a lure that can trap the one who gazes. The allure of Sinon's face is such a trap:

> But like a constant and confirmed devil
> He entertained a show so seeming just,
> And therein so ensconced his secret evil
> That jealousy itself could not mistrust
> False creeping craft and perjury should thrust
> Into so bright a day such black-faced storms,
> Or blot with hell-born sin such saintlike forms. (lines 1513–19)

The narrator's paradoxes are available for us to read, to puzzle through, and to cipher/decipher, but Lucrece, by contrast, is not able easily to detect in the painting the paradoxes whose labyrinth of words (Shakespeare the poet's meta-medium, so different from, and emulous of, the tapestry maker's silent and unwritten medium) the reader must negotiate. Seeing a tapestry is not like reading a text that describes it.

As she examines Sinon's image more intently and "advisedly" (line 1527), Lucrece comes to revise what she sees and to reverse her discourse accordingly, doubting the identity of the person represented. Her skepticism advances to the point of broaching the possibility that Sinon himself is not Sinon; he is rather an allegorical figure standing for the non-being of what appears to be—in other words, an allegorical figure for allegory per se.[18] Or, to put it in a slightly different way, Sinon is a subject of impersonation, and may indeed be an allegorical figure thereof:

[17] See Richard Meek 35–38.

[18] For Patrick Cheney, Sinon is a figure not only for Tarquin but also for Virgil and the incorporation of Virgilian epic into the poem, and Cheney also discusses the influence of Spenser's "deterministic nationalist teleology" (136). The depiction of the fall of Troy within the domestic space of Lucrece recalls the frescoes that Aeneas sees in the temple of Sidonian Dido. Willbern regards Sinon not just as a figure for Tarquin but for Collatine as well, since the latter's boasting of his wife's chastity is what lays the trap for her undoing (88–89).

> This picture she advisedly perused,
> And chid the painter for his wondrous skill,
> Saying some shape in Sinon's was abused;
> So fair a form lodged not a mind so ill.
> And still on him she gazed, and gazing still,
> Such signs of truth in his plain face she spied,
> That she concludes the picture was belied. (lines 1527–33)

The truth of appearances ("signs of truth") is in fact doubtful, since the sincerity that Sinon signals in his face is a deception. The lines above can be interpreted in two ways: (1) It is possible that Sinon is impersonating truth, or (2) It is possible that someone else is impersonating Sinon. In any event, in either case, Sinon is not Sinon. Sinon (or someone who looks like him) speaks lies to Priam that are plausible, pleasing, and verisimilar, coaxing him to allow the gift of the wooden horse to be brought in through the gates of the city. The representation of Sinon's physiognomy similarly fools Lucrece, at first glance, though she comes to discover her error in time to reverse it, unlike the Trojan king. It is her distance from the tapestry, her observing it from outside its two-dimensional warp and woof, that sets her apart from the woven/depicted figures and allows her not to be duped in the final analysis.

Lucrece's self-consciousness reaches its apogee once she understands that the test of the tapestry, the proof of its vision—the truth for her as spectator of the artwork—is the identification of Sinon not with himself but with Tarquin. An analogical reading reveals that Sinon's use of deceit to penetrate the walls of Troy parallels Tarquin's mask of complaisance as prelude to his rape of Lucrece. That he is an impersonator (not identical to himself) is what makes Simon a type for Tarquin. Once Lucrece decodes the visual message, immediately she mimics and echoes the paradoxicity of the narrator's rhetorical word-painting. In the stanza quoted below it is she, not just the narrator, who speaks truth in both speaking and penetrating the language of paradox, she for the first time in the ekphrasis. No longer the passive observer, Lucrece speaks back to the tapestry directly, in her own voice. The "advised" (line 1527) truth is not simply that looks are deceiving, whether in representational art or in real life. This is true; but more to the point is the fact that the heroine accedes to an understanding about the nature of language, namely that there exist propositions that cannot be but the opposite of what they assert—something that she could not articulate and was defenseless against in her encounter with Tarquin:

"It cannot be," quoth she, "that so much guile"—
She would have said "can lurk in such a look."
But Tarquin's shape came in her mind the while,
And from her tongue "can lurk" from "cannot" took.
"It cannot be" she in that sense forsook,
   And turned it thus: "It cannot be, I find,
   But such a face should bear a wicked mind." (lines 1534–40)

These utterances mark for Lucrece a complex understanding of the nature of duplicity, both visual and verbal. She understands that to be immersed in language is to be bespoken as a divided or barred subject. Language belies the image's self-identity. "Sinon" (the signifier) morphs into "Tarquin."[19] Visually innocent "look" morphs into menacing "lurk" via an aural chain of association (consonance) and slips of signifiers. The double negative ("cannot" ... "But") of the concluding couplet reverses the false clarity of the opening line. The dialectic of her ruminations leads Lucrece to conclude that, as Sinon betrayed Troy, so

"To me came Tarquin armed to beguild
With outward honesty, but yet defiled
   With inward vice. As Priam him did cherish,
   So did I Tarquin, so my Troy did perish." (lines 1544–47)

In these lines, paradox is diminished after its predominance in the preceding stanzas, giving way to simple and clear revelation by parallelism and analogy, expressed rhetorically in the figure of a *simile* that links Sinon and Tarquin as guests, host Priam and host Lucrece, Troy and the domus of Collatine. Looking at the tapestry over the course of her long speech, Lucrece is schooled in the duplicity of both faces and voices. Her looking is a schooling, an insight. Outward honesty is a foil for inward vice, epitomized in the triple pun on "beguild" as a gilding that covers over guile and guilt. For all its layers of complexity, the ambiguities of "beguild" are readable and decipherable in a way that the deconstructive antithesis of

[19] Tarquinius Superbus, the father of Tarquinius Sextus, pretended to have abandoned the war against the Gabii, leaving his son behind to feign that he had been cast out by his own side. The son became the general of the Gabii but then betrayed them (Livy I.53–54 and Ovid, *Fasti* 2.690–710). In his edition of the Fasti annotated by Marsus, Shakespeare would have found the marginal note, "Ut Sinon apud Virg." ("as Sinon in Virgil") (Jonathan Bate 79–80).

"let" and its ancillary images (the winds, the glove, the fort, the lock, the door, the eyelids) were not, leading as the latter did to moral impasse, aporia. The tapestry vouchsafes Lucrece the ability to give definitive voice to duplicity and thus to contain and to control it. Despite, or due to, the fact of having been raped by a deceptive talker, Lucrece can articulate truly the doubleness of language now that she has seen a version of her story represented (or re-represented) in art. The art of tapestry is framed by the ekphrastic art of the poet. The depiction of Troy teaches Lucrece that the depravity of human nature results from man's duplicitous ("beguild") means of expression. The speaking picture's didactic function results from the potential of visual art to be translated into ekphrastic speech according to the humanist formula *ut pictura poesis*. The tapestry that exists in non-linguistic form inspires accurate and pointed speech in Lucrece. And its revelation to the purposeful viewer of it directs her toward decisive action. Lucrece is enlightened, stoically resolute now for her suicide.

iii

At the end of *The Rape of Lucrece* no single word can express the paradoxical (but not antithetical) duality of the rape/suicide pairing, in the way that the word "let" served earlier as Tarquin's alibi for taking and mistaking every "No" to mean "Yes" (Fineman 186). Lucrece's rape and Lucrece's suicide do not collapse into each other indifferently, amorally, and antithetically; rather, Lucrece's suicide supersedes and undoes her rape. In the latter part of the poem the aporetic wordplay on "let" disappears, as do the equally aporetic images of winds and gloves, doors and eyelids, forts, and so on that put up a resistance that excited violent entry. Antithetical words and images like these cede place to a different because ultimately decipherable species of ambiguity, a less threatening paradoxicity that is in principle understandable and resolvable, like the visual feints in the tapestry. What occurs after the rape of Lucrece (objective genitive) gives the lie to, and upends, the abyssal and permissive *mise en abîme* of the "let" that gave rise to the rape in the first part of the poem.

Self-murder cleanses Lucrece of the pollution of sexual violation and of its infamous long-range consequences after death. In plunging the knife into herself, Lucrece nips in the bud the potential illegitimate life in her womb and instead drives herself toward a death that claims to be providential for both the individual and the polity. Tarquin's rape of Lucrece will produce no illicit inheritors, no spurious claimants to the throne.

When Brutus forces Tarquin and his royal father into exile, the narrator reveals that an unintended but fortunate consequence of the rape is the demise of the monarchy and the birth of the Roman republic in its place.[20] Brutus vows that "by this bloody knife, / We will revenge the death of this true wife" (lines 1840–41). Shakespeare's rhyming gives (glib) point to the theme: Knife vindicates wife; shame yields to fame. Both legitimate and potentially illegitimate heirs to the Tarquin dynasty are done away with thanks to the suicidal response to the transgressive violence perpetrated against aristocratic subjects like Collatine and Lucrece.

In taking her own life Lucrece violates herself. She repeats the act of violence in order to efface her rape and the subversive words and images that forbade but also excited, permitted, and necessitated it.[21] Shakespeare's heroine makes sacred again the temple (of the body) that was violated. Once she sees duplicity depicted in the tapestry and understands its modus operandi in Sinon and in Tarquin, Lucrece stabs herself. Plunging the phallic knife through her breast recalls, repeats, and undoes the rapist's penetration of her body with his penis, as he held her at falchion-point. Her death will give rise to a new regime. Stabbing herself recoups lost honor:

> My honour I'll bequeath unto the knife
> That wounds my body so dishonoured.
> 'Tis honour to deprive dishonoured life;
> The one will live, the other being dead.
> ………………………………
> Mine honour be the knife's that makes my wound. (lines 1184–87, 1201)

Lucrece's enduring legacy is her bequest of honor to the state, not her children or anything material that she bequeaths to her family. The "dishonoured life" that she takes pride in eliminating is her own. It is also, perhaps, that of an illegitimate fetus in her womb. Honor derives from the knife and its negation of life or lives, a negation performed at the local

[20] Cheney traces the republicanism of *The Rape of Lucrece* to Shakespeare's debts to Marlowe's translation of the first book of Lucan's *Pharsalia*. The fourth chapter of Cheney's book is entitled "*Publishing the show*: The Rape of Lucrece *as Lucanian counter-epic of empire*.

[21] Ian Donaldson points to lines which describe Tarquin's soul as a "princess" who has been assaulted and "spotted" (line 721) by the patrician's rape of Lucrece. The soul's "fair temple is defaced" (line 719) and lust has "battered down her consecrated wall" (line 723). See Sam Hynes 451–53.

level by the prefixes "*de-*" and "*dis-*" in the passage above. The double negative of piling negation upon negation is reparative. The illegitimate is aborted, in substitutive compensation for which "honour is new born" (line 1190).[22] Honor is a sublimation that displaces the soiled body and its soiled offspring or telos. The newly secured honor is permanent, bound for fame. It cannot collapse back into its opposite; it cannot follow the antithetical modality of "let" that prevailed as long as Tarquin's was the dominant verbal framework in the narrative up to and including the rape.

Lucrece's soul is released from the "poisoned closet" (line 1659) of the body as the knife ravages (ravishes) the latter:

> Even here she sheathed in her harmless breast
> A harmful knife, that thence her soul unsheathed:
> That blow did bail it from the deep unrest
> Of that polluted prison where it breathed. (lines 1723–26)

Sheath serves as a key switchword, carrying multiple valences in this passage. In Elizabethan English one meaning of *sheath* is vagina (*OED* 2a).[23] But in the repetition of the primal scene the vagina gets displaced to the breast, which is a second referent for *sheath*. The suicide that replays and reverses the rape releases the soul from its corporeal shell (a third referent of *sheath*). As a container, the sheath houses the violating penis or the restorative, re-sacralizing knife in the chest, according to context. The metaphorical meaning of knife and sheath vary according to their placement in the body. The metaphor varies according to the metonym (the locus). The unsheathing in line 1724 is releasing the soul from the body—specifically from the corporeal nexus of the breast but recalling (at a

[22] Lucrece assures Collatine that "This bastard graff shall never come to growth" (line 1062) and that Tarquin will never be able to boast that he is the father of a child that Collatine will dote upon. Duncan-Jones and Woudhuysen point out that there is no source for Lucrece's pregnancy. They believe that Shakespeare introduces the subject of a possible bastard child glancingly so that his readers will not have to dwell on the disturbing ethical quandary of Lucrece as murderer of an unborn child (44). Colin Burrow believes that Lucrece may want to kill the bastard graff (graft) because conception as a result of rape was often interpreted to mean that the woman consented to the sexual intercourse (69).

[23] Katharine Eisaman Maus notes a range of contradictions in Lucrece's suicide, including the fact that she proves her innocence by exacting the penalty for guilt and that the "sheath" (line 1723) of her breast, into which she plunges the knife, derives from the Latin word for vagina (72). Bate quotes a relevant line from Ovid's *Fasti*: "et aurata vagina liberat ensem"—"and from the gilded scabbard he draws his sword" (line 793) (70).

metonymic distance) the vagina too as somatic nodal point and thematic crux. Cutting the soul apart from the body in the act of suicide—reiterating the original violation when Tarquin brandished his "insulting falchion" (line 509) against Lucrece's neck—does not simply replay the penis penetrating the vagina in the primal scene of forced intercourse at knife-point; rather, it implies the more radical notion of effacing the effect of phallic penetration in the primal scene, as if Lucrece is not only martyred but *revirginated* (or returned to chastity, at least) in the process of stabbing herself in the breast. The labor of the knife at the breast undoes the harmful violences of the other two metonymic knives: the knife at the throat and the penis in the vagina.

Since she is a matron, Lucrece cannot be revirginated, and since she is raped it is hard to imagine how her marital chastity may be restored, especially in the eyes of those male interpreters like Augustine[24] for whom the intentions of a woman like Lucrece are always held in suspicion; but the paradox implicit in the idea of the restoration of chastity—of losing the loss that the rape occasioned—is the poem's ideological asymptote, its point of maximal suspension of disbelief. This is the acme of the heroine's sublime apotheosis. At one moment before the rape the narrator refers to his heroine's breasts as "a pair of maiden worlds unconquered" (line 408) to suggest that even though Lucrece is not a virgin, she remains chaste. She is like a town or fortress that has consented to admit no one within its walls except her lord and husband. The paradox that suicide restores purity, though complex and challenging, does not defy logic in the way that the primal, antithetical "let" did. The paradoxical and the antithetical are not the same. The restoring or reversal of the heroine's violation and loss makes of *The Rape of Lucrece* a precarious and distant cousin of Shakespeare's romances, in that the heroine is granted enduring posthumous renown, if not the bodily resurrection that happens so often in romances like *Pericles*, *The Tempest*, and *The Winter's Tale*. Tragedy is rewritten as comedy, provided that we onlookers espouse a Coleridgean suspension of disbelief. We must awaken our faith to the possibility of the (impossible) loss of loss. We must believe in what (we know) is not real.

[24]For discussion of how Augustine influenced the tradition of seeing Lucrece's suicide as an act of sinful pride, thus posing an obstacle that Renaissance humanists would later attempt to surmount, see Coppélia Kahn, "The Rape in Shakespeare's *Lucrece*," 62–63. Donaldson gives a lengthy account of Augustine's position on Lucrece's rape and suicide (21–39). In her chapter on *Antony and Cleopatra*, Kahn, *Roman Shakespeare*, presents the argument justifying Cato's suicide and shows how it served as a model for Antony's.

What is at stake in the unsheathing of the knife and the use of it to commit suicide is the deep fantasy that after a woman is raped, sacrificial violence may be reparative and restorative. Self-sacrifice returns the woman, in a figurative sense, to an original state of intactness. As an after-effect that retroactively undoes the original rape, Lucrece's death instances an unusual, uncanny mode of Freud's *Nachträglicheit* (Lacan's *après-coup*), which may also be translated in terms of the *posthumous*: that only at the moment of death, indeed at the cost of death, after the real fact of rape, is Lucrece able to re-establish her integrity by re-entering the primal scene of violation in order to re-encounter, there, the original traumatic loss. She embraces the trauma. At the moment of death, the self-murderer enjoys posthumous life and posthumous fame. The self-imposed death, which resolves the stressful post-trauma incumbent upon sexual violence and violation, is a prolepsis of all the eternalizations that will follow: in painting, in tapestry, in prose, in poetry.

Some paintings of the rape of Lucrece portray Tarquin raping his victim in her bedroom, whereas others represent the moment in the same bedroom when Lucrece herself (not her rapist) holds the knife to her breast—an aggressive heroine, confiding herself to the void. (This is the deferred action [*Nachträglichkeit*] of the *après-coup* that precludes, that absents, that forecloses the *après-coupe*.) The new-found uncanny *intactness* of Lucrece is emphasized in classical pictorial representations of her suicide (as in many of Lucas Cranach's thirty-five paintings of the rape of Lucrece) by showing the heroine with the knife posed against her breast, poised just before the moment of striking. That the artist chooses to crop the scene the moment before the spilling of any blood helps to draw a distinction between the original trauma and its subsequent sublimation. In *L'Age d'homme*, Michel Leiris comments on the odd way that the rape victim's holding of the knife suggests that she is preparing "to cancel, by a parallel act, the effect of the rape which she has suffered" (Donaldson 17).[25] David

[25] Shakespeare offers no freeze-frame of Lucrece just before she plunges the knife. He deploys both the ideal image before suicide, like Cranach, and the bloody aftermath, with the blood divided into red and black streams, and the black further divided into pure and impure rigols that remain distinct from each other (lines 1137–50). Louis Marin analyzes a practice very different from Cranach's idealization in Caravaggio's *Head of Medusa*, perhaps a portrait of the artist himself as a woman, in which the portrayal of the bloody moment just after decapitation foregrounds the gaze as a rift or gap in representation. This is mimesis performing its own impossibility, when Medusa and her viewer implode in the instantaneous moment of recognizing that they are caught in the trap or ruse of their own gaze.

Willbern sees Lucrece's suicide as a "self-rape" and a "symbolic coitus" between herself and Tarquin; Lucrece's stabbing herself with the knife "formally re-enacts the rape" (84). I agree with Willbern's formulation of symbols, except that the emphasis needs to be put (I think) more on the putative reversal of rape, not just its re-enacting and its symbolization of coitus.

The Stoic ideal is an image, akin to the ekphrastic revelation vouchsafed by the Trojan War tapestries. Stoic Lucrece's redemptive rape-suicide runs counter to Christianity and to modern feminisms, both of which tend to find repugnant the secular pagan martyrdom on display at the end of *The Rape of Lucrece*. Although the poem shows the suicide in all its bloody gore, this supplemental realism does not compromise or displace the idealism of Lucrece's integrity and fame. Shakespeare does not blame Lucrece for the rape, unlike Augustine. His poem consummates itself with no less clamor than a Roman military triumph. The poet embraces classical culture's insistent valorization of Honor, which entails that the violated woman must be sacrificed, whether she is guilty or not. If there is no hope for christic redemption in this pre-Christian world, there is nonetheless the prospect of secular glory. Renaissance humanists saw Lucrece's suicide, as Livy had in Augustan times, as a heroic action that repressed and sublimated the original shame for which the heroine bore no fault.[26] (The Augustan view contrasts with that of Augustine, the church father who condemned the earthly city that persecuted him and his kind.) That Lucrece's self-inflicted death is one way to denominate her "rape" is not only no misnomer, nor is it just a matter of Augustan apologia; it is also a necessity of syntax. The *of* in the rape of Lucrece is both objective and subjective genitive: the woman is both raped woman (object) and rapist (subject): Thus, Lucrece's rape of Lucrece. Repetition is reversal, what in

[26]Stephanie Jed translates and analyzes Coluccio Salutati's *Declamatio Lucretiae*. For Jed the humanistic celebration of Lucrece is inseparable from the violence done to her and from the necessity of her self-violation via suicide, analogous to how humanistic scholarship is obsessed with castigating (*castigatio*) the text in the effort to make it chaste (*castitas*). Eric Langley posits that narcissism and suicide are two forms of self-centering that entail self-dissolution. His sixth chapter discusses how Renaissance authors like Sidney, Donne, Shakespeare, Burton, and Milton revived the debate over suicide between Stoicism and Christianity, with specific reference to the question of whether the self possesses authority over itself. Langley cites many sermons in the English Renaissance that rely on Augustine's notion that classical suicides like Lucrece, Cato, and Seneca were despairing rather than heroic and were guilty of pride since they courted earthly fame for their actions.

psychoanalytic terms is a "working through"—a repetition with a redemptive difference, from shame to apotheosis, as Lucrece avers when she invokes the internal rhyme of the shame/fame binarism (a paradox, not an antithesis): "So of shame's ashes shall my fame be bred … / My shame so dead, mine honour is new born" (lines 1188–90).[27] Instead of giving birth to a disgraceful bastard, she fashions for herself, as her posthumous progeny, the fantastical phoenix of an illustrious and fecundating reputation. The new trauma of stabbing herself to death dissolves her history of trauma. The allegory of political triumph: The Tarquins are expelled and aborted; the Roman Republic is born. It is a Stoical, conservative apotheosis, an allegory of the Imaginary triumphing over the Real (the real of rape) and over the ideological enablers of the Real: the Symbolic language of the "let" and its panoply of fetishized accoutrements and supports that take the form of primal antitheses: the glove, the bedroom door, the locks on the door, the closed eyelids, the adverse winds, the unimpregnable yet impregnable fort, the bastion of thorns around the rose, the No's that mean Yes. Tragedy, trauma, dishonor, bathos, death, rape—all are sublimated in the unimaginable Imaginary. The unrealistic end of Lucrece (and of *The Rape of Lucrece*) is its teleology for the future, its reversion to the ideal and the imaginary.

References

Adelman, Janet. *Suffocating Mothers: Fantasies of Maternal Origin in Shakespeare's Plays,* Hamlet *to* The Tempest. Routledge, 1992.

Baldwin, T. W., editor. *On the Literary Genetics of Shakespeare's Poems and Sonnets.* U of Illinois P, 1950.

Bate, Jonathan, *Shakespeare and Ovid.* Oxford UP, 1993.

Belsey, Catherine. "Tarquin Dispossessed: Expropriation and Consent in 'The Rape of Lucrece.'" *Shakespeare Quarterly*, vol. 52, 2001, pp. 315–35.

Berry, Philippa. "Woman, Language, and History in *The Rape of Lucrece.*" *Shakespeare Survey*, vol. 44, 1992, pp. 33–39.

[27] Mark Breitenberg sees the rebirth of honor in Lucrece's act of suicide as the vindication of the Calvinistic emphasis on one's private relationship before God, as opposed to the more public notion implicit in a "shame culture" (107). Honor is inner conscience, not external approbation. Following the categories of Raymond Williams, Breitenberg regards the Calvinistic definition of honor as "emergent," whereas honor as shame is a "residual" or traditional notion in Elizabethan culture.

Breitenberg, Mark. *Anxious Masculinity in Early Modern England.* Cambridge UP, 1996.

Burrow, Colin, editor. *William Shakespeare: The Complete Sonnets and Poems.* Oxford UP, 2002.

Cheney, Patrick. *Shakespeare, National Poet-Playwright.* Cambridge UP, 2004.

Donaldson, Ian. *The Rapes of Lucretia: A Myth and its Transformations.* Oxford UP, 1982.

Dubrow, Heather. "A Mirror for Complaints: Shakespeare's *Lucrece* and Generic Tradition." *Renaissance Genres: Essays on Theory, History, and Interpretation*, edited by Barbara Lewalski, Harvard UP, 1986, pp. 400–17.

Duncan-Jones, Katherine and H. R. Woudhuysen, editors. *The Arden Shakespeare: Shakespeare's Poems.* Bloomsbury, 2007.

Enterline, Lynn. *The Rhetoric of the Body from Ovid to Shakespeare.* Cambridge UP, 2000.

Fineman, Joel. "Shakespeare's *Will*: The Temporality of Rape." *The Subjectivity Effect in Western Literary Tradition: Essays Toward the Release of Shakespeare's Will.* MIT Press, 1991, pp. 165–221.

Freud, Sigmund. *The Revised Standard Edition of the Complete Psychological Works of Sigmund Freud*, edited and translated by James Strachey, revised by Mark Solms. 24 vols. Rowman & Littlefield Publishers, 2024. (In-text references provide *RSE* page numbers immediately after *SE* page numbers).

———. "The Antithetical Meaning of Primal Words" (1910). *The Standard Edition of the Complete Psychological Works of Sigmund Freud*, edited and translated by James Strachey, vol. 11, Hogarth Press, 1957, pp. 153–61/*RSE* vol. 11, pp. 141–48.

Greenstadt, Amy. "'Read it in me': The Author's Will in *Lucrece.*" *Shakespeare Quarterly*, vol. 57, 2006, pp. 45–70.

Hulse, S. Clark. "'A Piece of Skilful Painting' in Shakespeare's 'Lucrece.'" *Shakespeare Survey*, vol. 31, 1978, pp. 13–22.

Hynes, Sam. "The Rape of Tarquin." *Shakespeare Quarterly*, vol. 10, 1959, pp. 451–53.

Jacobson, Miriam. "The Elizabethan Cipher in Shakespeare's *Lucrece.*" *Studies in Philology*, vol. 107, 2010, pp. 336–59.

Jed, Stephanie. *Chaste Thinking: The Rape of Lucretia and the Birth of Humanism.* Indiana UP, 1989.

Kahn, Coppélia. "The Rape in Shakespeare's *Lucrece.*" *Shakespeare Studies*, vol. 9, 1976, pp. 45–72.

———. *Roman Shakespeare: Warriors, Wounds, and Women.* Routledge, 1997.

Kelemen, Csilla. "Images of Passion, Rape, and Grief: A Comparative Analysis of Shakespeare's *Rape of Lucrece* and *Titus Andronicus.*" *Hungarian Journal of English and American* Studies, vol. 11, 2005, pp. 151–73.

Kökeritz, Helge. *Shakespeare's Pronunciation.* Yale UP, 1953.

Langley, Eric. *Narcissism and Suicide in Shakespeare and his Contemporaries.* Oxford UP, 2009.
Marin, Louis. *To Destroy Painting.* Translated by Mette Hjort, U of Chicago P, 1996.
Maus, Katharine Eisaman. "Taking Tropes Seriously: Language and Violence in Shakespeare's *Rape of Lucrece.*" *Shakespeare Quarterly*, vol. 37, 1986, pp. 66–82.
Meek, Richard. *Narrating the Visual in Shakespeare.* Ashgate, 2009.
Newman, Jane. "'And Let Mild Women to Him Lose Their Mildness': Philomela, Female Violence, and Shakespeare's *The Rape of Lucrece.*" *Shakespeare Quarterly*, vol. 45, 1994, pp. 304–26.
Roe, John, editor. *William Shakespeare: The Poems.* Cambridge UP, 1992.
Stone, James W. "'A carrion Death': The Theme of the Gold Casket in *The Merchant of Venice.*" *The Upstart Crow: A Shakespeare Journal*, vol. XXVIII, 2009, pp. 35–49.
Willbern, David. *Poetic Will: Shakespeare and the Play of Language.* U of Pennsylvania P, 1997.
Weaver, William P. "'O teach me how to make mine own excuse': Forensic Performance in *Lucrece.*" *Shakespeare Quarterly*, vol. 59, 2008, pp. 421–49.

CHAPTER 9

Hamlet, Freud, Laplanche: A Copernican Reading

John Fletcher

Indeed, if Freud is his own Copernicus, he is also his own Ptolemy [...] In Freud, one should speak, at almost every period, of an alternation between relapses into Ptolemaism and resurgences of the Copernican, other-centered vision. (Laplanche, *Essays on Otherness* 60)

A Metapsychological Prologue: Freud's Copernican Affiliation

As is well known, Freud affiliated psychoanalysis with the Copernican Revolution as a paradigm of scientific rationality. This he described as the first of a series of blows to human narcissism delivered by science, conceived of as a series of decenterings of the human subject. The first, Freud proposes, is in relation to the cosmos, delivered by Copernicus's heliocentric model of the solar system in which the earth and the other planets moved around the sun. This challenged the hitherto dominant geocentric model in which the earth was the center of a system around which the sun

J. Fletcher (✉)
London, UK

J. W. Stone, C. Bates (eds.), *Shakespeare and Psychoanalysis*, Palgrave Shakespeare Studies,
https://doi.org/10.1007/978-3-032-07897-1_9

and the planets moved, perfected in the *Almagest* or "great synthesis" of Ptolemy of Alexandria in the second century CE. As a second decentering, Freud added the Darwinian model of evolution, which decentered the human species in relation to the whole system of animal species, and the natural history of their emergences and disappearances, challenging the religious cosmogonies that had placed Man as a separate creation and as the apex of the natural world. Finally, as the third of the world-historic blows to human narcissism, Freud modestly places his own psychoanalytic revolution, which delivered the third psychological blow, decentering the human subject in relation to itself. This comes with Freud's discovery of the unconscious and the drives: "the ego is not master in its own house" ("A Difficulty in the Path of Psycho-Analysis" 143/133). Jean Laplanche has developed Freud's analogy of the Copernican and psychoanalytic revolutions as a critical tool for reading Freud himself, offering us the paradoxical proposition cited above as an epigraph: "if Freud is his own Copernicus, he is also his own Ptolemy [...] In Freud, one should speak, at almost every period, of an alternation between relapses into Ptolemaism and resurgences of the Copernican, other-centered vision." Laplanche traces Freud's continual alternation between, on the one hand, concepts and arguments that pose a radical decentering of the subject in relation to a primal other—which, in a letter to Wilhelm Fliess of 6 December 1896, Freud had called "the prehistoric, unforgettable other person who is never equaled by anyone later" (Masson 213)—and, on the other hand, a continually resurgent movement of Ptolemaic recentering on the individual, as the origin and center of his own endogenous development. Laplanche demonstrates that concepts such as the ego, narcissism, the unconscious, the drive (Freud's *Trieb* and not *Instinkt*) are marked by distinct and competing conceptualizations, in which an original decentering Copernican break is covered over by a recentering Ptolemaic revision, a revision that initiates a certain *fourvoiement* or "going-astray" of the concept along structurally determined lines.

At a moment of impasse in his work on the theory of traumatic seduction, Freud announced its abandonment in a letter to Wilhelm Fliess of 21 September 1897: "I no longer believe in my *neurotica* [theory of the neuroses]" (Masson 264). Three weeks later in a letter of 15 October 1897 he proposed an alternative to adult seduction: "A single idea of general value dawned on me. I have found, in my own case too, [the phenomenon of] being in love with my mother and being jealous of my father, and I now consider it a universal event in early childhood" (Masson 272), which he is only later in 1910 to call the "Oedipus complex" ("A Special Form of Choice of Object Made by Men" 171/158). It is at this point of transition from an exogenous to an endogenous model of psychic causality, in a crucial moment of Ptolemaic recentering, that Freud turns to Sophocles's *Oedipus the King*, which is usually twinned with Shakespeare's *Hamlet* in Freud's thought. Freud's interpretation of the two tragedies centers *Oedipus* on the protagonist's spontaneous, infantile impulses, incestuous and parricidal, supposedly enacted in the tragedy's back-story of Oedipus's unwitting killing of his father, Laius, and marriage to his mother, Jocasta. Similarly, *Hamlet* is centered on the protagonist's repressed oedipal impulses, reactivated by the actions of his uncle in murdering his father and seducing his mother. Freud's turn to these tragedies, and his interpretive erasure of the daemonic and spectral figures of the other in each tragedy, replicates the logic whereby three weeks earlier he had abandoned the theory of traumatic seduction by an adult in his theory of neurosis, for the "universal event in early childhood" of spontaneous jealous rivalry with the father over love for the mother (Masson 272). Freud's reading of *Oedipus* outlines a template for psychosexual development that he was to formulate systematically in his later work (as distinct from the psychopathology—hysteria, obsessional neurosis, paranoia—resulting from premature sexual experience, with which he had hitherto been preoccupied). In a Copernican rereading of Sophocles's *Oedipus*, I have previously attempted to retrieve and trace the central role of the ubiquitous figure of the daemon that drives Oedipus's actions but is dismissed by Freud's Ptolemaic interpretation (Fletcher, "Scenography of Trauma"). The present chapter is a parallel Copernican reading that seeks to resituate Freud's oedipal Hamlet in relation to the transmissions from the spectral figure of the paternal ghost, the other who presides over but then vanishes from Shakespeare's play.[1]

[1] I must acknowledge at this point a powerfully framed Copernican reading of the play by the Laplanchean translator and scholar, Nicholas Ray, who focuses on the differential transgenerational logics in the play's father-son relations and makes a persuasive critique of the problematic of modernity invoked by contemporary critics (171–218).

Part 1: *Hamlet* Without Freud: *A Tragedy of Delay*

Freud's interpretation turns on the phenomenon usually referred to as Hamlet's "delay," an ambiguous term that can be taken in an objective sense to indicate difficulties in the task assigned him (access to Claudius, the trustworthiness of the Ghost, etc.) or in a subjective sense to indicate personal reluctance (ethical objections to revenge) or incapacity (melancholia, introversion). Freud's preferred terms, however, are *inhibitions* and *hesitations*, clearly indicating a psychological process or state as central explanatory issues. There is a line of criticism from E. E. Stoll and A. J. A. Waldock in the early twentieth century through Phillip Brockbank and Ruth Nevo in mid-century to commentators in more recent editions, Alan Sinfield and Johnathan Bate, who consider the issue of delay misconceived or at best of secondary importance.[2] Consequently I will attempt to establish first the centrality of delay, formally as well as thematically, independent of any psychoanalytic reflection and before engaging with Freudian and post-Freudian perspectives.

Hamlet's Failed Revenge

Hamlet, both Prince and play, is something of an anomaly. Hamlet the Prince is an enigma, *especially* to himself; *Hamlet* the play presents the prince as an irresolvable problem, a revenger whose "dull revenge" has, in his own words, "let all sleep" (4.4.33, 59). Consequently, the play is itself a problem *as a play*. For nearly five long acts in this, the longest by far of all Shakespeare's plays (especially when the 1604 good Quarto and the 1623 Folio are conflated), Hamlet, though very busy, fails to act. He fails to carry through a mission demanded of him by the ghost of his father, and to which he had passionately pledged himself by the end of act 1. Instead of the driving dynamic of tragedies such as *Macbeth*, *Othello*, *King Lear*, or *Coriolanus*, we have Horatio's busy list of bungles and mishaps that he promises to disclose publicly at Hamlet's funeral obsequies, and which are themselves due to take place only *after* the play's ending. In the

[2]"So we might say the Prince is fairly punctual," notes Sinfield in a new Introduction to Spencer's New Penguin edition of the play (xxiv); "Nor does he delay nearly so much as he tells us he is delaying […] deeds take over from words, revenge is performed without further compunctious visitings of nature," comments Bate in his notes to the play (2020–22). One might search in vain, however, for Hamlet's compunctious visitings as regards Claudius, or indeed anyone else.

closing moments, in one last, final postponement, Horatio promises Fortinbras:

> So shall you hear
> Of carnal, bloody and unnatural acts,
> Of accidental judgements, casual slaughters,
> Of deaths put on by cunning and forced cause,
> And, in this upshot, purposes mistook
> Fallen on th' inventors' heads. (5.2.374–79)

Rather than a unified tragic action, Horatio promises to describe a catalogue of *failed* actions, of "accidental judgements," "casual slaughters," and "purposes mistook."

Of course, Hamlet does finally get his man. He reacts immediately and violently to the violence that has been done to him in the final scene of the duel. Hamlet had always been good at rapid reaction behavior under the pressure of events, stabbing whoever lurks behind the arras in his mother's closet (the wrong man, Polonius), sending Rosencrantz and Guildernstern to their deaths, and we might add leaping aboard the pirates' ship, and leaping also into Ophelia's grave to confront Laertes. A good man in an emergency, Hamlet's seizing the initiative, however, is essentially reactive, a reaction to the initiatives of others taken toward him. With one exception, the performance of *The Murder of Gonzago* before the King, Hamlet is reactive rather than proactive throughout. Consequently, he dies poisoned by the very man who had poisoned his father, as Freud notes, and in danger of taking with him to the grave his knowledge of Claudius's still secret crimes and Gertrude's adultery.

In his essay *Of Revenge* (1623), Shakespeare's contemporary, Francis Bacon, wrote:

> Revenge is a kind of wild justice [...] The most tolerable sort of revenge, is for those wrongs for which there is no law to remedy. [...] Public revenges are for the most part, fortunate [...] But in private revenges, it is not so. (13–14)

Bacon argues that revenge is only defensible where the crime is beyond the law to remedy and which is a public and an open revenge. For Justice to be done, it must be *seen* to be done. A justified revenge, if it is to be more than a private and vindictive tit-for-tat, is a public calling of the criminal to account and to punishment, when the law itself cannot do so. So Hamlet's last-minute killing of Claudius fails to make his death a matter of justice, however wild, because it has not been explained and justified in public. Understandably, the reaction of those present at Hamlet's killing of Claudius is to cry "Treason! Treason!" (5.2.317). Hamlet himself is acutely aware of this, which is why he struggles to prevent his friend Horatio from committing a stoic suicide like "an antique Roman":

> O God, Horatio, what a wounded name,
> Things standing thus unknown, shall live behind me!
> If thou didst ever hold me in thy heart,
> Absent thee from felicity awhile,
> And in this harsh world draw thy breath in pain,
> To tell my story. (5.2.338–43)

Hamlet's final request to Horatio is "to tell my story," because he himself has failed to do so publicly. His killing of Claudius on the rebound in the duel scene is not enough for a justifiable and proportionate revenge. A story must be told which makes sense of Hamlet's regicide, which exposes Claudius's crimes "to th'yet unknowing world" (373), and which brings satisfaction to the "perturbed spirit" of his murdered father. However, such a story—Hamlet's story—is never told in the public space of Elsinore during the time of the play. Even at the play's bungled close, the Ghost has yet to receive any public justice, wild or otherwise. Indeed, both Hamlet and his play seem to have forgotten the Ghost entirely by the final scene; there is no sigh of satisfaction from the "old mole" (1.5.162) under the stage, when his murderous and adulterous brother Claudius is dispatched.

Hamlet's Self-Reproaches

Hamlet's inaction is clearly a problem *for Hamlet himself*, and he rebukes himself passionately for his failure to act on at least three separate occasions. First, in his concluding soliloquy at the end of act 2, scene 2, after the Player's speech about Pyrrhus's killing of King Priam of Troy. Hamlet contrasts himself with the emotional eloquence of the Player, who breaks down in tears over the death of Priam, in sympathy with the grief of the long dead Hecuba. He reproaches himself for his inability to expose and denounce Claudius in public, his failure to "cleave the general ear with horrid speech, / Make mad the guilty and appall the free" (560–61).

Despite being "the son of a dear father murdered, / Prompted to my revenge by heaven and hell" (581–82), he can only in the privacy of his soliloquy rage against Claudius:

> Bloody, bawdy villain!
> Remorseless, treacherous, lecherous, kindless villain!
> O, Vengeance! (2.2.577–79)

These head-banging repetitions are merely a series of impotent verbal assaults on Claudius delivered in private, a momentary rhetorical tantrum, for which he immediately goes on to denounce himself—for cowardice, when he clearly is not a coward. Yet characteristically, Hamlet ends the soliloquy by deciding not to organize a plot like the genre's other revengers, with assistance from Horatio and those who have *actually seen* the Ghost, in order to bring the criminal Claudius to justice, but instead to put on a play.

A second moment of guilty self-reproach occurs in the closet scene with Gertrude (act 3, scene 4). In the midst of another paroxysm of denunciation of Claudius, this time to his mother—"A murderer, a villain [...] a king of shreds and patches" (3.4.97, 103)—Hamlet is suddenly interrupted by the reappearance of the Ghost. Instantly he changes tack and anticipates the Ghost's reproach to him:

> Do you not come your tardy son to chide,
> That, lapsed in time and passion, lets go by
> Th'important acting of your dread command?
> O, say! (3.4.107–10)

We then have the Ghost, precisely, chide his tardy son and reiterate his original command to remember and revenge: "Do not forget. This visitation / Is but to whet thy almost blunted purpose" (111–12). Consequently, this is not just a question of Hamlet's melancholic self-loathing, but an agreement between dead father and living son that Hamlet has failed, so far, to implement "th'important acting of your dread command." In other words, Hamlet's delay is established as a *dramatic reality*, not just something we might infer by puzzling over the time lapse between his assuming an antic disposition at the end of act 1 and his "mad" appearance in Ophelia's closet at the beginning of act 2.

The third moment of Hamlet's self-reproach is the last of his soliloquies, where he contrasts himself, not as in act 2 with the player weeping with Hecuba over the death of Priam, but with the figure of young Fortinbras leading his army over stage, to wage war over a worthless scrap of ground in order to vindicate his honor, while Hamlet witnesses his departure from a distance. The soliloquy was cut from the First Folio of 1623, and it appears only in the earlier good Quarto of 1604. It turns on and repeats Hamlet's bafflement at his own inability to act on his ghostly father's "dread command":

> How all occasions do inform against me
> And spur my dull revenge!
> ....
>   I do not know
> Why yet I live to say, "This thing's to do,"
> Sith I have cause, and will, and strength, and means
> To do't. (4.4.32–46)

Hamlet's self-bafflement is obvious here, as there are no excuses for his inaction. He is unclear in his own mind whether he has been guilty of thinking too much about the revenge he is committed to ("thinking too precisely on the event" (41)), or whether he has not been thinking about it at all ("bestial oblivion" (40)). He elaborates here at some length his shaming awareness of his father killed and mother stained, and his own puzzling failure to avenge their dishonor, through the pointed contrast with Fortinbras, the prince "with divine ambition puffed" (49).

Framing the Prince

The play uses both Fortinbras and Laertes, who are Shakespearean inventions not found in the sources of the Amleth legend, to frame Hamlet. The play's action consists of two movements, a longer first movement that concludes with Hamlet's being sent into England and with his final soliloquy prompted by Fortinbras's first brief appearance onstage, where act 3 should end. This is obscured by the standard act-divisions inherited from Nicholas Rowe's edition (1709), which are not Shakespeare's and interrupt the sequence of short scenes presenting the immediate aftermath of

Hamlet's killing of Polonius.[3] A second shorter two-act movement, with the madness and death of Ophelia and the return of Laertes and Hamlet to Denmark, also concludes with a second brief appearance of Fortinbras. This makes visible what Emrys Jones calls the "structural rhyming" (80) that Shakespeare had arranged between the conclusion of the play's first movement, where Fortinbras and his army appear crossing Danish soil, followed by Hamlet *en route* to England who only just misses him, and the conclusion of the play's second movement, with the arrival of young Fortinbras onstage, who only just misses Hamlet, who has just died. So Young Hamlet and Young Fortinbras each time miss each other. However, Fortinbras the warrior, whose name means Strong Arm, and who had been invoked twice in the play's opening scenes as a son seeking to avenge his father's defeat and death, thus end-stops the play's two parts, providing a striking contrast with the central figure of Hamlet. Shakespeare in effect makes the two appearances of Fortinbras onstage punctuation points in the play's progress, and Hamlet himself reflects painfully on this contrast between them in his final soliloquy.

A similar contrast is framed in the second movement of the play, this time with Laertes rather than Fortinbras. Laertes returns angrily to Denmark from Paris on the news of his father's death, and seems no sooner to have set his foot on Danish soil than he has roused an angry mob calling for Laertes to be King, stormed the palace, overcome the Royal Guard of Switzers and has Claudius at this mercy, defended only by the redoubtable Gertrude (who appears to pounce on Laertes: "Let him go, Gertrude!" Claudius has twice to appeal to her). Indeed, the second part of the play is organized around a contrast between Laertes and Hamlet on their respective returns to Denmark. This is a contrast in which Hamlet's situation as the son of a murdered father for whom he seeks revenge, is both mirrored and reversed with geometrical precision by the situation of Laertes, as Hamlet himself admits to Horatio: "for by the image of my cause I see / The portraiture of his" (5.2.77–78). Where Hamlet was the would-be avenging son in the first part of the play, he has now become the object of Laertes's filial revenge in the second part. The contrast between them suggests how relatively easy it is for a gung-ho, determined, and angry son, bent on avenging his father's death, to raise the necessary forces to take Claudius by surprise and call him to account. How much more readily this might have been achieved by the popular

[3]Jones discusses *Hamlet*'s two-part structure (78–80).

Prince Hamlet, son of the late King, on his return from Wittenberg and fresh from his encounter with the Ghost!

Thus, the problem of Hamlet's inaction is articulated self-consciously by Hamlet himself in the two soliloquies discussed above and is confirmed by the Ghost's rebuke about his "almost blunted purpose." This is enforced by a pair of systematic contrasts with these two proactive sons of dead and dishonored fathers. Hamlet's inaction can indeed be seen as a problematic dimension of Hamlet himself, a personal enigma, "the heart of my mystery." Before I explore this, however, I wish to consider the way that indirection, detour, proliferation, and compulsive postponement mark the formal character of the play as a whole.

The Dramaturgy of Delay

I have gratefully borrowed the above title from an essay by Robert Hapgood as a succinct summary of the patterns of proliferating speech and arrested action he points to, in which not only Hamlet but virtually all the characters are caught up. For if Hamlet delays the acting of his father's dread command in chronological time, it is also the case that the play delays the unfolding of its action *in dramatic time*; for the play proliferates scenes, speeches, interactions, intrigues, and minor characters, often ones in which Hamlet is the targeted object rather than the active subject. If Hamlet postpones and delays his revenge, it is equally the case that the play itself diverts and delays Hamlet in dramatic time. As in cinema a film can present what is a very brief action or short moment of chronological time so as to prolong the moment: the camera can go into slow motion, into replay or flash-back or indeed flash-forward, lingering over or detouring around a very small piece of plot, so as to elaborate it in cinematic time, thus delaying its forward movement. So also, while Hamlet's delay exists at the level of the bare plot, delay takes place in dramatic time as well, at the level of the play's theatrical articulation of the Hamlet story. This, the longest of Shakespeare's plays,[4] delays us the audience and draws out almost unbearably our expectations. It retards our movement through

[4]The so-called bad Quarto of 1603 runs only to 2200 lines, while the second, good Quarto of 1604 "newly imprinted *and enlarged to almost as much againe as it was*" (my emphasis), according to its title page, runs to 3800 lines. With the Folio Collected Works of 1623 cutting 230 but adding a further 70 lines to the second Quarto, neither of them would have been playable on the Globe's open-air stage in winter, running well over the available two to three hours afternoon playing time (Shapiro 339–41).

the plot with more and more minor characters, such as Reynaldo and the verbally diarrheic Osric, with interminable conversations when we were hoping for action, with long speeches on set topics (Hamlet's verse essay on the "dram of evil" in act 1 or Rosencrantz's redundant lecture on the "cease of majesty" in act 4), with Polonius's elaborate and self-entangling syntax and with the proliferation of multiple subordinate clauses in almost every verse-speaker in the play. In fact, at the micro-level of language, delay is written into the very DNA of Shakespeare's play, along with detour and proliferation, the complements of the play's strategies of postponement.

Hamlet is indeed a language-heavy play, its linguistic texture more densely worked with Latinate vocabulary, rhetorical elaboration and amplification, with alternating and clashing registers in both verse and prose, than any other in the Shakespearean canon. In his study of Shakespeare's vocabulary, Alfred Hart calculates that in *Hamlet* Shakespeare added over six hundred new words to his own working vocabulary, of which four hundred were not used again in any of his later plays, while one hundred and seventy of these new words were making their first recorded appearance in written English.[5] In this linguistic and rhetorical *tour de force*, one rhetorical figure is preeminent—that of hendiadys (from the Greek *en-dia-duo*: one through two)—which the Elizabethan rhetorician George Puttenham called a "figure of twinnes," making "two out of one" (188). George Wright, the modern scholar who has single-handedly retrieved this neglected rhetorical figure, has foregrounded its centrality to the language of Shakespeare's mature plays, with its peak incidence in *Hamlet*. The latter's sixty-six occurrences as calculated by Wright are followed by *Othello*'s twenty-eight, with another seven middle period plays in the range of ten to nineteen occurrences (173 and Table 1, 185–87). Wright supplements this with a further list of twenty-three borderline examples. Hendiadys emerges out of a pervasive pattern of paired words and phrases to be found in virtually any speech in the play. In Frank Kermode's apt metaphor, "the doubling devices give

[5] Hart is comparing Shakespeare's working vocabulary in the plays before *Hamlet* with those after it. The turnover is striking. The identification of Shakespeare's words as first recordings in English has been considerably altered by recent technology that enables the scanning of a vastly greater number of older texts. The first recording is not the same as an invention. The same scholarship has reduced the number of neologisms attributed to Shakespeare to 500; still a considerable testimony to his linguistic fertility (Jonathan Culpepper and Matthew Gillings).

the verse its tune, or might perhaps be thought a ground bass that sounds everywhere" (106). The paired words may be just synonyms or tautologies, adding little in meaning but, as often in Polonius's speech, a self-important orotundity—"And thus do we of wisdom and of reach, / With windlasses and with assays of bias / By indirection find direction out" (2.2.64–66)—or slight expansions and specifications: "this same strict and most observant watch" (1.1.71), "of unimproved mettle hot and full" (1.1.96), "out of the shot and danger of desire" (1.3.35), "the slings and arrows of outrageous fortune" (3.1.58).

The tendency of Shakespeare's doublings, however, especially in *Hamlet*, is to give rise to a new three-way interaction between a base image or idea and the paired attributes into which it is unfolded, and that deserves to be distinguished as hendiadys from the simpler and more common forms of pairing. Wright focuses only on the relations between the paired words, while the distinctive Shakespearean version is a three-term grouping that can be the support of a larger metaphor: "why the sepulchre [...] / Has oped his ponderous and marble jaws / To cast thee up" (1.4.48–51). The relations between its terms are sometimes suggestive but elusive—"the perfume and suppliance of a minute" (1.3.9)—or may tremble on the verge of a micro-drama of its own: "in the morn and liquid dew of youth / Contagious blastments are most imminent" (1.3.41–42). The latter tendency is most striking in the Ghost's warning to Hamlet of the effect his withheld speech about the secrets of his prison house would have: "whose lightest word / Would [...] / Make [...] / Thy knotted and combined locks to part," which develops a life of its own: "And each particular hair to stand on end / Like quills upon the fretful porpentine" (1.5.15–20). The parting of "the knotted and combined locks" by way of "each particular hair" leads us from the felt state of terror that is the aim of the speech, toward the pictured stasis of the "fretful porpentine." Vivid, picturesque, seen from the outside, the porpentine, however fretful, contrasts with Macbeth's radically different description of the body in a state of alarm:

> The time has been my sense would have cooled
> To hear a night shriek, and my fell of hair
> Would at a dismal treatise rouse and stir
> As life were in't. (5.5.10–13)

Here the drop in temperature on the skin surface, the prickling of the scalp as the hackles rise, evoke the experience of embodied terror, animated by an involuntary adrenaline rush. Where Macbeth's lines work to pinpoint and focus attention, the Hamlet idiom is driven by a habit of expansion and proliferation that often detours from its starting point. The individual doublet, and especially the hendiadys as a micro-generator of linguistic energy, feed into larger patterns of repetition. As Bert States observes: "over and over, we find characters falling into a *seriatim* rhythm in which they seem compelled to inventory a thing or process to within an inch of its life before passing on to more urgent matters" (513). This is aptly exemplified in Hamlet's first major speech: "'Tis not alone my inky cloak, good mother / nor […] nor […] no, nor […] nor […] / Together with […]" (1.2.77–82). In this famous manifesto of interiority—"I have that within which passes show" (85)—the speech's rhetorical space and energy are given over to the parade of "customary suits of solemn black," "windy suspiration of forced breath," "the river in the eye," and the "'haviour of the visage," "all forms, moods, shapes of griefs" (78–82), the very things that are being repudiated. Summed up in the speech's crowning hendiadys—"These but the trappings and the suits of woe" (86)—this negative abundance of what is being rejected points to Hamlet's metatheatrical paradox, that in repudiating "the actions that a man might play" (84), he is repudiating the very medium of theater, and counter-posing "that within which passes show," "the heart of my mystery" (3.2.373–74), not only to theater, but by implication to the public sphere of action itself.

The retarding effect of the play's amplifying rhetoric contributes to the larger pattern of interrupted and arrested action, of pause and standstill, tellingly described by Hapgood, which characterizes not just Hamlet's own postponed mission of revenge, but so often the actions and interactions of all the main characters. Even Fortinbras and Laertes, the two framing and contrasting figures of direct action, taking up arms to avenge their dead fathers, are both turned aside and deflected—old Norway "sends out arrest / On Fortinbras, which he obeys," the latter acquiring possession of the Danish kingdom only through happenstance, a turn of events and timing outside his own knowledge and control; while Laertes, having successfully stormed the royal palace and held the king to account, is talked around, volunteering to be Claudius's "organ" (4.7.69) in his plot against Hamlet, only to fail in the rigged duel, bringing about Hamlet's death but only after his own.

At the micro-level of action so easily missed, Hapgood points to the many delayed exits in scene after scene, in which characters seem incapable of leaving each other or the stage without lingering or returning to add further thoughts. Encountering his companions after the ghost's departure, Hamlet bids them "shake hands and part" (1.5 128) but does not exit with them for another sixty-odd lines, during which time he swears them multiple times to secrecy, forewarns them of his antic disposition, accompanied with seven different examples of the kind of knowing behavior they are *not* to engage in, while he is then rejoined by the ghost who, having already bid Hamlet "Adieu" three times, yet lingers "in the cellarage" to urge them four times to swear the oath of secrecy. So Laertes's departure from Ophelia begins "Farewell," but then takes another fifty odd lines to complete his warning against Hamlet's courtship, replete with no less than seven examples of hendiadys, when he is delayed yet further by Polonius who arrives for a twenty-six-line second leave-taking of his son—"A double blessing is a double grace. / Occasion smiles upon a second leave" (1.3.53–54)—followed by a forty-eight-line second warning to Ophelia against Hamlet. Hamlet himself in his moment of emotional disturbance with Ophelia dismisses her five times, "To a nunnery, go!," while announcing three times "Farewell" in the same fifty-line passage (3.1.121–50). In the closet scene with his mother, Hamlet bids her goodnight five times in a fifty-eight-line exchange, before lugging the guts of Polonius offstage. Similarly Hamlet's final exit from the stage is a series of incomplete repetitions: "I am dead, Horatio [...]," as he struggles first to tell his story: "Had I but time [...] O I could tell you— / Horatio, I am dead," but is defeated "as this fell sergeant Death / Is strict in his arrest"; only to commission Horatio to speak for him: "O, I die, Horatio" and finally to settle the succession on Fortinbras: "He has my dying voice" (5.2.327–50). Sergeant Death may well be strict in his arrest, but it is much protracted, and he is long about it.

However, the play's dramaturgy of delay is most strikingly exemplified in what for any other revenge plot would be its climactic moment: Hamlet, coming across the King, kneeling unguarded, at prayer in his closet in act 3, scene 3. This comes immediately after the play-within-the-play, where Claudius's guilt has been dramatically betrayed by his panicked reaction and hurried exit, noted by both Hamlet and Horatio. Hamlet now takes out his sword to dispatch the praying Claudius—"Now might I do it, pat [...] / And now I'll do't" (3.3.73–4)—but instead, with his sword drawn, he suddenly decides *not* to kill him as yet: "Up sword, and know thou a more horrid hent" (88). His soliloquy in explanation gives us both a bad argument and a fantasy of future opportunities. The bad argument is based on the theologically dubious presumption that Claudius will go to heaven because he is at prayer—"in the purging of his soul" (85)—that is, that he is repentant. Of the alternative possible scenes of a later killing that Hamlet promises his sword, one notes the exciting thought that he might strike Claudius "in th'incestuous pleasure of his bed" (90), a scene Hamlet's imagination returns to on more than one occasion. This is, of course, Hamlet's own decision to postpone his act of revenge in order not just to kill Claudius, but to send him *unrepentant* to Hell. However, it is the play—or Shakespeare—that with exquisite timing has Claudius then rise from his knees, at the very moment Hamlet leaves the stage, to declare that he cannot after all repent, because he still enjoys the benefits of his crime, his queen and his crown: "My words fly up, my thoughts remain below, / Words without thoughts never to heaven go" (97–98). Hamlet mistakes his most opportune moment, for which any revenger would give his eye-teeth, not only to kill Claudius but to damn him eternally. The play thus offers Hamlet this golden opportunity but then, teasingly, withdraws it from him. It hides Claudius's failure to repent behind the kneeling posture of prayer that it exhibits. In his edition of the play, Harold Jenkins comments: "The tableau of an opportunity let slip is unforgettable" (140). Hamlet, but equally Shakespeare's play, never misses an opportunity to miss an opportunity.

Part 2: *Hamlet* with Freud: *Freud's Oedipal Interpretation*

The dramaturgy of delay with its pervasive features of rhetorical amplification and arrested or postponed action does not mean that the play's insistent focus on Hamlet, his mental states and motivation should be downplayed. Significantly both Hamlet and Claudius reflect on the psychological dimension of failed action. In the anti-climactic prayer scene where Claudius fails to repent and Hamlet fails to kill him, Claudius displays a certain clarity about his failure. His impulse to pray and his guilt are locked together in conflict, so that he acknowledges: "like a man to double business bound / I stand in *pause* [...] and both neglect" (3.3.41–43; emphasis added), diagnosing the very checkmating of impulse that leads to paralysis. In Hamlet's central soliloquy "To be or not to be," though it is cast in generalizing terms and without explicit reference to his own situation, Hamlet also diagnoses a similar checkmating of impulse. His famous question of being or not being morphs into a wish for the sleep of death, "a consummation devoutly to be wished" that ends "the thousand natural shocks that flesh is heir to" (3.1.63–65). This death wish is then checkmated by the thought of the dreams that may come in the sleep of death that "must give us *pause*" (68; emphasis added). Hamlet's pause like Claudius's pause results in inaction: "thus [...] enterprises of great pitch and moment [...] lose the name of action" (88). Behind the failure of action lies a checkmate or blockage that "puzzles the will" (80), a moment of subjective paralysis that both men are clearly familiar with.

There is a pattern in Hamlet's passions and his inhibitions, but it is not a pattern that he himself is able to grasp. Of the psychological commentators on Hamlet, it is Freud whose comments in a famous passage from *The Interpretation of Dreams* throw some light on the patterns of repetition in which Hamlet is caught up. Freud contrasts Shakespeare's *Hamlet* with Sophocles's *Oedipus*, arguing that in the ancient Greek drama the fantasy of murdering the father and taking his place with the mother has been literally, if unwittingly, acted out by Oedipus, whereas in *Hamlet* such an oedipal fantasy is only present negatively, that is, we can detect its presence only through Hamlet's inhibitions, *what he fails to do*. Freud notes: "The plot of the drama, however, shows us that Hamlet is far from being represented as a character incapable of taking any action. We see him doing so on two occasions." And he asks:

> What is it, then, that inhibits him in fulfilling the task set him by his father's ghost? The answer, once again, is that it is the peculiar nature of this task. *Hamlet is able to do anything—except take vengeance upon the man who did away with his father and took that father's place with his mother, the man who shows him the repressed desires of his own childhood realized.* Thus the loathing that should drive him on to revenge, is replaced in him by self-reproaches, by scruples of conscience, which remind him that he himself is literally no better than the sinner whom he is to punish. Here I have translated into conscious terms what was bound to remain unconscious in Hamlet's mind. (265/235; emphasis added)

Freud's insight directs us to the position that Claudius, and uniquely Claudius, occupies: he is indeed the one man who has both killed Hamlet's father and taken his place with Hamlet's mother. Central to Freud's argument is this link between Claudius and Hamlet, which I will call a *negative or hostile identification*,[6] which establishes a powerful and very specific inhibition that disables Hamlet from acting against Claudius, his hated proxy and substitute. It also helps to explain his pervasive self-loathing—"What should such fellows as I do crawling between earth and heaven? We are arrant knaves all. Believe none of us" (3.1.127–129)—through its connection with his loathing for Claudius. His negative identification with Claudius is a turntable that redirects his loathing for Claudius back onto himself.

There is some further quite powerful evidence in the play that would support Freud's argument. The most obvious is Hamlet's relation to his mother, which Freud unaccountably ignores. Most audiences and readers have felt from Hamlet's first scene his powerful anger with his mother. Hamlet's anger, however, has an obsessional quality, because there is more to it than his perfectly justified objection to the haste with which Gertrude has married her brother-in-law, the new King, and the bland religiosity with which she urges Hamlet to stop mourning and, like her, forget his father:

> Thou knowest 'tis common. All that lives must die,
> Passing through nature to Eternity
> ....
> If it be,
> Why seems it so particular with thee? (1.2.72–73, 74–75)

The extra dimension that makes Hamlet's understandable anger more than it seems is his intense preoccupation with his mother's sexual desires. While Hamlet praises his father for his tenderness toward his mother, it is hard not to feel that, by contrast, Hamlet describes something both greedy and clinging in Gertrude's desire for his father:

> Heaven and Earth,
> Must I remember it? Why, she would hang on him
> As if increase of appetite had grown
> By what it fed on. (1.2.142–45)

[6]"[H]atred against a particular person or institution might operate in just the same unifying way [...] as positive attachment" (Freud, *Group Psychology* 100/93).

Despite his father's warning: "Taint not thy mind, nor let thy soul contrive / Against thy mother aught" (1.5.85–86) and his father's solicitude in the closet scene for Gertrude's distress, Hamlet's obsession turns back again to his mother as soon as the Ghost departs. He dwells with a lingering relish on her coupling with Claudius, addressed reproachfully to Gertrude herself:

> Nay, but to live
> In the rank sweat of an enseamed bed,
> Stewed in corruption, honeying and making love
> Over the nasty sty. (3.4.93–96)

Like two pigs on heat and rutting. Sniffing the maternal sheets ("enseamed," that is sweat-laden, greasy), Hamlet's incestuous obsessions have never seemed more gross and palpable. When Gertrude cries, "What should I do?" Hamlet's excited disgust betrays through its contradictory logic a demented possessiveness about his mother:

> Not this, by no means, that I bid you do:
> Let the bloat King tempt you again to bed,
> ....
> And let him for a pair of reechy kisses,
> Or paddling in your neck with his damned fingers,
> Make you to ravel all this matter out [...] (3.4.182–87)

Both Hamlet's desire to imagine what Claudius does with his mother between the incestuous sheets, and its negation, struggle with each other in the very syntax of his speech: "What should I do? / Not this [...] that I bid you do." Hamlet both bids and forbids his mother's sexual availability to Claudius. It is notable that throughout the scene Hamlet's preoccupation with his mother's "compulsive ardour" (87) and "heyday in the blood" (70), except for a brief unexplained allusion (29–30), eclipses any concern with his father's murder. The Ghost directs Hamlet toward Claudius and revenge and away from his mother. However, even after the Ghost's return to rebuke his son's "almost blunted purpose" (111), Hamlet fails to expose his father's murderer to his mother. He returns repeatedly to his mother's desire, both unable to stop demanding—"But go not to my uncle's bed" (160)—and unable to stop imagining it. His father features only as the highly idealized opposite of Claudius and the discarded object of his mother's desire.

This angry possessiveness toward a woman, accompanied by intense male rivalry is then displaced across and repeated in relation to Ophelia and Laertes. This is evident in the graveyard scene, where Hamlet hears himself first referenced by his mother as the possible husband of Ophelia, then cursed by Laertes as both the murderer of her father and responsible for her suicide. Finally, the sight of Laertes leaping into Ophelia's grave and embracing her body provokes a jealous, competitive rage and possessiveness in Hamlet, and apparently a similar leap.

> I loved Ophelia. Forty thousand brothers
> Could not with all their quantity of love
> Make up my sum. What wilt thou do for her?
> ....
> I'll do't. Dost thou come here to whine?
> To outface me with leaping in her grave?
> (5.1.265–67, 273–74)

Hamlet's counterchallenge to Laertes implies that the latter's rhetorically noisy grief is experienced as a challenge to Hamlet's unsettled identity: "What is he [...] This is I, / Hamlet the Dane" (5.1.250–54). However, this is a challenge that is more appropriately directed to Claudius who had already claimed that title and in relation to Laertes: "What is't, Laertes? / You cannot speak of reason to the Dane / And lose your voice" (1.2.43–5). What is at stake is neither simply citizenship nor ethnic identity but the symbolic embodiment of Denmark in a royal figure.[7] Hamlet's sudden assertion of his claim to his father's role as "Royal Dane" (1.4.45), in the midst of his rivalry with Laertes for Ophelia, confirms that in this violent drama of Hamlet-Laertes-Ophelia that erupts so unexpectedly, the more fundamental drama of Hamlet-Claudius-Gertrude is being played out again but in displaced form. Hamlet's disclaiming of his love for Ophelia and abuse of her in the nunnery scene—"You jig and amble, and you lisp [...] and make your wantonness your ignorance. Go to, I'll no more on't.

[7]When Horatio and Marcellus are challenged by the castle guard in act 1, scene 1, they reply: "Friends to this ground [...] and liegemen to the Dane" (15). While Hamlet hails his father's ghost as "Royal Dane" (1.4.45) and curses Claudius as he pours poison down his throat: "Here, thou incestuous, murderous, damned Dane / Drink off this potion" (5.1.319–20).

It hath made me mad" (3.1.145–48)—had begun the process by which his possessiveness and anger with his mother is transferred across to Ophelia and lays the ground for his sudden violent rivalry with Laertes.

Hamlet's Antic Disposition

Now psychoanalytic reflection might suggest that if Hamlet's act of revenge is postponed even when the perfect opportunity for it arises, or if it is simply not acted on and other things proliferate in its place, then those displacement activities must be interrogated in order to understand what is producing the paralysis and diversion of energies that lie behind Hamlet's delay. If we ask, between the moment where he pledges his father's ghost to remember and revenge his murder, and the moment when he is sent into exile: What has Hamlet been doing?, the answer in theatrical terms is quite a lot—indeed, he has scarcely been off-stage. He has elaborated his antic disposition by frightening Ophelia in her closet, gained quite a reputation in Elsinore as a disturbed and disturbing figure, and as a result become the dominant topic of conversation at court. There are *eight* different scenes in the play where Claudius, Polonius, Laertes, Gertrude, Ophelia, and Rosencrantz and Guildenstern in various combinations come together to discuss "the problem of Hamlet," to interpret his behavior and his motives, and to explain his apparent madness. "Hamlet's transformation" (2.2.5), "My too much changed son" (36), "Hamlet's lunacy" (49), these have become the hot topics of the moment. He has become indeed "the observed of all observers" (3.1.155), the discussed of all discussions. The first Hamlet seminar ever takes place in Elsinore.

When Hamlet's prototype character in Saxo-Grammaticus, the ancient Danish source for Shakespeare's play, one Amleth, adopts a disguise of madness, it is because his uncle had publicly murdered his father and taken his place, and he is forced to pretend to be feeble-minded and unthreatening, not worth killing. By contrast, Hamlet's antic disposition has succeeded in making himself an object of suspicion to Claudius, who comes to fear, quite rightly, "something in his soul / On which his melancholy sits on brood" (3.1.165–66). Even the slow-witted Guildenstern has worked out that Hamlet's is a "crafty madness" (3.1.8) strategically deployed. Whereas the standard politic avenger in Elizabethan and Jacobean revenge tragedy would seek to blend into the background and ingratiate himself with his intended victim (compare Vindice in *The Revenger's Tragedy*), Hamlet instead behaves provocatively, repeatedly signaling his hostility to Claudius. Indeed, the amount of Hamlet's energy and dramatic time taken up in the playing out of his supposed madness would seem to be drawing Hamlet away from and not toward the organization of a plot or intrigue, leading to the exposure and punishment of Claudius. Indeed, Hamlet's antic disposition seems to function as displacement activity, a substitute for the very action of revenge it is meant to forward.

The Play's the Thing

Alongside the lengthy soliloquies largely concerned with his own inaction, Hamlet's most extended preoccupation, along with his charade of madness, is with the players, greeting them, talking with them, giving them advice. He recalls, in particular, one play they had put on in the past and launches into "one speech in it I chiefly loved" (2.2.444), the lengthy Troy speech with Priam and Hecuba and Pyrrhus, Priam's killer, which he then passes on mid-speech to the player to complete. Taking up even more dramatic time is Hamlet's staging of the play, *The Murder of Gonzago*, along with his detailed advice to the players on what they should strive for or avoid in their acting. Indeed, Hamlet inserts an extra speech (arguably the Player King's long reflection on the failure of purpose and memory). During the performance of the inner play Hamlet keeps up a running commentary throughout, so obtrusively underlining its loaded references to both Gertrude and Claudius, as well as to himself, that Ophelia comments dryly: "You are as good as a chorus, my lord" (3.2.254).

The long theatrical sequences in both act 2, scene 2, and act 3, scene 2, show Hamlet at his most proactive, making something happen, in a way he does not do elsewhere in the play: the organizing and acting out of two theatrical fictions. Hamlet's passionate implication in both fictional situations is obvious. Each of them has center-stage the figure of a killer: first, Pyrrhus the blood-covered killing machine slaughtering old "grandsire Priam" (2.2.462) who attempts feebly to oppose him; then the murderer Lucianus, who pours poison into the ear of the Player King as he sleeps in his orchard. In their different ways both stories echo in displaced and thinly disguised form the killing of old King Hamlet by Claudius. Both Pyrrhus and Lucianus as King-killers are Claudius-figures. However, the complication is that Pyrrhus is also an avenging son, who kills Priam to avenge the death of his own father Achilles, who was killed by Priam's son Paris during the siege of Troy. Likewise, the figure of Lucianus the poisoner is said to be the Player King's nephew and so conflates both Claudius the poisoner-in-the-ear and Hamlet the current King's nephew. So, also, Pyrrhus the regicide, at the point of his butchering the old King, is suddenly arrested, paralyzed by the sound of the towers of Troy as they come crashing down:

> For Lo! his sword
> ....
> [...] seemed in the air to stick.
> So as a painted tyrant Pyrrhus stood,
> And like a neutral to his will and matter
> Did nothing. (2.2.475–80)

"Pyrrhus's pause" (485), his frozen moment in the killing of Priam, is Shakespeare's invention, as it does not appear in classical accounts of Priam's killing, such as Virgil's in the *Aeneid* Book 2. Pyrrhus's pause, however, does appear in classical accounts of his sacrifice of Polyxena, Priam's daughter, on the tomb of his father Achilles, whose ghost had demanded it.[8] Unlike the ancient scene of Pyrrhus hesitating out of pity for his victim or "dread" at his own deed, Shakespeare's killer is arrested by the traumatic force of Troy's physical collapse, which with "a hideous crash takes prisoner Pyrrhus's ear" (475). Consequently, Hamlet's "one speech in't I chiefly loved" presents us with an ancient prototype of an avenger paralyzed in mid-act by a violent incursion through the ear. Pyrrhus's pause is a momentary mirror-image of Hamlet's delay, redoubled later as Hamlet pauses in the very act of drawing his sword to kill Claudius at prayer, only to postpone the deed. Unlike Hamlet, however, Pyrrhus arouses his energies, "mincing with his sword" (512) the body of the prostrate Priam. In both these figures of Pyrrhus and Lucianus, there is then a fusion and confusion of Hamlet and Claudius, the avenger and the criminal. Hamlet's attraction to these narratives—his compulsion to re-enact them—with their fusion of opposed figures, like the condensations of opposites by the dream-work in the unconscious (*The Interpretation of Dreams* 279–305/248–71), exemplifies the hostile identification of Hamlet with his loathed antagonist Claudius. This is precisely the negative

[8]It can be found in Euripides's *Hecabe* and Seneca's *Troas*. Most likely Shakespeare encountered it in the Elizabethan translation of Seneca's *Troas* by Jasper Heywood (1559): "And lo a strange thing monster-like / that Pyrrhus even himself stood still, for dread and did not strike" (243).

identification in play between them that Freud's analysis points to but does not name as such. Such an identification produces the combination of emotional obsession and paralyzed inaction that we see in Hamlet's relation to Claudius.

Part 3: *Hamlet* with Laplanche: *The Spectral Figure of the Other*

For all the light that Freud's brief comments can throw on the enigma of Hamlet, it should be noted that they explain his failure to act on his father's demand entirely in terms of his relation in the present moment to his uncle Claudius. Freud has nothing to say about Hamlet's relation to his father, in particular, to the spectral figure of his father's Ghost who lays the duty of revenge on his son. It is rather surprising for Freud of all thinkers to ignore the figure of the father and in this play of all plays, with its not one but three dead fathers and three avenging sons, as well as a mourning suicidal daughter. It parallels the setting aside of the question of daemonic agency in Freud's Ptolemaic interpretation of *Oedipus*. Hence, a Copernican analysis that seeks to make good this absence in Freud's partial account of the play must turn to the scenes in act 1 where Hamlet encounters his father's Ghost. These constitute a traumatic encounter, one whose consequences ripple throughout the play. The Ghost refuses to answer Horatio's interrogation, but on his appearance to Hamlet, the latter begins with similar questions: is the Ghost from heaven or hell, charitable or wicked in its intents? Hamlet very quickly comes to the conclusion: "I'll call thee Hamlet, / King, father, royal Dane" (1.4.44–45). Hamlet rapidly and confidently recognizes the Ghost as his father, and his urgent questions all take his identity for granted. "It is an honest ghost, that let me tell you" (1.5.138), he insists to Horatio after their encounter. He clearly does not need to spend dramatic time at this point in testing the Ghost's identity.

When the Ghost then reveals his status and where he comes from, it is neither from Heaven nor Hell but from a third location, "the middle state of souls"[9] where he is

> Doomed for a certain term to walk the night,
> And for the day confined to fast in fires,

[9]From a seventeenth-century Catholic treatise by Thomas White (cited in Greenblatt 230n17).

> Till the foul crimes done in my days of nature
> Are burnt and *purged* away. (1.5.10–13; emphasis added)

In other words, the ghost is confined temporarily in a place that in the pre-Reformation Catholic tradition was called Purgatory, but which could not be invoked seriously as such on the Elizabethan stage. This was because Purgatory was abolished by the Protestant Reformation and virtually by Act of Parliament, when all the chantries and specially funded provisions for the saying of Requiem Masses for the dead, to shorten their time in Purgatory, were expropriated by Henry VIII and Edward VI in *The Dissolution of Colleges Acts* of 1545 and 1547. It is one of the unexplained anomalies of this play that Hamlet and Horatio, students at the University of Wittenberg, which was Martin Luther's university, a center of international Protestantism in the sixteenth century, should in coming home to Denmark meet up with a ghost from Catholic Purgatory. It was precisely with a rejection of the doctrine of Purgatory, and the indulgences that would mitigate the punishments of the dead held there, that Luther had begun the break from Rome that led to the Protestant Reformation.

As its name suggests, Purgatory was a temporary place of purging, where sins that had been confessed but for which the penance had not been performed or completed, were purged away by fire. The Ghost tells his son that he was murdered by his brother without any preparation for death:

> Thus was I sleeping by a brother's hand
> Of life, of crown, of queen at once dispatched,
> Cut off even in the blossoms of my sin,
> Unhouseled, disappointed, unaneled,
> No reckoning made, but sent to my account
> With all my imperfections on my head.
> O, horrible! O, horrible! Most horrible! (1.5.74–80)

The three technical terms "Unhouseled, disappointed, unaneled" refer to the three sacraments that Catholic tradition requires the dying person to receive: Hamlet senior was "unhouseled" because he had not received Holy Communion (the "housel" was the consecrated bread); he was "disappointed" (i.e., not properly "appointed") because he had not made Confession and received Absolution for his sins, and he was "unaneled" because he had not received at the point of death the final anointing or "aneling" of the Catholic sacrament of Extreme Unction.[10]

Theology aside, I will simply observe that this third place between Heaven and Hell—the middle state of souls—that remains unnamed in the play, but whose function is signaled by the verb "purged," solves a problem for Shakespeare. For if the Ghost had come from Hell, his command should definitely not be obeyed, as he would be damned; if he came from Heaven, he would not be demanding this archaic but still prevalent practice of blood revenge by one who is "born to set it right" (1.5.189), that is, the victim's son. In other words, location in a third place saves the Ghost from damnation and discredit and gives him the dramatic space to embody the call of ancestral obligation, and the demand that Hamlet fulfill his filial duty. Furthermore, what could be a more striking expression of the play's dramaturgy of delay? Purgatory is the play's ultimate state of delay, the deferral of the soul's final entry into Heaven until remorse, purging and penance for sin had been completed. Shakespeare here brings together two ideas in the ghost's speech. The ancient idea of a ghost that walks the night, as Old Hamlet does, because there is unfinished business, and whose life must be properly completed before he can be laid to rest. In this case his secret murder must be exposed and his murderous brother punished and deprived of his illicit possession of both queen and crown. This is combined with Purgatory as a "middle state" between Heaven and Hell, where the soul is in a state not of damnation but of suffering suspension, and where its accession to a final destiny in Heaven is indefinitely postponed. Thus, the principle of delay reigns supreme throughout the play, from the ubiquitous rhetorical trope of *hendiadys* and its amplificatory rhetoric to its ultimate theological expression in the state of Purgatory. Significantly, the Ghost does not plead for prayers for his soul to shorten his period of suffering, like other Purgatorial revenants (Greenblatt

[10]Catholic doctrine held that dying in a state of *mortal* sin (i.e., deadly to the soul), unconfessed and unabsolved, would send the sinner to eternal damnation in Hell, while Purgatory was the temporary destination for those dying with unconfessed *venial* or lesser sins, or with confessed mortal sins for which penance had not been completed. Shakespeare seems to have crafted his own version of Purgatory, as the Ghost refers to his "foul crimes" and being "cut off in the blossom of my sins," which with his distress at being deprived of a final confession—"no reckoning made"—suggests that they are serious mortal sins. Instead of Hell, however, he is "for a certain term [...] confined to fast in fires / Till the foul crimes [...] are burnt and purged away," arrested in the temporary state of purgation (1.5.11–13).

105–33), but pleads instead: "If thou didst ever thy dear father love— / [...] Revenge his foul and most unnatural murder" (1.5.23–25).

Traumatic Intromission from the Other

In his return to the model of traumatic seduction, Jean Laplanche in his General Theory of Primal Seduction posits the foundational transmission of enigmatic signifying sequences in the initiation and structuring of human subjectivity. These tactile, auditory, visual as well as verbal signifiers are implanted in the primitive skin ego of the infant (Anzieu and Scarfone), through the ordinary gestures of childcare and nurturing. Among these he differentiates a violent variant, which he calls "intromission": parental signifiers highly charged with unprocessed affect and fantasy, swamping the recipient and blocking the normal processes of translation and binding, incorporation and repression (Laplanche, *Essays on Otherness* 133–37; Fletcher, "Seduction and the Vicissitudes of Translation" 1259–68). Where the ordinary implantation of primal seduction initiates the formation of the primitive containing boundaries and surfaces of the skin ego and provokes the evolving ego's defenses of repression and sublimation, "its violent variant [...] blocks this [...] and puts into the interior an element resistant to all metabolization" (137). This condemns the recipient to the compulsive repetition of the original scene of intromission and invasion. Laplanche notes that intromission targets the vulnerable orifices (of which the ear under assault is most prominent in *Hamlet*). It is in relation to these different modalities of transmission initiated by the adult other, to intromission as well as to implantation, that the classical oedipal configurations described by Freud need to be repositioned clinically and reformulated theoretically.

The Ghost ends the announcement of his exact location in the afterlife by saying that he is forbidden to disclose the secrets of his prison house, otherwise:

> I could a tale unfold whose lightest word
> Would harrow up thy soul, freeze thy young blood,
> Make thy two eyes like stars start from their spheres,
> Thy knotted and combined locks to part,
> And each particular hair to stand on end
> Like quills upon the fretful porpentine.
> But this eternal blazon must not be
> To ears of flesh and blood. (1.5.15–22)

The Ghost here engages in a rhetorical strategy called *apophasis*, in which a speaker mentions something by saying he will not mention it, or, in performative mode, implements something by saying that he will avoid it. The Ghost withholds the secrets of his prison-house, but the sensory power of this description of their potential devastating effects on a listener, itself has the power to induce in Hamlet the very traumatized effects he warns against. He exercises obliquely the power of what I will call traumatic speech; a traumatic speech whose "lightest word," he tells Hamlet, can provoke freezing blood, starting eyes, standing hair in its recipient, that is, it can push the body into extreme spasm, and take over and derange the mental and bodily processes of his listener.

These are the classic symptoms of a state of *fright*, which Freud, in his discussion of trauma in its relation to the compulsion to repeat, distinguishes from both specific *fears* attached to particular objects and *anxiety* that circulates without a fixed object (*Beyond the Pleasure Principle* 12/12). Fright is the reaction of the subject taken by surprise, without time to prepare a defense, and who is overwhelmed by the impact of a powerful experience it cannot assimilate. As such it is cognate with the notion of trauma as the violent infraction of the subject's boundaries, whether a physical trauma or wounding of the body and its containing surfaces, or a psychical breaking in of the ego's defenses by an influx of excitations and affects that cannot be integrated or translated into the terms of the ego's defense system ("Trauma," Laplanche and Pontalis 465–66). The grotesque extremity of the Ghost's evocation both prefigures his own fate as victim in the tale he next unfolds to Hamlet, as well as proleptically inscribing a traumatized receptivity in Hamlet as the listener to that tale.[11]

However, it is when he goes on to describe to his son what his brother Claudius has done to him, evoking the poisoning in such an intimate and detailed a way, that he re-lives the poisoning once again and so transmits it and its effects to Hamlet.

> Sleeping within my orchard,
> My custom always of the afternoon,

[11]When the ghost returns to rebuke Hamlet, Gertrude describes his reaction in similar terms: "Forth at your eyes your spirits wildly peep, / And as the sleeping soldiers in th'alarm, / Your bedded hair like life in excrements / Start up and stand on end" (3.4.120–23).

> Upon my secure hour thy uncle stole,
> With juice of cursed hebenon in a vial,
> And in the porches of my ears did pour
> The leperous distilment; whose effect
> Holds such an enmity with blood of man
> That swift as quicksilver it courses through
> The natural gates and alleys of the body,
> And with a sudden vigour doth posset
> And curd, like eager droppings into milk,
> The thin and wholesome blood: so did it mine;
> And a most instant tetter bark'd about,
> Most lazar-like, with vile and loathsome crust,
> All my smooth body [...]
> O, horrible! O, horrible! Most horrible! (1.5.59–73, 80)

This is the play's "primal scene," to borrow a formulation from Freud's theory of traumatic seduction, that is, a scene of traumatic invasion by the other, where the traumatized subject is overwhelmed and immobilized by a force that cannot be processed or integrated (Masson 239, Laplanche and Pontalis 335–36, and Fletcher, *Freud and the Scene of Trauma* 220–24). It establishes "a *Vorbild*, precisely a prototype or protoscene that has its primal status in relation to scenes that are to come later" (Fletcher 223). Laplanche's concept of intromission specifies this traumatizing process as proceeding from highly charged adult (usually parental) transmissions that intrude, possess, and immobilize the recipient. The long rhetorical crescendo that enacts the drama of physical poisoning climaxes in the Ghost's final state of spiritual destitution, with its triple cry of horror. From the beginning of the passage the emphasis is on the old King's unguarded vulnerability: taking his customary afternoon nap (a valetudinarian touch) "within my orchard [...] on my secure hour," he is taken advantage of through the ear, the orifice that, unlike the eye, cannot be closed.[12] The Ghost discloses the full trauma of a violently interrupted life, as he is "cut off" and deprived of all his passionate attachments to life and queen and crown. Like the state of fright he had just previously invoked, he was caught undefended, with his guard down, which climaxes in his state of spiritual unpreparedness—"no reckoning made"—that sends him

[12] Ray offers a striking elaboration of the significance of the ear and its auditory regime in both *Hamlet* and sixteenth-century writing (189–94).

without benefit of sacraments to Purgatory.[13] The repeated emphasis on defenselessness and being taken by surprise suggests an intimate connection between the manner of his murder (poisoned in his sleep with all its imaginary bodily consequences), and its spiritual outcome (an arrested state of purgatorial stasis and repetition-compulsion).

The physiologically impossible fantasy of a poisoning through the ear that leads to a poisoning of the whole body through the bloodstream does two things. It parallels the aural violence of the Ghost's previous hair-raising speech to its hypothetical listener in a state of fright; here the analogy is between traumatizing speech and poisoning through the ear. It also renders corporeal the Ghost's own experience of traumatic dispossession. The poisoning climaxes in a mortal crisis of the whole body as the poison "as swift as quicksilver [...] courses through the gates and natural alleys of the body," like a city whose internal spaces are invaded and possessed by the enemy. The medico-culinary analogies of possets and curdling milk describe the whole volume of his blood as transformed from the "thin and wholesome" to the clotted and thickened. Similarly, we get contrasting states of the body's surfaces as "all my smooth body" morphs "lazar-like" into a "vile and loathsome crust." Thin blood, smooth body into clotted blood, crusted body. Elizabethan medicine would not have had anything like a modern understanding of the circulation of the blood, which was first publicly formulated by William Harvey only in 1616.[14] Nevertheless, just as the Ghost's "lightest word" of the secrets of Purgatory "would freeze thy young blood," so also Claudius's poison violently induces a condition of arrest, stasis and a congealing or freezing of the vital movements of the blood on which life depends.

The Ghost relives this trauma and in doing so transmits its traumatic force *through the ear* to the listening Hamlet and to the wider body of Denmark: "the whole ear of Denmark / Is by a forged process of my death / Rankly abused" (1.5.36–38). Hamlet's response is to pledge a remembrance that will take over the entire content of his brain, or so he says. He will wipe everything else away:

[13] Hamlet justifies his later intention not just to kill Claudius but to damn him as well, by invoking his father's complaint: "'A took my father grossly, full of bread, / With all his crimes broad blown, as flush as May" (3.3.80–81). Also, his formulation of Rosencrantz and Guilderstern's death sentence specifies, "Not shriving time allowed" (5.2.47) where shriving refers to confession and absolution, thus matching his father's fate.

[14] Harvey first outlined this in a lecture to the College of Physicians in 1616. He published his full statement of his theory in *De Motu Cordis* (1628).

> And thy commandment all alone shall live
> Within the book and volume of my brain,
> Unmixed with baser matter. (1.5.102–104)

Thus the Ghost's traumatic primal scene of bodily invasion takes prisoner Hamlet's ear, as with Pyrrhus's pause, and will live on in sole command of his brain. Instead, however, of enabling Hamlet to act to eliminate this toxin, by exposing and bringing Claudius to Bacon's "wild justice," what seems to happen is the paralysis of Hamlet's very capacity for new action, and so his entrapment in a process of traumatic repetition. To remember the Ghost *for Hamlet* is to relive the Ghost's poisoning and to repeat its transmission.

We get our first glimpse of this in the report we hear of Hamlet in the very next scene, from the "affrighted" Ophelia to her father:

> My lord, as I was sewing in my closet,
> Lord Hamlet, with his doublet all unbraced;
> No hat upon his head; his stockings foul'd,
> Ungarter'd, and down-gyved to his ankle;
> Pale as his shirt; his knees knocking each other;
> And with a look so piteous in purport
> As if he had been loosed out of hell
> To speak of horrors, he comes before me. (2.1.77–84)

Ophelia does not know about the ghost or his situation in Purgatory, so her testimony is all the more powerful: it was, she says, "as if he had been loosed out of hell / To speak of horrors." Hamlet appears to her as if a revenant from the afterlife "to speak of horrors," but he says or can say nothing. The father's mortal trauma possesses the son. The deranged, and in this scene, speechless Hamlet has come to embody the Ghost but unlike him is unable to speak the secrets he carries and transmits. Its effect on Ophelia is that of a ghostly contagion, for as Nicholas Ray has acutely noted, her report is "freighted with implicit stage directions: 'And with his other hand *thus* o'er his brow [...] And thrice his head *thus* waving up and down.' Ophelia doesn't just describe [...] she is compelled to re-enact that re-enactment in her turn" (194).

Traumatic Speech

It is this same power of an invasive and traumatizing speech, the speech of intromission, that we have heard Hamlet aspiring to in his soliloquy at the end of act 2, scene 2. Hamlet responds intensely to the player's emotional breakdown, overwhelmed with sympathy for Hecuba over the horrors of the destruction of Troy and the butchery of Priam. The player has relived and recirculated this ancient historic trauma through the heightened theatrical speech that Hamlet had remembered: "One speech [...] I chiefly loved [...] It was Aeneas's tale to Dido [...] especially when he speaks of Priam's slaughter" (2.2.444–46). The scene of the murder of the King-father has riveted itself in Hamlet's memory so much that he knows the passage by heart. He begins the speech himself with the grotesque figure of Pyrrhus "Roasted in wrath and fire / And thus o'ersized with coagulate gore" (2.2.461–62), before handing the tragic narrative over to the player. In the player's performance, the traumatizing passions of the speech overwhelm and immobilize him. The moment of breakdown is the actor's identification with Hecuba: "Come to Hecuba" (501), Hamlet had impatiently urged. The Trojan Queen's "instant burst of clamour" (515) at her husband's mutilation and killing is in stark contrast to Gertrude's bland acceptance of her husband's death in the opening court scene, with her rebuke to Hamlet's provocative mourning. In an emotional ricochet from earth to heaven and back again, Hecuba's grief provokes tears "in the burning eyes of heaven / And passion in the gods" (517–18), which rebounds to earth again to overwhelm the actor in tears, arresting him in the moment of his interrupted performance.

Roused by this repetition of the trauma of Troy, Hamlet wishes also to make the stage, the theater itself, the very site of trauma, of its transmission and circulation:

> What would he do,
> Had he the motive and the cue for passion
> That I have? He would drown the stage with tears
> And cleave the general ear with horrid speech,
> Make mad the guilty and appall the free,
> Confound the ignorant, and amaze indeed
> The very faculties of eyes and ears. (2.2.548–63)

Again we have the fantasy of the power of speech to invade and derange, through a "fiction, a dream of passion" to traumatize its recipient: to "cleave the general ear with horrid speech," to make mad, appall, confound, and amaze the very faculties of eyes and ears.[15] In other words, Hamlet aspires to that "horrid speech" whose traumatizing effects the Ghost had refrained from unleashing on him, only to do exactly that in reliving the trauma of his own poisoning. It is the compulsion to use the stage to transmit and repeat the Ghost's primal trauma that is the driving force, I would suggest, for Hamlet's decision to put on the play-within-the-play. Hitherto, he has been quite confident of the Ghost's identity.

> I have heard
> That guilty creatures sitting at a play
> Have by the very cunning of the scene
> Been struck so to the soul that presently
> They have proclaimed their malefactions;
> For murder, though it have no tongue, will speak
> With most miraculous organ. (2.2.586–92)

In the play's performance Hamlet imagines that what speaks will be the deed itself: "for murder will speak [...] with most miraculous organ" (593–94). Through "the very cunning of the scene"—which I have called the scenography of trauma (Fletcher, "Scenography of Trauma")—the re-enacted deed will have the power to conscript the guilty creature to bear witness against himself.

What actually happens when Hamlet stages *The Mousetrap*, however, is rather different. As Lucianus enters, Hamlet announces: "This is one Lucianus, nephew to the King [...]" and minutes later, impatient with the actor, he shouts across the play to Claudius: "A poisons him i'th' garden for his estate [...] you shall see anon how the murderer gets the love of Gonzago's wife" (3.2.253, 270–73). Hamlet's aggressive voice-over commentary clearly signals a threat to Claudius: "I know your secret, how you killed my father," but also "I am the nephew who is going to kill my uncle" (and perhaps, implicitly, "Thus I will win back the love of the

[15] In his angry rivalry with Laertes over Ophelia's grave, Hamlet demands: "What is he [...] whose phrase of sorrow / Conjures the wandering stars and makes them stand / Like wonder-wounded hearers?" (5.1.250–53), and he later admits to Horatio: "But sure the bravery of his grief did put me / Into a towering passion" (5.2.79–80). Here it is not the stars (unmentioned by Laertes) but Hamlet, who in his "towering passion" is a "wonder-wounded hearer" of Laertes's delayed "speech o'fire" (4.7.90). Laertes has seized both the prerogative of traumatic speech, as well as Ophelia's body, from Hamlet.

Queen from you"). Hamlet's goading plot summary forestalls the play's action, unable to let the "very cunning of the scene" by itself operate on Claudius's emotions. In response to Hamlet's implied threats Claudius promptly rises and flees the scene. In fact, no public exposure of the crime takes place, the murder does not speak with most miraculous organ. Instead, Claudius's secret crime and Hamlet's secret knowledge of it both remain unvoiced, withheld, mirroring each other. Once again, while transmitting their disturbance Hamlet does not speak the secrets he is possessed by.

Half-way through the performance Claudius had asked, somewhat warily, "Is there no offense in it?" and Hamlet replied: "No, no, they do but jest, poison in jest" (243). The poison is only a jest, but the jest *is* poison and so Claudius will *ingest* poison. There will be no catharsis, no purging, no elimination of the toxin. This has the effect of paralyzing Hamlet's ability to act openly, publicly, and cathartically. With this poisonous performance the stage is no longer a place of exposure and public judgment, but instead becomes a secret instrument of private vengeance, the site of a secret return to sender: an eye for an eye, an ear for an ear, poison for poison. The inner play's "poison in jest" is returned to Claudius, not visually through the actions of the dumb show at the beginning to which he does not respond, but as Hamlet observes to Horatio: "Didst perceive […] Upon the *talk* of poisoning?" (296–98; emphasis added), that is, through the ear. It is of course Hamlet's "talk," his repeated comment—"you shall see anon […]" (249–50, 272–73)—that anticipates the play's action and so provokes Claudius's reaction. In the immediately following prayer scene, we see the two antagonists locked in their separate states of paralysis, unable to repent and unable to revenge. Locked into this compulsion-to-repeat, in the play's final scene both Hamlet and Claudius will die mutually poisoned, in an exchange of poison.

Two lines of psychoanalytic thought converge on this moment: Freud's account of Hamlet's hostile and paralyzing identification with Claudius the usurper of his oedipal fantasy; and a Laplanchean-Copernican account of the Ghost's paternal intromission of the traumatic scene into the ear of Hamlet, the recipient who is thereby conscripted to repeat both the scene itself and its mode of transmission—poisoning through the ear. While the performance of the inner play secretly repeats the scene of Claudius's crime, the figure of Lucianus, the ear-poisoning nephew, inscribes Hamlet himself into the play's primal scene, a composite figure who aims like Claudius both to kill the King and to seduce and possess the Queen. It is this compulsive repetition of the scene that drives Hamlet's self-defeating identification with Claudius/Lucianus. The "very cunning of the scene" conscripts, not Claudius who betrays his guilt to Hamlet by his alarmed exit while remaining silent, but Hamlet himself in his identification with Lucianus, summoned into the scene as both the revenging nephew and the ear-poisoning uncle, whom he is both commissioned but unable to kill.

Hamlet's Interim

The play's concluding scene is marked by the same characteristics of inaction, explosive reaction, interruption, and postponement that we have seen throughout. Hamlet had no sooner recounted to Horatio Claudius's previous failed plot against his life in exiling him to England, than he has agreed to act as Claudius's representative in the proposed duel, with the latter placing high wagers on his winning and ceremonially drinking to his success. In response to Horatio's warning that the news soon to arrive from England leaves him little time, Hamlet confidently asserts: "It will be short. The interim is mine" (5.2.73). This is instantly followed, however, by a hundred lines of linguistic mockery and rivalry with Osric, ending with Hamlet's agreement, in Hapgood's apt words: "to enter into a fencing match with the man whose father he has killed, sponsored by the man who has killed his father and ordered his own death" (138). We have here a reversal of the familiar pattern of revenge drama, for it is not Hamlet, the commissioned and sworn revenger, who orchestrates through his inner play the concluding plot that brings the criminal to wild justice. As throughout the play, and so in Hamlet's "interim"—the time between his return to Denmark and his death—the initiative is taken by Claudius not by Hamlet. It is Claudius the criminal who organizes the public spectacle of the duel, the equivalent of the revenger's inner play or masque, that erupts in a final round of accidental judgments, casual slaughters and purposes mistook, in which both participants and spectators are killed.

Despite the King's sponsorship of the duel, Hamlet uses the language of brotherhood (5.2.237–38) and speaks of it rather as a "brother's wager" (247) with Laertes. This, as Ray points out, turns the duel into a second fratricide that repeats the original crime, "with Hamlet now placed—like his father before him—as the ignorant victim" (215) of the machinations of both his uncle and his "brother," Laertes; or as Freud observed, "suffering the same fate as his father of being poisoned by the same rival"

(Masson 272). Ray's Copernican reading points to the way the ghost's intromissive possession of his son, previously glimpsed in the silent Hamlet's visit to Ophelia's closet, "as if he had been loosed out of hell / To speak of horrors" but unable to do so, continues into this final scene. The poisoned Hamlet in his final speech to Horatio, in all its unfinished repetitions, carries striking echoes of the Ghost's speeches in the opening scenes. I cite Ray's examples: "I am dead Horatio" / "I am thy father's spirit"; "Had I but time [...] O I could tell you" / "I could a tale unfold"; "If ever thou didst hold me in thy heart" / "If thou didst ever thy dear father love"; "tell my story" / "Remember me."

What is anomalous is that this subsuming of the son into the voice of the dead father whom he echoes, takes place in a final scene in which the son's killing of his father's murderer is carried out without any reference to the paternal Ghost who has demanded and authorized it. The father is absent, not just as an explicit reference point in the final discourse of the son that echoes him, but absent also as an urgent and passionate presence in his own right, a traveler not shy of returning on more than one occasion from the undiscovered country of the after-life. Not just his son, but the play also forgets the perturbed spirit who has haunted it from the beginning.

Ray's solution to this anomaly is to suggest that Hamlet's killing of Claudius is prompted by Laertes's last-minute repentance and revelation of the plot against him: "The treacherous instrument is in thy hand / [...] Thy mother's poisoned. / I can no more. The King, the King's to blame" (5.2.310, 13–14). This "effectively supersedes the Ghost's command and [...] says absolutely nothing of him" (Ray 216–17). Ray also argues that the killing is done "in the name of the dead mother" (217), as it is to Gertrude alone and not his father that Hamlet refers, as he forces the poisoned wine down Claudius's own throat: "Is thy union here? / Follow my mother" (5.2.320–21).

While I find completely persuasive the Copernican logic at work in the play that Ray traces, I remain unpersuaded by these two final interpretations. Laertes's exposure of Claudius's treachery, while it does indeed provoke Hamlet's instant, reactive turning of the poisoned cup and sword against Claudius, does not really have a bearing on the apparent absence of the Ghost or of any invocation of him. What the play presents is both the simultaneous absence of the Ghost and any reference to him, alongside his intromissive possession of his son. What is at stake here are the different forms of repetition in play. Freud had first formulated the compulsion to repeat in his work on the clinical transference and the transference neurosis that develops in the analytic situation, and he returned to it in relation to trauma and the death wish.[16] In both cases, of clinical transference and traumatic repetition, the disablement of memory is the condition for the unwitting acting out of scenes that the subject is unable either to remember or to stop repeating, and which are profoundly self-destructive. In this case we have both Hamlet's confession: "Thou wouldst not think how ill all's here about my heart" (5.2.206–207), alongside his determined acceptance of the lethal invitation, from the man who had sought to kill him, to fight a duel with the man whose father he has killed. It is hard not to feel that Hamlet's resignation—"The readiness is all" (216)—for all his invoking a "divinity that shapes our ends" (10), is a fated complicity with Claudius's designs on him. In other words, Hamlet both forgets the Ghost and enacts his fate; poisoned, he speaks from the same post-mortem position. For Hamlet, like the Ghost, the rest is indeed silence.

The tone of Hamlet's two brief references to his mother makes rather implausible the suggestion that his killing of Claudius is done in the name of the dead mother: "Is thy union here? / Follow my mother" (5.2.320–21), as he forces the King to drink; "Wretched Queen, adieu!" (327), his last words to his mother. Nothing here would suggest that the killing of Claudius is at the demand or authorization of Gertrude. The "union" has multiple meanings: a unique and precious pearl, "Richer than that which four successive kings / In Denmark's crown have worn" (267–68), an ancestral symbol, Claudius's giving of which hints deceptively that the succession will finally go to Hamlet. It is also the means by which the poison is introduced into the cup of wine, and the "union" is as well the marriage of Claudius and Gertrude, their union ironically confirmed in their death by the same poison. The Hamlet who had pleaded with his mother, "but go not to my uncle's bed" (3.4.160), now sends Claudius after her in a *mariage noir*: "Is thy union here? / Follow my mother" (5.2.320–21). His final dismissal of her as "wretched" is both a final acknowledgment by Hamlet that Claudius and Gertrude belong together as a couple, and a renunciation of his obsessional attachment to

[16] "The patient does not *remember* anything of what he has forgotten and repressed, but *acts* it out. He reproduces it not as a memory but as an action; he *repeats* it, without, of course knowing he is repeating it" (Freud, "Remembering, Repeating and Working-Through" 150/147–48).

her, in the very moment in which he both avenges but repeats his father's fate.

The acting out of the inner play's "poison in jest" through a literal returning to Claudius, the original poisoner, of "a poison tempered by himself" (5.2.322), both interrupts its further circulation as Ray points out, and helps to explain an important feature of the play's final moments: "Hamlet's final words [...] in effect reverse the performative dynamics of [the dead father's] posthumous address" (217). There is no intromissive relay of metaphorical poison as a legacy to the listening Horatio. In Hamlet's appeal "to tell my story" (343) there is no call to revenge and no paradoxical re-enactment of the deed to be avenged. Horatio's farewell blessing—"Good night, sweet Prince, / And flights of angels sing thee to thy rest" (5.2.353–54)—could not be more antithetical to the Ghost's burdened demands on his son, both poisoned and poisoning, or to Hamlet's traumatized receptivity. It is hard to see, however, even a *delayed* completion, as Hapgood and others do, in these final moments, with Hamlet arrested in mid-sentence by "this fell sergeant Death" (330): "Had I but time [...] O, I could tell you [...] The rest is silence" (330, 331, 352). Completion does not seem the right word amidst so much unfinished business, Hamlet never having confronted Claudius or Gertrude with his father's murder, let alone having exposed it in public. Despite Horatio's bid to make good Hamlet's wild justice: "let me speak to the yet unknowing world / How these things came about" (373–4), his determination to "Truly deliver" (380) the public exposure of Claudius's secret crimes, entrusted to him by Hamlet, is itself caught up in the play's dominant pattern of interruption and postponement. It is not to be performed or heard in Elsinore, within the time of Shakespeare's play. Horatio's anticipatory prospectus of bungled and failed actions yet to be told, functions in place of the standard tragic encomium, as a final blazon of the play's dramaturgy of delay and non-completion.

Works Cited

Anzieu, Didier. *The Skin Ego* [1995]. Translated by Naomi Segal. Karnac Books, 2016.

Bacon, Francis, Lord Verulam, *Essayes or Counsels, Civill & Morall.* Edited by Israel Gollancz. J. M. Dent, 1905.

Bate, Jonathan, and Eric Rasmussen, editors. *The RSC Shakespeare: The Complete Works.* Macmillan, 2007.

Culpepper, Jonathan and Matthew Gillings, "Five Myths about Shakespeare's Contribution to the English Language," posted on *The Conversation*, August 31, 2022. https://theconversation.com/five-myths-about-shakespeares-contribution-to-the-english-language-189402.

Fletcher, John. *Freud and the Scene of Trauma*. Fordham UP, 2013.

———. "The Scenography of Trauma: a 'Copernican' reading of Sophocles' *Oedipus the King*." *Textual Practice*, vol. 21, no. 1, 2007a, pp. 17–41. (Reprinted in Fletcher, *Freud and the Scene of Trauma*, pp. 123–36; and Fletcher and Ray, editors, *Seductions and Enigmas: Laplanche, Theory, Culture*, pp. 209–39).

———. "Seduction and the Vicissitudes of Translation: the Work of Jean Laplanche." *Psychoanalytic Quarterly*, vol.76, no. 4, 2007b, pp. 1241–91.

Fletcher, John, and Nicholas Ray, editors. *Seductions and Enigmas: Laplanche, Theory, Culture*. Lawrence and Wishart, 2014.

Freud, Sigmund. *The Revised Standard Edition of the Complete Psychological Works of Sigmund Freud*, edited and translated by James Strachey, revised by Mark Solms. 24 vols. Rowman & Littlefield Publishers, 2024. (In-text references provide *RSE* page numbers immediately after *SE* page numbers).

———. *Beyond the Pleasure Principle* (1920). *The Standard Edition of the Complete Psychological Works of Sigmund Freud*, edited and translated by James Strachey, vol. 18, Hogarth Press, 1955, pp. 1–64/*RSE* vol. 18, pp. 3–61.

———. "A Difficulty in the Path of Psycho-Analysis" (1917). *SE* vol. 17, 1955, pp. 135–44/*RSE* vol. 17, pp. 125–33.

———. *Group Psychology and the Ego* (1921). *SE* vol. 18, pp. 65–143/*RSE* vol. 18, pp. 63–133.

———. *The Interpretation of Dreams* (1900). *SE* vols. 4 and 5, 1953/*RSE* vols. 4 and 5.

———. "Remembering, Repeating and Working-Through" (1914). *SE* vol. 12, 1958, pp. 145–56/*RSE* vol. 12, pp. 141–53.

———. "A Special Form of Choice of Object Made by Men" (1910), *SE* vol. 11, 1957, pp. 163–75/*RSE* vol. 11, pp. 151–61.

Greenblatt, Stephen. *Hamlet in Purgatory*. Princeton UP, 2001.

Hapgood, Robert. "Hamlet nearly absurd: The Dramaturgy of Delay." *Tulane Drama Review*, vol. 9, no. 4, 1965, pp. 132–45.

Harvey, William. *De Motu Cordis*. William Fitzer, Frankfurt, 1628.

Hart, Alfred. "Vocabularies of Shakespeare's Plays." *Review of English Studies*, vol. 19, no. 74, 1943, pp. 128–40.

Heywood, Jasper, translator. *Seneca his Tenne Tragedies* [1581]. Edited by Charles E. Simms. The Spenser Society, 1887.

Jenkins, Harold, editor. *Hamlet*. Methuen, 1982.

Jones, Emrys. *Scenic Form in Shakespeare*. Clarendon Press, 1971.

Kermode, Frank. *Shakespeare's Language*. Penguin, 2000.

Laplanche, Jean. *Essays on Otherness*. Edited by John Fletcher. Translated by John Fletcher, Leslie Hill, and Luke Thurston. Routledge, 1999.
Laplanche, Jean, and J.-B. Pontalis. *The Language of Psychoanalysis*. Translated by Donald Nicholson-Smith. Hogarth Press, 1973.
Masson, Jeffrey Moussaieff, translator and editor. *The Complete Letters of Sigmund Freud to Wilhelm Fliess 1887–1904*. Harvard UP, 1985.
Puttenham, George. *The Arte of English Poesie* [1589]. Facsimile reproduction of 1906 reprint, Kent State UP, 1970.
Ray, Nicholas. *Tragedy and Otherness: Sophocles, Shakespeare and Psychoanalysis*. Peter Lang, 2009.
Scarfone, Dominique. "'It was *not* my mother': From Seduction to Negation." *Jean Laplanche and the Theory of Seduction*, special issue, *New Formations*, no. 48, 2002–2003, pp. 69–76.
Shakespeare, William. *Hamlet*. Edited by T. J. B Spencer, with an Introduction by Alan Sinfield. Penguin, 2005.
Shapiro, James. *1599: A Year in the Life of William Shakespeare*. Faber and Faber, 2005.
States, Bert O. "Word-Pictures in *Hamlet*." *The Hudson Review*, vol. 26, no. 3, 1973, pp. 510–22.
Wright, George T. "Hendiadys and *Hamlet*." *PMLA*, vol. 96, no. 2. 1981, pp. 168–93.

CHAPTER 10

Emulous Fidelity: Shakespeare, Jack Spicer, and *Troilus*

Daniel Katz

Shakespeare's *Troilus and Cressida* has, of course, traditionally been read as a play about infidelity. Indeed, the play asks to be read as such, proposing Cressida herself as the very figure of this fault: "Make Cressid's name the very crown of falsehood / If ever she leave Troilus!" (4.2.101–102), the heroine exclaims. Earlier, Pandarus puts it even more plainly, asserting that if ever Cressida should be untrue, all "false women" should be known as "Cressids" (3.2.198). In this light, the play is the origin story of how Cressida becomes the very emblem, indeed the generic name, of the False Woman (something which, historically, never happened with that name in the same way it has with the name of the character, Pandarus, who suggested that fate), and therefore, the very type of the unfaithful woman. In this chapter, I will read the play somewhat differently, arguing that it also asks, if somewhat surreptitiously, to be read as a study of nothing other than fidelity, but of another kind. In so doing, I will follow the lead of Jack Spicer, who, in his own retelling of the story in his play *Troilus*, pressures

D. Katz (✉)
London, UK
e-mail: d.katz@warwick.ac.uk

J. W. Stone, C. Bates (eds.), *Shakespeare and Psychoanalysis*, Palgrave Shakespeare Studies,
https://doi.org/10.1007/978-3-032-07897-1_10

some of the key cruces in Shakespeare, allowing them to be seen in another light.

Spicer himself was primarily a poet, and his play *Troilus* was one of his very rare extended undertakings in another form, and probably the one he took most seriously. The play was mostly written over the first six months of 1955, a crucial time for Spicer, who turned thirty in January of that year and was preparing to leave the San Francisco Bay Area to seek his fortune as a writer in New York—a fortune he failed to find there. *Troilus* was never performed, but as he got ready for his move, Spicer considered it perhaps the major asset in his portfolio and continued to regard it as one of his most important pieces of writing for several years afterward. His interest in the story itself was long-standing. Some of Spicer's acquaintances remember him reciting long passages of Chaucer's *Troilus and Criseyde* by heart (see Ellingham and Killian 211), and he apparently pronounced it the greatest poem in the English language on several occasions. Additionally, as a student at the University of California at Berkeley, he wrote a somewhat uninspired but quite meticulous long essay on specifically theatrical renderings of the story: "A Preliminary Excursion into Comparison of Shakespeare's and Dryden's Troilus and Cressida in a Quixotic Attempt to Discover Neoclassical Poetic Technique, or, Some Little Truth Found Too Early."[1] The paper contains many point-by-point comparisons of corresponding scenes from the two plays (always to the detriment of Dryden) and certainly got Spicer thinking about what kinds of things might happen were Shakespeare's version to be rewritten.

And rewriting, recasting, adapting, or translating were central to Spicer's writing practice more generally. To borrow the term Spicer's close friend Robert Duncan used about his own processes, much of Spicer's most important work is "derivative" rather than original in the usually accepted sense, or to use Spicer's own preferred term, in "co-respondence" with other authors or works.[2] Thus, the two most complete and finished plays Spicer wrote other than *Troilus* were also both adaptations: of Hawthorne's tale "Young Goodman Brown" in one case and of Euripides's *The Bacchae* in the other. Even more important, what he considered his

[1]The essay can be found in the Spicer archives at the Bancroft Library, University of California, Berkeley, BANC MSS 2004/209.

[2]For Duncan's sense of the "derivative," see the excellent collection edited by Collis and Lyons. Spicer's concept of "co-respondence" is crucial to his book *After Lorca*, found in *My Vocabulary Did This To Me*, pp. 105–54.

own breakthrough book of poetry, *After Lorca* of 1957, is mostly a book of translations, though it includes some hidden "ghost-written" unattributed Spicer poems, and a series of letters to Lorca, where "Jack" muses on the exchange between them. For Spicer, "finding" oneself as a writer meant losing oneself among the texts of others, and the adaptation or recasting of other bodies of work remained crucial to him until the end, as seen in works like his *Billy the Kid*, or even more, *The Holy Grail*. A careful reader of T. S. Eliot, Spicer offers one of the signal early instances of readings of Eliot's "tradition" which serve to untether authorship more than ground it in a coherent order. As "Jack" explains in one of his letters to Lorca, tradition "means generations of different poets in different countries patiently telling the same story, writing the same poem, gaining and losing something with each transformation—but of course never really losing anything. [...] Invention is merely the enemy of poetry" (*My Vocabulary* 110–11). From this optic, translation as a form of imitation is no longer an exception to the norm of authorial work, but rather its most exemplary form.

What makes all this especially relevant for the context of Spicer's *Troilus* is that Shakespeare's play itself is obsessed throughout with similar questions. Forms of imitation—of behaviors, desires, and even in one case, of individuals' linguistic mannerisms—recur again and again, and are specifically considered by Ulysses both as dangers to authority and as phenomena that can be exploited tactically. It is far from a surprise that René Girard, the theorist of "mimetic desire," would single this play out for special attention. In the Arden edition at least, the word "imitation" appears twice, "emulation" four times, and "emulous" five times. All these words relate, as the play makes clear, to a psychic state at the heart of the play's concerns: that of "envy," a word Shakespeare uses six times also. In this respect, Spicer's own project is in some ways already found *within* the play it revisits: in the very act of writing his jokey play with its moments of high camp and near pastiche, Spicer might be said to imitate Shakespeare's own Patroclus, who, as Ulysses asserts in astonishing language in act 1, scene 3, "pageants" the Greek leaders, imitating and mocking their language and gestures. But if as an imitation of sorts Spicer's play writes itself into the dynamics that Shakespeare's play explores, it also perhaps provides new ways of thinking of the "emulous." Crucial in Shakespeare's play is that the question of what it means to imitate is related to that of what it means to envy, and both of these questions in turn are tied to the problem of what it means to love. Imitation in this play is at once a form of love *and* a form of violence; quite possibly it is a form of love as violence, or violence as love. Indeed, the play is no less concerned with physical violence than it is with love, and with the contradictory codes of obligation, responsibility, and debt that govern both. That is to say that "fidelity" in the collective and hierarchical social order—something the play parallels with the "fidelity" that binds the amorous couple—is explicitly based on a complicated economy which at once enforces emulation and also prohibits it.

Several observations follow from the above. The first is that "fidelity" is also a crucial term in translation theory, and one no less vexed. In the passage from *After Lorca* cited above, Spicer radically questions such a concept of fidelity because he also questions the notion of originality. Originality, or what we might call "intellectual property" today, becomes the enemy of poetry, and thus throws the question of a translator's fidelity on its head. And this leads to a following, parallel question: To what extent does the notion of erotic fidelity also rest on a conception of erotic property, which Spicer, and possibly Shakespeare, wish to challenge? Meanwhile, if fidelity leads us to jealousy, and the latter to problems of "emulation" or forms of mimetic desire, let us not forget that the entire question of the ambivalent dynamics of imitation is, of course, central to psychoanalytic theory under the rubric of identification, itself a core theoretical component of Freud's view of subjectification by way of the Oedipus complex. Shakespeare's play stresses these dynamics as fundamental at once to social organization (and not least to social organization as organized violence) as well as to the dynamics of erotic object choice. What this means is that the hallowed opposition in some psychoanalytic theory between the realm of sublimation and repression governing the social order on the one hand, and the private libidinal drive of the erotic on the other, is harder to maintain. Indeed, a tendency of both Shakespeare and Spicer is to challenge the concept of the "private" or "personal" more globally. But before pursuing these questions further, a brief overview of Spicer's play is in order.

Consisting of four acts, Spicer's *Troilus* follows Shakespeare in many significant ways, while intervening in some of the manners one would expect in the context of mid-century "New American poetry" aesthetics. Spicer's language is mostly demotic American and casual in tone, but markedly witty, including in the Elizabethan sense. Donne was one of Spicer's favorite poets and complex rhetorical and intellectual figures abound (one of Spicer's chief criticisms of Dryden was that he reduced the philosophical complexity of Shakespeare's play). The wit is often decidedly camp and irreverent, and Spicer, an out-of-the-closet queer poet writing for a community of the same, is explicit in his treatment of the relationship between Achilles and Patroclus. The camp humor and mundane mid-century American lexicon help Spicer to capture very effectively the surprisingly modern managerial tediousness with which Shakespeare imbues the Greek leaders' councils, as Spicer recasts them explicitly as a corporate board meeting in act 1. Meanwhile, heavily stressing generational difference throughout his play, he frames the sociality obtaining among the young Trojan fighters by giving it the trappings of American university student life of the 1950s. Stage directions present the fighters "sitting half-dressed on a bench in what looks vaguely like a locker-room" (*Be Brave* 249), or tell us that the Greek and Trojan fighters are "dressed in costumes of the sort American colleges would use if sword-fighting to the death were an intercollegiate sport" (242).

Though Spicer reduces the acts to four and radically intervenes at the play's end, his *Troilus* largely replicates the most important structural architecture of Shakespeare's play, and all of Shakespeare's crucial scenes have a clear counterpart. Aside from the major alteration to the narrative's conclusion, the one major exception to this mirroring is Spicer's act 1. Generally, there is broad correspondence: Spicer's first scene maps onto act 1, scene 3 in Shakespeare, which contains Ulysses's famous speech on degree, while in his scene 2 Spicer introduces the young fighters of the Trojan camp, clearly reprising elements from scenes 1 and 2 in Shakespeare. But despite this, Spicer's act 1 includes an important difference: while Shakespeare begins with Troilus already enamored of Cressida, Spicer follows Chaucer instead and, like him, dwells on the origins and etiology of the affect of love. Of particular note here is the way Spicer pushes a consideration of destiny and fate, more or less in keeping with conventional twentieth-century scholarly notions of Greek thought, into a realm that is more properly that of parapraxis. If the very first lines of Shakespeare's play establish that Troilus is not "master of his heart" (1.1.4), Spicer's Troilus, fancy-free, in contrast questions his more experienced relatives about the concept of love itself. After having first asked Paris "when did you first decide" to fall in love with Helen, Troilus makes his major claim: "people don't fall in love by accident" (252). He explains, "there's a point where you decide—where you say 'I'll let myself fall in love.' Once you say that, it's too late, you can't change your mind again. But there's that point where you consciously let go and let the rest follow" (252). As he continues to argue with Paris and Aeneas, Cressida is mentioned as a more or less random hypothetical example of a woman Troilus might fall in love with. And indeed, the next time we see Troilus, he is confessing to Pandarus that he is in love with Cressida but "didn't know" it.[3] Asked by Pandarus to extrapolate, he continues: "It only makes me sound stupider. I'd been with Aeneas and Paris and we were talking about love and Cressida was mentioned. I didn't know her. [...] anyway, this started me thinking about her. And then I had a dream about her last night" (262). Reversing the roles in Shakespeare's telling, Troilus then has to convince the skeptical and none-too-willing Pandarus to set up a meeting, which he finally agrees to do. In act 2, scene 1, Cressida appears for the first time in the play, having dinner with Troilus and Pandarus in the latter's "bachelor apartment" (265). The young would-be couple make small talk while Pandarus scampers in and out from the kitchen, bringing food and clearing dishes. The scene ends this way:

> TROILUS: Have some more wine. (He starts pouring it into her glass). It's a beautiful apartment, the pictures... (He has been pouring wine into a full glass. He notices it spilling onto the table and tries to stop it and in doing so upsets all the wine from the glass onto CRESSIDA's lap. She takes a napkin and starts wiping the wine from her dress.) I love you, Cressida.
> CRESSIDA: You love me.
> TROILUS: Do you love me?
> CRESSIDA: I think so. (At this moment PANDARUS comes in from the kitchen.) Uncle, there's been an accident. (267)

The importance of this scene for Spicer's play is severalfold. To begin, it functions as a rebuttal to Troilus's earlier theory of love and firmly places love in the realm of the "accidental"—that which resists conscious control, but just as importantly that which is contrary to fate, destiny, purpose, and order. Love is on the side of contingency, which Spicer's play will rather clumsily associate with freedom. At the same time, the scene as described reads like an obvious parapraxis (or dream sequence), in which the material accident, albeit symbolically, fulfills the unconscious desire. Love is not only an accident, but it takes the form of accident, and expresses itself in accidental actions. It is an uncontainable excess, a literal overflowing onto its object, which it sullies: if the analogy to the physical act is too obvious to dwell on, note that this paradigm gives us something very

[3]That Troilus's desire arises from a markedly homosocial exchange, stressed as such, is hardly coincidental. Thanks to James Stone for this observation.

different from the idealization of the love object which seems to dominate in Shakespeare's telling of the tale. At the same time, Troilus makes the wine glass "speak," as it were, his desire. And this form of non-verbal "speaking" of desire is something which Shakespeare's Cressida, in an unwilled willing which smacks of parapraxis too, cannot prevent her own body from doing, at least according to Ulysses, who depicts her allure as shouting uncontainably from the details of her body: "There's language in her eye, her cheek, her lip, / Nay, her foot speaks; her wanton spirits look out / At every joint and motive of her body" (4.5.56–58). Through the lens of Spicer, can we read Cressida's later betrayal of Troilus as a kind of accident, occasioned by a seductive body speaking its own language of desire? Or is Ulysses himself too quick to shut down the question of Cressida's desire, in opposition to Troilus, who tends to present the mystery as simply unsoundable? Either way, in both Shakespeare and Spicer, the origins of desire cannot be separated from the problematics of imitation and identification. In Spicer this is handled more through the topos of suggestion—an offhand reference to Cressida leads to Troilus's "accident." But Shakespeare's play is more deliberate here: when Pandarus sets about kindling Cressida's desire for Troilus, he does so by suggesting that Helen is in love with him: "I think Helen loves him better than Paris" (1.2.104), Pandarus tells her, and presses the idea at some length, suggesting that in winning Troilus, Cressida will have outdone the paragon not only of female beauty, but of power. In other words, Pandarus uses Helen as a mediating figure to fashion Cressida's desire through the establishment of a rival, in a manner very similar to the way Ulysses will try to use Ajax with regard to Achilles. Indeed, it is striking that the scene with Pandarus and Cressida, in which Helen's desire is constructed as a model to spur on Cressida's, is immediately followed by the "council" of the Greek leaders, where the question of emulation and its disordering force is stressed more powerfully than anywhere else in the play. This creates less an opposition than a parallel between the "private" realm of love and the "public" concerns of statecraft and warcraft. It also establishes a crucial irony: Ulysses, the eloquent denunciator of "emulation," is also the figure who is most canny in using its own power for his own ends. And this means that if "emulation" can be seen as a threat to Agamemnon's enterprise, as Ulysses says, what Ulysses actually does on the contrary suggests it is also indispensable to it.[4]

[4]David Bevington notes this, too, in his Introduction to the Arden edition (25).

In that connection, one of the most strikingly modern aspects of Shakespeare's play is the extent to which it presents its warriors as alienated from the war in which they fight. Hector goes so far as to suggest that they simply give Helen back, arguing that every lost Trojan "hath been as dear as Helen" (2.2.20), and maintaining that Troy is in fact in the wrong, contravening "moral laws" (2.2.184) because Helen, as Menelaus's wife, belongs to him. If this is a blatant affirmation of the idea of woman as erotic property that Cressida's subsequent actions, like those of Helen before her, can be seen to challenge, it nevertheless opens the seemingly "modern" problem of the soldier beholden to fight by laws of duty or kinship for a cause believed to be morally wrong. If Hector in the end refuses to act in accordance with his moral judgment, it is because of a further consideration which he admits takes precedence: the war is now "a cause that hath no mean dependence / Upon our joint and several dignities" (2.2.192–93). That is, for Hector this immoral and wasteful war from which it is impossible to withdraw is no longer really about Helen at all, an idea Spicer picks up on, when his Paris, annoyed at being blamed for the war by his fellows, says to Aeneas, "Can't you get it through your thick skull that Helen is just an excuse? Do you and everyone else in this goddamn town have to go around shouting Greek propaganda? [...] We're fighting about commerce and so are they. [...] They want to destroy us and Helen's only a convenient excuse" (249). For both Spicer and Shakespeare, the reality is much more tawdry than the protagonists would like to believe, and Hector's "dignity" is anything but dignified. Let us examine Hector's conundrum closely. To begin, his annoyance stems from allowing himself to be governed by a code of conduct whose importance he recognizes as supreme and sovereign over his own desires—we might be tempted to read this in terms of the unhappy submission to repression and the superego which Freud thematizes in *Civilization and its Discontents*. But note that the code to which Hector submits is not a moral one, but on the contrary is in his eyes in opposition to the moral code to which he would like to adhere. Hector is upset because he feels it is his duty to do the wrong thing, as it were. But what would Hector lose by refusing to do this thing? Troilus immediately spells it out for him, reminding Hector that the chief cause of their combat is "glory" (2.2.195), and that Helen is "A spur to valiant and magnanimous deeds" (2.2.200), likely to bring "fame" (2.2.202) to those who undertake them. Following Troilus's exhortation, Hector renews his dedication to the cause and divulges the "challenge" he has sent to Achilles to meet him in individual combat. Striking here is that the narcissistic satisfaction of "glory" that Troilus outlines seems not a stronger force than Hector's moral code but more a compensation for Hector in return for abandoning what he is certain is right. The conflict, in other words, is not between the "Id" and the "Superego," or personal ambition and the collective good, or individual libidinal drive and collective social sublimation. Rather, it is the contradiction between two conflicting ego ideals competing in one tormented and violent body.

In these respects, Hector's position provides an interesting framing for the attitude of Achilles as Ulysses addresses it, notably in his famous speech on "degree." As we have seen, in order to continue to fight Hector must sacrifice one ideal to another, which he cannot do without grave misgivings, at the demands of a superego that is not wholly sovereign. The dynamic played out here already hints at the conditions which make him the tragic hero he becomes later, when he would rather die than betray a code of honorable combat, unlike Achilles. But what is crucial to bear in mind is that the glory/shame system, which for Hector replaces the morality/immorality system, is equally governed by regulatory ego ideals. In other words, an opposition between, say, "duty" and "selfishness" is precisely not what is in play.

Now, let us turn to Ulysses's speech. On the one hand, he argues that hierarchical order, or what the play calls "degree," is the sole bulwark against what would otherwise be the generalized violence of the war of all against all, "an envious fever / Of pale and bloodless emulation" (1.3.133–34), in which there would be no check on sheer force, leaving all under the sway of "appetite, an universal wolf" (1.3.121). In the phrase above, "emulation" is associated precisely with jealousy, or as Arden glosses it, a "grudge against the superiority of others" (165), though in Shakespeare's time the word meant "three overlapping but distinct things," according to the *OED*, as it also carried the senses of "ambitious rivalry" and "the endeavour to surpass or equal others." These divisions mirror the divisions of rivalry itself, in which, as the dynamics of identification teach us, the loving desire to double the object and the violent desire to supplant it cannot be easily parsed. Thus, while condemning "emulation" as the enemy of the Greek cause in Troy, it is nothing other than emulous strivings that Ulysses uses in his stratagem of raising Ajax's reputation among the Greeks to the point that Achilles will feel the need to return to battle to confirm his supremacy. In fact, the very "emulation" he condemns in the speech on degree he encourages when goading Achilles into action, telling him that his past deeds "Made emulous missions 'mongst the gods themselves" (3.3.190), which means that he not only made the gods wish to imitate him, but, according to Arden, caused the gods to join the Trojan War. For Ulysses, then, "emulation" is not only a corrupting influence but also an indispensable force: it is the force that impels Achilles to prove himself better than Ajax, or better than Hector, for that matter. And from this perspective, "degree" appears as something rightly curious, and fully ideological. "Degree," for example, affirms that even should Achilles prove himself in some ways "better" than Agamemnon, he should not dare to expect he can have what Agamemnon has (for example, Briseis, in other versions of the tale), or take his place. Seen this way, one of Ulysses's privileged examples of the "chaos" that would follow from the abasement of "degree" is in no way accidental: "And the rude son should strike his father dead" (1.3.115). In other words, Ulysses's logic follows the classic logic of the Oedipus complex for Freud, in which the son must *emulate* his father while renouncing the goal of being him, or taking what he has, in a classic double-bind. In the concrete terms of Ulysses's maneuvers, this means Achilles must be reminded that while his relationship with Agamemnon must absolutely not be "emulous," on the other hand his relation to Ajax must absolutely be so.

But in terms of the broader problem of mandatory emulation and rivalry in relation to fixed hierarchy, let us turn to Freud, who is clear on how this contradiction is resolved in the normative situation he proposes. For Freud, the child's superego is based not on the parent as rival, but on that rival's relationship to their own rival, that is, to their parents' own superego: "Thus a child's super-ego is in fact constructed on the model not of its parents but of its parents' super-ego" (*New Introductory Lectures* 67/60). In making this point, Freud goes on to stress the conservative or even anti-historical propensities of the superego and, thus, of the human psyche (something which other schools of thought might formulate as "residual ideology"). But there is another element which is more important for us: the implication that what the child therefore identifies with is the parents' *submission* to their own superego, and that the Oedipal resolution is thus triangulated doubly: the third point is not only the "father" in relation to the "mother," but the superego that the child perceives as operative within the father. The child does not internalize the parent as all-powerful tyrant, in the form of the superego, but rather *identifies* with the parent as one who himself or herself *submits* to a force that limits their own power, and their own desires. The child submits to the father who has *not* struck his own father dead. While rivalry rewards sheer power (who is stronger—Achilles or Hector?), law is based on power's abrogation by the powerful. These are the problems which Hector recognizes when he insists that the war be in some way justified, and his way out is through the ideal of "glory." This is because "glory" is in fact the term that offers a (false) resolution to the competing systems that Ulysses, in speech and in deed, proposes (that is, the "degree" system and the "emulation" system), which together amount to the tendentious principle that maintains Agamemnon's authority on the one hand, while insisting that Achilles prove his supremacy on the other. "Glory" would be a way of allowing the first system to contain the second, a mechanism to bind a world of rivalry in which "Each thing meets / In mere oppugnancy" (1.3.110–11) (as Ajax might meet Hector, or Achilles might meet Ajax) into a symbolic system that rewards emulous victory while at the same time constraining it. This is the resource Ulysses will use when arguing with Achilles that his value must be *seen*. And as for the contradictions in Ulysses's machinations, these can be found in his speech itself. That is to say, while Shakespeare clearly presents the speeches of Agamemnon and Nestor as tedious and clichéd (Spicer not unreasonably implicitly recasts them as the kind of thing a high school football coach might say), Ulysses can easily be read in contrast as a voice of some real authority. However, a close look at his words makes this harder to maintain. Certainly, his speech is coherent when he voices concerns that bad examples when unpunished provoke imitators, which destroys hierarchy. But his presentation of the absoluteness of hierarchy itself, as an order based on something other than demonstrated value as established through rivalry, conflict, or "oppugnancy," is not argued at all. Indeed, his argument, like the concept, is tautologous:

> How could communities,
> Degrees in schools and brotherhoods in cities,
> Peaceful commerce from divadable shores,
> The primogeneity and due of birth,
> Prerogative of age, crowns, sceptres, laurels,
> But by degree stand in authentic place? (1.3.103–108)

Not only is there a tautology in the syntax, which asks how "degrees" can stand without "degree," but also in the logic: since "degree" is the name Ulysses gives to the place which is "authentic," to ask how that place can be kept without degree is not to ask a real question. Evidence that Ulysses's entire train of thought here might in fact be tendentious can be found in his final criticisms of Achilles and Patroclus, who, he claims, show great contempt for "The still and mental parts, / That do contrive how many hands shall strike" (1.3.200–201) to which they give "not a finger's dignity," dismissing strategic labor as "bed-work, mapp'ry, closet war" (1.3. 204–205). In other words, they express contempt and disdain for the very qualities in which Ulysses, it so happens, excels (Spicer's twist on Ulysses as the champion of the "still and mental" is to cast him as poet).

But "emulation" is as crucial to the "love plot" as to the war plot, and to examine this I would like to turn to the two most crucial scenes for the former and compare the treatments of them in Shakespeare and Spicer. Shakespeare's act 4 depicts Troilus and Cressida after their night of love, when the couple is informed that Cressida is to be taken to the Greek camp to join her father. Here Cressida swears her eternal fidelity to Troilus—"Make Cressid's name the very crown of falsehood / If ever she leave Troilus!" (4.2.101–102), while Troilus rightly worries that Cressida, despite her protestations, will never be able to resist the charms of Greek manhood; he correctly foretells the disaster that will befall him. In his reading of this scene, René Girard stresses the importance of rivalry for the construction of Troilus's desire. He argues that act 4, scene 2, depicts Troilus, having won his suit and his desire sated, now clearly bored with his conquest, to whom he displays a distinct lack of passion. For Girard, only when the prospect of losing her to another appears does his desire revive. Interestingly, however, he completely ignores the desire of Cressida herself. Here the picture is very different: she repeatedly professes her fidelity to Troilus, and her sorrow at being parted from him: "Have the gods envy?" (4.4.27), she asks in trying to find an explanation for their cruel fate. And when Troilus admonishes her, "Be thou true of heart" (4.4.57), she reproves him sternly for even being tempted to doubt her. But Troilus continues to insist, in a crucial exchange. He first stresses the great attractiveness of the Greeks:

> The Grecian youths are full of quality;
> Their loving well composed with gifts of nature,
> And flowing o'er with arts and exercise.
> How novelty may move and parts with person,
> Alas, a kind of godly jealousy—
> Which, I beseech you, call a virtuous sin—
> Makes me afeard. (4.4.75–81)

Once again using the rhetoric of emulation, rivalry, and envy, it is Troilus who firmly plants the idea of Cressida's infidelity into Cressida's own mind. This only continues when in an extraordinary speech, Troilus compares himself unfavorably to his rivals:

> In this I do not call your faith in question
> So mainly as my merit. I cannot sing,
> Nor heel the high lavolt, nor sweeten talk,
> Nor play at subtle games—fair virtues all,
> To which the Grecians are most prompt and pregnant. (4.4.82–87)

Troilus goes on to tell Cressida, "But be not tempted," and when she answers, "Do you think I will?" Troilus responds, "No / But something may be done that we will not; / And sometimes we are devils to ourselves" (4.4.90–3).

A great deal is in play here. First, of course, Troilus's speech is heavily ironic dramatically in prefiguring the outcome of the events, but also rhetorically in that the speech brings about the events it is meant to counter. This is crucial: it is Troilus who first insists that Cressida is capable of betraying him (something that simply does not occur to her), and it is Troilus, too, who insists that the Greeks are in some ways more attractive than he. Troilus plants the seed of Cressida's subsequent infidelity. But once we acknowledge this, we have to ask if Cressida has been unfaithful at all, because she has in fact been nothing but faithful to Troilus's conceptions and fears. It might be said that in a catastrophic and ironic act of emulation, she has endorsed Troilus's own conception of himself and of the Greeks. To put it in other terms, her love for Troilus expresses itself in hysterical fashion, by the very act of her falling in love with Troilus's own ego ideals, this being an outcome programmed by Troilus himself. "Something may be done that we will not," Troilus says, seeming to understand that Cressida's future betrayal will not originate from the place of conscious willing, but rather be, to use Spicer's language, an "accident" derived from Troilus's own sense of abjection in comparison to his own amorous ideal.

None of this appears at all in Spicer, who does however introduce a "deception" on Cressida's part in that his version has her know the night before that she will be leaving on the morrow, and she in consequence withholds the information from Troilus so as not to spoil their night together. Spicer's Troilus is mostly calm at the moment of parting. The closest we come to Shakespeare's scene is an exchange between Troilus and Pandarus after Cressida has left with the Greeks, in which Pandarus asks, "You don't doubt her?" (286), and Troilus answers, "I don't doubt her, I doubt things that happen. This happened. Things like this are going to happen until the day both of us die" (286)—a speech echoing in some ways Shakespeare's Troilus's "something may be done that we will not." However, in the very next scene Spicer pointedly insists on something left more implicit in Shakespeare, that is, the idea of Cressida as subject to the violence of Troilus's own construction of her. This occurs during a long exchange between Thersites and Zeus, in which the former refers to Cressida as "Troilus's masturbation fantasy" (289), and Zeus replies, "She did seem to start out as an invention of Troilus, maybe even a fantasy. But she started to tell him something in the tower" (289). This is a reference to Spicer's act 2, scene 4, in which Cressida informs Troilus she is "afraid" because "I can't feel the same way about you that you feel about me" and that "sometimes I feel guilty that I can't love you enough" (281). But in the broader context of the play, this reads less crucially as an acknowledgment of an imbalance of feeling between the two lovers, and more as a tentative affirmation of a different articulation of the erotic economy, something that becomes clear when we examine how the two plays handle the crucial scene where Troilus is made to witness Cressida's betrayal of him with Diomedes.

In Shakespeare's play, Troilus's shocked reaction—as, hidden from sight, he watches Cressida give to Diomedes the sleeve he had offered her as a token of his love—presents a famous crux. Troilus, explicitly unable either to accept what he is seeing or to deny it, seems ultimately to do neither. After asking Ulysses and probably himself to "Rather think this not Cressid" (5.2.139), he continues:

> This she? No, this is Diomed's Cressida.
> If beauty have a soul, this is not she;
> If souls guide vows, if vows be sanctimonies,
> If sanctimony be the gods' delight,
> If there be rule in unity itself,
> This is not she. O, madness of discourse,
> That cause sets up with and against itself!
> Bifold authority, where reason can revolt
> Without perdition, and loss assume all reason
> Without revolt! This is and is not Cressid.

> Within my soul there doth conduce a fight
> Of this strange nature, that a thing inseparate
> Divides more wider than the sky and earth,
> And yet the spacious breadth of this division
> Admits no orifex for a point as subtle
> As Ariachne's broken woof to enter. (5.2.144–59)

How can we read Troilus's anguished yet paradoxical assertion, "This is and is not Cressid"? Laura Levine suggests this phrase bespeaks the impasse Troilus has reached regarding Cressida's knowability, which is a problem throughout the play. Torn between two "dogmatic" alternatives, neither of which he can accept, Troilus abandons the idea of the "rule of unity" altogether: "there is no oneness, no 'rule in unity itself' that would allow him to make a claim one way or the other about Cressida. Rather, 'cause sets up with and against itself' and all he can say is 'This is, and is not, Cressid'" (65). In this respect, Cressida could be seen as the figure of the impossibility of oneness, of unity of meaning, altogether. Ann Lecercle's reading seems to move in this direction as she points out the way Shakespeare stresses not only the intrinsic non-self-identity of Cressida, but also that very non-self-identity's inseparability into manageable discrete entities: "His [Troilus's] verbal interpretation is predicated syntactically in its *incipit* on the simplest of paradoxes ('This is and is not Cressid'); *a contrario* its conclusion relies on the most contortedly complex of amphiboles: 'And yet the spacious breadth of this divison / Admits no orifex for a point as subtle / As Ariachne's broken woof to enter'" (157). The radically divided Cressida cannot be separated from herself.

Of course, Cressida's essential unknowability, or integral division into two incompatible states she nevertheless occupies at once, can be read another way too. For this corresponds precisely to the logic of disavowal as outlined by Freud in "On Fetishism," in which the fetishist both knows and does not know that the mother is without the phallus. And moreover, the scene of Troilus's rapt and tormented witnessing of the amours of a couple from which he is the radically excluded third term seems like a classic example of the kind of primal scene Freud privileges, for example, in the Wolfman case, and others where the mother's castration provokes disavowal or delusion in response. This is not to argue that at stake in Shakespeare's play is castration—a reading that strikes me as brittle and doctrinaire—but rather that it shows that for Troilus, when confronted with an intolerable crisis, the either/or alternative of "is or is not" breaks down, replaced by the "splitting" in the ego able to assert the contradiction of "is *and* is not."[5]

But there is another possibility too, which is simply that Cressida's essence is not in fact defined by fidelity to Troilus—that he has given himself an alternative that is false or insoluble, by asking the wrong question (and this not only because, as argued above, her act of infidelity can be seen as ultimately faithful to Troilus's own investment in an ego ideal which he denies himself, as she sacrifices herself and their vows for Troilus's secret narcissistic love). Spicer's handling of the scene brings these possibilities to the fore. His Troilus does not so much collapse in crisis as bear witness in defeated resignation, as he watches Cressida hand not a sleeve but rather a ring, gage of their love, to Diomede (as Spicer names him). Later he will learn that Cressida herself had helped stage the scene, because, Calchas tells Troilus, "she thought it would be easier for you if you hated her" (296). The stratagem does not work, because as Troilus tells Calchas, "I don't care what Cressida does with the Greeks" (296). Seeming to take his cue from Shakespeare's Troilus, who exclaims "this is Diomede's Cressida" in trying to convince himself that the Cressida he sees with Diomede is somehow a different one, Spicer gives his Troilus this speech:

> What I want is my Trojan Cressida—I'd watch worse scenes than the one you staged for me to get *her* back. You thought you were being so clever arranging it so I'd see her being unfaithful. Unfaithful! Every single minute she's away from me she's unfaithful. Every second that we're not kissing each other, every instant that we're not laughing into each other's eyes she's unfaithful. Monstrously unfaithful. I don't care what she does outside of Troy, who she gives rings to or who she sleeps with. I want her back. I want my Trojan Cressida back. (296)

But Calchas tells him that even if Cressida certainly does not love Diomede as much as she once did Troilus, "She just doesn't want to go back to being your Trojan Cressida. You never did understand her" (297). In a crucial passage for Spicer, Calchas goes on to encourage Troilus to trade Cressida for art, as it were, that is, to sublimate. With the help of Apollo, whom Calchas serves as a priest, Troilus is told he might replace his lost

[5] One can easily imagine a Lacanian reading in which the sleeve would play the role of phallus, exchanged between the three Oedipalized protagonists. But such an identification risks closing down what Shakespeare's uncompromising rhetoric has opened.

Eurydice (Troilus's figure for Cressida, who in his view refuses to be rescued from the Hell he hoped to take her out of) with the Eurydice "inside yourself. He [Apollo] can help you find balance and pleasure" (297). After Troilus bitterly refuses this, there follows this exchange:

> CALCHAS: You have locked your heart like a city.
> TROILUS: Who taught me to lock my heart? Who built the walls around my city? You and the rest of your balance worshippers, your friends of Apollo. You gave me a war to play with when I was a child. You taught me how to build walls. Then you brought me Cressida and I moved the walls to make room for her—and so you took her away. Now my heart is empty and big like a deserted city and you tell me I've locked my gates. (298)

At the end of the scene, Troilus exclaims, "Orpheus goes down into hell to find Eurydice and finds a sermon. Shit on Apollo! I came here for Cressida, not a plaster statue" (298).

This scene has numerous implications. First, note that Troilus's final gesture is to refuse to allow Cressida to be sublated into allegory—he will not accept that she is simply a figure for what Calchas calls the "true Eurydice, the thing my daughter was a copy of" (297), which is meant to reside inside Troilus's soul. Here, the rhetoric and logic of imitation, doubling, displacement, and emulation is decisively spurned. The Cressida that Troilus seeks is not an allegory, a projection, or a stand-in. Yet, as in Shakespeare, she is also not "one," and Spicer's Troilus makes no claim on her as a totality—only the Trojan Cressida, and no other, is of concern to him. Spicer's framing of betrayal is so absolutist as to morph into its opposite: once one accepts that anything short of constant, uninterrupted, total union is a betrayal, then all forms of betrayal short of this impossible ideal are relegated to the same plane. "Troy" is the name Troilus gives to the space of impossible, fusional, dyadic intimacy in which Troilus feels he can make total claims on Cressida, and this is why Calchas tells him, "You have locked your heart like a city." The city was a crucial trope for Spicer throughout much of his writing life, and it often was associated with bonds of loyalty, fellowship, responsibility, and love.[6] In a letter to his close friend and rival, the poet Robert Duncan, Spicer writes, "It seems to me poets have a bond of responsibility to each other even more sacred than that of

[6]See Michael Davidson, *The San Francisco Renaissance*, and Daniel Katz, *The Poetry of Jack Spicer*, for more on this.

lover to lover," and goes on to express the wish to "learn a map of this city we walk in so seldom. The responsibility between lovers is, after all, an act of love. All the rest is traffic noise. Why should I tell you this? You were the first person to show me that the city was there."[7]

Spicer's city in *Troilus*, locked or open, is then probably not, despite some appearances, Freud's "closed fortress" of the ego, but rather a bizarrely cloistered space of intimacy and recognition, a space outside of which the members of the couple act outside the bonds of responsibility they have accepted toward each other. To view the Trojan Cressida as the companion who walks with Troilus through this city would allow Spicer's Troilus to accept two Cressidas, one within and one without, one that is his and one whose alterity is forever unavailable and unsoundable, whether she is found in Diomede's arms or not. But at the play's end, he has neither.

The last pages of Spicer's *Troilus* are labored and show the lyric poet which he was unable to intervene as meaningfully in plot construction as one might wish. The play's close centers on fate, destiny, and the will of the gods, as Troilus, in an effort to thwart all of the above, slays Patroclus himself to upend the gods' plans. The play finishes with an almost parodic *deus ex machina*, as Zeus is given the final words to a play that stops more than it ends. But prior to Spicer's somewhat slapdash conclusion, the play throws in a short interlude where Patroclus and Cressida chat while tending to the Greek wounded, soon to be joined by Achilles. Achilles and Patroclus reminisce about the coastlines of the Greek islands, and how different the ocean is there from that in Troy—again, an important image for Spicer, who as a self-consciously Californian poet thematized the Pacific coast again and again. But Cressida interrupts their lyric musings:

> Last night when I watched the ocean I tried to think what it was. Diomede had his arm around me. I think he was asleep. [...] I tried to think of it as Troilus would have, as another land of the dead out there beyond me, or, as you two did, as something black and limitless, or even as a woman. [...] But all I saw was an ocean with pieces breaking off from it in meaningless patterns, some coming close to our torch, some ending far away from it. Just a cold dark fact that no metaphor could make significant. It didn't even mean to be meaningless. (301–02)

[7] Unpublished letter quoted in Katz, *The Poetry of Jack Spicer*, p. 89.

When Patroclus suggests, "That must have been frightening to feel," Cressida answers, "It was wonderful. I had nothing to do with the ocean and the ocean had nothing to do with me. There were no gods around to watch us" (302).

Here Cressida evokes a scene of love which is not a spectacle—either for a spurned lover or for the gods. But even more, she stresses the restorative power of the absence of meaning—not only of the ocean, but presumably of her and her acts. If, as Laura Levine has argued, for Shakespeare Cressida becomes the emblem of a Renaissance crisis in epistemology, Spicer leaves her much closer to the Snow Man of Wallace Stevens (a poet whose work Spicer knew extremely well): emblem of "nothing that is not there and the nothing that is." If Spicer's play never fully develops this theme or topos, then it does suggest that this is the space of Cressida's escape from the meanings which Troilus, or Shakespeare's Pandarus, would impose on her actions, actions that remain under constant observation both visually and intellectually. But as Spicer knows, the fact that the ocean did not even mean to be meaningless itself has a meaning. As he was to write in one of his greatest poems several years later, "The ocean / Does not mean to be listened to. A drop / Or crash of water. It means / Nothing" (*My Vocabulary* 373). This is the space where Cressida can be and be not, and where the narcissistic ideals that govern rivalrous desire are emptied. "No one listens to poetry," this poem tells us, before repeating the phrase with a new connotation, created only by the difference made by the spacing of a line-break: "No / One listens to poetry" (373). It is here, in *Language*, that Spicer finds a rhetoric for what is and is not, for what one does and does not, that emulates Shakespeare and rewrites Spicer's own earlier work. Cressida's ocean becomes his own.

Works Cited

Collis, Stephen, and Graham Lyons. *Reading Duncan Reading: Robert Duncan and the Poetics of Derivation.* U of Iowa P, 2012.

Davidson, Michael. *The San Francisco Renaissance: Poetics and Community at Mid-Century.* Cambridge UP, 1989.

Ellingham, Lewis, and Kevin Killian. *Poet Be Like God: Jack Spicer and the San Francisco Renaissance.* UP of New England, 1998.

Freud, Sigmund. *The Revised Standard Edition of the Complete Psychological Works of Sigmund Freud*, edited and translated by James Strachey, revised by Mark

Solms. 24 vols. Rowman & Littlefield Publishers, 2024. (In-text references provide *RSE* page numbers immediately after *SE* page numbers).

———. *New Introductory Lectures on Psychoanalysis* (1933). *The Standard Edition of the Complete Psychological Works of Sigmund Freud*, edited and translated by James Strachey, vol. 22, Hogarth Press, 1964, pp. 1–182/*RSE* vol. 22, pp. 3–160.

Girard, René. "The Politics of Desire in *Troilus and Cressida*." *Shakespeare and the Question of Theory*, edited by Geoffrey Hartmann and Patricia Parker, Routledge, 1985, pp. 188–209.

Katz, Daniel. *The Poetry of Jack Spicer*. Edinburgh UP, 2013.

Lecercle, Ann. "Interpretation and 'logique du sens': the Problem Plays' Problematizing of Language." *Actes des congrès de la Société française Shakespeare: la langue de Shakespeare*, vol. 31, 2014, pp. 151–63.

Levine, Laura. "This Is, and Is Not, Knowledge: Cressida and the Titillation of Male Curiosity in Shakespeare's *Troilus and Cressida*." *Women and Curiosity in Early Modern England and France*, edited by Line Cottegnies, John Thompson, and Sandrine Parageau, Brill, 2016, pp. 61–75.

Shakespeare, William. *Troilus and Cressida*. Edited by David M. Bevington. Bloomsbury Arden Shakespeare (third series), 2006.

Spicer, Jack. *Be Brave to Things: The Uncollected Poetry and Plays of Jack Spicer*. Edited by Daniel Katz. Wesleyan UP, 2021.

———. My Vocabulary *Did This To Me: The Collected Poetry of Jack Spicer*. Edited by Peter Gizzi and Kevin Killian. Wesleyan UP, 2008.

CHAPTER 11

Skepticism and Dysphoria: On Two Tales of Winter

Paul A. Kottman

> How can I doubt that these hands or this whole body are mine? To doubt such things, I would have to liken myself to brain-damaged madmen who are convinced they are kings when really they are paupers, or say they are dressed in purple when they are naked, or that they are pumpkins, or made of glass. Such people are insane, and I would be thought equally mad if I modelled myself on them. (Descartes, First Meditation 1)

> [...] a clumsy action in isolation by no means has a fixed meaning, but offers itself as a method of representing some intention or other, depending on the circumstances [...] On festive occasions such as a wedding it is common to break something on purpose, accompanying the breakage by wishes of good luck. (Freud, *Psychopathology of Everyday Life* 165)[1]

[1] I cite this translation of the text by Anthea Bell, rather than that by James Strachey in the *Standard Edition*, simply because it was easier to have at hand when I was working on this essay, and I found it to be very good.

P. A. Kottman (✉)
New York, NY, USA
e-mail: kottmanp@newschool.edu

J. W. Stone, C. Bates (eds.), *Shakespeare and Psychoanalysis*, Palgrave Shakespeare Studies,
https://doi.org/10.1007/978-3-032-07897-1_11

> Félicie: "*Pourquoi? Pour rien, comme ça, par connerie. C'est un lapsus* [...] ("Why? No reason, just plain stupidity. It was a lapsus ...") (Rohmer)

> Truth can never be confirm'd enough,
> Though doubts did ever sleep. (*Pericles* 5.1.201–202)

In his catalogue and discussion—thanks to which we now speak of "Freudian slips"—Freud invites us to consider "inadvertent actions" as "the symbolic representation of an idea." By this he means that "clumsy movements which appear to be accidents" belong, despite appearance, to the domain of human intentionality. What looks accidental can be what Freud calls "semi-intentional" and "can be very skillfully put to the service of unacknowledged intentions" (161).[2] While varied and diverse, such inadvertent actions have, Freud suggests, precisely "two characteristics: violence and a sure aim." That is: inadvertent-semi-intentional slips (what to call them?) enact a targeted, specific kind of damage "and fulfill their purpose with a certainty that cannot always be attributed to conscious or voluntary movements" (161).

These characteristics of inadvertent actions make them catnip to our best dramatists—like Sophocles or Shakespeare—for whom "fate" names a predicament in which susceptibility to accidents is our exposure, not just to the laws of physics, but to regions of intentionality beyond that which can be consciously acknowledged at a given moment. It seems also to have been Freud's view, further, that Sophocles and Shakespeare themselves—inadvertently?—present dramatic depictions of slips that reveal domains of intentionality common to us all. Highly particularized accidents or clumsy actions—plausible enough, but unlikely to happen again—turn out to belong to unconscious intentions at work in human life generally. Sometimes, it falls to victims and perpetrators of inadvertent actions to reveal problems that concern all of us.

❦

In Shakespeare's *The Winter's Tale*, as I presume readers of this chapter know, Leontes acts out with "violence and a sure aim" in accusing

[2] "Anyone who believes that semi-intentional self-inflicted injuries do happen—if I may be allowed that rather clumsy way of putting it—will be prepared to accept that besides conscious and intentional suicides there are also cases of semi-intentional suicide attempts [...]" (172).

Hermione not only of general sexual infidelity but, in particular, of carrying Polixenes's child. It is only upon learning of his son Mamillius's death that Leontes seems to drop his denial of his own paternity, seems to (re) suspend his disbelief, and begin again to believe in himself and others. In Rohmer's *Conte d'hiver* (1992), Félicie inadvertently gives the wrong address to Charles, the man she loves and the father of her child, making herself unfindable by him. She enacts a targeted, specific kind of damage—separating Charles from her and their daughter for what turn out to be five years. Charles and Félicie are eventually reunited by what looks like coincidence on a city bus in Paris—a plausible enough accident. But, because it is a genuine reunion we witness, and not just a "bumping into each other," the accident appears inseparable from intentionality.

In his discussion of Shakespeare's play and Rohmer's film, Stanley Cavell helpfully suggests that Félicie's "lapsus" in giving Charles the wrong address "reveals in Félicie a kind of skepticism" (*Cities of Words* 425) that, while differently manifested and enacted when compared with Leontes's madness in *The Winter's Tale*, might be helpfully considered alongside it. Cavell invites us to consider Rohmer's film as showing us something about Shakespeare's play that, although it cannot be shown without remembering what Shakespeare shows us, also cannot be shown by Shakespeare's play alone. Rohmer's film, that is, needs Shakespeare's play to be what it (the film) is. This need is explicitly acknowledged in the scenes of the film in which *The Winter's Tale* is shown being performed in a theater and then discussed on the car ride home from the playhouse. But it is equally true, Cavell intimates, that Shakespeare's play needs Rohmer's film, too. In what follows, I want to see what might be gained by admitting that understanding Shakespeare's *The Winter's Tale* today requires seeing the play as incomplete without Rohmer's film.

Incomplete how?

Freud's catalogue of "inadvertent actions" can lead us to think—and indeed Freud himself seems to have thought—that one thing that would remain incomplete is a fuller taxonomy of the *kind* of slip (or, translated into Cavell, the kind of skepticism) we are dealing with. In other words, we need some kind of catalogue if we are to achieve a fuller picture of what inadvertent actions are and of what they might mean—for instance, as betrayals of one's disbelief. My working hypothesis, borrowing Cavell's suggestion, is indeed meant to add to Freud's catalogue: slips and inadvertent actions are betrayals of where we stand with respect to our belief or confidence or trust in ourselves and others and the world, and hence evidence of the significance of that belief, of our dependence on such confidence and trust. But Freud also insists that a catalogue alone (a "classification of instances") does not, as he puts it, "encourage" "psychological understanding." To gain psychological understanding, we need "instead to trace some individual examples back to the conditions in which they occurred" (155).

Trace back how?

Is this where our dramatists and fabulists can help? Perhaps. Although it is striking that—in the very next sentence—Freud immediately turns to what he calls "self-observations" and "self-observations by others" as resources. Freud's claim to self-observation puts me in mind of Descartes, who begins his Third Meditation by writing: "I will get into conversation with myself, examine myself more deeply, and try in this way gradually to know myself more intimately" (9).

Which raises a further question, worth noting at least in passing: What are the forms that self-observation might take? To undertake self-observation in *writing*—especially, as in the cases of both Descartes and Freud, whose self-observing texts offer themselves as a method that others might undertake—is to suggest or even to promise a kind of legibility, connecting one self-observing "self" to other such "selves." The introspections of Descartes or Freud, written out in French or German, propose themselves as methods for meeting the introspective demands of others, too. In this way, these texts (perhaps inadvertently) imply that self-observation-as-method must be mediated, in these instances by the written form that method takes.

But do methods of self-introspection succeed only if written down? In *Conte d'hiver*, Félicie complains to Loic, "to you, only what is written is true," and she calls this a gulf between them. So are there other media for self-observation? What about talk therapy, or a humanities seminar? Do theatrical drama (Shakespeare) or film (Rohmer) present instances, or even methods, of self-observation? Shakespeare's soliloquies, of course, have a history of being performed as though the characters were overhearing themselves, or observing themselves (in a mirror, say), or touching themselves. Consider Leontes's early soliloquy:

> Affection, thy intention stabs the center.
> Thou dost make possible things not so held,
> Communicat'st with dreams—how can this be?
> With what's unreal thou coactive art,

And fellow'st nothing. Then 'tis very credent
Thou may'st co-join with something; and thou dost,
And that beyond commission, and I find it,
And that to the infection of my brains
And hard'ning of my brows. (1.2.138–46)

If performances of such soliloquies are forms of self-observation or introspection, then what does their medium imply about their prospects *as method*? If Leontes is giving voice to his thoughts—saying whatever comes into his mind—is his thinking separable from the reporting of sensation, or stabbing "affection," or a "hardening of brows"? Does it matter who overhears him, or how they do so? In a theater, or the office of an analyst, or a conversation on the beach?

Rohmer's style of filmmaking strikes me as one way of exploring these questions. In Rohmer's films, we mostly watch and hear people reporting self-observations to each other—talking to each other about their lives, about whatever is happening to them or felt to be happening to them. In *Conte d'hiver*, for instance, Félicie returns from Nevers and tells Loic—as if updating him—about her abrupt break-up with Maxence, about the clarity with which she "saw her thoughts" in the cathedral, about what the experience means to her intention to live in a way that is not incompatible with being with Charles in the future. And in that scene, Félicie's experience, which had been shown to us wordlessly in an earlier scene from the film, is described (like Descartes's) as a "meditation."[3]

If psychological understanding of inadvertent actions (slips of disbelief) requires us "to trace some individual examples back to the conditions in which they occurred," then we might do well to consider—for the sake of scientific method—what different forms or media teach us about possible methods and modes for self-observation.

❦

But let me return from this digression to the main issue of Shakespeare's and Rohmer's incompleteness without each other. According to Cavell,

[3] At a certain point in the film, when Félicie is discussing with Maxence what may have happened to Charles, she responds very pointedly: "*Je suppose*" ["I suppose."] Given that the film later cites Pascal's wager, and that Félicie describes her reverie in the cathedral as a "meditation," it is hard not to hear Rohmer's film as echoing Pascal and Descartes in Félicie's mouth.

Leontes's florid skepticism is a "derangement," a "world-shattering skepticism" (*Cities of Words* 437), whereas Félicie's quiet lapsus in giving Charles the wrong address betrays "a milder form of skepticism, an expression of the everyday mistrust of the world, a sort of mistrust of existence and of what there is to say about existence" (438). And furthermore, according to Cavell, both Félicie's lapsus and Leontes's rage can be productively considered in the light of "what Freud called a slip, an *acte manqué* [...] a parapraxis" (437).[4] Cavell sees both Leontes and Félicie as having "slipped" in the sense of having done or said something "crazy" and tempestuous—something targeted and destructive to themselves and to those they love. "*Pourquoi? Pour rien, comme ça. Par connerie. C'est un lapsus* [...] [Why? No reason, just plain stupidity. It was a lapsus...]" says Félicie; Leontes speaks of "the wrong I did myself" (5.1.9).

Pairing Leontes and Félicie in this way forced Cavell, late in his philosophical career, to revise his well-known, earlier work on skepticism in Descartes, Hume, Kant, Wittgenstein, and Shakespeare—especially his book, *The Claim of Reason* (1979), which concludes with an interpretation of *Othello*. In that earlier work, Cavell had argued that skeptical doubt—as presented by these authors—interrupts ordinary day-to-day life, threatening its continuity and its very worth. In these canonical authors, the younger Cavell argued:

> skepticism *contrasts* with what [...] we can see as ordinary or everyday life. Skepticism breaks into that life with a surmise that I cannot live with, that the world and I and others are radically unknown to me. I *must* find a way to put this doubt aside [...]. (*Cities of Words* 426)

However, what *Conte d'hiver* reveals—and this is, I think, what the mature Cavell came to identify as Shakespeare's *need* for Rohmer's film—is that:

> our temptations to skepticism, or say to a knowledge beyond human powers, are unannounced and may be at work anywhere [...] woven into the

[4] Cavell admits that neither Félicie's nor Leontes's actions seem *quite* like what Freud has in mind in his discussion of inadvertent actions. For one thing, when it comes to Leontes's destructive derangement, "nothing with so massive a consequence actually counts for Freud as a slip, any more than it could count as such" (*Cities of Words* 437–38). Given that Freud is tempted to see "clumsy" self-inflicted injuries as "semi-intentional suicide attempts," I am not sure that Cavell's judgment about Freud's meaning is entirely correct; but leave that aside for the moment.

restlessness of vacations at the beach as well as into the business of getting along every day with others back in town, walking along the streets with them, and through tunnels and down and up stairs in their company, riding with them in trains, and subways, and buses, and automobiles. (*Cities of Words* 426)

To see both Félicie and Leontes as having "acted inadvertently"—such that the inadvertency reveals a tendency to skepticism that can take mild and less mild forms—we confront the fact that skeptical doubt does not contrast with ordinary life but rather infuses it. Skepticism "may be at work anywhere" in the countless ways human beings are prone to self-doubt, to crises of confidence in themselves or others. Doubt thus appears as an unconscious intentionality—a temptation or tendency—that breaks into everyday life in something like the way that "Freudian slips" worm their way into our speaking and acting.[5] "The consequences of melodramatically tragic action, to which human folly subjects us," concludes Cavell, revising his earlier treatise, "is active pervasively, below the level of notice, in the world of everyday existence" (*Cities of Words* 426).

I find it poignant that Cavell—who wrote so much on skepticism and so autobiographically, and thus I imagine felt personally called to the question—discovers this Rohmerian correction to his own work so late in his career. It amounts to an admission on Cavell's part of a late discovery of his own finitude—of his own philosophical finitude (skepticism and the "ordinary" are his two great themes)—in finding his own *oeuvre* so stamped by the denial of skepticism's ordinariness.[6]

[5]This seems a good place to recall Thomas Mann's apt description of psychoanalysis as a "revolutionary" "blithe scepticism" which "infiltrates life." "The analytic revelation is a revolutionary force. With it a blithe scepticism has come into the world, a mistrust that unmasks all the schemes and subterfuges of our own souls. Once roused and on the alert, it cannot be put to sleep again. It infiltrates life, undermines its raw naivete, takes from it the strain of its own ignorance, de-emotionalizes it, as it were, inculcates the taste for understatement [...]" (427–28). Mann anticipates by two decades Paul Ricoeur's famous description of Freud's "school of suspicion (*école du soupçon*)" (33).

[6]Consider this passage from Cavell's own autobiography, an entry from June 8, 2004. Cavell is remembering the painful end of a youthful romance with a woman by whom he had felt betrayed: what he calls "an occasion for ending [his] connection with Alexandra." He writes: "In the end what I said, and found I meant, was that I no longer wanted to be crazy with doubtful and unappeasable desire, that I wanted a commitment, faith in one another, something neither of us could convincingly offer the other." He goes on in the next sentence to say: "I think I would not now have phrased things quite this way before living fairly recently with Éric Rohmer's *A Tale of Winter* [...]" (*Little Did I Know* 397).

❦

What Freud's catalogue, Shakespeare's searing drama, Rohmer's "style," and Cavell's interpretive remarks all have in common is an effort to make perspicuous—to bring to our notice, inviting us to believe in—tendencies to skepticism, that otherwise risk being mistaken for (in Freud) mere accident, or (in Descartes or Shakespeare) for madness or insanity. Or less reassuringly (in Rohmer), for the ordinary, day-to-day business of taking public transportation, or figuring out where to sleep for the night, or at what time to wake up in the morning (with which lover? in which house? in which room?).

Cavell's appreciation for Rohmer's "correction" to *The Claim of Reason*—namely, the Rohmerian view that skepticism does not contrast with ordinary life but, rather, can infuse it—implies that even Descartes, Hume, and Shakespeare could not adequately see or reckon with the *everydayness* of skepticism. For these giants of the Western canon, skepticism had appeared as a fever, opposed to the viability of day-to-day life: Descartes made clear that the kind of skeptical procedure he enacted in the *Meditations* cannot be tried every day, practiced as a way of life, or woven into the fabric of day-to-day existence. When it comes to Shakespeare, to say that the doubts of Othello or Leontes interrupt their lives is, to put it mildly, an understatement. Hume, for his part, went so far as to say that "the great subverter of [...] excessive scepticisme is [...] the occupation of life" (158–59).

Taken together, across the four centuries that separate Shakespeare from Rohmer, this body of work invites us not to be skeptical about skepticism: not to be skeptical about the pervasiveness and destructiveness of our mistrust of ourselves and others, or the targeted and damaging "clumsy actions" that betray our suspicions about the world, ourselves, and others. Freud, recall, begins this chapter of his 1901 text by declaring that he cannot be "the first to have suspected that there is significance and intention behind the small functional disturbances in the daily life of healthy people" (*Psychopathology of Everyday Life* 155).

Given all this, it seems worth asking: Why has the everydayness of skepticism been so hard to believe in? And what would a diminished skepticism about skepticism amount to, in daily life? What would believing in our lack of faith require, entail, unfurl, look like or sound like? To give the question a Freudian twist: What is the (practical-therapeutic) upshot of believing that our inadvertent actions are laden with intentionality? Or a Shakespearean-Rohmerian twist: What is the (practical-ethical) upshot of awakening faith in the ordinariness of our modes of disbelief?

❦

To hold skepticism apart from the everyday is to imagine that there are—or, to believe that there must be—regions of existence which are not subject (or are no longer subjectable) to doubt. Belief in the everydayness and pervasive destructiveness of skeptical doubt, put another way, is impeded by the achievement of a confidence that *something*, someone, somewhere, is beyond doubting. Consider again how these impediments were depicted in early modernity: in Descartes, this was made explicit in the way in which the "non-ordinariness" of radical doubt, the threat of the *mauvais génie*, led to the proof of the existence of God. For Descartes, the denial of the everydayness of skepticism required or entailed something like religious belief in that which, ultimately, cannot be denied or doubted.

In Shakespeare's *The Winter's Tale*, as in *Othello* or *Cymbeline*, it is significant that both Othello and Leontes (or Posthumous)—having radically doubted—finally come to avow the limits of their skepticism by recognizing something with respect to the central women in their lives. Thanks in large measure to Emilia, Othello realizes, albeit "too late" (5.2.83) that he believes in Desdemona's fidelity as well as in his love for her. For Leontes, what makes day-to-day life possible after the destructiveness of his doubting is a quasi-religious confidence in "true Paulina" (5.1.81), which leads him back to Hermione. In letting himself be guided by Paulina, especially when it comes to what Paulina claims to know about Hermione—in a woman's knowledge of another woman of the same generation, knowledge from which Leontes (now) takes himself to be excluded—Leontes finds the basis of his skepticism determined, limited, by the fact that these women do not share his earlier doubts.

In Shakespeare's plays, then, what holds skeptical doubt apart from the everyday is vouchsafed in a susceptibility to skepticism in (certain) men that is stopped by these men's eventual confidence in the "truth" of women: a truth which the men cannot claim to know through experience and can only believe in (or not).[7] Whether Othello or Leontes appears "stuck" in doubting, or appears to overcome his skepticism, is measured,

[7] See Barbara Johnson's remark: "If human beings were not divided into two biological sexes, there would probably be no need for literature" (13).

precisely, by his faith (or lack of it) in Desdemona, Emilia, Paulina, and Hermione.

Go back to the question I asked a moment ago: Why has the everydayness of skepticism been so hard to believe in?

If *Othello* or *The Winter's Tale* is a guide, then one explanation for this has been the pervasiveness of a viewpoint on human affairs that sees skepticism, or doubt and mistrust of others, as taking root in men. Or, to be a bit more precise: as taking root in men in relation to (though differently to) women, as concerns the limits of male knowledge about the sexual life of women, or (in Shakespeare's works such as *Cymbeline* or *The Winter's Tale*) the vicissitudes of pregnancy.[8] For instance: Leontes's trust in Paulina plays something like the role that proving God's existence plays for Descartes: it posits an outsider to doubt in a way that makes doubting appear contained by, "cured" by (as in Hume) the everydayness of belief, perhaps carried out in the capacity of men and women to find ways to live with one another. And it is made even more explicit in the way that each of the women in *The Winter's Tale* must prove themselves, so to speak, against explicit accusations of witchcraft. That is to say, they are burdened with needing to defend against the doubt that they are, in fact, women—or, more inflated: that there *are*, in fact, women on earth.[9]

[8] As I was just noting, such male skepticism is (in Shakespeare) defined by—in the sense that it "meets its limits in"—the expressed viewpoint of formerly doubted women (Desdemona, Imogen, Paulina, Hermione) taken to be finally unknowable (by men) and thus investable with deep confidence or radical doubt by men. I do not mean to suggest that there are not also other doubts expressed by Shakespeare's characters—for instance, by Macbeth about the value of life or human existence. But I do mean to invoke the kinds of doubts and their precise violence, expressed by male characters, in *Othello, The Winter's Tale*, or *Cymbeline*—along the lines captured in Posthumous's declaration in *Cymbeline*, after Iachimo causes him to doubt his wife's fidelity: "Is there no way for men to be, but women / Must be half-workers? We are all bastards, / And that most venerable man, which I / Did call my father, was I know not where / When I was stamp'd. Some coiner with his tools / Made me a counterfeit: yet my mother seem'd / The Dian of that time: so doth my wife / The nonpareil of this. O vengeance, vengeance!" (2.4.153–60).

[9] Accusations of witchcraft in early modern England often expressed anxieties about sexual difference; that is, doubts about whether women really *are* women, about whether *there are* women. Relevant and significant here is Freud's admiration for the early modern physician Johann Weir (1515–1588), who had argued centuries before Freud that witch-hunts should be replaced with what would now be called "mental health" interventions, and that witches ought to be viewed as symptomatic of "the credulity and fragility of the female sex" (which Weir took to be "fantasies" to which women in particular were susceptible). See Freud's letter to The Antiquary Hinterberger (Masson 224–25); and the discussion in Swales 345–49.

A general point to be made here is that, in the mature Shakespeare, the overcoming of skepticism and the achievement of a livable certainty amounts to overcoming doubts about sexual difference and its vicissitudes.[10] Accepting one's finitude, put another way, entails coming to a nonviolent practical acceptance (on the part of Shakespeare's men, at least) of their exclusion from what women know, especially of sexual experience, pregnancy, or the bearing of children. The reality of sexual difference may not stop skepticism from intruding into everyday existence—indeed, doubts about sexual difference (e.g. suspicions of witchcraft) open the door to skepticism's incursions. Nevertheless, Shakespeare's work suggests, a hard-won acceptance of one's own finitude vis-à-vis accepting *one's own* sexual difference (at least, for the men in Shakespearean drama) might stop skepticism from taking over everyday life entirely.

❦

If this is not wrong, then it follows that seeing more clearly the everydayness of skepticism requires reckoning with the forms that skepticism can take not only in men, but in women as well.[11] Indeed, this seems crucial to Rohmer's own practice as a filmmaker.

For more on the linguistic and historical context of discourse around witches, especially in relation to *The Winter's Tale*, see Rideout. For another way into the question of whether "there are women" in Shakespeare, one that takes the issue of "the reality of fiction" as a way of thinking about skeptical doubt, see Beckwith.

[10] James Stone has argued that doubts about sexual difference, which he identifies also in the work of Judith Butler, characterize the gender fluidity of Shakespeare's early comedies in contrast to "the embodied depths of tragedy" in Shakespeare's later work. "Tragedy passes beyond [...] subjectifying self-division, to the principle of difference which patriarchal, misogynistic discourse takes women to be" (4–5). Stone's book thus argues for a significant shift in Shakespeare's work, from the early comedies through the tragedies and into the later works—a shift that, I am suggesting with Cavell (and, I think, in contrast to Stone), involves a deepening reckoning with the pervasiveness of skepticism's vicissitudes in sexual difference, in ways that are not adequately captured by treating sexual difference, or male doubts about women, as the result of "misogynistic discourse." Shakespeare seems to me to identify misogynistic discourse and patriarchy as festering symptoms (of skepticism) rather than as the source of the suffering of it.

[11] It is illuminating, I think, to compare Rohmer and Freud on this point, to see whether Rohmer offers a more hopeful prognosis than the obdurate "bedrock" of penis envy that Freud claims to observe in certain female patients. I therefore want to set the interpretation of *Conte d'hiver* in the following pages alongside Freud's mature assessment that "a repudiation of femininity" is very difficult to treat psychoanalytically. Freud writes: "At no other

In saying all this, I must be careful to say that there are of course doubts to which human beings are susceptible irrespective of sex or gender—doubts about the worth of living, about what others say or believe, and so on. However, if one of the obstacles to "believing in the everydayness of skepticism" has been something like the canonical "Shakespearean" view of men as doubting, and of women as subject to either male doubt or male faith, precisely in the domain of sexual life and (in *The Winter's Tale*) the vicissitudes of sexual reproduction, then it seems worth reckoning with the fact that sexual difference, sexual identity, sexual maturation, sexual life, and the bearing of children have been, and remain in our culture, sites of doubt about oneself and others, sometimes infusing everyday life with a skepticism that has come to be called *dysphoric*.

❦

Consider, as one way to approach such a reckoning, what Cavell has to say about this:

> That *The Winter's Tale* differs from [*Othello*] in which skepticism produces only tragedy [...] I find marked specifically by a peculiarity of Leontes's basis for doubt (whether his children are his), which is (unlike the doubts in the major tragedies, which are about faithfulness more generally, or about the worthiness to be loved, or about the worth of human existence, or about the nature of one's spouse) not a doubt that a woman is apt to be vulnerable to. What would it look like for Hermione to doubt whether her children are hers? I am careful to say that it does not follow that women in general are not vulnerable to what philosophy calls skeptical doubt, only that where

point in one's analytic work does one suffer from an oppressive feeling that all one's repeated efforts have been in vain, and from a suspicion that one has been 'preaching to the winds,' than when one is trying to persuade a woman to abandon her wish for a penis on the grounds of its being unrealizable [...] it is the source of outbreaks of severe depression in her, owing to an internal conviction that [...] nothing can be done to help her. And we can only agree that she is right, when we learn that her strongest motive in coming for treatment was the hope that, after all, she might still obtain a male organ, the lack of which was so painful to her [...] The decisive thing remains that the resistance prevents any change from taking place—that everything stays as it was. We often have the impression that, with the wish for a penis [...] we have penetrated through all the psychological strata and have reached bedrock, and that thus our activities [of patient analysis] are at an end. [...] We can only console ourselves with the certainty that we have given the person analyzed every possible encouragement to re-examine her attitude to it" ("Analysis Terminable and Interminable" 252–53/227–28).

> they are, their doubt of existence is apt to be expressed otherwise than toward their progeny, and in some emotion other than doubt. (They may have some anxiety about the father of their child). (*Cities of Words* 425)

In declaring his own belief about the doubts to which "women in general" are apt, Cavell suggests that these do not include doubts (of the sort attributed to Leontes by Cavell) about whether a woman's children are in fact hers.

Now, one might immediately and reasonably object to Cavell's conclusion by raising an apparent fact of which Cavell is, I assume, quite aware: not all women have borne or will bear children. So, does Cavell mean to say that any woman *qua* woman (regardless of whether she is herself a mother) will not doubt whether the children of *other* women are in fact *theirs*? Perhaps. But since Leontes also does not doubt whether Perdita is *Hermione's* (only whether the baby is *his*), this conclusion would leave us no way to think about the difference between the kinds of doubts to which men and women are apt. Indeed, it leaves us doubting whether there is a difference—unless we want to conclude, wryly, that women never doubt whether a man's child is *his*. This, I think, cannot be what Cavell means.

In a generous mood, one might take Cavell to *mean to say* something like this: insofar as pregnancy and childbearing are experiences from which the (roughly) half of humanity we call "men" are exempt, there must be doubts to which men and women are, differently, prone when it comes to the vicissitudes of certain bodily and sexual experiences, pregnancy, and the bearing of children. But what Cavell *actually* declares is: the fact of the vicissitudes of certain sexual experiences, pregnancy, and the bearing of children make "women in general" "apt" to express doubt "otherwise than toward their progeny, and in some emotion other than doubt." In this way, Cavell apparently aligns himself with Leontes—for whom, as we have seen, the nondoubting relationship that Hermione has to Perdita's being "hers" both (initially) fuels Leontes's initial skeptical rage and (late in the play) ostensibly limits that rage's final scope. In sum, Cavell's belief in the doubts to which a woman may not be susceptible underwrites his belief in the limits of skepticism, as well as in the fact of sexual difference generally. But this only leaves us right back where we were at the end of our discussion of Shakespeare a moment ago, without—I think—adequately allowing us to see a bridge between Shakespeare and Rohmer.

So, to take a different approach, let us hear Cavell's suspended question about Hermione differently from the way Cavell himself does. The question is: "what would it look like for Hermione to doubt whether her children are hers?"

Although Cavell thinks that this is not a doubt Hermione (or any woman) is apt to entertain, Rohmer offers us—I think—a way to tarry longer with the question of what it would look like for a woman to doubt whether her children are hers, even when she does not doubt that her children are, so to speak, "*his*." (Recall: Félicie never doubts that Elise's father is Charles, and indeed goes out of her way to emphasize Charles's paternity at every chance, for instance in her placement of Charles's photograph in Elise's bedroom.)[12]

Whereas Cavell conflates (1) bearing children (a general capacity to undergo the biological fact of pregnancy and childbirth) with (2) *bearing the bearing* of children, Rohmer is careful to hold the two apart. ("Dysphoria," the dictionary tells us, derives from Greek *dusphoria*, from *dusphoros* "hard to bear.") Rohmer thus allows us to see the difference between these two moments—bearing children and the bearing of bearing children—as opening space for doubt, as well as space for a possible suspension of disbelief.

Consider one example: In Rohmer's 1976 film *The Marquise of O*, the marquise (having taken a sleeping potion before going to bed)[13] does not know that she has been raped and thus does not believe that she is pregnant when her body starts to show physical evidence of the pregnancy, with the social-psychological implications that follow. The ethical and psy-

[12] It is worth mentioning that Charles, when finally presented with his child, does not doubt or question, either. He immediately sweeps Elise into his arms. As if Rohmer were emphasizing: where there have been doubts here, they have belonged to the mother, Félicie, and not to Charles. In saying this, as I shall try to make clear, I do not mean that Félicie doubts that she has given birth to Elise—rather, her doubts appear lodged in whether she can, in front of Charles and in relation to him, *bear* bearing or having borne Elise.

[13] This detail was added by Rohmer to the plot of the Kleist story on which the film is based, raising the stakes of the marquise's *self*-doubt by (arguably) assuring the audience that she could not possibly have recalled the rape. If the marquise were aware of having been raped, Rohmer seems to imply, then the stakes and implications of any resulting self-doubt would be quite different. Does the marquise, Rohmer leaves us wondering further, later recall what the film presents to the audience as an erotic dream the marquise seems (at least, possibly) to be having, and which the count seems to witness before he rapes her? Or, in that moment, is the film showing us only the count's fantasizing? More vexingly still: does the conclusion of the film disclose some kind of shared or newly sharable recollection of that night? Something that would reveal the dream to have been—as Freud suggests dreams can be—a wish?.

chological stakes of the film turn on whether the marquise can believe *her own* innocence or chastity, *while also believing* the biological evidence her body itself *is* and then—once that belief, with difficulty, is provisionally secured—be believed by her parents or others when she protests her innocence *while giving birth*.

The point here is not simply that the marquise is not "responsible" for the pregnancy, in the sense of not having consented to the sexual violation that caused it—since that alone is not enough for her to secure her "mind" from the doubts that arise in the form of her own body. *The Marquise of O* suggests rather that, contra the letter of Cavell's assertion above, "women in general" may be quite vulnerable, indeed may even be anatomically vulnerable, to skepticism "toward their progeny" and precisely as "the emotion of doubt." The biological fact of pregnancy and childbirth can be acknowledged, while nevertheless being experienced as radical self-doubt in a woman and a radical doubt *of* her by all who know her. Any overcoming of that doubt—*trust*, in any relevant sense—cannot be adequately secured just by securing knowledge of (nor by simply denying) the biological or anatomical facts, nor in the social "recognition" (or denial) of the significance of those facts, since the marquise's child can be recognized as legitimate or illegitimate whether belief (and self-belief) in the marquise herself is secured or not.

Which means, something *in* the marquise's *own* lived experience of this pregnancy and childbirth and her doubts about it (which the film marks as distinct from her relation to her older two children) must be internally reckoned with by her, and then by others, in ways it is arguably the task of Rohmer's film to help us observe and perhaps even study.[14] Does *The Marquise of O* offer a method of self-observation?

Consider *Conte d'hiver*. We do not observe Félicie pregnant or giving birth. The first five years of Elise's life are what the film's narrative brackets off from our view. Instead, we watch and listen as Félicie reflects on her pregnancy and Elise' birth. For instance, when Maxence asks Félicie why she did not abort the pregnancy as soon as she realized that Charles could not be there, Félicie answers that an abortion would have run contrary to what she calls her "intimate convictions." "I hate what goes against nature," she says at this point—as if to say that her convictions about the

[14] In *Conte d'hiver*, this is also discussed in terms of "metempsychosis"—to be understood here, as Cavell aptly puts it, "not [as] finding a new body but finding [one's] own body anew" (*Philosophy the Day After Tomorrow* 72).

biological fact of her pregnancy, convictions that she calls "intimate," were reason enough to see it through. This declaration of "intimate convictions" is given an important, apparently improvised, qualification shortly thereafter in the film when Félicie, talking with her sister this time (and not with Maxence), reflects that she could not bear having a child with Loic, probably could not bear having a child with Maxence (*"Enfin, je ne sais pas. On verra"* ["Actually, I do not know. We'll see."]), whereas she could bear having a child with Charles. As if to say that what is required to make bearing Elise bearable (not just physically possible)—what underwrites intimate conviction—is the nature of her relation to the child's father.

What Félicie does seem to wonder about, as she reflects on her pregnancy, is why she committed the inadvertent slip—giving Charles the wrong address—which prevented her from having or raising their child with him, prevented them from continuing together as a couple. She reflects that she noticed her slip-up six months after the fact, when filling out maternity forms while she was still pregnant and working. (Cavell interprets this to mean that Félicie "connects the slip with her pregnancy" and that "both may be thought to be accidents" (*Cities of Words* 434). If so, then pregnancy—as in *The Marquise of O*—might itself be an inadvertent betrayal of disbelief, or an ordeal that can, but might not, bring about a suspension of disbelief.) As Félicie reflects, she recalls further that—before she realized that she had committed a slip-up—she in fact regarded Charles as dead rather than as having forgotten her. I take this assertion to mean that Félicie absolutely believed in Charles's love of her, and that whatever doubts were being symptomized in her slip-of-the-tongue were not, she now thinks, doubts or anxieties about him or his intentions. ("I know what he thought," she says firmly).

So, what was in doubt? Is anything in doubt?

We find out more as Félicie goes on to reconstruct the days and months following her realization of her error (six months after saying goodbye to Charles at the train station). She notes that she was still working and pregnant when she realized her error (that is, she was not yet at home with the child).[15] She notes further that her house, 36 rue Victor Hugo in Levallois, was being demolished in those days, and so she had to move in with her mother. She trekked as well to Courbevoie (the location of the wrong

[15] Cavell, I think, makes a significant assumption in his viewing of the film which I need to mark here since I will return to it later: he thinks that Félicie knew that "she was already three months pregnant" when she and Charles said goodbye (*Cities of Words* 440).

address she had given), where there was also a house at 36 rue Victor Hugo, to see if a letter from Charles could be found, but that house was under demolition as well. Rohmer, I take it, really wants us to notice that Félicie was not "at home" in those days, or that homes assigned to her were not solid, safe, durable. Or, at least, that the meeting of Félicie's material needs was at that time unsettled, far from certain. Félicie concluded from this further that, if Charles had sent her a letter (as she declares she is sure he must have done), then the letter would have been returned to him and hence Charles would have deduced that it was not her "fault" ("*pas ma faute*").[16]

That *what* was not her fault? The original slip up? Charles's inability to find her? Charles's own behavior? The demolition of 36 rue Victor Hugo? For what does Félicie think Charles might blame her? Where to find fault? For the pregnancy? For not being impregnable, that is, for being penetrable and fertile?

Félicie had in those days what she calls another "handicap"—the fact that she did not know or could not recall Charles's surname; he had what Félicie recalls only as a Dutch or a Danish-sounding surname.[17] Charles may have known Félicie's surname, but that would not have helped him in his search since Félicie, in those days, was always lodging at houses registered to other owners (just as Charles himself had no stable address in those days). Moreover, Félicie's mother uses her maiden name (her *nom de jeune fille)*, and her sisters are married (with, presumably, different surnames). "I am," Félicie concludes with a look of despair, "the girl no one can find" (*Je suis la fille introuvable*).[18]

In French, of course, *la fille* can mean "the girl" or "the daughter."[19] Given that Félicie has here invoked her mother (who uses her maiden name) and her married sisters (who use their husbands' surnames), we notice perhaps for the first time in the film that we know nothing about Félicie's father, from whom she, alone, presumably retains her surname.

[16] She also notes that reaching this conclusion, which she claims is "logical," gave her "courage." "That's assuming a lot," responds Maxence, mockingly.

[17] The name of the actor who played Charles is Frédéric van den Driessche. In presenting 'characters,' how do narrative films disclose the finite historical reality of actors?.

[18] "Poor thing, you really have no chance," responds Maxence, as if pronouncing fate.

[19] Félicie does not say *femme*—which can mean "wife" as well as "woman." Later in the car, with Loic, she remarks that she reacted to the Shakespeare performance like *une petite fille*. At the end of the film, Félicie declares that she could accept being called *la patronne* with Charles, a name that she could not bear being called by Maxence.

The nature of their relationship to one another remains a mystery to us. Is Félicie calling herself, in distinction to her sisters, "the unfindable daughter"—as if this were a family nickname? As if, were her father to be asked, "which daughter is Félicie?" he would answer: "she's the unfindable one." As if a missing or absent father and an unfindable daughter were a kind of pair.[20] Would her father know how to find her, were he to look for her? When it comes to her own daughter, Félicie vehemently insists (to her sister) that Elise will know who her own "true" father is, even if only through a photograph. ("A child should know what her father is like," she proclaims.)

The English subtitles say, "I am the girl no one can find." But the French—*Je suis la fille introuvable*—can be heard to mean either: I am the *unfindable* girl; or, I am the unfindable *girl*. The difference would be between being the "girl, not found by anyone" and being "not findable, as a girl."

There may be, that is, a doubt about being findable as a girl (in the feminine condition, on the way to being a *femme*). To be *la fille introuvable* may suggest a game of hide-and-seek or someone lost-and-then-found (like Perdita in *The Winter's Tale*, which is the parallel Cavell draws here). Or it may suggest not the need to recoup a loss but a need for discovery. After all, "*trouver*" also has the meaning of discovery, and even of "finding or believing something to be thus and so" (*Je trouve que* ...). Does Félicie stand not just in doubt of being locatable, but of being found and believed, or finding herself, to be a girl?

What do we make of the fact that, at this very point, she interrupts her reflections? She had been talking to Maxence the way that one might talk to one's psychoanalyst. And here, with her declaration of being "the unfindable girl," she breaks off her story. She was, she says, "dumb" (*conne*)—"stark raving dumb." Maxence corrects her: "one says 'stark raving mad' (*folle à lier*), not "stark raving dumb" (*conne à lier*)." This leaves us to wonder: when Félicie chides herself for being "dumb" (*conne*), as she does more than once in the film, is she slipping in the Freudian sense? Does she mean to say, without quite being able to say it, that she is mad (*folle*)? We know that Félicie can pronounce the word "mad" (*folle*) because we hear her proudly declare that she can only live with someone she loves madly ("*à la folie*"), and she even tells Maxence later that she is

[20] Félicie fills out her imagination of her family with Loic, too; she later says that perhaps she and Loic were brother and sister in a former life.

mad "*moi, je suis folle.*" So, is there something stopping Félicie at this moment—having just called herself "*la fille introuvable*"—at the cusp of explicitly admitting herself to be mad?

How ordinary is it for a girl, such as Félicie, to doubt not only that she is findable but also that she is findable as a girl? If she is entertaining doubts or insecurities about whether, or how, she might be found as a girl, then how would she manifest, or ward off, those doubts? To return to my earlier discussion: Is there a *method* here?

Well, what else do we witness Félicie do?

One thing she does—as a way of living with her doubts, or as a way of trying to overcome them—is to go about choosing between men, in the plural, or between *types* of partners (which is how Félicie sometimes talks about Loic and Maxence: as intellectual, or egghead, or tasteful, or beefy, or dominant, or sweet). In choosing between Loic and Maxence, for instance, Félicie tells her mother that she experiences greater sexual satisfaction with the latter. "I don't like being dominated mentally, but physically [...] *j'aime*," she tells her mother—affirming that with Loic she feels intellectually diminished, whereas with Maxence she finds physical pleasure. "I am certain I enjoy *that*," she seems to be asserting, as if looking in her experience of her own sexual pleasure, in the form of being physically dominated, for a source of conviction. And yet later, when she breaks up with Maxence, she tells him that her newfound desire not to be held by force by him is "physical," that she no longer wishes to be "held by force, especially today." And when she breaks up with Loic, the tenderness of his embrace causes her to sway—to feel "weak," as she later puts it. Is Félicie's pleasure a source of conviction, the location of a firm resolve in herself, or in him? Or a sensation of swooning or falling? Related to "not being stopped" by them, as she later puts it?

Félicie was carrying on, it appears, as if developing one's own tastes and predilections—and then maximizing their satisfaction accordingly, through the "choices" one makes—could be a method for living with doubts or overcoming them. As if life could be approached by "choosing," in the same way that one approaches shopping, which is something Félicie does in the place of going to church, we later learn. A "matter of taste," Félicie calls it. Indeed, Rohmer explicitly presents the activity of shopping as a way of living with a lack of religious belief or conviction—"*enfin, mes convictions* ..." says Félicie, her voice trailing off, before asking Loic to pray for her, to pray "in her place," while she goes shopping.

In these ways—that is, thanks to such "methods" and to these men who give her what she calls "courage," though not love—Félicie seems to arrive in the Nevers cathedral at the conclusion that her mad love of Charles is itself, importantly, not a matter of decision-making or choice. She finally appears convinced that she loves Charles madly, without "choice" entering the equation. Perhaps, by "choosing" her way through life, she has arrived at a point at which she no longer feels herself to be in doubt about what or whom she desires.

❦

But then why—the question lingers—did she give Charles the slip, and then later confess to have been "dumb" (mad?) How did she come to think of herself as the "unfindable girl," or perhaps, as unfindable as a girl?

No one around Félicie seems to doubt that she is a girl or, for that matter, to doubt that she is now the mother of a five-year-old girl. There is no overt cross-dressing or theatrical gender-bending. And yet, if the preceding remarks and pages of this chapter can lend support to what I am now going to say, perhaps Rohmer is here allowing us to see the very ordinariness of Félicie's skepticism or dysphoria. Can we also call it an insecurity? A crisis of confidence?

Have I lost my mind? Do we not see that Charles already knows that Félicie is a girl? And that she knows he knows it? We see them naked, on the beach and in bed. What more proof do we need?

But the point is not that *we* need convincing. We are, rather, entertaining the possibility that we are watching Félicie convince herself, or become convinced, that she can be found as a girl, by undergoing doubts and slips and accidents and self-declared madness. Along the way, we might notice details, such as the fact that Félicie wears a sharp black-and-white suit to Christmas dinner and afterward gives away her dresses to her sister. As she and her sister talk, while Félicie empties her wardrobe, we hear her declare that she has always hated her nose ("*j'avais toujours horreur de mon nez*"). We can guess, ahem, what a nose stands for. Indeed, Félicie clarifies, or makes explicit, that she prefers long and straight noses (like Charles's) to noses that bend (like her own, or Loic's).[21]

In Shakespeare's *The Winter's Tale*, Leontes notes that others say his son's nose is "a copy out of mine"—as if some evidence, some proof of

[21] See note 11 above, on Freud's discussion of penis envy.

paternity (and of masculinity) might be on offer.[22] Remembering Descartes's question—"how can I doubt that these hands or this whole body are mine?"—we might insert a question of our own: Of what is having (or not having) an identifiably ownable limb, or family-trait, proof? Félicie takes her disapproval of her nose, and Loic's nose, to be—she says—"not proof, but rather a sign" that she would not want a child with him and, thus, does not love him. Is acceptance, or "horror," of one's body—or horror or desire of another's body, the identification of another's body as *their* body—to be taken as a sign, or as proof? Of what?

Félicie's train of thought connects the identifiable horror of her own nose, and her adjudication of the relative straightness of her lovers' noses, to the acceptability of having a child by any of them. As I noted earlier, what seems to be in doubt is not whether Félicie could accept the arrival of a child in general—we already know that she is intimately convinced of the value of letting nature take its course—but whether she could *bear* bearing a child *with* one of these men. Can she stand bearing a child stamped in her with the shape of some man's "nose," which would then have to be raised by her alone, or with her own mother's help, or together with him, or with one of them? Could she bear all that with a smile or laughter? Or at least with tears of joy—as the film's conclusion proposes—rather than tears of suffering?

We hear Félicie laugh only twice in the film. The second peel of laughter records the "tears of joy" which end the film. The first laugh was in a moment of postcoital bliss with Charles at the beginning of the film, just after Charles had pointed out that she was being "imprudent" (in having had unprotected sex with him, presumably). Cavell refers to this scene as the "enigma" of Félicie's laughter, and offers, I think, a somewhat tendentious interpretation of the facts. He sees her laughter as "partly [...] a risk for mad happiness [...] but essentially there is no risk, since she knows she is already three months pregnant" (*Cities of Words* 440). Cavell's calculation of the timing of the pregnancy is open to question, since Rohmer shows us two scenes of intercourse between Charles and Félicie: one seems to be early in the summer, and the other toward summer's end. Félicie says

[22] Whereas Leontes seems to see in Perdita a resemblance to the youthful Hermione, without immediately acknowledging her as his daughter or even as "the daughter of a King" (5.1.208). Perdita's womanhood and beauty are given explicit and repeated remarking: "Women will love her, that she is a woman / More worth than any man; men, that she is / The rarest of all women" (5.1.110–12).

that she realized her slip "filling out a birth certificate six months after she and Charles parted," when she was "still working and pregnant." None of this helps *us* to determine the precise dates of the pregnancy or birth, nor to assess at what point in time Félicie realized that she was pregnant. The most we can say is that she might have known that she was pregnant by Charles at any point in what we are shown of their summer together. Her laughter in bed with Charles of course *could* be, as Cavell wants, an enigmatic expression of Félicie's happy knowledge of her pregnancy—though this raises the question, again, of why she would keep that knowledge (and with it, *that* happiness) from Charles. But it could equally be the carefree laughter—the laughter before tears—of a girl who did not then see, as Charles did, her behavior as "imprudent." If there is any realization of "imprudence" on Félicie's part, then it comes later—comes more slowly—to her than it does to Charles, though it comes more indelibly.

Let me put it this way: the fact that Charles saw, in that moment, a risk, such that sharing that danger with Félicie would prompt her to laugh, and to clasp his hand, seems to testify to a fundamental difference in their first-personal sexual experience with one another, of one another. And *that* experience is not *ours* to experience, even as the film discloses it to us.

None of this is to conclude that Félicie did not have a premonition, did not somehow sense that she then was pregnant with Charles's child at the time of their parting on the train platform. Yet there is no way for *us* to know whether she was then three months pregnant. And if *we* cannot turn to the calendar (as Cavell wants to do) for definitive evidence of what knowledge she harbored at that time, then we must be more circumspect. That Félicie was pregnant when they parted is not in doubt. What has been in doubt, again, is whether she could *bear* having a child *with him*. At issue is *her own* experience (and Charles's experience) of the secret bond between their sexual intimacy and her pregnancy, and the possible disclosure of that experience to each other as well as to Rohmer's camera: which is to say, of their own experience of their sexual difference, and its possible modes of disclosure. For, *bearing* having a child with Charles would amount to Felicie's finding herself, with him, to be *une fille* found out as such by him—the man who seems to have felt, before she did, the risk she was taking with him.

Turning to the end:

"Close your mouth," says Félicie to Elise, applying lip balm to herself and her child in the moment she sits down in front of Charles on the bus. Watching them, Charles recognizes Félicie's face as hers. Elise speaks first, saying "papa." Félicie, for her part asks—as if disbelieving—"You are in France?" Charles asks immediately: "Is that your daughter?" Félicie ignores this question and instead declares "If you knew how dumb I am." Charles, assuming Félicie is referring to Elise (that is, assuming that she is answering the question of whether the child is hers), says "you could have told me, I would have understood." But Félicie continues, explaining that by "dumb" she means that she told him the wrong address. In short: in the sequence of the dialogue and its train of thought, Félicie's answer to Charles's question about whether her child is hers is the confession of the slip. As if owning up to the slip and answering his questions about the presence of Elise were one and the same conversation.

Rohmer's camera then shows Elise looking at her "papa" with another woman—Dora, Charles's companion on the bus, around whom Charles puts his arm and to whom he continues to speak. Félicie sees this, too. At this moment, I think, Félicie's doubts about whether she can bear having a child with Charles are more visible than at any other place in the film: Félicie abruptly takes Elise's hand and quickly exits the bus without a word, leaving Charles to race after her, almost shut off from following her by the closing door of the bus. (Imagine either Leontes or Hermione, having just been reunited at the close of *The Winter's Tale*, running straight for the hills with Perdita. Or imagine, further, Polixenes shadowing the end of *The Winter's Tale* locked in an embrace with Hermione in the way that Dora appears entwined with Charles on the bus.)

Are you "mad"? asks Charles, catching up to Félicie. She is, as she puts it, "demanding" with men. And we hear Charles say to Dora that the past five years have brought "problems" to him, too. Although Charles manages to offer Félicie the reassurance that she needs to stop running for the moment, they are nevertheless clearly being tested by one another.

What is to be gained by awakening our faith in the ordinariness of disbelief?

It is tempting to imagine, as Cavell seems tempted to imagine, that Félicie's doubts had been resolved in the Nevers cathedral, by her "meditation," by her moral perfectionism and her hard-won determination not to live in a way that is incompatible with Charles's return to her. The film invites us to bear witness to Félicie's slow and methodical overcoming of her doubts, her coming to "believe" in her intimate convictions, and the final reward of that hard-won "faith" in the second coming of Charles.

Félicie's convictions, her suspension of disbelief in the value and truth of her experiences, are indeed all hard-won. But whether that victory brings laughter as well as tears is not up to her alone.

Do we wait for one another? Subject ourselves and each other to test after test? Lest we take our lives and loves for granted?

Acknowledgements My thanks to Catherine Bates, John Gillies, Gregg Horowitz, Helena Kottman, Karl A. Kottman Jr., Adam Phillips, and James W. Stone for encouraging and critical responses to a draft of this essay.

Works Cited

Beckwith, Sarah. "Are There Any Women in Shakespeare's Plays? Fiction, Representation, and Reality in Feminist Criticism." *New Literary History*, vol. 46, no. 2, 2015, pp. 241–60.

Cavell, Stanley. *Cities of Words: Pedagogical Letters on a Register of the Moral Life*. Harvard UP, 2004.

———. *The Claim of Reason: Wittgenstein, Skepticism, Morality, and Tragedy*. Oxford UP, 1979.

———. *Little Did I Know: Excerpts from Memory*. Stanford UP, 2010.

———. *Philosophy the Day After Tomorrow*. Harvard UP, 2005.

Descartes, René. *Mediations on First Philosophy* (1641). Translated by Jonathan Bennett. www.earlymoderntexts.com, 2017.

Freud, Sigmund. *The Psychopathology of Everyday Life* (1901). Translated by Anthea Bell, Penguin, 2003.

———. *The Revised Standard Edition of the Complete Psychological Works of Sigmund Freud*, edited and translated by James Strachey, revised by Mark Solms. 24 vols. Rowman & Littlefield Publishers, 2024. (In-text references provide *RSE* page numbers immediately after *SE* page numbers.)

———. "Analysis Terminable and Interminable" (1937). *The Standard Edition of the Complete Psychological Works of Sigmund Freud*, edited and translated by James Strachey, vol. 23, Hogarth Press, 1964, pp. 209–54/*RSE* vol. 23, pp. 191–228.

Hume, David. *Enquiries Concerning Human Understanding and Concerning the Principles of Morals*, edited by L. A. Selby-Bigge, Oxford UP, 1975.

Johnson, Barbara, *The Critical Difference: Essays in the Contemporary Rhetoric of Reading*, Johns Hopkins UP, 1980.

Mann, Thomas. "Freud and the Future." *Essays of Three Decades*, translated by H. T. Lowe-Porter, Knopf, 1948, pp. 411–28.

Masson, Jeffrey Moussaieff, translator and editor. *The Complete Letters of Sigmund Freud to Wilhelm Fliess, 1887–1904*. Belknap Press, 1985.

Ricoeur, Paul. *Freud and Philosophy: An Essay on Interpretation*. Translated by Denis Savage, Yale UP, 1970.

Rideout, Mark C. "'With What's Unreal Thou Coactive Art': Gender and the Forces of Illusion in *The Winter's Tale* and *The Tempest*." *Selected Papers of the Ohio Valley Shakespeare Conference*, vol. 7, 2014, pp. 138–55.

Rohmer, Éric (Director). *Conte d'hiver*. Les Films du Losange, 1992.

Shakespeare, William. *Othello*, edited by E. A. J. Honigmann, Bloomsbury, 1999.

———. *Pericles*, edited by F. David Hoeniger, Bloomsbury, 1990.

———. *The Winter's Tale*, edited by John Pitcher, Bloomsbury, 2010.

Stone, James W. *Crossing Gender in Shakespeare: Feminist Psychoanalysis and the Difference Within*. Routledge, 2010.

Swales, Peter. "Freud, Johann Weier and the Status of Seduction: The role of the witch in the conception of fantasy." *Sigmund Freud: Critical Assessments*, edited by Laurence Spurling, Routledge, 1989, pp. 331–58.

CHAPTER 12

Afterword: Beyond the Pillow Problem

Drew Daniel

It is time to read the room. In particular, the shared project of the psychoanalytic reading of the works of William Shakespeare must confront what I want to call "the pillow problem." As I sit and write these words, I look over my left shoulder to the armchair where, nestled beneath the reading light and a watercolor of flowers, a throw pillow reclines beside a sleeping cat. Appearing on both sides, the throw pillow bears upon its screen-printed surface a telling illustration which I will now zoom in upon and describe. In the foreground, William Shakespeare reclines upon a couch in a velvet doublet with puffy sleeves, his hands contentedly folded on his belly, his eyes gazing upward, his mouth primly closed, as if arrested en route to language; behind him, flanked by Persian rugs and a tiny pantheon of vaguely African and pseudo-classical statuettes, Sigmund Freud sits in a brown wool suit, absorbed, listening for the next remark, taking notes, his eyes obscured by opaque glasses that conceal his expression. We are invited to examine, even snuggle up beside, this imagined encounter.

D. Daniel (✉)
Department of English, Johns Hopkins University,
Baltimore, MD, USA
e-mail: drewdaniel@jhu.edu

J. W. Stone, C. Bates (eds.), *Shakespeare and Psychoanalysis*,
Palgrave Shakespeare Studies,
https://doi.org/10.1007/978-3-032-07897-1_12

That this preposterous, transhistorical cartoon of Freud psychoanalyzing Shakespeare—so familiar, so comforting, so harmlessly banal—happens to appear upon a throw pillow is a matter of one-click consumer whim. The image is easily found online at the various emporiums that sell coffee mugs and t-shirts with whatever image a solitary Google searcher has recently sought out. Search-engine-driven capitalism will emblazon any image upon any product in order to complete a sale, so as to turn the merest passing tremor of curiosity into another micro-transaction, another drop in a glittering sea of profit and exchange. One can purchase a yoga mat with an image of the bombing of Dresden or the Rubens painting of the beheaded Medusa from the same vendor for the same amount.

If I claim to draw precedent from the tapestry in *The Rape of Lucrece* for this ekphrasis upon décor, my would-be object lesson begs a basic question: What is "the pillow problem" anyway? The problem is precisely the absence of any problem. The "pillow problem" is the comfortable *of course-ness* that suffuses this scene, its readymade, received rightness, its cozy glow. That is, the fact that there are now enough potential consumers of Shakespeare-and-Freud throw pillows to warrant their fabrication and sale does not just index the financial and professional comfort enjoyed by those who "do" Shakespeare and Freud for a living, and need something to slump against as they do it, and it does not just index the randomness of the late capitalist imaginary hustling phantasmagoria into a drop-shipped box either. It is my wager that the pillow problem also tells us something about the hidden costs of hermeneutic success: domestication. The conjunction of Shakespeare and Freud has become—literally—just another part of the furniture.

I do not say this to be the wicked fairy who comes to curse the wedding feast. *I say this precisely because I think this volume—in its complexity, variety, and stubborn force—is not an instance of but a pointed riposte to "the pillow problem."* These deliberately discordant, thorny, difficult, and sometimes mutually contrary responses to the conjunction of Freud and Shakespeare manifest the richness and capacity of these fields when they are brought together in order to experiment with the affordances of each discourse as they activate and cross-multiply each other. This volume strives to assess how and in what way a cluster of Shakespearean texts and intertexts might imaginatively enact, embody, prefigure, or resonate with Freud's manifold discourses and the broad tributaries of subsequent theoretical and clinical practice that radiate outwards from the Freudian author function. In testing what relationships are possible, and at what cost, and for whom, this volume offers, in other words, a no-less-pleasurable alternative to comfort: rigor. Instead of reclining comfortably upon the settled verities of the Shakespeare-and-Freud duo as a ready-to-hand conjunction that can be taken for granted—as a pillow to be reclined upon—this volume rightly insists upon challenge, risky and sometimes fleeting encounters, and the attempt to bypass easy pleasures for precise claims when they are possible, and for speculative and imaginative responses when they are not.

The role of the respondent typically fails in one of two ways: if you flatter, the stakes of encounter drop because one is simply being polite and professional. If you snarl, you risk being both offensive and obvious: of course, any chapter could always go farther, could always become an entire book of its own if permitted to meander and overspill. Of course, any anthology could be larger and contain more works, more topics, more texts. Accordingly, I am going to note what I see as shared methodological issues and patterns that arise from these chapters as they cluster into affinity groups, and at my conclusion to point—I hope constructively—outwards and onwards to indicate what is missing. I realize that there is a certain occupational hazard that any response to psychoanalytic papers courts the hysteric's discourse, a professorial "that is not it!" in which one resists the readings of others simply because it always feels good to do so.

❦

In keeping with Shakespeare's tragicomedic crosscurrents of pleasure and mourning, the genial conviviality of this collection is inflected, if not destroyed, by the brute and unanswerable fact of loss: Christian Smith's death renders bittersweet the substantial gift of his opening chapter. "The Role of Shakespeare in the Development of Freud's Theory" situates us precisely at the flex point of self-difference within Freud's legacy, the hinge at which the abandonment of "*neurotica*" precipitated the breakthrough of Oedipus into Hamlet and Hamlet into psychoanalysis, in the letter to Fliess which Smith illuminates and probes. I am moved to read Smith's solicitation of a possibility nascent within Freud's essay on "The Theme of the Casket Choice" (1913), which he puts forward in the speculative mode:

> Perhaps the *Kästchenwahl* essay provides a theoretical spark from which one could write a general psychoanalytic theory of comedy. Comedy (Eros) could be seen as a reaction-formation that represses tragedy (Thanatos).

> The life drive that powers the comedic plot could be interpreted as a defensive inversion of the death force that shadows the unconscious. Shakespeare presaged this notion by weaving many tragic fibers into the fabric of his comedies. (37)

Some might argue that such a speculative proposal points towards a space already occupied in part by the readings of *The Comedy of Errors* in Alenka Zupančič's *The Odd One In: On Comedy* (2008); but that book, as generative as it is, does not fundamentally achieve what Smith predicts here with respect to the permeative suffusion of the death drive within Shakespeare's comedies. It is my hope that readers of this volume will activate this possibility in the future. Going further, the belatedness of any Afterword in the face of mortal loss makes me more attentive to the temporality of dialogue between chapters that Smith has already conducted in his revisions, as when his chapter reaches out to Dominique Scarfone's excavation of the complex contextual situatedness of Hamlet's "readiness" as it recirculated within Freud's thought. Smith's willingness to rewrite Shakespeare via a slight but pointed adjustment is itself a most Freudian way of responding to the provocations of Shakespeare while adding something inevitably new; Smith's final gesture is to transpose "the readiness is all" to an optative, future-oriented reconsideration of the effects of the analytic hour itself as a means "to put the subject in readiness for all" (41).

If Stone's chapter reminds us that psychoanalysis is a discourse in which "[r]epetition is reversal" (189), such a maxim prepares us for the way that the "same" subject—the "readiness" that Freud both reinscribes and betrays through his manifold revisions—is subject to complementary but distinct readings by both Christian Smith and Dominique Scarfone. Scarfone's return to the question of how to render this "readiness" across its passages from Shakespeare's English to Freud's German revisions and on to Bonnefoy's French translations offers a rich and agile example of psychoanalytic close reading and the critical fashioning of a multiauthor assemblage that turns upon a telling affective slippage in connotation between "readiness" and "*bereitschaft*" and "*disponibilité*." Drawing from the work of Michel de M'Uzan for its articulation of the "chimera" as the generative outcome of the clinical encounter between the unconscious of the analyst and the unconscious of the analysand, Scarfone makes the "chimera" portable here in order to widen the distance between "preparedness" and "readiness." Is this the difference, perhaps, between a defensive crouch and the open ears projected onto Freud as depicted in the design upon the throw pillow? I am reminded of the mocking words of the

Prologue to Molière's *Le Malade imaginaire*, which taunts medical doctors with the pert crack that "Votre plus haut savoir n'est que pure chimère" [Your highest knowledge is nothing but fantasy]. Of course, Molière transposes the corporeal assemblage of the mythical monster onto the epistemological patchwork of seventeenth-century medical practice as a deflationary gesture, part of his assault on the professional prestige of the doctors he despised. But perhaps we could return to—and reverse—the valence of Molière's satirical judgment: where psychoanalysis is concerned, the emergence of the chimera is to be welcomed as the paradoxical, depersonalized, and constructive fabrication of a different kind of readiness.

Perched in response to Juliet in her crypt, Madelon Sprengnether's chapter opens out to ask the largest of intellectual historical questions. When did we become modern? When did the "self" as we understand that term emerge? To such questions, one always wants to reply with a "who is the 'we' that asks?" I push back against this line of questioning not to dispute that historical changes inflect subjectivity but precisely to double down upon Madelon Sprengnether's valuable insistence upon the ambient tension between the transhistorical dimension of psychoanalysis as a strong theory and the headwind of historical change that cuts across the terrain for which that theory offers explanation. With respect to the particulars of such a "when," it seems to me that, in solidarity with our colleagues in medieval or classical studies, one could always move the goalposts earlier: Don't the distinctly self-ironizing gestures that we encounter in Chaucer's pilgrims or in Ovid's lovers or in the savagely self-anatomizing classical satirists such as Lucian and Juvenal also exemplify these habits of awareness about the capacity to deceive that we also find in Petrarch, and Shakespeare's Juliet, and in other examples of what Samuel Fallon encourages us to identify as early modern literary "paper monsters"?

That said, there is a tendency within psychoanalytic writers, and not only in Freud, to assert that there is a special relationship between psychoanalytic thinking and the early modern period. Consider as case in point Lacan's insistence upon the special "paternity" shared by a tradition that joins the sixteenth century to Freudian discourse:

> not to recognize the filiation or cultural paternity that exists between Freud and a new direction of thought—one that is apparent at the break which occurred toward the beginning of the sixteenth century, but whose repercussions are felt up to the end of the seventeenth century—constitutes a fundamental misunderstanding of the kind of problems Freud's intellectual project addresses. (97)

Untwisting the double negative, to recognize this paternity is to understand the Freudian project as somehow continuous with the shattering disclosures of the Reformation (a reformation of the Reformation?). The context here is Lacan's assertion that Luther's writings on the divine hatred of humanity prefigures the ethical disclosure of psychoanalysis itself insofar as they force us to rethink the relationship between ethics, pleasure, and transgression. While a fuller analysis of this gesture would need to triangulate this allegation of paternity via Lacan's relation to his Catholic surround and Freud's complex Jewishness, I cite it here merely to indicate the presence of an "early modern Freud" as something that, in the torrent of the seminar, Lacan regards as a *fait accompli*. Such a claim is congenial insofar as it sets parameters that are isometric with those that tend to bracket the literary criticism of early modern England: 1500 to 1700. Sprengnether's suggestion that Juliet constitutes one exemplary moment in the broader emergence of modern subjectivity pulls us backward in a double-sense: we are back to Harold Bloom's claims for Shakespeare's exemplarity (also discussed in the Introduction), but back farther still to Burckhardt. Yet in pressing the question, Sprengnether also alerts us to a foundational problem for psychoanalytic responses to early modern culture: Are they sustained by an ambient assumption that there is an always over-determined "special relationship" between "our" period and our chosen theoretical apparatus? Here is where the very comfort of the connections we fashion becomes, for me, uncomfortable.

Temporal folds are essential to the field's overlay of the 1590s onto 1897 onto the present, but some chapters leap farther than others. I was particularly struck by John Fletcher's willingness to move across media history via his comparison with cinema as he moves from the inward experience of Hamlet's delay to its establishment outside that character's perspective through the exteriorization of "dramatic time" within the play. This seems to me both compelling in its insight into the experience of staging the play, and quintessentially Freudian, in its resemblance to Freud's own reading strategies in "Some Character-Types Met with in Psycho-Analytic Work" (1916). In that essay, in a dilatory passage that Freud later admits constitutes a "digression into literature" (331/334), Freud investigates *Macbeth*, pursuing not only the play-text but also the Holinshed sources and speculations about how those sources might have inspired Shakespeare, and makes a particularly revealing observation about the compression of action in that fast-paced play: "the economy of time in the tragedy expressly precludes a development of character from any motives but those inherent in the action itself" (322/326). Fletcher is surely right to indicate that "while Hamlet's delay exists at the level of the bare plot, delay takes place in dramatic time as well, at the level of the play's articulation of the Hamlet story" (202). Accordingly, Fletcher's reading of *Hamlet* seems to me to at once confirm and invert the logic at work in Freud's remarks about *Macbeth*. In *Sculpting in Time*, filmmaker Andrei Tarkovsky referred to rhythm not as a matter of editing between shots but as the "the pressure of the time" (117) generated by his own notorious long takes and tracking shots; in the wake of Fletcher's chapter, what is noticeable about *Hamlet* is the experience of time's languorous extension, the manifestation of delay not simply as a matter of interiorized inhibitions but as a kind of collectively shared exposure to duration that is the flipside of the "haste" imputed to Gertrude's and Claudius's marriage. In Elsinore, time drips and oozes, more like molasses than like the punctual and predictable descent of grains of sand within an hourglass.

Part of the pleasure of reading this collection is the way that individual chapters sometimes seem to prompt responses to or rethinkings of claims made in other essays within the edited collection itself. A case in point occurs when Heather Hirschfeld's chapter glosses Freud's account of thinking as activity:

> Thinking, according to Freud, is one of the pre-eminent means of such accommodation, a way out of hallucinated enjoyment and thus a way into contact with things and people outside of the self. As he writes in "Formulations," thinking is "endowed with characteristics which ma[ke] it possible for the mental apparatus to tolerate an increased tension of stimulus while the process of discharge [is] postponed" (221/218). Indeed, thinking becomes action itself; it is, as Freud says, "essentially an experimental kind of acting" (221/218). (82)

What is particularly compelling here is the sense that such a Freudian reading of the status of thinking might open out, rather than simply contradict, John Fletcher's analysis of Hamlet's "delay." The distinction between thinking and acting, the presupposition that thinking as such constitutes a refusal to act, a deferral, a strategy of avoidance—however intuitive, given the long and overdetermined history of critical responses to Hamlet and *Hamlet* that have emphasized that delay as constitutive—might be reconsidered if we are to take Hirschfeld's claims made via Bion and Freud seriously. I bracket for now the sense that telling intellectuals that thinking, too, constitutes a form of activity might be altogether too congenial as a balm for the self-lacerations about political impotence that seem to afflict scholarly people as such, and particularly at this moment of pronounced crisis about the status and institutional survival of the academic milieu.

Hirschfeld's account of Bion builds out towards a reading of the dark "scenes of cognition" (87) within *Measure for Measure*, which she reads with brio. But upon examining her account of Angelo's literalism as a "thought disorder" (89), "a mental alternative to thinking because thinking is impossible" (89), I was left wondering about the status of literalism, both within the play and outside the play as a tacit methodological strategy for literary critical response. Whether we examine Helena's satisfaction of Bertram's conditions via the bed trick in *All's Well That Ends Well* or Portia's insistence in *The Merchant of Venice* upon the strict letter of the law in her perverse insistence that Shylock is entitled to Antonio's pound of flesh but may not spill a drop of blood or take one jot above or below precisely one pound, across the "problem plays" as a group, literalism often functions as a *deus ex machina* at the level of plot.

However unthinking, this driving insistence upon the letter certainly, intuitively, clicks Hirschfeld's Bion-ian reading into place. But it also seems to me to constitute a literalism wielded via impressive skill of the premeditated, thoughtful, interventionist sort that, to my eyes, seems to also look rather like thinking, an intuition that might trouble the security of the alleged distinction between actively engaged thought and its disordered antithesis. I do not bring this up as a rejoinder to Hirschfeld's reading of the play, but to pose the problem of the literal as itself something that Shakespearean psychoanalytic criticism might be in a position to examine with a special sort of care regarding the slippages of status that the same object—even something as multivalent as "thinking" reduced to a keyword—can occasion. Doing so now, in the age of the digitally scanned contents of EEBO and the easy searchability of digital concordances of major authors, also exposes something about the nature of interpretive desire in the age of digital textuality: there is a sense in which these labor-saving devices have subtly altered the status of our close reading practices. Now one can search for every appearance of the word "think" within a play with greater facility than ever. Is looking at the surfacing of these keywords itself an example of literalism or not? Who thinks through us, with us, or perhaps for us when we think in this manner?

Excavating both its mythographic origins and its Lacanian afterlife, Catherine Bates's journey across *Venus and Adonis* commences with a striking triangulation of Adonis as (eventually) the Symbolic, Venus as the Imaginary, and the Boar as the threatening Phallus, and keeps expanding in its explanatory reach from this opening gambit. It must be said that Lacanian responses to this poem have an extensive provenance. An "oldie but a goodie," I have always been partial to Catherine Belsey's essay "Love as Trompe L'Oeil: Taxonomies of Desire in *Venus and Adonis*" (1995) because of its thorough deconstruction of Adonis's rhetorical opposition between love and lust on historicist grounds; Belsey marshals usage evidence from the period to make a convincing argument that these terms have only become antithetical in the modern era. Thirty years later, Bates's reading encouraged me to reconsider the centripetal force of Belsey's interpretation; specifically, Bates's persuasive overlay of the Imaginary and Symbolic onto the pairing reworks their relationship along new temporal lines as a developmental drama necessarily reenacted by each subject:

> Preoedipal "love" can only be imagined from the place of oedipalized "lust" and is thus the ghostly product of it (ghostly because literary, poetic, imagined, represented). Adonis is right to sense an absolute difference between the Imaginary and Symbolic registers: his immaturity (unmistakable in the tone of his pert little speech) shows in his inability to grasp this point, or to see and accept the inextricable relation between the two. (143)

Through her etymological maneuver via the concept of "venery" as both hunting and lustful play, Bates is able to address the scission between these contrary registers—their genuine opposition as an organizing binary—while also acknowledging the relationality that connects them together in a far more complex way. As if this were not enough, the essay in its final crescendo makes a persuasive case for this erotic epyllion constituting not so much a plague-motivated detour in search of aristocratic privilege as the germinating seed of all that was to flower in Shakespeare's subsequent career. In her willingness to indicate, and analyze, the way that a basic psychic structure can be traced across the arc of Shakespeare's own development, I was reminded of the capacious reach of Janet Adelman's classic monograph *Suffocating Mothers: Fantasies of Maternal Origin in Shakespeare's Plays,* Hamlet *to* The Tempest (1992). Both that work and this chapter share a willingness to posit a deep structure to Shakespeare's lifelong project.

While it may be speculative to posit that sharing labors as co-editors has produced sympathetic reading strategies, the convergences between

Stone's chapter and Bates's are noticeable: what "venery" was in Bates—a highly revealing switch point that manages to collapse contrary meanings—becomes a topic of direct methodological engagement in Stone's account of antithetical words across *The Rape of Lucrece*. In a surprising twist, Stone also finds a buried kinship between this early poem and the longer trajectory of Shakespeare's developmental arc, finding seeds of the romances in the deeper structure of the "loss of loss" (187) within both the early poem and the later plays. But connection points abound between Stone and other chapters as well: Lucrece's ekphrastic encounter with Sinon, charged as it is with the overlay of Tarquin's assault, becomes a lesson in the absorption of the possibility of deception implicit in the use of language, an interest that dovetails with Sprengnether's interest in duplicity as part of the emergence of "modern" subjectivity. A question that emerges for this reader is whether there is a standing tension between the fundamental binary of "antithetical words" and the always promiscuously open possibility of polysemy as a multiplicity that would be more-than-two: if a word can accumulate additional connotations as it moves across history (witness the fate of the word "tag," for a recent instance), and if any word can through unconscious processes operate as a site of condensation and displacement and thus come to connote in excess of its strict definition, then is this capacity for accumulation likely to overwhelm, or at least clutter, the pure binary of antithesis as such?

Among the affinity groups that this Afterword clusters, the most intuitive is the shared interest of Katz's and Kottman's chapters in transhistorical adaptations that extend the Shakespearean corpus into multiple cross-media afterlives. These, too, seem to me to index Stone's interest in repetition as a "working through," in this case the harrowing of the Shakespearean author-function as Shakespeare's words become optional, ghostly, subject to revision and distortion by Jack Spicer and Éric Rohmer as they anatomize and adapt found material, exorcising bardolatry through palimpsestic revisionary play. Katz's evocation of Cressida as faithful to something within Troilus's own fantasy offers, perhaps, a figure through which to use Spicer's fidelity to Shakespeare to think about Katz's own creative fidelity to Freud, a deployment of concepts that is also a creative skirting or deviation from doctrine when that doctrine does not serve the text under analysis. The most revealing moment of this creative fidelity is surely Katz's moment of granting the possibility that castration might be in play while also blocking that reading off as "brittle and doctrinaire" (247). This kind of critical honesty about owning up to critical fatigue with certain perhaps too pat psychoanalytic interpretive moves felt, to this reader, both bracing and delicate. It felt like the moment when the pillow problem surfaced and was rejected.

Kottman's reading of Cavell's reading of Rohmer's response to Shakespeare offers a potentially dizzying spiral of transmedial influence; Freud threads the needle that quilts these mediated layers together. Piecing things together, I was most attendant to the moments of self-critique that surface within Kottman's text at the points when Rohmer's character Félicie reconsiders her inhabitation of her own gender: "How did she come to think of herself as the 'unfindable girl,' or perhaps, as unfindable as a girl?" (272). By placing in conjunction "Félicie's skepticism or dysphoria" (272), the essay seems to me to cruise a broader methodological question that I do not think psychoanalytic literary criticism, whether in its Shakespearean form or *tout court*, can afford to put off any longer: the question of how, and in what way, our field might best learn from the flowering of trans studies.

This is not a simple task, as the duel in print between Jacques Alain-Miller and Paul Preciado makes apparent. Despite the polemical rancor displayed in that exchange, there are constructive paths forward; consider, as cases in point, Patricia Gherovici's *Transgender Psychoanalysis: A Lacanian Perspective on Sexual Difference* (2017) and the full-scale rethinking of castration in Grace Lavery's *Pleasure and Efficacy: Of Pen Names, Cover Versions, and Other Trans Techniques* (2023). These works model a possibility that psychoanalysis might exceed its troubling legacy of clinical harm with respect to transgender people, a legacy that has caused McKenzie Wark to argue in *Parapraxis* for reparations for trans people from Lacanian analysts. Within early modern studies, the work of Colby Gordon on dysphoria in his book *Glorious Bodies: Trans Theology and Renaissance Literature* (2024)—and in particular his chapters on John Donne and John Milton in that book—offers a possible model for how to think gender dysphoria within early modern subjectivity. What is missing, so far, is a way to connect early modern trans studies specifically with psychoanalytic forms of critical reading. There is a space on the chessboard for such a move to happen.

Lest such remarks seem to have blown us off course from Rohmer studies entirely, it might be worth also pointing out that Rohmer is the director of a film which seems to me long overdue for a reading in conversation with early modern trans studies. Rohmer's final film *Les Amours d'Astrée et de Céladon* (2007)—a stunningly executed, strategic adaptation of

Honoré d'Urfé's monstrously extensive pastoral text serialized between 1607 and 1627—turns centrally upon a gendered disguise plot loosely analogous to Sidney's *Old Arcadia*. While scholars of transgender performance such as Sawyer Kemp have rightly pointed out that mere clothes-swapping plots do not by themselves necessarily constitute a trans text, it seems to me that the sorrowful affects associated with cisnormativity that often precipitate such disguise do solicit trans readings. The dysphoria that Kottman finds in *Conte d'hiver* (1992) might be spread across a wider swathe of Rohmer's work—and, for that matter, Shakespeare's as well.

I have saved David Hillman's and Adelais Mills's excavation of ~~Coriolanus~~ (under a Derridean erasure) for last because it seems to me to reach beyond the strict contents of this volume to interact with the Appendix that is both attached and yet outside it in a particularly apt and telling manner. The logic of the supplement, so generative for Derridean practices of reading generally and for the extravagant maneuver of the "tranche" specifically, seems also relevant to the way that the Appendix's insistence upon the strict enumeration and parsing of exactly where Freud speaks of exactly which Shakespearean texts finds its conceptual obverse in Hillman's and Mills's acute encounter with *Coriolanus* as that which must remain extimate to any and all accounting of Shakespearean/Freudian relationality. In their adjacency and noncorrespondence, when considering how the Appendix and the Hillman and Mills chapter interact, I am reminded of the phenomenon observed by child psychologist Mildred Parten of so-called parallel play (250) in which two children, while not actually interacting with each other, nevertheless sit together and play side by side. I do not invoke this nursery scene as a disparagement of the chapter's two co-authors, who seem to me to have played together beautifully in this essay, but to emphasize the conjunctions at work within Shakespeare and Freud in a new way, and, specifically, to think about the chapter's capacity to enact a Freudian/Derridean reading of a Shakespeare play that Freud—we now see, thanks to Hillman and Mills—should have written about but, for reasons that now become clearer, did not acknowledge.

❦

So what do these chapters have in common, over and above their shared commitment to the reconsideration of Shakespeare and Freud as overlapping and mutually implicated author-functions? I would suggest that, as with The Meters's celebrated definition of "funk" as a musical genre, it is as much about the notes you do not play as it is about the notes you do. In the case of this volume, there is very little defensiveness about the historical validity of the combination of these discourses. To go ahead and discuss the elephant in the room, this might in turn reflect the decline in prestige of New Historicism as the perceived antagonist to psychoanalytic readings of early modernity that put the field into a defensive crouch forty years ago (a matter discussed with sensitivity by Stone and Bates in their own introduction). Tides go in and out, and it is now the case that a "return to Freud" is trumpeted across a number of humanities disciplines which are drawing new conclusions from Freud's texts and the practices they inspire. While space prohibits me from listing all the scholars involved, the deployments of psychoanalysis in recent early modern scholarly monographs as diverse as Eric Song's *Love Against Substitution* (2022), Christine Varnado's *The Shapes of Fancy* (2020), or Steven Swarbrick's *The Environmental Unconscious* (2023) make it clear that thoughtful scholars in early modern studies do not find the old prohibitions against the application of psychoanalytic ideas to early modern literary texts inhibiting, or even worth bothering to argue against. Instead, there is a spirit of continuity and increased pressure upon how to overcome the bare premise of "application" in order to arrive at something that feels both psychoanalytically compelling and generative of new literary insight. The field is better off for this new abandonment of defensiveness, and I see a similar spirit expressed collectively in these chapters.

That said, there is a darker question that one might pose about notes that are not being played, and it also speaks to the question of the moment and whether and how to meet the moment. Specifically, the flowering of premodern critical race studies is the defining movement in early modern studies at present: this is where the innovative scholarship, pathbreaking arguments, and critical heat are in this decade, and the key recent monographs within this field have all engaged with Shakespeare as a central figure in the period (I am thinking here of Urvashi Chakravarty's *Fictions of Consent* (2022), Noemie Ndiaye's *Scripts of Blackness* (2022), Ian Smith's *Black Shakespeare* (2022), and Miles Grier's *Inkface* (2023), but this list could be a lot longer). So, with respect to the viability of the ongoing intersections between psychoanalysis and Shakespeare studies, we have to ask ourselves: Why is race largely absent from this anthology and from this critical conversation, as generative as it is?

Given the current flourishing of work on psychoanalysis and race by Donald Moss, David Marriott, Stephen Frosh, Lee Edelman, and Ankhi

Mukherjee—to pick otherwise dissimilar scholars who simply share that they are mostly not early modernists—why does the confluence of Shakespeare studies and psychoanalytic reading still await strong work on the psychoanalysis of Shakespearean racecraft? If Ian Smith, in *Black Shakespeare*, has identified a need for "racial literacy" (14) as fundamental to the scholarly task of engaging early modern racecraft on the page and in the classroom, is there perhaps a reticence or a dearth of such racial literacy among even such perspicuous scholars of Shakespeare and Freud as are gathered here? Given the foundational contributions of Hortense Spillers, or, to reach farther back, Frantz Fanon, to the considerations of how racializing discourses inflect political structures of fantasy and ricochet across psychic life, it is not sufficient to simply throw up our hands and humbly admit that we cannot do everything, particularly given how frequently the texts under analysis eroticize whiteness and fantasize about nonwhite otherness. Psychoanalytic readings of Shakespeare should not take place in what Juliana Spahr and Stephanie Young, with reference to the poetic avant-garde, have usefully named as "the Mainly white room." We can and ought to do better.

At my close, I want to return to the pillow problem with which I began, if only to preempt a possible misreading. In a time of triumphant fascism and the sudden deportation of graduate students who are disappeared for speaking out against injustice, and in a time when home ownership is out of reach for millions, the evocation of a cozy domestic scene as something to sneer at and reject might seem both crudely gendered and poorly timed, a reflex of would-be edgy critical machismo that sits badly within a field that has had its own long-standing poor PR on that score. What is wrong with cozy décor? What is wrong with comfortably reclining on a pillow? Doubling down, we could also say that the slur "pillow princess" applied to sexual partners who are tediously passive, who just lie there, as it were, is itself a reflex of misogyny, a denigration of those on the sexual bottom, that reflects a culture that cannot stop overcompensating through its willful dream of active, powerful, probing masculinity. The received history of literary criticism is itself a gendered scene lit up by a tension between the manly philosophical hunting of buried references and rampant abstractions best left to the boys club of sturdy professionals and the feminized sighs and tears of belle-lettristic, Paterian appreciation. My objection is not to throw pillows, or, indeed to comfort, as such.

Rather, I cite the object that bears the image, and the image itself, as an index of an all-too-ready set of assumptions about the relationship of

Shakespeare to Freud, about a certain unidirectional, inevitable triumphalism about that intimacy and influence. Pushing off from the example of the chapters in this volume, I believe that we must reconsider the Shakespearean-Freudian field anew, in our readings, in our classrooms, in our seminars, in our writing, if we are going to truly activate the kinetic potential of two adjacent but distinct fields in the present time. I also hope that, for the readers of this volume, undiscovered connections, readings, critiques and responses sprout forth that productively estrange and develop this field further. Pushing off from the pillow, this volume helps us reconsider the nature, and necessity, of Shakespearean psychoanalytic "readiness." It has taught me that there is always more than one way to read the room.

Works Cited

Adelman, Janet. *Suffocating Mothers: Fantasies of Maternal Origin in Shakespeare,* Hamlet *to* The Tempest. Routledge, 1992.

Belsey, Catherine. "Love as Trompe L'Oeil: Taxonomies of Desire in Venus and Adonis." *Shakespeare Quarterly*, vol. 46, no. 3, 1995, pp. 257–76.

Chakravarty, Urvashi. *Fictions of Consent: Slavery, Servitude and Free Service in Early Modern England.* U of Pennsylvania P, 2022.

Fallon, Samuel. *Paper Monsters: Persona and Literary Culture in Elizabethan England.* U of Pennsylvania P, 2019.

Freud, Sigmund. *The Revised Standard Edition of the Complete Psychological Works of Sigmund Freud*, edited and translated by James Strachey, revised by Mark Solms. 24 vols. Rowman & Littlefield Publishers, 2024. (In-text references provide *RSE* page numbers immediately after *SE* page numbers).

———. "Some Character-Types Met With in Psychoanalytic Work" (1916). *The Standard Edition of the Complete Psychological Works of Sigmund Freud*, edited and translated by James Strachey, vol. 14, Hogarth Press, 1955, pp. 309–33/*RSE* vol. 47, pp. 315–36.

Gherovici, Patricia. *Transgender Psychoanalysis: A Lacanian Perspective on Sexual Difference.* Routledge, 2017.

Gordon, Colby. *Glorious Bodies: Trans Theology and Renaissance Literature.* U of Chicago P, 2024.

Grier, Miles. *Inkface: Othello and White Authority in the Era of Atlantic Slavery.* U of Virginia P, 2023.

Kemp, Sawyer. "Shakespeare in Transition: Pedagogies of Transgender Justice in Performance." *Teaching Social Justice Through Shakespeare: Why Renaissance Literature Matters Now*, edited by Hillary Eklund and Wendy Beth Hyman, Edinburgh UP, 2019, pp. 36–46.

Lacan, Jacques. *The Seminar of Jacques Lacan: The Ethics of Psychoanalysis, Book VII*. Translated by Dennis Porter. W. W. Norton, 1997.
Lavery, Grace. *Pleasure and Efficacy: Of Pen Names, Cover Versions, and Other Trans Techniques*. Princeton UP, 2023.
Miller, Jacques-Alain. "Docile to Trans." Lacan.com url: https://www.lacan.com/pdfjam2021.pdf
Molière, *The Imaginary Invalid*. Translated by Henri van Laun. Dover, 2004.
Ndiaye, Noémie. *Scripts of Blackness: Early Modern Performance Culture and the Making of Race*. U of Pennsylvania P, 2022.
Parten, Mildred. "Social participation among school-age children." *The Journal of Abnormal and Social Psychology*, vol 27, no. 3, 1932, pp. 243–69.
Preciado, Paul P. *Can the Monster Speak? Report to an Academy of Psychoanalysts*. Translated by Frank Wynne. MIT Press, 2021.
Smith, Ian. *Black Shakespeare: Reading and Misreading Race*. Cambridge UP, 2022.
Spahr, Juliana and Stephanie Young. "The Program Era and the Mainly White Room" *The Los Angeles Review of Books*, September 20, 2015. url: https://lareviewofbooks.org/article/the-program-era-and-the-mainly-white-room/
Swarbrick, Steven. *The Environmental Unconscious: Ecological Poetics from Spenser to Milton*. U of Minnesota P, 2023.
Tarkovsky, Andrei. *Sculpting in Time: Reflections on the Cinema*. Translated by Kitty Hunter-Blair. Bodley Head, 1986.
Varnado, Christine. *The Shapes of Fancy: Reading for Queer Desire in Early Modern Literature*. U of Minnesota P, 2020.
Wark, McKenzie. "Dear Cis Analysts: A Call for Reparations." *Parapraxis*, Winter 2022. url: https://www.parapraxismagazine.com/articles/dear-cis-analysts
Zupančič, Alenka. *The Odd One In: On Comedy*. MIT Press, 2008.

Appendix

Chronological record of quotations from, allusions to, and mentions of Shakespeare and his works in Freud's writings.
Compiled by Christian Smith and supplemented by Catherine Bates.

Key

Boehlich	Boehlich, Walter (ed.), Pomerans, A. (trans.), *The Letters of Sigmund Freud to Eduard Silberstein, 1871–1881*. Belknap Press, 1992.
Freud/Stern	Freud, Ernst L. (ed.), Tania Stern and James Stern (trans.), *The Letters of Sigmund Freud, 1873–1939*. Hogarth Press, 1961.
Freud/Robson-Scott	Freud, Ernst L. (ed.), Elizabeth Robson-Scott, William Robson-Scott (trans.), *The Letters of Sigmund Freud and Arnold Zweig*. Hogarth Press, 1970.
Jones	Jones, Ernest, *The Life and Work of Sigmund Freud*. 3 vols. Hogarth Press, 1953–57.
McGuire	McGuire, William (ed.), Ralph Manheim and R. F. C. Hull (trans.), *The Freud/Jung Letters: The Correspondence Between Sigmund Freud and C. G. Jung*. Princeton UP, 1974.

J. W. Stone, C. Bates (eds.), *Shakespeare and Psychoanalysis*, Palgrave Shakespeare Studies,
https://doi.org/10.1007/978-3-032-07897-1

Masson	Masson, Jeffrey Moussaieff (ed. and trans.), *The Complete Letters of Sigmund Freud to Wilhelm Fliess, 1887–1904*. Belknap Press, 1985.
Meng	Meng, Heinrich, and Ernst L. Freud (eds.), Eric Mosbacher (trans.), *Psychoanalysis and Faith: The Letters of Sigmund Freud and Oskar Pfister*. Basic Books, 1963.
Paskauskas	Paskauskas, R. Andrew (ed.), Riccardo Steiner (intr.), *The Complete Correspondence of Sigmund Freud and Ernest Jones, 1908–1939*. Belknap Press, 1993.
Waugaman	Waugaman, R. M., "An unpublished letter by Sigmund Freud on the Shakespeare authorship question." *Scandinavian Psychoanalytic Review* 39 (2016): 148–51.
RSE	*The Revised Standard Edition of the Complete Psychological Works of Sigmund Freud*, edited and translated by James Strachey, revised by Mark Solms. 24 vols. Rowman & Littlefield Publishers, 2024.
SE	*The Standard Edition of the Complete Psychological Works of Sigmund Freud*, edited and translated by James Strachey. 24 vols. Hogarth Press, 1953–66.

All references to Shakespeare are to *The Riverside Shakespeare*, edited by G. Blakemore Evans, et al. Houghton Mifflin, 1997.

Year	*Shakespeare*	*Reference*	*Freud*	*Reference*	*Type*	*Cross-references*
1872	Hamlet (character)	*Hamlet*	Letter to Eduard Silberstein 4 September	Boehlich 16	Mention	
1873	"If music be the food of love"	*Twelfth Night* 1.1.1	Letter to Eduard Silberstein 20 August	Boehlich 40	Adaptation	
1874	"Words, words, words"	*Hamlet* 2.2.192	Letter to Eduard Silberstein 13 August	Boehlich 49	Quotation	1926 *SE* 20.187/*RSE* 20.167
1878	"What! Will the line stretch out to the crack of doom"	*Macbeth* 4.1.117	Letter to Wilhelm Knöpfmacher 6 August	Freud/Stern 6	Quotation	
1882	"Journeys end in lovers meeting …"	*Twelfth Night* 2.3.43–52	Letter to Martha Bernays 14 July	Freud/Stern 13	Quotation	
1882	"What's Hecuba to him"	*Hamlet* 2.2.559	Letter to Martha Bernays 23 July	Freud/Stern 19	Allusion	
1883	Cordelia (character)	*King Lear*	Letter to Martha Bernays 13 July	Freud/Stern 40–41	Mention	
1885	"there's the rub"	*Hamlet* 3.1.64	Letter to Martha Bernays 25 June	Freud/Stern 156	Quotation	
1895	"My heart is in the coffin here with Caesar"	*Julius Caesar* 3.2.106	Letter to Wilhelm Fliess 27 April	Masson 128	Quotation	
1895	Lady Macbeth (character)	*Macbeth*	"Obsessions and Phobias"	*SE* 3.79/*RSE* 3.72	Mention	
1897	Titania and Bottom (characters)	*A Midsummer Night's Dream*	Draft N (enclosed with letter to Wilhelm Fliess 31 May)	*SE* 1.256/*RSE* 1.282	Mention	
	"The poet's eye, in a fine frenzy rolling"	*A Midsummer Night's Dream* 5.1.12	As above	*SE* 1.256/*RSE* 1.282	Allusion	

(continued)

(continued)

Year	*Shakespeare*	*Reference*	*Freud*	*Reference*	*Type*	*Cross-references*
1897	"the readiness is all"	*Hamlet* 5.2.222	Letter to Wilhelm Fliess 21 September	Masson 264–66	Variation	
1897	Hamlet (character)	*Hamlet*	Letter to Wilhelm Fliess 15 October	Masson 272–73	Discussion	
	"Thus conscience does make cowards of us all"	*Hamlet* 3.1.82	As above	Masson 272–73	Quotation	1930 *SE* 21.134n/*RSE* 21.121n
	"use every man after his desert, and who should 'scape whipping?"	*Hamlet* 2.2.528–29	As above	Masson 272–73	Quotation	1917 *SE* 14.246 & n/*RSE* 14.220 & n; 1928 *SE* 21.189/*RSE* 21.175; 1936 Freud/ Robson-Scott 127
1898		*Hamlet*	Letter to Wilhelm Fliess 15 March	Masson 303–04	Mention	
1899	"thou owest God a death"	*1 Henry IV* 5.1.126	Letter to Wilhelm Fliess 6 February	Masson 343–44	Misquotation	1900 *SE* 4.205 & n/*RSE* 4.182 & n; 1915 *SE* 14.289/*RSE* 14.288
1900	"Though this be madness, yet there is method in't"	*Hamlet* 2.2.205–06	*The Interpretation of Dreams*	*SE* 4.60/*RSE* 4.53	Allusion	1909 April 16 McGuire 219; 1911 *SE* 12.21/*RSE* 12.19; 1937 *SE* 23.267/*RSE* 23.242

Year	Shakespeare	Reference	Freud	Reference	Type	Cross-references
1900	"There needs no ghost, my lord, come from the grave / To tell us this"	*Hamlet* 1.5.124–25	*The Interpretation of Dreams*	*SE* 4.175/*RSE* 4.155	Quotation	
1900	Desdemona's handkerchief	*Othello*	*The Interpretation of Dreams*	*SE* 4.177/*RSE* 4.157	Mention	
1900	"thou owest God a death"	*1 Henry IV* 5.1.126	*The Interpretation of Dreams*	*SE* 4.205 & n/*RSE* 4.182 & n	Misquotation	1899 Feb 6 Masson 343–44; 1915 *SE* 14.289/*RSE* 14.288
1900	The red and white roses representing York and Lancaster in the Wars of the Roses	*3 Henry VI* 1.2.32–34, 2.5.97–100	*The Interpretation of Dreams*	*SE* 4.212/*RSE* 4.188	Mention	
1900	"It was the nightingale and not the lark"	*Romeo and Juliet* 3.5.2	*The Interpretation of Dreams*	*SE* 4.234/*RSE* 4.208	Adaptation	
1900	"The undiscover'd country, from whose bourn / No traveller returns"	*Hamlet* 3.1.78–79	*The Interpretation of Dreams*	*SE* 4.255/*RSE* 4.226	Quotation	1916 *SE* 15.161/*RSE* 15.140
1900		*Hamlet*	*The Interpretation of Dreams*	*SE* 4.264–66/*RSE* 4.234–36	Discussion	
	"sicklied o'er with the pale cast of thought"	*Hamlet* 3.1.84	*The Interpretation of Dreams*	*SE* 4.265/*RSE* 4.235	Quotation	
		Timon of Athens	*The Interpretation of Dreams*	*SE* 4.265/*RSE* 4.235	Mention	

(*continued*)

(continued)

Year	Shakespeare	Reference	Freud	Reference	Type	Cross-references
		Macbeth	*The Interpretation of Dreams*	*SE* 4.266/*RSE* 4.236	Mention	
1900	"As Caesar loved me, I weep for him …"	*Julius Caesar* 3.2.24–27	*The Interpretation of Dreams*	*SE* 5.424/*RSE* 5.378	Quotation and discussion	1900 *SE* 5.484/*RSE* 5.433; 1909 *SE* 10.180/*RSE* 10.138–39
1900	"I am but mad north-north-west …"	*Hamlet* 2.2.378–79	*The Interpretation of Dreams*	*SE* 5.444/*RSE* 5.397	Quotation	
1900	Lion (character played by Snug the joiner)	*A Midsummer Night's Dream* 5.1.219–26	*The Interpretation of Dreams*	*SE* 5.462/*RSE* 5.413	Mention	
1900		*Julius Caesar*	*The Interpretation of Dreams*	*SE* 5.483/*RSE* 5.431–32	Mention	
1900	Prince Hal (character)	*2 Henry IV* 4.5	*The Interpretation of Dreams*	*SE* 5.484/*RSE* 5.433	Mention	
1900	"as he was ambitious, I slew him"	*Julius Caesar* 3.2.26–27	*The Interpretation of Dreams*	*SE* 5.484/*RSE* 5.433	Quotation	1900 *SE* 5.424/*RSE* 5.378; 1909 *SE* 10.180/*RSE* 10.138–39
1901	"Truly, my name is Cinna …"	*Julius Caesar* 3.327–34	*The Psychopathology of Everyday Life*	*SE* 6.117n/*RSE* 6.102n	Quotation	
1904	"… you would pluck out the heart of my mystery …"	*Hamlet* 3.2.363–72	"On Psychotherapy"	*SE* 7.262/*RSE* 7.271	Quotation and discussion	
1905		*Hamlet*	"Psychopathic Characters on the Stage"	*SE* 7.309–10/*RSE* 7.299	Discussion	

Year	*Shakespeare*	*Reference*	*Freud*	*Reference*	*Type*	*Cross-references*
1905	"brevity is the soul of wit …"	*Hamlet* 2.2.90–91	*Jokes and Their Relation to the Unconscious*	*SE* 8.13/*RSE* 8.13	Quotation	
1905	"Discharge thyself of our company, Pistol!"	*2 Henry IV* 2.4.137	*Jokes and Their Relation to the Unconscious*	*SE* 8.36/*RSE* 8.32	Quotation	
1905	Banquo (play on name)	*Macbeth*	*Jokes and Their Relation to the Unconscious*	*SE* 8.36/*RSE* 8.32	Allusion	
1905	"hold, as 'twere, the mirror up to nature …"	*Hamlet* 3.2.21–22	*Jokes and Their Relation to the Unconscious*	*SE* 8.37/*RSE* 8.32–33	Quotation	
1905	"Thrift, thrift, Horatio, the funeral baked-meats / Did coldly furnish forth the marriage tables"	*Hamlet* 1.2.180–81	*Jokes and Their Relation to the Unconscious*	*SE* 8.42, 44/*RSE* 8.37, 38	Quotation	
1905	"For Brutus is an honourable man …"	*Julius Caesar* 3.2.82	*Jokes and Their Relation to the Unconscious*	*SE* 8.73/*RSE* 8.64	Quotation	
1905	"Every inch a king"	*King Lear* 4.6.107	*Jokes and Their Relation to the Unconscious*	*SE* 8.76/*RSE* 8.67	Variation	
1905	"A jest's prosperity lies in the ear / Of him that hears it, never in the tongue / Of him that makes it"	*Love's Labour's Lost* 5.2.861–63	*Jokes and Their Relation to the Unconscious*	*SE* 8.144/*RSE* 8.126	Quotation	

(*continued*)

(continued)

Year	*Shakespeare*	*Reference*	*Freud*	*Reference*	*Type*	*Cross-references*
1905	Falstaff (character)	*1 Henry IV*	*Jokes and Their Relation to the Unconscious*	*SE* 8.231 n/*RSE* 8.201n	Discussion	
1907		*Hamlet*, *Macbeth*	"Delusions and Dreams in Jensen's *Gradiva*"	*SE* 9.17/*RSE* 9.13	Mention	
		King Lear	"Delusions and Dreams in Jensen's *Gradiva*"	*SE* 9.43/*RSE* 9.33	Mention	
1907		*Hamlet*, *Macbeth*	Letter to Heinrich Hinterberger (undated)	Freud/Stern 268–69	Mention	
1908	"Let me have men about me that are fat"	*Julius Caesar* 1.2.192	Letter to Carl Jung 3 May	McGuire 145	Quotation	
1909	"for such kind of men, the less you meddle or make with them, why, the more is for your honesty"	*Much Ado About Nothing* 3.3.52–53	"Analysis of a Phobia in a Five-Year-Old Boy" ("Little Hans")	*SE* 10.144/*RSE* 10.110	Quotation	
1909	"… as he was ambitious, I slew him"	*Julius Caesar* 3.2.24–27	"Notes Upon a Case of Obsessional Neurosis" ("The 'Rat' Man")	*SE* 10.180/*RSE* 10.138–39	Quotation and discussion	1900 *SE* 5.484/*RSE* 5.433; 1900 *SE* 5.424/*RSE* 5.378
	"Doubt thou the stars are fire …"	*Hamlet* 2.2.116–18	"Notes Upon a Case of Obsessional Neurosis" ("The 'Rat' Man")	*SE* 10.241n/*RSE* 10.183n	Quotation and discussion	

Year	*Shakespeare*	*Reference*	*Freud*	*Reference*	*Type*	*Cross-references*
1909		*Hamlet*	*Five Lectures on Psychoanalysis*, Lecture 4	*SE* 11.47/*RSE* 11.45	Mention	
1909	"There are more things in heaven and earth, Horatio, / Than are dreamt of in your philosophy"	*Hamlet* 1.5.166–67	Letter to Carl Jung 16 April	McGuire 219	Allusion	1910 *SE* 11.137 & n/*RSE* 11.123 & n; 1918 *SE* 17.12/*RSE* 17.11; 1921 *SE* 18.178/*RSE* 18.168; 1933 *SE* 22.31/*RSE* 22.28
	"Though this be madness, yet there is method in't"	*Hamlet* 2.2.205–06	As above	As above	Allusion	1900 *SE* 4.60/*RSE* 4.53; 1911 *SE* 12.21/*RSE* 12.19; 1937 *SE* 23.267/*RSE* 23.242
1909		*Hamlet*	Letter to Ernest Jones 1 June	Paskauskas 25	Mention	
1909	Shakespeare's name		Letter to Ernest Jones 31 October	Paskauskas 32	Discussion	
		Macbeth	As above	As above	Mention	
1910	"There are more things in heaven and earth, Horatio, / Than are dreamt of in your philosophy"	*Hamlet* 1.5.166–67	"Leonardo Da Vinci and a Memory of his Childhood"	*SE* 11.137 & n/*RSE* 11.123 & n	Allusion	1909 April 16 Maguire 219; 1918 *SE* 17.12/*RSE* 17.11; 1921 *SE* 18.178/*RSE* 18.168; 1933 *SE* 22.31/*RSE* 22.28

(*continued*)

(continued)

Year	*Shakespeare*	*Reference*	*Freud*	*Reference*	*Type*	*Cross-references*
1910	Macduff (character)	*Macbeth* 5.7.15	"A Special Type of Choice of Object Made by Men"	*SE* 11.173/*RSE* 11.160	Discussion	1916 *SE* 14.321/*RSE* 14.324–25; 1916 *SE* 16.397/*RSE* 16.350
1910	"At least we'll die with harness on our back"	*Macbeth* 5.5.51	Letter to Oskar Pfister 6 March	Meng 35	Allusion	1911 September 1 McGuire 442
1910		*Hamlet*	Letter to Ernest Jones 20 November	Pausaukas 77	Mention	
1911	"Though this be madness, yet there is method in't"	*Hamlet* 2.2.205–06	"Psycho-Analytic Notes on an Autobiographical Account of a Case of Paranoia" (The Schreber Case)	*SE* 12.21/*RSE* 12.19	Allusion	1900 *SE* 4.60/*RSE* 4.53; 1909 April 16 McGuire 219; 1937 *SE* 23.267/*RSE* 23.242
1911	"At least we'll die with harness on our back"	*Macbeth* 5.5.51	Letter to Carl Jung 1 September	McGuire 442	Allusion	1910 March 6 Meng 35
1912	"I pray you tarry; pause a day or two …"	*The Merchant of Venice* 3.2.1–18	added to *The Psychopathology of Everyday Life*	*SE* 6.97–98/*RSE* 6.84–85	Quotation and discussion	1916 *SE* 15.37–38/*RSE* 15.34–35
1913		*The Merchant of Venice*	Letter to Sandor Ferenczi 9 July	Freud/Stern 301	Mention	
1913		*The Merchant of Venice*	"The Theme of the Three Caskets"	*SE* 12.291–301/*RSE* 12.289–98	Discussion	
		King Lear	"The Theme of the Three Caskets"	As above	Discussion	

Year	*Shakespeare*	*Reference*	*Freud*	*Reference*	*Type*	*Cross-references*
1913	Macbeth (character)	*Macbeth*	*Totem and Taboo*	*SE* 13.38/*RSE* 13.43	Mention	
	Richard III (character)	*Richard III*	*Totem and Taboo*	As above	Mention	
	"My words fly up, my thoughts remain below: / Words without thoughts never to heaven go"	*Hamlet* 3.3.97–98	*Totem and Taboo*	*SE* 13.84n/*RSE* 13.83n	Quotation	
	"Full fathom five thy father lies …"	*The Tempest* 1.2.397–402	*Totem and Taboo*	*SE* 13.155n/*RSE* 13.142n	Quotation	
1914		*Hamlet*	"The Moses of Michelangelo"	*SE* 13.212–13/*RSE* 13.206	Discussion	
1914	"if reasons were as plentiful as blackberries"	*1 Henry IV* 2.4 239	"On the History of the Psycho-Analytic Movement"	SE 14.24/*RSE* 14.20	Misquotation	1915 *SE* 14.287/*RSE* 14.286
1915	"if reasons were as plentiful as blackberries"	*1 Henry IV* 2.4 239	"Thoughts for the Times on War and Death"	*SE* 14.287/*RSE* 14.286	Misquotation	1914 *SE* 14.24/*RSE* 14.20
1915	"thou owest God a death"	*1 Henry IV* 5.1.126	"Thoughts for the Times on War and Death"	*SE* 14.289/*RSE* 14.288	Misquotation	1899 February 6 Masson 343–44; 1900 *SE* 4.205 & n/*RSE* 4.182 & n
1916	Richard III (character)	*Richard III*	"Some Character-Types Met with in Psychoanalytic Work"	*SE* 14.314–15/*RSE* 14.317–18	Discussion	
	"But I, that am not shaped for sportive tricks …"	*Richard III* 1.1.14–31	"Some Character-Types Met with in Psychoanalytic Work"	*SE* 14.314/*RSE* 14.317–18	Quotation and discussion	

(*continued*)

(continued)

Year	*Shakespeare*	*Reference*	*Freud*	*Reference*	*Type*	*Cross-references*
	Lady Macbeth (character)	*Macbeth*	"Some Character-Types Met with in Psychoanalytic Work"	*SE* 14.318–19, 321–24/*RSE* 14.322–23, 25–27	Quotation and discussion	
	"Come, you spirits / That tend on mortal thoughts, unsex me here …"	*Macbeth* 1.5.40–48	"Some Character-Types Met with in Psychoanalytic Work"	*SE* 14.318/*RSE* 14.322	Quotation	
	"I have given suck, and know / How tender 'tis to love the babe that milks me …"	*Macbeth* 1.7.54–59	"Some Character-Types Met with in Psychoanalytic Work"	*SE* 14.318/*RSE* 14.322	Quotation	
	"Had he not resembled / My father as he slept, I had done it"	*Macbeth* 2.2.12–13	"Some Character-Types Met with in Psychoanalytic Work"	*SE* 14.319/*RSE* 14.322	Quotation	
	"Nought's had, all's spent, / Where our desire is got without content …"	*Macbeth* 3.2.4–7	"Some Character-Types Met with in Psychoanalytic Work"	*SE* 14.319/*RSE* 14.323	Quotation	
	"Fie, my lord, fie! a soldier, and afeard? …"	*Macbeth* 5.1.36–37	"Some Character-Types Met with in Psychoanalytic Work"	*SE* 14.319/*RSE* 14.323	Quotation	
	"What's done cannot be undone"	*Macbeth* 5.1.68	"Some Character-Types Met with in Psychoanalytic Work"	*SE* 14.319/*RSE* 14.323	Adapted quotation	

Year	*Shakespeare*	*Reference*	*Freud*	*Reference*	*Type*	*Cross-references*
	Macbeth (character)	*Macbeth*	"Some Character-Types Met with in Psychoanalytic Work"	*SE* 14.319–24/*RSE* 14.323–27	Quotation and discussion	
	"She should have died hereafter …"	*Macbeth* 5.5.17–18	"Some Character-Types Met with in Psychoanalytic Work"	*SE* 14.319/*RSE* 14.323	Quotation	
	"Upon my head they placed a fruitless crown …"	*Macbeth* 3.1.60–63	"Some Character-Types Met with in Psychoanalytic Work"	*SE* 14.320n/*RSE* 14.324n	Quotation	
	"Bring forth men-children only! …"	*Macbeth* 1.7.72–74	"Some Character-Types Met with in Psychoanalytic Work"	*SE* 14.321/*RSE* 14.324	Quotation	
	Macduff (character)	*Macbeth* 5.7.15	"Some Character-Types Met with in Psychoanalytic Work"	*SE* 14.321/*RSE* 14.324–25	Allusion	1910 *SE* 11.173/*RSE* 11.160; 1916 *SE* 16.397/*RSE* 16.350
	"He has no children!"	*Macbeth* 4.3.216	"Some Character-Types Met with in Psychoanalytic Work"	*SE* 14.321/*RSE* 14.324	Quotation	
	"Sleep no more! Macbeth does murder sleep"	*Macbeth* 2.2.32–33	"Some Character-Types Met with in Psychoanalytic Work"	*SE* 14.324/*RSE* 14.327	Quotation	
	"Macbeth shall sleep no more"	*Macbeth* 2.2.39	"Some Character-Types Met with in Psychoanalytic Work"	*SE* 14.324/*RSE* 14.327	Quotation	
	"all great Neptune's ocean"	*Macbeth* 2.2.57	"Some Character-Types Met with in Psychoanalytic Work"	*SE* 14.324/*RSE* 14.327	Quotation	

(*continued*)

(continued)

Year	*Shakespeare*	*Reference*	*Freud*	*Reference*	*Type*	*Cross-references*
	"A little water clears us of this deed"	*Macbeth* 2.2.64	"Some Character-Types Met with in Psychoanalytic Work"	*SE* 14.324/*RSE* 14.327	Quotation	
	"All the perfumes of Arabia will not sweeten this little hand"	*Macbeth* 5.1.50–51	"Some Character-Types Met with in Psychoanalytic Work"	*SE* 14.324/*RSE* 14.327	Quotation	
1916	"I pray you tarry; pause a day or two …"	*The Merchant of Venice* 3.2.1–18	*Introductory Lectures on Psychoanalysis*, Lecture 2	*SE* 15.37–38/*RSE* 15.34–35	Quotation and discussion	1912 *SE* 6.97–98/*RSE* 6.84–85
1916		*Macbeth*	*Introductory Lectures on Psychoanalysis*, Lecture 5	*SE* 15.96/*RSE* 15.84	Mention	
1916	"the undiscovered country from whose bourn / No traveller returns"	*Hamlet* 3.1.78–79	*Introductory Lectures on Psychoanalysis*, Lecture 10	*SE* 15.161/*RSE* 15.140	Quotation	1900 *SE* 4.255/*RSE* 4.226
1916	Hamlet (character)	*Hamlet*	*Introductory Lectures on Psychoanalysis*, Lecture 21	*SE* 16.335/*RSE* 16.295–96	Mention	
1916	Macduff (character)	*Macbeth* 5.7.15	*Introductory Lectures on Psychoanalysis*, Lecture 25	*SE* 16.397/*RSE* 16.350		1910 SE 11.173/*RSE* 11.160; 1916 SE 14.321/*RSE* 14.324–25

Year	*Shakespeare*	*Reference*	*Freud*	*Reference*	*Type*	*Cross-references*
1917	"use every man after his desert, and who shall 'scape whipping?"	*Hamlet* 2.2.528–29	"Mourning and Melancholia"	*SE* 14.246 & n/*RSE* 14.220 & n	Quotation	1897 October 15 Masson 272–73; 1928 *SE* 21.189/*RSE* 21.175; 1936 Freud/ Robson-Scott 127
1918	"There are more things in heaven and earth, Horatio, / Than are dreamt of in your philosophy"	*Hamlet* 1.5.166–67	"From the History of an Infantile Neurosis" ("The Wolfman")	*SE* 17.12/*RSE* 17.11	Quotation	1909 April 16 McGuire 219; 1910 *SE* 11.137 & n/*RSE* 11.123 & n; 1921 *SE* 18.178/*RSE* 18.168; 1933 *SE* 22.31/*RSE* 22.28
1919	"Lesser than Macbeth, and greater …"	*Macbeth* 1.3.65–67	"'A Child is Being Beaten'"	*SE* 17.187/*RSE* 17.182–83 & n	Allusion	
1919		*Hamlet*, *Macbeth*, *The Tempest*, *A Midsummer-Night's Dream*	"The Uncanny"	*SE* 17.230/*RSE* 17.225	Mentions	
		Hamlet, *Macbeth*, *Julius Caesar*	"The Uncanny"	*SE* 17.250/*RSE* 17.242	Mentions	
1920		*Richard II* 2.2	added to *The Psychopathology of Everyday Life*	*SE* 6.100n/*RSE* 6.86n	Mention	

(*continued*)

(continued)

Year	*Shakespeare*	*Reference*	*Freud*	*Reference*	*Type*	*Cross-references*
1921	"There are more things in heaven and earth, Horatio, / Than are dreamt of in your philosophy"	*Hamlet* 1.5.166–67	"Psycho-Analysis and Telepathy"	*SE* 18.178/*RSE* 18.168	Quotation	1909 April 16 McGuire 219; 1910 *SE* 11.137 & n/*RSE* 11.123 & n; 1918 *SE* 17.12/*RSE* 17.11; 1933 *SE* 22.31/*RSE* 22.28
1922	"I called my love false love; but what said he then? …"	*Othello* 4.3.55–57	"Some Neurotic Mechanisms in Jealousy, Paranoia, and Homosexuality"	*SE* 18.224n/*RSE* 18.216n	Quotation	
1925		*Hamlet*	"An Autobiographical Study"	*SE* 20.63–64/*RSE* 20.55–56	Discussion	
1926	"Words, words, words"	*Hamlet* 2.2.192	"The Question of Lay Analysis"	*SE* 20.187/*RSE* 20.167	Quotation	1874 August 13 Boehlich 49
1928		*Hamlet*	"Dostoevsky and Parricide"	*SE* 21.177, 188–89/*RSE* 21.165, 175	Discussion	
	"use every man after his desert, and who should 'scape whipping?"	*Hamlet* 2.2.528–29	"Dostoevsky and Parricide"	*SE* 21.189/*RSE* 21.175	Quotation	1897 October 15 Masson 272–73; 1917 *SE* 14.246 & n/*RSE* 14.220 & n; 1936 Freud/Robson-Scott 127
1930		*King Lear*	Letter to Richard Flatter 30 March	Freud/Stern 395	Discussion	

Year	*Shakespeare*	*Reference*	*Freud*	*Reference*	*Type*	*Cross-references*
1930	Shakespeare ("the man from Stratford")—doubt of authorship		Added to *The Interpretation of Dreams*	*SE* 4.266n/*RSE* 4.236n	Discussion	1930 *SE* 21.211/*RSE* 21.199; 1934 March 25 Jones 3.487–88; 1935 *SE* 20.63n/*RSE* 20.55n; 1935 Waugaman; 1937 January 18 Freud/Robson-Scott 139; 1937 *SE* 23.65n/*RSE* 23.60n; 1938 *SE* 23.192n/*RSE* 23.173n
1930	Shakespeare—doubt of authorship		"Address Delivered in the Goethe House at Frankfurt"	*SE* 21.211/*RSE* 21.199	Discussion	1930 *SE* 4.266n/*RSE* 4.236n; 1934 March 25 Jones 3.487–88; 1935 *SE* 20.63n/*RSE* 20.55n; 1935 Waugaman; 1937 January 18 Freud/Robson-Scott 139; 1937 *SE* 23.65n/*RSE* 23.60n; 1938 *SE* 23.192n/*RSE* 23.173n

(*continued*)

(continued)

Year	*Shakespeare*	*Reference*	*Freud*	*Reference*	*Type*	*Cross-references*
1930	["oh inch of nature!"]	[*Pericles*] "This very Shakespearean phrase is not in fact to be found in the canon of Shakespeare" but in George Wilkins, *The Painfull Adventures of Pericles Prince of Tyre* (1608)	*Civilization and its Discontents*	*SE* 21.91n/*RSE* 21.83n	Explanatory note added by Strachey	
	"Shakespeare's time"		*Civilization and its Discontents*	*SE* 21.93/*RSE* 21.85	Discussion	
	"Thus conscience does make cowards of us all"	*Hamlet* 3.1.82	*Civilization and its Discontents*	*SE* 21.134n/*RSE* 21.121n	Quotation	1897 October 15 Masson 272–73
1933	"There are more things in heaven and earth, Horatio, / Than are dreamt of in your philosophy"	*Hamlet* 1.5.166–67	*New Introductory Lectures on Psycho-*Analysis, Lecture 30	*SE* 22.31/*RSE* 22.28		1909 April 16 McGuire 219; 1910 *SE* 11.137 & n/*RSE* 11.123 & n; 1918 *SE* 17.12/*RSE* 17.11; 1921 *SE* 18.178/*RSE* 18.168
1934	"A plague on both your houses"	*Romeo and Juliet* 3.1.106	Letter to Ernst Freud 20 February	Freud/Stern 420	Quotation	
1934		*King Lear*, *Othello*, *The Merchant of Venice*	Letter to James S. H. Bransom 25 March	Jones 3.487–88	Discussions	

Year	*Shakespeare*	*Reference*	*Freud*	*Reference*	*Type*	*Cross-references*
	Shakespeare—doubt of authorship		As above	As above	Discussion	1930 *SE* 4.266n/*RSE* 4.236n; 1930 *SE* 21.211/*RSE* 21.199; 1935 *SE* 20.63n/*RSE* 20.55n; 1935 Waugaman; 1937 January 18 Freud/Robson-Scott 139; 1937 *SE* 23.65n/*RSE* 23.60n; 1938 *SE* 23.192n/*RSE* 23.173n
1935	"The time is out of joint – O cursed spite, / That ever I was born to set it right!"	*Hamlet* 1.5.188–19	Letter to Arnold Zweig 2 May	Freud/Robson-Scott 106	Allusion	
1935	Shakespeare—doubt of authorship		Added to "An Autobiographical Study"	*SE* 20.63n/*RSE* 20.55n		1930 *SE* 4.266n/*RSE* 4.236n; 1930 *SE* 21.211/*RSE* 21.199; 1935 Waugaman; 1937 January 18 Freud/Robson-Scott 139; 1937 *SE* 23.65n/*RSE* 23.60n; 1938 *SE* 23.192n/*RSE* 23.173n

(*continued*)

(continued)

Year	*Shakespeare*	*Reference*	*Freud*	*Reference*	*Type*	*Cross-references*
1935	Shakespeare—doubt of authorship		Letter to Percy Allen 7 November	Waugaman		1930 *SE* 4.266n/*RSE* 4.236n; 1930 *SE* 21.211/*RSE* 21.199; 1937 January 18 Freud/Robson-Scott 139; 1937 *SE* 23.65n/*RSE* 23.60n; 1938 *SE* 23.192n/*RSE* 23.173n
		King Lear	As above	As above	Mention	
1936	"use every man after his desert, and who should 'scape whipping?"	*Hamlet* 2.2.528–29	Letter to Arnold Zweig 31 May	Freud/Robson-Scott 127	Quotation	1897 October 15 Masson 272–73; 1917 *SE* 14.246 & n/*RSE* 14.220 & n; 1928 *SE* 21.189/*RSE* 21.175
1937		*Hamlet*, *Macbeth*, *Othello*, *King Lear*	Letter to Arnold Zweig 18 January	Freud/Robson-Scott 139	Mentions	

Year	*Shakespeare*	*Reference*	*Freud*	*Reference*	*Type*	*Cross-references*
	Shakespeare—doubt of authorship		As above	As above	Discussion	1930 *SE* 4.266n/*RSE* 4.236n; 1930 *SE* 21.211/*RSE* 21.199; 1935 *SE* 20.63n/*RSE* 20.55n; 1935 Waugaman; 1937 *SE* 23.65n/*RSE* 23.60n; 1938 *SE* 23.192n/*RSE* 23.173n
1937	"William Shakespeare of Stratford"		*Moses and Monotheism*	*SE* 23.65n/*RSE* 23.60n		1930 *SE* 4.266n/*RSE* 4.236n; 1930 *SE* 21.211/*RSE* 21.199; 1935 *SE* 20.63n/*RSE* 20.55n; 1935 Waugaman; 1937 January 18 Freud/Robson-Scott 139; 1938 *SE* 23.192n/*RSE* 23.173n
1937	"Your bait of falsehood take this carp of truth"	*Hamlet* 2.1.60	"Constructions in Analysis"	*SE* 23.262/*RSE* 23.237	Allusion	

(*continued*)

(continued)

Year	*Shakespeare*	*Reference*	*Freud*	*Reference*	*Type*	*Cross-references*
	"Though this be madness, yet there is method in't"	*Hamlet* 2.2.205–06	"Constructions in Analysis"	SE 23.267/*RSE* 23.242	Allusion	1900 *SE* 4.60/*RSE* 4.53; 1909 April 16 McGuire 219; 1911 *SE* 12.21/*RSE* 12.19
1938		*Hamlet*	*An Outline of Psychoanalysis*	*SE* 23.192/*RSE* 23.173	Discussion	
	Shakespeare—doubt of authorship		*An Outline of Psychoanalysis*	*SE* 23.192n/*RSE* 23.173n	Discussion	1930 *SE* 4.266n/*RSE* 4.236n; 1930 *SE* 21.211/*RSE* 21.199; 1935 *SE* 20.63n/*RSE* 20.55n; 1935 Waugaman; 1937 January 18 Freud/Robson-Scott 139
1938	"the rest is silence"	*Hamlet* 5.2.358	Letter to Alexander Freud 19 April	Freud/Stern 442	Allusion	

Analysis

- Total references to plays: 139
- Total references to Shakespeare the man, his times, and so on: 10
- Total references: 149
- Period covered 1872–1938: 66 years
- Shakespeare and/or his plays referred to in 41 of those years
- Average references to Shakespeare and/or his plays per year: 2.25
- Longest period with no references: 1885–1895 (10 years)
- Years with most references: 1916 (× 25), 1900 (× 17), 1905 (× 10)
- Texts with most references: "Some Character-Types Met with in Psychoanalytic Work" (1916), *The Interpretation of Dreams* (1900), *Jokes and Their Relation to the Unconscious* (1905)
- Freud's favorite quotations: "There are more things in heaven and earth, Horatio, / Than are dreamt of in your philosophy" (*Hamlet* 1.5.166–67) × 5 (1909, 1910, 1918, 1921, 1933); "Though this be madness, yet there is method in't" (*Hamlet* 2.2.205–06) × 4 (1900, 1909, 1911, 1937); "use every man after his desert, and who should 'scape whipping?" (*Hamlet* 2.2.528–29) × 4 (1897, 1917, 1928, 1936)
- Plays referred to: 19 (50% of total plays)
- Plays with most references and % in descending order:

	Play	*occurrences*	*% of total references to plays (rounded)*
1.	*Hamlet*	52	38%
2.	*Macbeth*	35	25%
3.	*Julius Caesar*	9	6.5%
4.	*King Lear*	8	6%
5.	*1 Henry IV*	6	4%
6.	*The Merchant of Venice*	5	3.5%
7.	*Othello*	4	3%
8.	*A Midsummer Night's Dream*	4	3%
9.	*Richard III*	3	2%
10.	*Romeo and Juliet*	2	1.5%
11.	*2 Henry IV*	2	1.5%
12.	*The Tempest*	2	1.5%
13.	*Twelfth Night*	2	1.5%
14.	*Timon of Athens*	1	<1%

(*continued*)

(continued)

	Play	*occurrences*	*% of total references to plays (rounded)*
15.	*3 Henry VI*	1	<1%
16.	*Love's Labour's Lost*	1	<1%
17.	*Much Ado About Nothing*	1	<1%
18.	*Richard II*	1	<1%
19.	[*Pericles*]	1	<1%

- Plays not mentioned by Freud: *All's Well That Ends Well*; *Antony and Cleopatra*; *As You Like It*; *Coriolanus*; *Cymbeline*; *Henry V*; *1 Henry VI*; *2 Henry VI*; *Henry VIII*; *King John*; *Measure for Measure*; *The Comedy of Errors*; *The Merry Wives of Windsor*; *The Taming of the Shrew*; *The Two Gentlemen of Verona*; *The Two Noble Kinsmen*; *The Winter's Tale*; *Titus Andronicus*; *Troilus and Cressida*

Index

J. W. Stone, C. Bates (eds.), *Shakespeare and Psychoanalysis*, Palgrave Shakespeare Studies,
https://doi.org/10.1007/978-3-032-07897-1

www.ingramcontent.com/pod-product-compliance
Ingram Content Group UK Ltd.
Pitfield, Milton Keynes, MK11 3LW, UK
UKHW020937180926
475692UK00004B/82

9783032078964